Mastering the ISDA® Collateral Documents

Mastering the ISDA® Collateral Documents

A practical guide for negotiators

Second edition

PAUL C. HARDING AND CHRISTIAN A. JOHNSON

Pearson

Harlow, England • London • New York • Boston • San Francisco • Toronto • Sydney • Dubai • Singapore • Hong Kong
Tokyo • Seoul • Taipei • New Delhi • Cape Town • São Paulo • Mexico City • Madrid • Amsterdam • Munich • Paris • Milan

PEARSON EDUCATION LIMITED

Edinburgh Gate
Harlow CM20 2JE
Tel: +44 (0)1279 623623
Fax: +44 (0)1279 431059
Website: www.pearsoned.com/uk

First published in 2002 (published as *Mastering Collateral Management and Documentation*)
Second edition published 2012

ISBN: 978-0-273-75717-7

British Library Cataloguing-in-Publication Data
A catalogue record for this book is available from the British Library

Library of Congress Cataloging-in-Publication Data
A catalog record for this book is available from the Library of Congress

Typeset in 11.5pt Garamond by 30

About the authors

Paul C. Harding is a graduate of London University and has worked in several UK and foreign banks in London in credit, marketing and documentation roles. Since 1990 he has been involved with derivatives documentation and was a well-known negotiator in the City of London with Barclays Capital Securities Limited and Hill Samuel Bank Limited where he was head of Treasury Documentation.

In February 1997 he founded Derivatives Documentation Limited, a derivatives consultancy and project management company based in the City of London and providing negotiation, recruitment and training services in derivatives documentation (www.derivsdocu.com). Its clients include many of the world's leading banks.

In November 2001 Paul's book, *Mastering the ISDA® Master Agreement* was published by Financial Times–Prentice Hall. This was followed by his *Mastering Collateral Management and Documentation* in conjunction with Christian Johnson which was published by Financial Times–Prentice Hall in November 2002. In 2004 they co-wrote *A Practical Guide to Using Repo Master Agreements* which was published by Euromoney Books.

His book on the 2002 ISDA Master Agreement was published in December 2003 also by Financial Times–Prentice Hall and in June 2004 his *A Practical Guide to the 2003 ISDA® Credit Derivatives Definitions* was published by Euromoney Books.

A third edition of *Mastering the ISDA® Master Agreements (1992 and 2002)* was published by Financial Times–Prentice Hall in April 2010.

In March 2011 Financial Times–Prentice Hall published *Mastering Securities Lending Documentation* co-written by Paul Harding and Christian Johnson.

Christian A. Johnson is a professor at the University of Utah College of Law and was previously a professor at Loyola University Chicago School of Law for 13 years. Professor Johnson teaches courses on corporate finance, banking and taxation. He graduated from Columbia Law School and was the Executive Editor of the *Columbia Law Review*. He practised law with Milbank Tweed Hadley & McCloy in New York and Mayer, Brown, Rowe & Maw in Chicago before teaching.

Christian Johnson has published extensively on corporate finance, lending and banking. He is also a frequent speaker and panelist on corporate finance and banking issues and has served as an expert witness in these areas. Professor Johnson is also a regular instructor for Euromoney Training on these subjects. Finally he has over 18 years of experience in negotiating and documenting corporate finance transactions such as securities lending, repurchase transactions and over-the-counter derivatives, having represented several large money centre banks, Federal Home Loan Banks and hedge funds in negotiations.

His previous collaborations with Paul Harding are listed above.

Disclaimer

This book is intended to provide an informational and illustrative overview of its subject, mainly to non-lawyers, and is not at all intended to provide legal or tax advice in respect of any particular situation, contractual relationship or contemplated transaction. The laws and regulations applicable to OTC derivatives transactions are complex and subject to frequent change. Users of this book should consult their legal and other advisers as they deem appropriate in the preparation and negotiation of OTC derivatives documentation. The authors of this book regard the examples given herein as illustrative only and assume no responsibility for any use to which ISDA standard documentation or any definition or provision set forth in this book may be put.

Contents

Acknowledgements

PAUL HARDING

First and foremost I would like to thank my family for their involvement with this book.

I should like to thank my wife Sheila again for all her support in keeping me focused and on track while writing this book. As usual she knew when to urge me to press on and when to give me space. She invariably helped me keep things in perspective especially when the going got tough. I thank her for all her patience and sacrifices over the past few months.

I also thank my daughter, Abigail for much typing at the later stages of producing this book and for solving various technical problems ably.

I am extremely grateful for the input of various professionals on the book. Nigel Underwood, Head of Collateral Management Control at Rabobank International in London provided very useful input to Chapter 2.

A big thank you is also due to Neil Murphy of Algorithmics, an IBM company, who helped develop the screen shots for Chapter 2 and who also reviewed the chapter and made many excellent amendments. Neil combines experience as a former collateral manager with knowledge of the functionalities of market leading collateral software. His approach was always unfailingly practical.

So Chapter 2 was much trawled over and combines the best efforts of us all!

I should like to thank Simon Leifer, Senior Derivatives Lawyer at Commerzbank AG London branch for his useful comments on the English law section of Chapter 3.

My grateful thanks are also due to Paul Berry, Head of Financial Institutions Credit, Global Banking and Markets, The Royal Bank of Scotland plc and a true credit professional whose detailed insights on the risks impacting collateral were invaluable in his useful contribution.

The thanks of both authors are offered to the International Swaps and Derivatives Association, Inc. for their permission to reproduce the ISDA Credit Support Annexes under English and New York Law in the text and Annexes.

We should also like to thank the editorial staff at Financial Times–Prentice Hall for all their excellent editing and support. Special thanks are due to Christopher Cudmore and Linda Dhondy.

Last but not least, it was, as usual, a real pleasure working with my co-author Christian Johnson who was always positive and practical.

CHRISTIAN JOHNSON

I begin by thanking my lovely wife Cori for her patience with me and the late nights as the book progressed and took shape.

I want to thank the numerous professionals that have mentored me in the past, in particular Vincent Hillery and Barry Taylor Brill (neither of whom have reviewed the contents of this book). I also want to thank the literally dozens of negotiators that I have sparred with in the past in putting in place collateral documentation, allowing me to hone and fully develop my understanding of New York ISDA Credit Support Annex. I also want to thank the countless law students and participants in educational programmes that have further sharpened my understanding through thoughtful questions and discussion.

Finally, I want to thank Paul Harding for inviting me once again to work with him on this book. Paul has been the driving force and principal architect behind this work. Paul always brings extraordinary energy and enthusiasm to any project that he undertakes. In particular, Paul brings a lifetime of experience that was particularly useful and helpful in editing my contributions regarding New York law and the New York Law Credit Support Annex. Most importantly, Paul's vision for this book and the others that we have worked on together has made difficult transactional documents accessible and understandable for a generation of negotiators, lawyers and other professionals.

Publisher's acknowledgements

We are grateful to the International Swaps and Derivatives Association, Inc. (ISDA) for permission to reproduce the 1994 ISDA Credit Support Annex (New York Law) and the 1995 ISDA Credit Support Annex (English Law). These Works must not be reproduced without written permission of ISDA.

ISDA® is the registered trademark of the International Swaps and Derivatives Association.

Screenshots from Algo Collateral Operations solution courtesy of Algorithmics, an IBM company. Copyright 2011 Algorithmics Software LLC. All rights reserved. Reprinted with permission from Algorithmics.

Authors' foreword

As Ogden Nash might have said, had he thought of it:

"It's only nateral
To take collateral
And that's becoz
It lessens your loss."

Collateral is now very big business, with some US$2.9 trillion of it (mostly in cash and G7 government securities) supporting OTC derivatives risk at the end of 2010 (latest ISDA figures). This represents some 70% of the global derivatives market on a replacement value basis.

Collateral does not in the authors' view eliminate credit risk entirely. The market value of OTC derivatives positions fluctuates constantly as do collateral values (especially securities), but it certainly supports risk exposure and can reduce it considerably. However, it is no substitute for a full analysis of your counterparty's creditworthiness. Obviously, it is most useful in a default or insolvency situation which is why collateral takers perform detailed legal analysis to find out what steps may be necessary in each jurisdiction to perfect and perhaps enforce their rights in their collateral. To this end, ISDA has published 45 legal opinions to its members and commissioned a further 4.

This book has been written for people with 0–3 years' experience in collateral documentation covering OTC derivatives risk exposure. It will also prove useful for individuals that are getting back up to speed on difficult collateral issues.

It is divided into eight chapters.

Chapter 1 defines terms, collateral and explains why collateral is taken. It also states the main types taken and which products are typically covered. It also describes how collateral documentation, and particularly that published by ISDA, has evolved over the past 17 years.

Chapter 2 is about collateral management itself. The authors considered that readers should have some knowledge about what happens on a collateral management desk in a bank. We hope this will provide useful background for a study of the collateral documentation itself. The chapter has several examples of screen shots that have been developed with the invaluable assistance of Algorithmics, an IBM company, in London.

Chapter 3 outlines the legal issues affecting the taking and enforcement of collateral in Europe and the USA. Paul Harding wrote the section on the European law position and Christian Johnson wrote the New York law part of this chapter. In Europe, laws relating to collateral have been on the move in recent years and tighter regulation in both Europe and the USA will only add to the need to be well informed on this subject.

Chapter 4 describes the credit issues surrounding collateral, such as the need to establish detailed policies to cover numerous risks including market risk, liquidity risk and concentration risk among others. It also describes rules relating to collateral under the Basel II Accord.

In Chapter 5, we get to the ISDA documentation itself. In this chapter, the ISDA English Law Credit Support Annex is fully reviewed on an extract with facing page commentary basis. The constituents of Paragraph 11 (the Elections and Variables Paragraph), which is similar to an ISDA Master Agreement Schedule are also analysed and examples given of different types of wording seen in the market. Paul Harding wrote Chapter 5.

Chapter 6 was written by Christian Johnson. It analyses the provisions of the ISDA New York Law Credit Support Annex in the same format as Chapter 5. It ends with a comparison and contrast between the two documents.

In both Chapters 5 and 6, the examples in the respective Elections and Variable Paragraphs of wording seen in the market are illustrative only. They are not meant to be imported wholesale, piecemeal or uncritically into these Paragraphs but could be seen as a starting point for developing your own wording for the requirements of your own negotiations.

While these two Credit Support Annexes are used by the market in nearly 90% of cases, there are other ISDA Credit Support Documents, i.e. the English Law Credit Support Deed and the Japanese Law Credit Support Annex, which are also occasionally used. The English Law Credit Support Deed is summarised in Chapter 7.

Chapter 8 of this book discusses developments in the collateral documentation market since 2002 when the first edition of this book was published and also covers ISDA's work on market best practices, dispute resolution procedures, portfolio reconciliation and use of electronic messaging for collateral calls.

The book concludes with the following four Annexes that are meant to provide useful information in one place. They are:

- *Annex 1* A facsimile of the ISDA Credit Support Annex (Bilateral Form-Transfer. Subject to English Law) (reproduced with the permission of the International Swaps and Derivatives Association, Inc.).

- *Annex 2* A facsimile of the ISDA Credit Support Annex (Bilateral Form. Subject to New York Law) (reproduced with the permission of the International Swaps and Derivatives Association, Inc.).
- *Annex 3* List of countries where ISDA has obtained collateral legal opinions.
- *Annex 4* Relevant extracts from the New York Uniform Commercial Code.

What does the book not contain? Due to constraints on space it was decided not to include a chapter on the *2001 ISDA Margin Provisions* as to date they have been very little used in the market. The last figure the authors saw was that just over 300 of these agreements had been put in place over 8 years out of a global total of about 150,000 collateral agreements. Anyone who is interested in *2001 ISDA Margin Provisions* can read Chapter 8 of the previous edition of this book.

What else is not covered in this book? We have attempted no description of how taxes impact on collateral taken in England and the State of New York, because we believe this is a matter for specialists. Nor have we discussed in any depth, guarantees or letters of credit that are relatively rarely used in the context of collateral for OTC derivatives transactions and which we consider are better treated in more general banking books. The use of equities as collateral is also not much discussed.

We have also not covered the ISDA Credit Support Annex under Japanese Law due to its specialist nature and usage. We have also not tackled local law collateral agreements because of our lack of language skills and because local writers have already covered them in most cases. Otherwise, we hope our coverage of collateral documentation is comprehensive at the time of writing.

Any opinions expressed are those of the authors themselves and do not necessarily reflect those of their employers.

We hope you enjoy this book and find it useful.

Paul Harding
Christian A. Johnson

1

Introduction

Definition of terms

Why collateral is taken

Product risk exposure covered

Evolution of collateral documentation

DEFINITION OF TERMS

What is collateral? In this book it is security for OTC derivatives risk exposure. Just as your house is security or collateral for your mortgage, so cash and government bonds can be collateral or security for risk exposure under swaps and other OTC derivatives products.

One of the dictionary meanings of the word "collateral" is:

connected with but aside from the main subject.

The main subject is counterparty credit risk. Collateral is no substitute for a full risk analysis of your counterparty. For us the message is:

By itself, collateral will not turn a poor credit risk into a good credit and it *never* eliminates credit risk all the time because market rates and prices are changing all the time. It just improves your rate of recovery – usually substantially.

Indeed, it could be said in a cross-border situation that the reduction in credit risk through taking collateral is sometimes counterbalanced by an increase in legal risk, documentation risk and operational risk.

Taking collateral is not risk-free because a bank can lose money under a fully collateralised transaction. This could theoretically happen where a counterparty defaulted at the same time as the value of corporate bond collateral plummeted because a corporate bond issuer also defaulted then. This is an example of joint default risk or double default risk.

Money could also be lost if a custodian failed and had not segregated bonds in his keeping properly: he said he would segregate them but did not actually do so.

Parties can also forfeit the right to liquidate collateral if they fail to use proper market standard documentation. Using the correct documentation becomes even more important if the collateral is transferred cross border.

Non-bank parties lost Independent Amounts (initial margin) posted to and reused by Lehman Brothers before they collapsed (please see page 413 for more on this). As we shall see in Chapter 2 collateral is not just about capture, it is very much about control too.

How could we define collateral? My definition is:

Legally watertight, valuable liquid property supporting a risk.

There has to be a legally watertight right to the collateral so you can enforce it; it has to be valuable so as to be worth something; liquid so you can sell it; property so you can own it or control it. However, with all these qualities it only supports a risk. It does not eliminate it completely all the time because market rates and prices are constantly changing.

In my definition, collateral *is* collateral – side by side with the main risk. It is not the be all and end all. A detailed risk analysis of your counterparty is of paramount importance.

WHY COLLATERAL IS TAKEN

Why do parties take collateral from each other?

- To improve but not eliminate credit risk continuously.
- To reduce risk exposure in order to do more business with each other when limits are under pressure.
- Because one party may only be able to deal with another on a collateralised basis due to its counterparty credit ratings policy.
- To be able to net risk exposure for regulatory capital purposes by transferring or pledging eligible assets. The Basel II Capital Accord allows this if the taking of collateral is backed up by positive legal opinions in the jurisdictions concerned.

These motivations are not completely separate and are often interlinked but normally one factor will dominate in any given situation and usually this will be the desire to reduce credit risk.

What types of collateral do parties typically take from each other? The following are most commonly taken:

- cash in mainstream currencies;
- G7 government bonds;*
- corporate bonds;
- bank standby letters of credit.

* *The G7 countries are Canada, France, Germany, Great Britain, Italy, Japan and the United States.*

The key concerns for parties receiving collateral is that it can be easily transferred and easily valued. In fact, many people will only agree to accept cash or US government securities as collateral because of these two concerns.

PRODUCT RISK EXPOSURE COVERED

The following are the main products that could be covered under collateral agreements, depending upon the needs of the parties:

- interest rate swaps and options;
- cross currency swaps;
- forward rate agreements;
- commodity derivatives;
- equity derivatives;
- bond options;

- credit derivatives;
- forward foreign exchange;
- currency options.

Only the biggest players currently have the systems to collateralise all these products. Transactions with very short-term maturities such as spot foreign exchange trades (which settle in two Local Business Days' time) are often not collateralised at all.

However, there is an increasingly strong trend towards cross product collateralisation (e.g. derivatives, repo, forward foreign exchange), which is likely to grow in the future as institutions manage collateral on a fully integrated basis across all these products. This is logical because if a counterparty went bust, it would affect its obligations under all its trading agreements and not just under one of them. It is, therefore, important that as many products as possible are eventually brought under a common collateral management and reporting structure, especially in times of crisis.

Taking security for counterparty credit risk has been common practice for centuries in moneylending, pawnbroking and from the nineteenth century in housing finance.

EVOLUTION OF COLLATERAL DOCUMENTATION

The first swap transaction (in the familiar market form) took place in 1981 between IBM and the World Bank with Salomon Brothers acting as the intermediary. It was a currency swap.

Taking collateral for OTC derivatives exposure began in the USA in the mid-1980s. There was no standardisation in legal documentation and control was via Excel or earlier spreadsheets. Calculating risk exposure and collateral took place monthly or weekly at best.

Taking collateral for derivatives exposure in Europe started in the early 1990s and followed the US precedent closely. The process worked but was highly manual and rather laborious. It is much more automated nowadays as we shall see in Chapter 2.

Cash and government securities with a remaining maturity up to ten years were the most acceptable collateral and parties only gradually ventured outside their domestic currency for each group when they could link in a foreign exchange feed to their spreadsheets. Each major player had its own legal documentation and preferences. This was largely pledge documentation, which usually took a long time to negotiate.

In late 1994 the International Swaps and Derivatives Association, Inc. ("ISDA") tried to bring some standardisation to market documentation by issuing, after extensive consultation, its New York Law Credit Support Annex which operates as a pledge or security interest but also allows collateral to be reused or sold by the taker (the Secured Party). A *User's Guide* focusing on the completion of Paragraph 13 (the Variables Paragraph which is similar to an ISDA Master Agreement Schedule) was published in 1995.

In late 1995 ISDA published its Credit Support Annex under English Law under which full legal title to and ownership of the collateral is transferred from the collateral giver, who is called the Transferor, to the collateral taker, who is called the Transferee. The English Law Annex has a similar structure as the New York Law Annex and uses much of the same vocabulary but it is legally different in nature.

At the same time ISDA also issued its Credit Support Deed under English Law under which the Secured Party has a security interest in the collateral but cannot reuse it (this is expressly forbidden in Paragraph 6(d) because the Pledgor retains an ownership interest in it). This changed with the adoption of the European Directive on Financial Collateral Arrangements in England in late 2003.

Also in 1995 ISDA published its Japanese Credit Support Annex, a security interest document which works on a lending and/or pledge basis with set-off rights. This document was revised in 2008.

The market quickly adopted the ISDA documentation so much so that today 92% of global collateral documentation used is published by ISDA.

The Asian currency crisis, the Russian debt default and the failure of Long-Term Capital Management, a major hedge fund, all of which occurred in 1997/98, gave impetus to tighter credit controls and greater interest in credit risk reduction techniques such as taking collateral.

Many banks will not trade with a counterparty until an appropriate collateral agreement has been put into place. This is typically the case with hedge funds and other unrated counterparties.

We shall be examining the ISDA English Law Credit Support Annex and the New York Law Credit Support Annex in depth in Chapters 5 and 6 as well as highlighting the differences between them.

The English Law Credit Support Deed is discussed in summary form in Chapter 7. Chapter 8 discusses developments in the market since 2002 when the previous edition of this book was published.

While acknowledging their differences, each ISDA Collateral Document has certain common features:

- calculation of collateral calls and returns;
- the mechanics and timing of transfers;
- method and timing of valuations by whoever is the Valuation Agent;
- collateral substitutions;
- dispute resolutions;
- enforcement on default;
- representations and warranties;

- allocation of expenses;
- reuse of collateral or not;
- default interest;
- an Elections and Variables Paragraph or a Margin Supplement to operate the arrangement.

With approximately 70% of the OTC derivatives market now subject to collateral documentation, it is important that such documentation is robust, legally watertight and enforceable.

With the advent of centralised clearing in 2011 and 2012 it is likely that more collateral will be taken in more ways. This subject is explored further in Chapter 8 on new and future developments which also covers ISDA's work on dispute resolution procedures, portfolio reconciliation and use of electronic messaging for collateral calls.

2

Collateral management from a European perspective

Defaults

Branches

External collateral management services

SOME FACTS AND FIGURES

If collateral is king, control of it is key and that is the function of a collateral management unit.

Every year ISDA publishes a Margin Survey that reports on volumes and trends in the global collateral market. The *ISDA Margin Survey 2011* estimated some interesting figures that have a bearing on the scope of collateral management, viz:

- Nearly 150,000 signed collateral agreements existed at the end of 2010.
- 92% of these collateral agreements were ISDA documents.
- 84% of these collateral agreements were two-way (e.g. both parties could potentially post collateral) and 16% were one-way.
- Overall, firms collateralised about 70% of their OTC derivatives risk exposure.
- Product-wise 93% of credit derivatives were collateralised; 79% of interest rate and currency swaps; 72% of equity derivatives; and 58% of foreign exchange transactions.
- Estimated global collateral value for OTC derivatives risk exposure at the end of 2010 was US$2.9 trillion (US$2,900 billion).
- In the 10 years between 2000–10 the amount of collateral in circulation grew at a compounded annual rate of 30% against a 14% compounded annual growth rate of gross risk exposure over the same period.
- 86% of major dealers base collateral thresholds on credit ratings.
- US$ and Euro cash were taken 80% as collateral and UK, US, EU and Japanese government bonds 9%. Cash is being taken more and more for operational convenience.
- Overall 71% of Independent Amounts (see page 15 for an explanation of this term) is commingled with normal collateral. The remaining 29% is segregated in various ways.
- Large dealers reused 74% of the collateral they received to meet collateral calls from other counterparties.
- 73% of market players now reconcile their deal portfolios on a regular basis. The Fed 14 dealers (see page 12 for a definition of this term) do this every business day.
- The Fed 14 had US$41 billion held as margin by central clearing counterparties at the end of 2010. US$36 billion was where dealers acted as executing brokers and US$5 billion as derivatives clearing members.
- Outsourcing of some collateral functions is done by 20% of major dealers. This is mainly done for reconciliation purposes.

Traditionally collateral management was classified as an operations function. However, some banks now regard it as a credit or derivatives risk management function while others see it as part of their liquidity management. Nonetheless, however individual institutions may wish to categorise it, the important thing is that collateral management must be able to perform its functions effectively in normal times and in crises.

Following the 2008 credit crunch collateral managers operate in a world where the demands from regulators, industry bodies (e.g. ISDA) and clients all place significant demands on resources (people and systems). The speed and scope of these changes involve continuous monitoring of market developments to ensure that the collateral management unit is following not only market 'best practice' but also regulatory requirements.

Portfolio reconciliations have become the focus of particular attention by the leading regulators leading to a major system-based solution to daily portfolio reconciliations (via triResolve) used by both the major broker-dealer banks and the buy side (e.g. hedge funds and asset managers). This has resulted in greater transparency in the underlying trades. The need for a robust, well-controlled, portfolio reconciliation process can be seen as a pre-requisite for many organisations.

ISDA has published a number of papers giving collateral managers guidance on operational best practice. Examples are *Best Practices for the OTC Derivatives Collateral Process* (30 June 2010) together with a specific paper from the Collateral Steering Committee on *Collateralized Portfolio Reconciliation Best Operational Practices* (20 January 2010). Aligning your collateral management process and procedures, including applicable timelines, to these industry recommendations is seen as a sound and prudent step.

In recent years there has been a trend to move collateral management units into the Operations area (for reduced costs and closer alignment with settlements/valuations departments). Investment in technology has definitely helped this move, allowing for a more streamlined and controlled process. Once large firms had invested in technology they were then easily able to manage growth in CSA volumes. Some firms also see the collateral management unit as providing a client service and so some have created high-level service offerings specifically aimed at buy-side clients like hedge funds and asset managers.

The credit crisis has moved collateral firmly centre stage and given it a much higher profile because of its risk mitigation function.

WHAT COLLATERAL MANAGEMENT UNITS DO

Collateral management units therefore have much to do including the following:

- to record details of the collateralised relationship in the collateral management system;
- to monitor customer risk exposure and collateral received or posted on the agreed margin frequency (normally every business day);
- to undertake sanity checks on data received (e.g. mark-to-market figures used to determine CSA risk exposure) ensuring that data is available, its integrity and validating it;
- to call for margin as required on the agreed frequency (normally every business day) taking into account collateral already held, Independent Amounts, Thresholds, Minimum Transfer Amounts and rounding (these terms are explained on pages 15–17);
- to transfer eligible collateral to its counterparty where a valid call has been made. The collateral manager will try to source this internally first where bond collateral is involved;
- to review the same matters if a collateral call is received from a counterparty and meets call response deadlines;
- to check that collateral to be received from a counterparty is of an eligible type agreed in the collateral documentation;
- where a custodian is involved, to ensure that the collateral is transferred by the counterparty to the custodian within the normal settlement timescale; where a custodian is not used the collateral management unit does this for its own account;
- to deal with any failures to deliver bond collateral and cash margin;
- to call for Independent Amounts where required by a risk manager;
- to apply the agreed "haircuts" (discounted values) to collateral being called or received;
- to reuse collateral (called collateral rehypothecation) where permitted in line with policy and liquidity guidelines;
- to return surplus collateral when requested in accordance with the documentation's terms;
- to deal with requests for collateral substitutions from clients and to manage their own substitution needs. These are often driven by Front Office requirements, corporate events or bond maturities;
- to ensure that each party holds appropriate standard settlement instructions;
- to pay over coupons on bonds promptly after receipt to collateral providers where this does not create or increase a margin call. This function is very often outsourced to the corporate actions or settlements department that already deals with this function for other areas (e.g. repos and securities lending);

- to calculate and pay over interest on cash collateral at agreed intervals and to monitor its receipt;
- to deal with disagreements or disputes over risk exposure calculations and collateral valuations as they arise in accordance with the collateral documentation and market practice including ISDA's Dispute Resolution Process (see Chapter 8);
- to act as Valuation Agent where agreed in the collateral documentation. In practice this means being proactive on behalf of both parties to the CSA;
- to reconcile portfolios of Transactions at regular intervals. This happens when a new counterparty is taken on or when new products are being collateralised and specifically in any case when a dispute over a collateral call arises. One notable recent market change has been the increased priority given to the importance and timing of reconciliation. New ISDA market recommendations require scheduled reconciliations according to the size of trade portfolios. The Fed 14* (also called the G14) reconcile their deal portfolios with each other every business day;
- to co-ordinate risk exposure and collateral valuations of various branches if the collateral management function is centralised in one place in the world;
- to deal with default situations in conjunction with the legal and credit functions and with senior management;
- to deal with assignments, unwinds, credit events and trade compression in line with best practice;
- to become involved as necessary in collateral agreement negotiation. Specifically the collateral management unit should (either directly or indirectly) have control over the operational aspects of the CSAs and ensure that their terms can be adequately monitored and controlled;
- to provide client and internal reporting;
- to perform special collateral projects.

* *The Fed 14, also called the G14, are Bank of America-Merrill Lynch, Barclays Capital, BNP Paribas, Citigroup, Credit Suisse, Deutsche Bank, Goldman Sachs, HSBC, JPMorgan Chase, Morgan Stanley, The Royal Bank of Scotland plc, Société Générale, UBS and Wells Fargo.*

So a collateral management unit is very busy, and we will shortly study many of these elements individually. First, however, I want to underline the importance of having written collateral policies and operating procedures in place because without them collateral management would just be "making it up as it goes along". It is becoming more common for a Service Level Agreement ("SLA") to be put in place with all key interfaces and dependencies to ensure adequate and acceptable levels of performance can be implemented and monitored and for appropriate escalation procedures to be clearly defined. Regulatory developments (e.g. the US Dodd-Frank Act) are likely to make this mandatory in applicable jurisdictions.

The collateral management functions mentioned above are controlled by a collateral management system. This is essentially a series of interlinked automated databases that bring together all the elements agreed in the collateral agreements so that they can be implemented on a day-to-day basis. Essentially the front office deal valuation systems feed into the collateral database.

Collateral systems range in complexity and breadth of functionality. At the lowest level, a firm might use Excel spreadsheets or an Access database to calculate net risk exposure and collateral requirements. At the highest level, dedicated vendor platforms and/or in-house systems provide highly automated tools for management of the end-to-end collateral process via a series of workflows and straight through processing. These can provide CSA storage, automated trade capture, collateral calculation, collateral eligibility checks, interest payments, substitutions, reporting etc. Such systems provide scalability while giving Senior Management and Risk comfort that collateral-related tasks are being performed to accepted market standards.

THE IMPORTANCE OF POLICIES AND PROCEDURES

Control is key with collateral and a robust control regime including monitoring and escalation is vital in managing collateral (to avoid a false sense of security) and should contain the following elements:

- a well-defined and enforceable general collateral policy in writing, approved by senior management and understood and widely distributed in the organisation. It should be regularly updated (we would say every six months) and provide built-in procedures for departures from it. Such concessions would usually be approved by a credit department. Such a policy would also speed up the negotiation process considerably if some negotiation boundaries are clearly established. This policy should also cover such aspects as product coverage that can be supported; applicable trading locations/offices; eligible collateral types and the approval process for deviations from it;
- a set of clear and flexible operating procedures;
- clear communication lines with the counterparty;
- standardised legal documentation where possible. This can be initiated by a documentation request process that states desired credit terms; products to be covered; and specific legal requirements (based on industry legal opinions);
- default "fire drills". Since the insolvency of Lehman Brothers in September 2008, many banks have written step-by-step procedures

on what to do if a counterparty fails to deliver collateral and it is decided to terminate all Transactions under the related ISDA Master Agreement. In addition, legal departments in some banks have composed template documentation that can be adapted and used in these circumstances;

- as much automation (ideally by straight through processing) as possible.

In my opinion time spent in getting these matters right is time well spent. Credit, Legal, Front Office, Middle Office, Operations and Collateral Management must all be happy with the end result. Collateralisation is nowadays very much a team effort in an organisation.

At this stage I should like to acknowledge my grateful thanks to Nigel Underwood of the Collateral Management Control Unit of Rabobank International, London for his input on the practical aspects of this chapter and also to Algorithmics, an IBM company, for its kind permission to illustrate the text with screen shots and for its input on the practical aspects of collateral management arising from its experience of implementing such systems in numerous institutions of different sizes. The Algo Collateral Operations solution is representative of the software available to collateral managers and the screen shots are illustrative of the information they need and use.

SETTING UP A COLLATERALISED RELATIONSHIP

Once all the terms of the collateral agreement are agreed and the documentation completed, it is necessary for the bespoke elements of the collateral arrangements between the parties to be input in the collateral management system. These include:

- the Base Currency;
- whether the collateral arrangements are one-way or two-way (unilateral or bilateral). Unilateral CSAs are common with supranational institutions (i.e. collateral flowing one way to the supranational institution) or with corporates/hedge funds (i.e. one-way flow to highly rated financial institutions who are their counterparties). It should be noted that after the Lehman Brothers insolvency in 2008 there was a trend towards two-way margining driven by the demands of regulators and buy-side clients. Recently some governments (e.g. Portugal) have been offering two-way margining.
- the type or nature of eligible collateral;
- the level of haircuts (Valuation Percentages) applying to the collateral;
- the level of Independent Amounts, Thresholds, Minimum Transfer Amounts and rounding;

- frequency of valuing risk exposure and collateral;
- notification times;
- dispute resolution procedures;
- collateral delivery periods (these could be shortened, for example, with hedge funds, where practicable);
- the type of quotations to be sought for bond collateral in a dispute (e.g. bid or mid-market valuations): when "Value" is determined it should include accrued interest (Best Practice 2.4);
- the rate of interest to be paid (including any potential spread) on cash collateral: the "Value" of cash collateral should, as a general rule, exclude accrued interest (Best Practice 2.4).

It might be useful to explain some of these terms at this point:

Independent Amount

Depending upon the wording you use in the ISDA collateral agreement this term either means collateral given by your counterparty as initial margin and excluded from the collateral balance or it is equivalent to maintenance or variation margin (i.e. an amount that is included in the collateral balance). The *2001 ISDA Margin Provisions* more helpfully differentiate between these types of Independent Amounts by calling them Lock-Up Margin and Additional Margin Amount respectively. However, few in the market use the *2001 ISDA Margin Provisions* and so terms like initial margin and Independent Amount are still commonly used.

Independent Amounts can either be set for an individual transaction or calculated on an entire portfolio of trades. They are typically defined by the Risk Department at the time of the trade execution, but are also defined in the CSA in some cases. When set at the trade level they are either fixed sums or percentages of the notional amounts of underlying transactions and both are set by credit departments. Sometimes they are linked to specific trade types (e.g. credit default swaps) or based upon the tenor of the trade. Large individual trades may need review by the credit department where the trades are highly structured and involve periodic amortisation, for instance. If set at a portfolio level they tend to be based on an externally calculated measure such as Value at Risk (VaR).

Independent Amounts are typically applied with lower-rated counterparties such as hedge funds. They are designed to provide greater protection should a counterparty default and it is necessary to unwind transactions. It would be normal for the hedge fund to maintain a certain level of Independent Amount with the counterparty while at the same time the counterparty may be posting variation margin to the hedge fund under a two-way ISDA collateral agreement.

In the English Law CSA Paragraph 10 the net risk exposure the Transferee has on the Transferor at any one time is called the Credit Support Amount. This is defined as:

- the Transferee's Exposure, plus
- all Independent Amounts applicable to the Transferor, if any, minus
- all Independent Amounts applicable to the Transferee, if any, minus
- the Transferor's Threshold, if any.

Example

Party A upon calculating the valuation of the swap transactions he has entered into with Party B finds that he has a risk exposure of US$5,000,000 on Party B. Neither party has any Independent Amounts and Party B's Threshold is US$500,000. This means that Party A can make a collateral call on Party B for US$4,500,000 (assuming that Party B's Minimum Transfer Amount is below this figure, which it probably is).

However, where the Credit Support Amount in respect to a party results in a negative figure for that party it shall be deemed to be zero (i.e. no collateral call can be made on it).

In the New York Law CSA the Credit Support Amount is calculated in essentially the same way.

Independent Amounts/initial margin have seen a high level of focus (post the Lehman Brothers insolvency) resulting in ISDA publishing a specific document on the subject in its *Independent Amounts* white paper (1 March 2010). More recently, specific requirements have been proposed by US regulators in the Dodd-Frank Act for segregation of initial margin for non-cleared Transactions. This will be a legal entitlement that must be offered to the applicable client and will require notification and affirmation (see Chapter 8 on developments since 2002).

Threshold

This is the monetary figure agreed in the collateral agreement below which a call for collateral cannot be made. It represents the unsecured risk exposure you are prepared to accept upon your counterparty and is considered with the Minimum Transfer Amount. The Threshold may be fixed at a level stated in the CSA or be linked to a credit ratings table. Then it will vary depending upon the formal credit rating of the collateral giver. However, fixed amount Thresholds are now often used and not just with lower-rated or unrated counterparties but also with banks and non-banks in some cases.

In the wake of the Lehman Brothers insolvency the collateral market witnessed a strong drive towards two-way margining and lower Thresholds (in many cases zero). The momentum for this change came from end-users, buy-side clients and regulators as the perception of risk changed and the use of collateral became more "risk mitigant" in nature rather than "deal enabling".

As a corollary, these lower or even zero Thresholds were often accompanied by higher Minimum Transfer Amounts.

Other recent developments have seen one-way margining against banks where the counterparty is unable for regulatory reasons to enter into two-way margining; for example, UCITS funds where their constitutional documents do not allow them to take on credit risk on their counterparties and so they would need zero Thresholds on them.

Minimum Transfer Amount

Collateral transfers cost time and money and so it is useful to have a minimum monetary figure (e.g. US$500,000) below which a collateral call is not made. This is often called a "nuisance amount" and is usually set at a high enough level to avoid all but significant collateral calls. In the USA Minimum Transfer Amounts can exceed US$1 million. While a Minimum Transfer Amount can be linked to a credit ratings table the trend for a while following Lehman's insolvency was to use a fixed amount, although this was not always mutual. For example, a highly-rated counterparty might for operational reasons seek a higher trigger amount than its counterparty before it was required to deliver/return collateral.

Rounding

A rounding convention is normally used so that the transfer of uneven amounts of collateral (e.g. US$578,946.92) is avoided. Typically such amounts are rounded up for deliveries and down for returns to the nearest US$1,000 or multiples of US$10,000.

Set out below are some screen shots that show how these matters could be input in the Algo Collateral Operations solution. For the purposes of this exercise please assume that our Collateral Management Unit is that of PCH Bank and the counterparty is XYZ Bank plc.

While all these boxes in Figure 2.1 overleaf may be specific to the Algo Collateral Operations solution, the key matters are the definition of both the Principal and Counterparty in the CSA; the Base Currency (Agreement Currency on the screen) is US Dollars; and identification that it is a bilateral CSA (Posting Party = Both). Further useful information includes the location of Principal and Counterparty which can help a collateral manager identify and prioritise margin calls to make based on his counterparty's location.

Figure 2.1

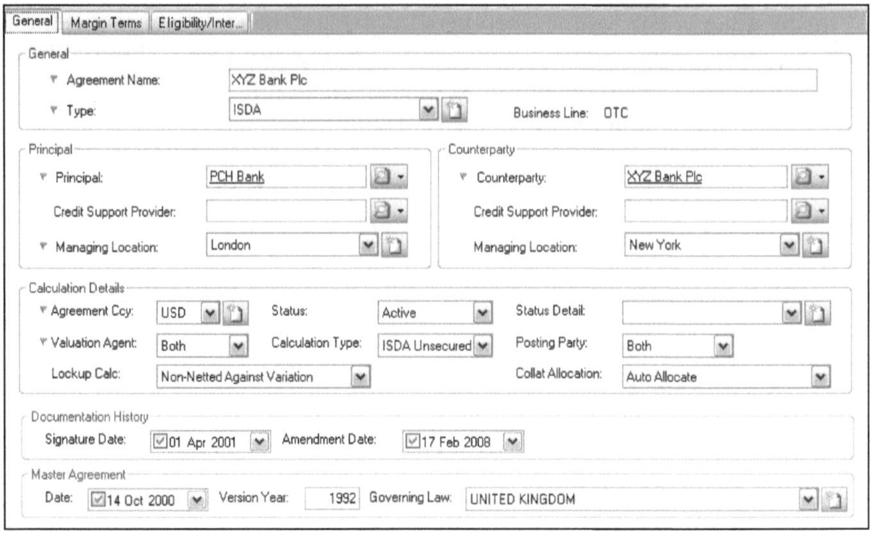

Eligible Credit Support

Figure 2.2 shows that cash in US Dollars and US government securities are Eligible Credit Support under the collateral agreement between PCH Bank and XZY Bank plc. The haircuts (i.e. the agreed discounts to face value) are shown for both held and posted collateral (the Posted Valn %).

This screen shows that both Principal and Counterparty can receive US$ cash (with no haircut) and US Treasuries with tenors of up to 1 year (1% haircut); between 1 and 5 years (2% haircut); between 5 and 10 years (3% haircut); and between 10 and 30 years (5% haircut). These haircuts would be deducted from 100% to give the Valuation Percentage as defined in the CSA.

Figure 2.2

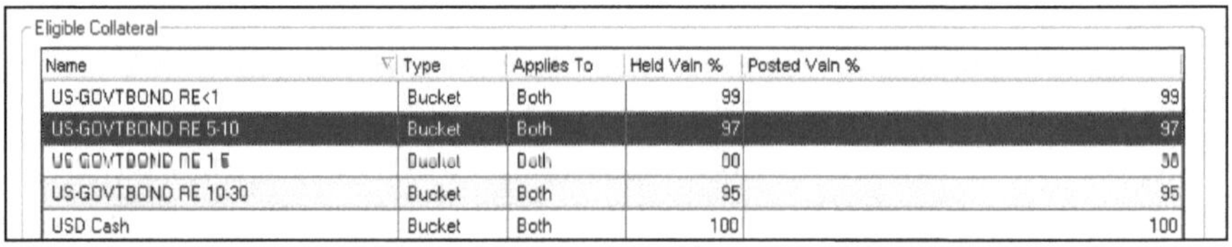

Eligible Collateral

Name	Type	Applies To	Held Valn %	Posted Valn %
US-GOVTBOND RE<1	Bucket	Both	99	99
US-GOVTBOND RE 5-10	Bucket	Both	97	97
US-GOVTBOND RE 1-5	Bucket	Both	[illegible]	[illegible]
US-GOVTBOND RE 10-30	Bucket	Both	95	95
USD Cash	Bucket	Both	100	100

Threshold, Minimum Transfer Amounts, Independent Amounts and Rounding

As mentioned above, these amounts may be fixed or linked to credit ratings. Figure 2.3A shows an example of fixed amounts. In this example both Principal and Counterparty have the same fixed Threshold but they can be different reflecting different creditworthiness between parties.

Figure 2.3B shows where these are linked to external credit ratings. In the CSA parties may select which credit rating agencies to reference and the actual Threshold and Minimum Transfer Amount. Typically the major rating agencies (Moodys, S&P and Fitch) are referenced but it is possible to use others. The type of credit rating is also defined in the CSA. While Long Term credit ratings are most widely used, parties may choose others (Short Term, Financial Strength, etc.). A Credit Department should decide which is appropriate.

In the example PCH Bank is rated Aa2/AA/AA+ and XYZ Bank plc is rated Aa3/AA-/AA. The standard market convention is to use the lowest credit rating to determine the Threshold and Minimum Transfer Amount, thus taking a more conservative approach.

It is also possible to include an Independent Amount linked to a credit rating. This will be payable by the relevant party upon being downgraded to the relevant level. In Figure 2.3C overleaf the counterparty XYZ is required to post an Additional Amount of US$2 million should it be rated Baa2/BBB/BBB. The fact that only counterparty XYZ is required to post such an amount reflects the relative difference in creditworthiness between the two parties.

Figure 2.3A

(Fixed amounts)

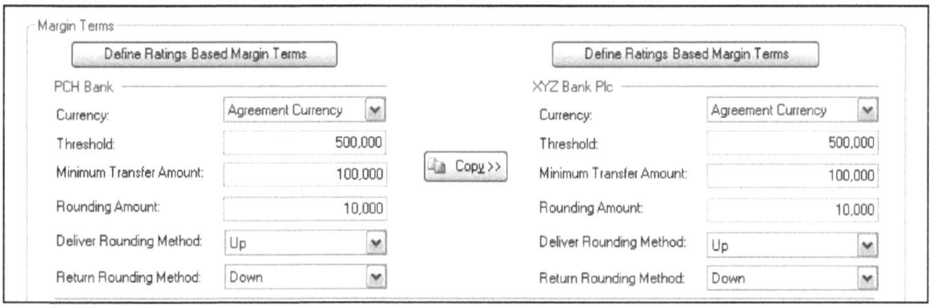

Figure 2.3B

(Rating linked)

Moody	Fitch	S & P	Threshold	MTA	Rounding Amount	Additional Margin	Lock Up Margin
Aaa	AAA	AAA	50,000,000	1,000,000	10,000	0	
Aa1	AA+	AA+	40,000,000	1,000,000	10,000	0	
Aa2	**AA**	AA	**30,000,000**	**1,000,000**	**10,000**	**0**	
Aa3	AA-	AA-	10,000,000	500,000	10,000	0	
A1	A+	A+	10,000,000	500,000	10,000	0	
A2	A	A	5,000,000	500,000	10,000	0	
A3	A-	A-	5,000,000	500,000	10,000	0	
Baa1	BBB+	BBB+	1,000,000	250,000	10,000	0	
Baa2	BBB	BBB	1,000,000	250,000	10,000	0	
Baa3	BBB-	BBB-	0	100,000	10,000	0	
Ba1	BB+	BB+	0	100,000	10,000	0	

Figure 2.3C

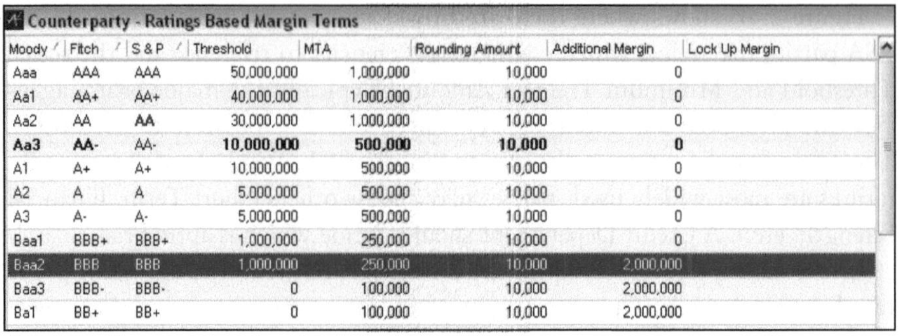

Counterparty - Ratings Based Margin Terms

Moody	Fitch	S&P	Threshold	MTA	Rounding Amount	Additional Margin	Lock Up Margin
Aaa	AAA	AAA	50,000,000	1,000,000	10,000	0	
Aa1	AA+	AA+	40,000,000	1,000,000	10,000	0	
Aa2	AA	AA	30,000,000	1,000,000	10,000	0	
Aa3	**AA-**	AA-	**10,000,000**	**500,000**	**10,000**	**0**	
A1	A+	A+	10,000,000	500,000	10,000	0	
A2	A	A	5,000,000	500,000	10,000	0	
A3	A-	A-	5,000,000	500,000	10,000	0	
Baa1	BBB+	BBB+	1,000,000	250,000	10,000	0	
Baa2	BBB	BBB	1,000,000	250,000	10,000	2,000,000	
Baa3	BBB-	BBB-	0	100,000	10,000	2,000,000	
Ba1	BB+	BB+	0	100,000	10,000	2,000,000	

Reprinted with permission from Algorithmics, an IBM company.

Interest Rate and payment frequency

(See Distributions below for a more detailed explanation.)

Figure 2.4 shows the agreed Interest Rate for cash collateral together with the frequency at which Interest will be paid. This will usually be monthly in the market but the English Law CSA Paragraph 11 template wording provides that it can also occur whenever a Return Amount of cash collateral is made by the collateral taker to the collateral giver. Whether this is possible will depend upon the parties' systems.

On this screen, cash collateral in US$ is eligible and interest will be paid at Fed Funds flat (identified by the 0 spread). Interest will be paid on the first calendar day of each month (see the Monthly Recurrence field). How interest is calculated can often cause disputes between collateral managers because the collateral agreement is not always specific enough. Is interest to be calculated on a calendar day or on a business day basis? Or is it to be calculated on a simple or compound basis? The simple basis is the market convention.

Figure 2.4

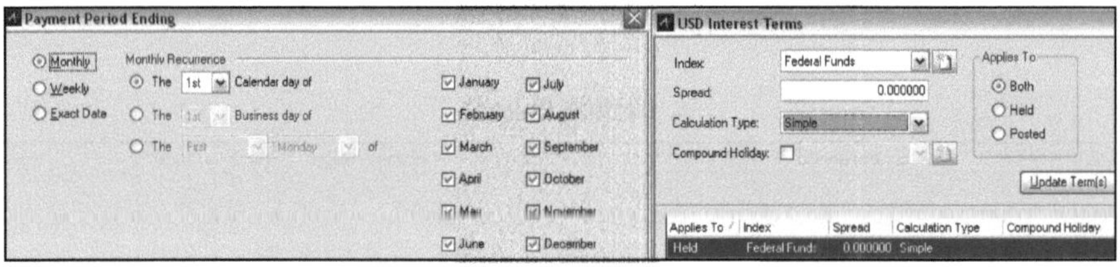

Reprinted with permission from Algorithmics, an IBM company.

EXPOSURE MONITORING AND COLLATERAL VALUATION AND CALLING

This is one of the most important functions of a collateral management unit.

Each Local Business Day the unit should receive an automated list of tasks showing which customers need to be called for collateral and which collateral calls the unit can expect from its counterparties. This is the result of the collateral calculation that takes into account total net risk exposure, the current collateral position and the credit terms of the CSA.

Typically a collateral manager will want to see all amounts involved in the margin calculation clearly displayed. This allows him to validate or approve that the numbers are as expected. Further drilldown into these numbers should also be possible for verification. Since the counterparty making the margin call is typically the Valuation Agent it may also be required to provide a report of all trades and mark-to-market ("MTM") valuations to the client. This should be possible from the collateral management system automatically. If a dispute arises such a report will be required for verification of the portfolio and MTM valuations through a reconciliation. Details of the underlying transactions and collateral breakdown are frequently sent to counterparties either attached to a margin demand and/or upon request. It should be noted that more counterparties are requesting this data even if no margin call is due.

There is no fixed standard for reporting of portfolios between clients but ISDA has made recommendations on minimum fields to report (ISDA *Minimum Market Standards for Collateralized Portfolio Reconciliation*, 20 January 2010). These are intended to make the reconciliation process more automated. Firms using a vendor system such as Algo Collateral Operations and/or triResolve will have the benefit of an automated reconciliation option that can speed up time taken for resolution of disputes.

There is not much standardisation in the market of the elements or presentation of this portfolio information but vendors are attempting to provide generic reports that can be shared between counterparties. For example, Algo Collateral Operations users can all exchange data in a single format thus simplifying the reconciliation process. In recent years, firms have invested large amounts in reconciliation, including vendor solutions such as triResolve, thus reducing earlier problems such as data format/content inconsistency. (See also the Portfolio Reconciliations section below.)

Within the collateral management system it should be possible to identify not just the margin calls to make and receive but also the underlying detail within the calculation of each. Figure 2.5 overleaf summarises the precise position for an individual customer (in this case XYZ Bank plc).

This report shows details of aggregate trades and their present mark-to-market value (Net Exposure in Prin Favor). These items feed in automatically from the trading systems, risk systems or any other system where the value of the transactions is calculated. The report also shows collateral received or posted, where applicable, and revalued using the latest bond prices for securities and interest rates for cash balances with the proper haircut or Valuation Percentage applied.

In this example PCH Bank is in the money for US$36,341,983.76 with XYZ Bank plc or, in other words, it is exposed to XYZ Bank plc for US$36,341,983.76. Given the current Threshold of US$10,000,000, and applying the relevant Minimum Transfer Amount and Rounding Amounts

Figure 2.5

XYZ Bank Plc

Margin Calculation

ISDA Unsecured Calculation as of 01/04/2011 10:05:41 (London) in USD.

Net Exposure in Prin Favor :	36,341,983.76
Net Additional Margin :	0.00
Threshold :	10,000,000.00
Collateral Posted :	0.00
Collateral Held :	0.00
Minimum Transfer Amount :	500,000.00
Rounding Amount :	10,000.00
Rounding Method :	Up
Variation Deliver to Prin :	**26,350,000.00**
Variation Demand Call Amount :	**26,350,000.00**

Reprinted with permission from Algorithmics, an IBM company.

from the CSA, the calculated margin call is US$26,350,000. Please note that the call amount is rounded up in this example which is market standard.

At this point PCH Bank will send a Collateral Notice to XYZ Bank plc by email. Such a notice might take the form of Figure 2.6.

As mentioned above, the collateral manager will normally email the Collateral Notice to the counterparty and may follow this up with an email or telephone call to see if they agree with the call figure. Differences are inevitable because the risk exposure may have been calculated by each of them at slightly different times using differently constituted yield curves. Such differences can be large, for instance with cross currency swaps, as these involve FX rates as well as yield curves. Trades may also have been overlooked by one of the parties (perhaps because of a booking/misbooking issue

Figure 2.6

To: XYZ Bank Plc
Contact(s): Collateral Manager (collateral@XYZBank.com)
RE: XYZ Bank Plc

This notice is confidential, unauthorized use is forbidden. Please destroy if you are not the addressee.

Pursuant to the ISDA agreement between PCH Bank and XYZ Bank Plc we hereby confirm notice of the following Margin Call requirement(s) as of Close of Business 31 March 2011. All figures below are in USD.*

Notification of Margin Call

Net Exposure in Prin Favor :	36,341,983.76
Net Additional Margin :	0.00
Threshold :	10,000,000.00
Collateral Posted :	0.00
Collateral Held :	0.00
Minimum Transfer Amount :	500,000.00
Rounding Amount :	10,000.00
Rounding Method :	Up
Variation Deliver to Prin :	**26,350,000.00**
Variation Demand Call Amount :	**26,350,000.00**

Reprinted with permission from Algorithmics, an IBM company.

or as a result of a trade assignment). The ISDA *Best Practices for the OTC Derivatives Collateral Process* Section 7 deals with this subject. When collateral is held this must also be valued, and the source of prices for any bond position may also cause differences in the overall margin call calculation.

In the vast majority of cases, collateral calls are agreed without problem with no need for an email/telephone chaser, but where this is not the case the parties can invoke a dispute resolution procedure (see pages 116–21).

Of course, it is possible that XYZ Bank plc could be in a position to make a collateral call on PCH Bank on another Local Business Day. Figure 2.7 shows how PCH Bank would be advised of this from the Algo Collateral Operations system.

Figure 2.7

XYZ Bank Plc

Margin Calculation

ISDA Unsecured Calculation as of 05/04/2011 11:33:25 (London) in USD.

Net Exposure in Prin Favor :	29,341,450.09
Net Additional Margin :	0.00
Threshold :	10,000,000.00
Collateral Posted :	0.00
Collateral Held :	26,350,000.00
Minimum Transfer Amount :	100,000.00
Rounding Amount :	10,000.00
Rounding Method :	Down
Return to Cpty :	**-7,000,000.00**
Variation Antic Demand Call Amount :	**-7,000,000.00**

Reprinted with permission from Algorithmics, an IBM company.

The next day the risk exposure has gone down from US$36,341,983.76 to US$29,341,450.09.

The previous requirement for US$26,350,000 has been received ("Collateral Held"). This creates a situation where PCH Bank is now overcollateralised by US$7,000,000. It is the standard convention to round down Return Amounts and so PCH Bank may expect a collateral call for US$7,000,000 from XYZ Bank plc.

If both parties are acting as their own Valuation Agents it is possible but unlikely that XYZ Bank plc may not call at all. If it does not, PCH Bank is under no obligation to point out to XYZ Bank plc that it could make a collateral call. Where a third party Valuation Agent is involved a call would be certain. However, third party Valuation Agents are only used by 20% of market players.

Based on the information recorded in the collateral management system a collateral call notice would be generated.

When an Independent Amount is required, it will be included in the margin call calculation. In the example below (Figure 2.8), XYZ Bank Plc is required to post Additional Margin of US$14,000,000 to PCH Bank. This has been added to the Exposure Amount before application of the Threshold in order to calculate the total collateral requirement. In this case, both MTM and Additional Margin are in the same direction.

Figure 2.8

XYZ Bank Plc

Margin Calculation

ISDA Unsecured Calculation as of 05/04/2011 11:39:32 (London) in USD.

Net Exposure in Prin Favor :	29,341,450.09
Net Additional Margin Due to Prin :	14,000,000.00
Threshold :	10,000,000.00
Collateral Posted :	0.00
Collateral Held :	26,350,000.00
Minimum Transfer Amount :	500,000.00
Rounding Amount :	10,000.00
Rounding Method :	Up
Variation Deliver to Prin :	**7,000,000.00**
Variation Demand Call Amount :	**7,000,000.00**

Reprinted with permission from Algorithmics, an IBM company.

TRANSFERS

Where cash is the only collateral, transfers are relatively easy involving as they do the electronic transfer of currencies normally on the same or following Local Business Day.

With bonds, transfers are more tricky. First of all the collateral manager needs to check, as he would with cash, that the securities he will receive are acceptable under the collateral agreement. If using a collateral management system, this should be checked automatically. If not, this will require manually checking the CSA to see which collateral types are eligible. If the collateral is not eligible this should be flagged and a request will be sent to the counterparty for an acceptable form of collateral.

The collateral manager should also check the price and the applicable haircut, if any, on a proposed bond. It is, however, the responsibility of the collateral giver to deliver correctly haircutted collateral amounts. If the bonds are lodged with a custodian or central securities depository system like Euroclear or Clearstream, they will either have to be transferred to the collateral manager's custodian or to his institution's account at Euroclear or Clearstream. Transfers to an external custodian can take up to three Local Business Days depending upon the terms of the collateral agreement. However, it is possible to make same day transfers if this is agreed early enough. Internal transfers can take place on the same day within Euroclear or Clearstream if matching instructions for the transfer are received by the cut-off time (e.g. 6.30 p.m. Brussels time for Euroclear Euclid or 4.00 p.m. for non-Euclid) or on the next business day if received after that time. Again we often see a separation of duties here between the collateral manager who will agree the call and the details of the collateral that will be posted by/to the counterparty and the settlements department who will take over from here and alert the collateral manager where a failure of receipt or delivery occurs.

Where this is the case charges for late delivery are likely to be made as per Paragraph 9(a) of the English Law CSA or Paragraph 11(a) of the New York Law CSA. With bonds the default interest provisions of Section 9(h)(i) of the 2002 ISDA Master Agreement will apply due to the close links between the two documents.

In making risk exposure calculations, collateral managers in Europe need to take account of any collateral already called for and in transit.

REUSE OF COLLATERAL

Under the ISDA Credit Support Annexes, collateral received is regularly reused by the collateral taker who, as owner, has a completely free choice as to how he deals with it. He can sell it, hold it, lend it out or reuse it. Most is used to meet incoming collateral calls. Often it is also reinvested with other desks within a bank, for example the repo desk. If the collateral portfolio is well managed, profits can be made. Given the larger volumes of collateral being used since the credit crisis, the associated increased cost of funding collateral is driving some firms to focus more on collateral optimisation. However, whether this is really a task for the collateral management unit depends upon the policy of the individual institution. This matter is discussed further on page 426 in Chapter 8. In addition it is covered in ISDA's *Best Practices for the OTC Derivatives Collateral Process* document of 30 June 2010 and is among the Dodd-Frank Act regulatory issues in 2011.

COLLATERAL SUBSTITUTIONS

Sometimes a collateral giver may need his securities collateral back to meet a delivery commitment to another party or a repo or stock loan needs to be unwound. In such cases, he would seek to replace the original bonds with new collateral but not necessarily of the same type or currency. For example, a party might request return of US government T-Bills, and replace them with UK government Gilts assuming the latter are eligible collateral under the CSA.

In some countries current law and tax practice might influence you to substitute the bond collateral before a coupon payment date as you could face tax liabilities if an interest payment is made to you. Similarly a collateral taker might request this if he could face a withholding tax liability on a manufactured dividend to be paid to a collateral giver.

Where the collateral giver makes a collateral substitution request, it is essential he obtains the consent of the collateral taker under the English Law CSA and this is advisable under the New York Law CSA especially where an English incorporated collateral giver is involved.

This is because where ownership of the bond has passed to the collateral taker, he has to have a free choice to consent to the substitution or the arrangement could be legally reclassified as a floating charge which might fail for lack of registration in England in a liquidation (see page 40). Despite this the industry is considering moving towards not requiring consent in substitutions as happens in the securities lending world but no final decision has yet been made on this.

Collateral substitution requests are normally made by email and may be followed by a telephone call. Normally the receiving collateral manager will agree it by email if this is not commercially inconvenient.

The collateral manager will consider if the bonds proposed for substitution are acceptable collateral (with particular focus on the post haircut value) and will consent if they are. Collateral managers would not refuse consent purely because the bonds for substitution had been repoed or had been posted to another counterparty. In these circumstances the collateral manager would have agreed with the repo desk that these bonds would be returnable upon request or the collateral manager will initiate a substitution with the counterparty to whom they have posted the bonds.

Assuming consent is given, the collateral taker will always check that he has received the new substitution bonds before he will release the collateral being substituted. If receipt of the substitution collateral can be verified early enough in the day the retransfer of the original collateral can be started on the same day. Before the collateral taker releases the bonds to be substituted he will, of course, be overcollateralised and the collateral giver will have a double risk exposure on the collateral taker in case he goes bankrupt before he returns the substituted bonds. So same day retransfer is desirable in these circumstances. Because of that a party may prefer to do substitutions with another client holding the same type of collateral and with whom they have a good working relationship and know that they can operationally meet the deadlines.

Cash collateral is sometimes substituted where a collateral giver requests this for the purposes of its own funding profile.

The market has largely relied upon cash to meet collateral obligations. This is mainly because it is simple to value (no haircuts) and transfer. Its use also considerably reduces the need for substitutions. However, the cost of using cash is often more expensive for firms given that they might not have large cash balances and may also be required to pay interest at market rates. Again, since the credit crisis, firms are reviewing the way in which they fund their collateral obligations, looking to ensure they minimise costs while at the same time adopting an operationally efficient programme.

Sections 9.3 and 9.4 of ISDA's *Best Practices for the OTC Derivatives Collateral Process* document also deals with substitutions.

DISTRIBUTIONS

Distributions cover payment of interest on cash collateral and coupons on bonds either receivable or payable.

Interest on cash collateral and any interest coupons on securities are always passed on to the collateral giver. This is because market practice is to regard the collateral giver as the owner of the securities *for economic purposes* and, by the collateral taker passing on distributions, to place the collateral giver in the same position he would have been in had he not transferred or pledged the securities collateral over the coupon payment date.

When bond coupons are paid, the collateral value of the bond will reduce because accrued interest is included in the bond price. Payment of bond coupons can therefore create a margin call and the ISDA collateral agreements allow the collateral taker to hold on to these payments in those circumstances as part of the collateral balance he holds (see commentary on Paragraph 5 of the English Law CSA on page 123). However, often in practice, the manufactured dividend is paid over even if a collateral call may ensue. Retention of the coupon is more likely to happen if there is a concern over the counterparty's creditworthiness rather than for operational reasons.

Payment of interest on cash collateral is agreed at a benchmark rate (e.g. EONIA or Fed Funds Rate) with or without a spread at an agreed interval (e.g. often on the second Local Business Day of a month for the previous calendar month). Section 11 of ISDA's *Best Practices for the OTC Derivatives Collateral Process* document expands on this subject.

During negotiation of collateral agreements between significant market players the payment date for interest is often one of the areas requiring compromise due to the particular functionalities of each party's operating systems. Non-bank counterparties might seek to include a spread in the interest calculations since they often do not have the same access to the money markets as banks and are thus not able to earn Fed Funds/EONIA on cash deposits. Therefore if they agreed to pay such interest rates on any cash collateral held they would lose money.

EONIA means European Overnight Index Average and is the interest rate banks will pay for overnight deposits in Euros. Fed Funds Rate is the interest rate at which US banks with surplus reserves lend to other banks which are temporarily short of reserves. It is set by the US Federal Reserve

Board. It is useful to point out that the Fed Funds Rate for the close of business on the previous Local Business Day is not available until New York opening time, so interest calculations for USD positions have to wait until early afternoon for European collateral managers. It is also common practice to send out detailed interest statements which will list the interest accrued per day. Best practice is for such statements to be sent on the first Local Business Day of the following month. Collateral managers are looking to promote electronic messaging as a means of communicating and agreeing interest payments on an industry-wide basis.

As regards distributions on bonds this is, as usual, slightly more complicated.

Under the English Law CSA the Transferee needs to transfer coupon payments on the Settlement Day following their payment. The Settlement Day is the first Local Business Day on which a trade in the relevant bonds would customarily settle. In practice they will try to do this on the same Local Business Day as they are received.

DISPUTES

Most disagreements are resolved before they reach the stage of a formal dispute.

Collateral disagreements centre on the calculation of risk exposure for the collateral call or the valuation of the collateral itself, or sometimes the CSA terms used for collateral calculation. The first of these is by far the most common type of dispute. Such disputes can arise for three main reasons viz:

Mark-to-model differences

This is where the parties calculate risk exposure at different times along the zero yield curve. Where the parties operate in different time zones one will close earlier than the other and if close of business prices are used they are bound to be different. Such differences also arise where an incorrect yield curve or trade details are input in the trading system. This could affect the whole day's trading records. Differences in valuation models also arise when valuing complex and highly structured trades.

Different trade population

This simply means that the parties have overlooked or omitted some trades in their collateralised portfolios. This might be due to upstream system issues, for example not feeding the correct trades into the collateral management system. Alternatively it could be due to incorrect capture of the correct portfolio details. For example, FX Spot trades are typically excluded from the overall risk exposure but if one counterparty includes them in the portfolio this will have an impact on the total risk exposure figure. A clear definition of Exposure within the CSA should avoid this risk. Sometimes transactions like swaptions are recorded as a single trade by one party and as two trades (i.e. a swap and an option) by the other. This point is considered further in the section on Portfolio reconciliations that follows. Different trade populations are the most common source of exposure disputes, hence the need for regular and proactive portfolio reconciliations in line with industry best practice.

Aggregating

This is where a mark-to-model difference affects each trade, compounding the difference across the whole portfolio. For example if your model gives an exposure valuation difference of US$10,000 for each trade then if a Portfolio has 500 trades the result would be a US$5 million difference.

ISDA's collateral documents individually contain a dispute procedure under which undisputed amounts are transferred to the collateral taker and the remaining amount at issue falls under a structured process involving primarily obtaining independent risk exposure quotations from dealers within agreed deadlines. The process is described in detail in the commentary on the relevant sections of the English Law CSA and the New York Law CSA respectively on pages 116–21 and 272–5.

Section 5 – Collateral Dispute Resolution in ISDA's *Best Practices for the OTC Derivatives Collateral Process* offers further guidance in this respect.

However, most disputes are resolved informally in one of three ways viz:

- **a mutually agreed tolerance level is included in the collateral document. The level may be expressed as a percentage or in US$ terms;**
- **each firm will "split the difference" of the disputed amount and will deliver only the undisputed amount as required by the collateral document;**
- **both parties agree to the undisputed amount only and revalue portfolios again the following day for comparison. If an exposure amount differs by a consistent amount, this amount is used to calculate a tolerance level.**

As we shall see in Chapter 8 on developments since 2002, an ISDA working group is proposing a Collateral Dispute Resolution Procedure for the market (see pages 418–23).

Disputes on collateral values are relatively rare and usually arise from exotic or not very liquid bonds and prices are difficult to obtain. Normally the difference is simple – a fault in pricing information or the wrong haircut. If it persists, the collateral taker usually requests the collateral giver to substitute the disputed collateral.

PORTFOLIO RECONCILIATIONS

Reconciliations are very important because parties need to know that the same trades are being collateralised and hence the level of collateral is correct. Most differences occur for two reasons: differences in trade valuation (especially with longer-dated trades or more exotic products) or in trade population.

In its *Collateral Survey 2000* ISDA reported that only 57% of market players reconciled their portfolios before trading on a collateralised basis. Therefore, alarmingly, at the start of the past decade 43% went in blind on Day 1. Reconciliation of deal portfolios is now far more disciplined helped by better automation. In its *Margin Survey 2011* ISDA reported that 100% of the Fed 14 and 73% of all market players regularly performed some form of portfolio reconciliation. It remains good practice to perform reconciliations and this often happens where the parties decide to extend their collateral arrangements to new products. It is also normal at the start of the collateralised relationship in order to reduce the risk of a dispute at that time. As mentioned earlier, the Fed 14 have undertaken to regulators to reconcile their deal portfolios with each other every business day.

Reconciliations are one of the regular and most time consuming features of a collateral manager's work and most frequently arise with mark-to-market exposure differences. For this purpose an automated reconciliation programme can be used which will initially record matched trades on a permanent basis. When a periodic reconciliation is done, if one of these trades is not shown this will be flagged by the system and can be investigated.

However, the most common problem in the past is that parties' trade portfolios are not in one common standard format and so collateral managers reconciling such portfolios spent much time reconfiguring the counterparty's trade information so that it could be compared to their own. Use of standard market platforms such as Algorithmics' Algo Reconciliation or triResolve from triOptima enable firms to reduce this issue since they allow them to create templates that auto-match regardless of data format. Moreover, there are now industry standards for the elements or presentation of this portfolio information (ISDA *Minimum Market Standards for Collateralized Portfolio Reconciliation* 20 January 2010).

DEFAULTS

What every collateral manager dreads is the non-delivery of collateral leading to a default situation under which all Transactions are closed out under the ISDA Master Agreement. Conversely, where there is an unremedied Event of Default under an ISDA Master Agreement, this will also trigger the collateral agreement's termination provisions.

Either of these circumstances entails a lot of urgent work involving the collateral management unit, the dealer(s) concerned, the Legal Department (who will send out the necessary notices), credit officers, Middle Office and Back Office. The impact of the default upon the bank's profit and loss account will be calculated by the Financial Control function and progress will be reported to senior management. Defaults of this nature are extremely rare but when they arise they can be large and have dramatic implications not only in-house but also across the market.

Collateral management units can factor in a period for the liquidation of their collateral. This might be calculated as shown in the table below.

Activity	Time	Day	
Collateral Valuation	Close of Business	Monday (1)	–1
Collateral Call	By 1.00 p.m.	Tuesday (1)	1
Counterparty to reply	By 5.00 p.m	Wednesday (1)	2
If agreed, OK. If not, dispute procedure applies. Dispute now assumed. Undisputed amount transferred and market quotations for exposure sought	By 5.00 p.m.	Thursday (1)	3
Agreement	By 1.00 p.m.	Friday (1)	4
Settlement T+2 (bond collateral)	By close of business	Tuesday (2)	6
Settlement fails. Event of Default notice issued		Wednesday (2)	8
Three Local Business Days' grace allowed for settlement under Section 5(a)(i) of the 1992 ISDA Master Agreement	By close of business	Monday (3)	11

The Bank for International Settlements has a "margin period of risk" for OTC Collateral of 10 business days.

In the above table a shorter period would apply to payments of cash collateral because there is no need for a two Local Business Day settlement period as for bonds. Moreover, if a 2002 ISDA Master Agreement is used there is a shorter one Local Business Day or one Local Delivery Day grace period for the Failure to Pay or Deliver Event of Default (Section 5(a)(i)).

Valuation Agent

The Valuation Agent is stated in the collateral document. In a collateral agreement between banks the Valuation Agent will be the party calling for either a delivery or return of collateral. However, where a large bank has a collateral arrangement with a small corporate it will invariably want to be the Valuation Agent for all purposes as it is likely to be best placed to calculate the risk exposure. It must act in good faith and in a commercially reasonable manner in this role. A Valuation Agent calculates risk exposure and makes collateral calls for both parties. In standard situations where this arrangement does not apply, if a collateral giver could claim return of collateral but does not do so, the collateral taker is under no obligation to return it. In contrast, where one party acts as Valuation Agent for both it is under an obligation to make such a collateral return call. Sometimes a Valuation Agent's role can be split with a third party. For instance, the Valuation Agent may value the trade portfolio and the third party will value the collateral. The use of third party collateral agents is becoming more common.

BRANCHES

Where a bank regularly takes collateral from customers in various financial centres around the world, each may have its own collateral management function operating under the global collateral policies of the central collateral management unit (probably located at the bank's head office) with permitted necessary local variations.

Monitoring of collateral on a global basis is not a perfect science. Take, for example, a large international bank that has three collateral management teams in Singapore, New York and London. Such a bank will typically manage a CSA in the region or branch nearest to its client's location. Thus, a European bank with three such collateral teams, but dealing with a Tokyo based counterparty, will probably manage the collateral using its Singapore team that has the advantage of being in the same time zone to make margin calls.

For such a large institution, trades will typically be booked in many branches across the globe. Often trades will be valued in the local branch due to system constraints. A potential impact is that trades booked in New York might not be valued until after the Singapore team has started its business day. Furthermore, the trades will be valued using rates/prices at close of business in New York. In contrast the Tokyo counterparty may have valued the trades using rates/prices at close of business in Tokyo. This will cause a difference in valuation and potentially in the margin call. Such differences are difficult to resolve since they are due to the operational setup of each institution and may cause daily differences.

As a result a collateral management unit in any of these locations might report different risk exposure on the same counterparty on the same day. Because no intra-day calling takes place and because counterparties are normally allocated to collateralised branches on a geographical basis and only one collateral management unit will call them, this is not a major problem. However it is fair to say that the global picture only stands still at weekends and on 1 January.

In addition, some major banks, with the necessary systems, would make one global collateral call. For this reason consistent internal risk management reporting is vital.

EXTERNAL COLLATERAL MANAGEMENT SERVICES

Where a corporate or a small bank lacks the internal resources or volume to establish its own collateral management unit it can still engage in collateralised business using a third party service.

JP Morgan Chase, Kas Bank NV, Blackrock and Barclays Capital all offer collateral management services as do Euroclear Bank N.V./S.A. through its Integrated Collateral Management Service and Clearstream through its Collateral Management Service.

The use of a third party collateral management service provider is likely to occur when one party (perhaps because of its size and/or operational capability) wishes to have its "own" collateral management system rather than just propose that the other (larger party) be Valuation Agent under the collateral document.

Assuming both parties are small and that they want to use an external collateral management service, they still enter into an ISDA Master Agreement and an ISDA collateral document with each other in the normal way. They also enter into a triparty agreement with the external collateral management service provider that covers operating arrangements with all counterparties in its securities clearing system. Where the two parties are just appointing a third party to act on their behalf this would be covered in a side letter with indemnity wording incorporated as applicable.

The external collateral management service provider will do the following:

- receive net exposure figures from either or both counterparties;
- seek to resolve any disputes about these;
- value collateral and check adequacy of cover;
- check eligibility of proposed collateral assets;
- transfer collateral assets according to the collateral document terms and the predefined preferences of both counterparties;
- accept same day delivery of collateral from outside its clearing system and make intra account transfers as appropriate within it;
- process substitutions;
- route coupon payments to the holder of securities;
- hold collateral assets in its own custody system;
- identify best available reuse of collateral opportunities;
- produce comprehensive daily valuation reports.

Such a service saves on infrastructure, technology and administrative costs for each party (although they still each have to value the risk exposure) but it does come at a price and will probably only be used as a precursor to each party establishing its own collateral management unit.

In the United States such a service is provided by Bank of New York Mellon, JPMorgan Chase and Citibank among others.

More normally only one of the parties will use such a service rather than both of them.

3

Legal issues relating to collateral from the European and US perspectives

EUROPEAN PERSPECTIVE BY PAUL HARDING

US PERSPECTIVE BY CHRISTIAN JOHNSON

EUROPEAN PERSPECTIVE BY PAUL HARDING

INTRODUCTION

In recent years laws relating to collateral have been on the move.

Back in December 1999, ISDA's Collateral Law Reform Group reported that despite legislative improvements before 1999 it remained the case that:

> **...current laws and rules throughout the European Union relating to the use of collateral are in many instances complex, inconsistent, impractical and/or out of date.**

That undesirable state of affairs resulted in uncertainty about the effectiveness of collateral arrangements and led to inefficiency, higher costs and increased risk.

GENERAL ISSUES

Because most collateral agreements are two-way or bilateral, the two parties to the collateral agreement (which we will assume is an ISDA Credit Support Annex under English Law) need to answer two basic questions first of all:

1 Do they each have the legal capacity to enter into OTC derivatives transactions and provide collateral? This is to confirm they are not acting beyond their powers or *ultra vires*.

2 Is close-out netting fully enforceable in their respective jurisdictions and if the underlying ISDA Master Agreement is multibranch and collateral is to be given or received, is close-out netting effective in those branches' jurisdictions?

In connection with the first point where an English company is concerned, Section 39 of the UK's 2006 Companies Act will generally protect third parties against *ultra vires* acts of their English (and Welsh) corporate counterparties but this is not so in many other jurisdictions. Counterparties of an English company have statutory protection and can safely assume (unless they definitely know otherwise) that the English company has the legal capacity to enter into OTC derivatives transactions and has taken all necessary internal action to authorise this. Therefore if you have negotiated in your ISDA Master Agreement Schedule for your English corporate counterparty to provide you with a board resolution confirming its legal capacity and authority to enter into OTC derivatives and it does not do so, you do not need to trigger a Breach of Agreement Event of Default. You can rely on the protection afforded by Section 39 of the 2006 Companies Act.

Close-out netting is very important, because it is against the closed-out net exposure that the collateral is applied in a default or bankruptcy situation. So close-out netting needs to be robust if collateral is to be enforced successfully. This can be gauged from netting legal opinions for each jurisdiction (whether commissioned by ISDA or by you).

The market has focused on two approaches to taking collateral – the security interest approach and the title transfer approach. Of these two approaches, the traditional one has been the creation of a security interest or pledge.

Security interest

Here the party giving the collateral is called the pledgor and the party receiving the collateral is called the pledgee. It is important to remember that the pledgor retains legal ownership of the collateral pledged to the pledgee.

Historically, collateral perfection requirements have taken various forms in different countries including the execution of the pledge document itself, its filing or registration, the use of a segregated account to hold bonds and/or the delivery of notices to third parties. With bonds, precise perfection requirements depend upon whether they are debt or equity; bearer or registered; in certificate (rare nowadays) or electronic book entry form; or held with a single custodian or through a chain of them. For many reasons, including uncertainty as to which rules applied (and when) and the difficulty of complying with these requirements in fast-moving bond markets or in relation to book entry securities held through a chain of custodians, these rules often impeded or delayed the perfection of pledge collateral arrangements and still do in some countries today. However, failure to comply with them could result in the invalidity or unenforceability of the collateral under the pledge.

Fortunately, the implementation of the European Directive on Financial Collateral Arrangements (2002/47/EC) (the "Collateral Directive") (see pages 45–7 for details) has streamlined this process in the countries that have adopted it.

Most financial institutions holding bonds as collateral want to deal freely with them until they are required to re deliver equivalent bonds under the collateral arrangement. This includes the freedom to sell, lend or repo the bonds to a third party subject always to the return of equivalent fungible bonds (i.e. of the same issue and issuer) to the collateral giver provided it performs its obligations under the ISDA Master Agreement in full. By dealing freely with the bonds the pledgee can use them efficiently and potentially increase its returns and lower its costs.

However, before December 2003 when England adopted the Collateral Directive (through the Financial Collateral Arrangements (No.2) Regulations 2003 (the "2003 Regulations"), under pledge arrangements in England the pledgee could not use the collateral as he only has a partial interest in it and not outright ownership. Therefore, any use of the collateral risked destroying the pledge. However, the 2003 Regulations meant that security interests within the scope of the Collateral Directive do not need to be registered with Companies House and are not subject to an administration moratorium in the pledgor's administration (see page 40).

The position has always been different under a New York Law CSA where reuse of collateral is the norm unless specifically prohibited. However, in both jurisdictions a pledgee generally has a fiduciary obligation to the pledgor for the safe custody of collateral.

Title transfer

The title transfer approach is based on netting and set off and was developed as an alternative to the cumbersome rules for the creation and perfection of pledge collateral and the restrictions on its use. In fact in Europe title transfer has become the market standard approach to take collateral.

Under title transfer collateral arrangements, the collateral giver is usually called the transferor and the collateral taker is called the transferee. Because the transferee of title transfer collateral, for example in the form of bonds, is their legal owner, it can do what it likes with them, subject only to a contractual obligation to return equivalent fungible bonds to the transferor when its risk exposure on the transferor is reduced or eliminated. Because it is the owner, it is also free of fiduciary obligations to the transferor for the safe custody of the collateral. However, it will look after it professionally in its own interests. So the transferor transfers full title in the collateral (whether it be bonds or cash) to the transferee and gives him the right to net or set off his risk exposure on the transferor under the Master Agreement if the transferor defaults or becomes insolvent. However, if the transferor performs its obligations in full, it is entitled to the return of fungible bonds from the transferee or repayment of cash in the same currency.

It is important to note that the transferor has an insolvency risk on the transferee. This is because the transferor only has a contractual claim against the transferee in relation to title transfer collateral and therefore would rank as an unsecured creditor for the value of the collateral if the transferee became insolvent. Under a pledge, as we know, a pledgee only has a partial interest in pledge collateral and the pledgor remains its legal owner. Therefore, in the insolvency of the pledgee, the pledgor will technically be able to redeem the collateral out of the pledgee's bankruptcy estate (this proved easier said than done with the Lehman Brothers' insolvency – see page 157) on the basis of its continuing ownership interest in the collateral which is, therefore, not available to the pledgee's general creditors. A transferor cannot do this with his transferee.

While title transfer collateral works well with modern methods of trading, holding and transferring bonds, in some jurisdictions there is thought to be a risk that it could be recharacterised as pledge collateral or a security interest.

RECHARACTERISATION

Recharacterisation arises from a court decision that the nature of a transaction is different from the way it is presented in the documentation covering it. Recharacterisation undermines legal certainty. An action for recharacterisation could be brought, for instance, by a liquidator of an insolvent collateral giver.

Under English law recharacterisation of title transfer collateral as pledge collateral might have had the following drawbacks in the past:

- Administration is a bankruptcy process in the UK where an administrator applies to a court for a breathing space to reorder a bankrupt company's affairs over a period of three or six months to see if it can be rescued. Administration does not affect a title transfer arrangement like an English Law CSA but before 2003 and the UK's adoption of the Collateral Directive it could affect pledges and any title transfer arrangement recharacterised as a pledge. In those circumstances a pledgee was unable to enforce his rights until the administration period ended. Title transfer collateral is not caught by the asset freeze under sections 10 and 11 of the Insolvency Act (1986).
- If the title transfer collateral arrangements were recharacterised as a floating charge they would have ranked lower in the liquidation pecking order behind both fixed charges (i.e. security interests) and preferential creditors (e.g. HM Revenue & Customs). Moreover, a floating charge could be invalidated in a liquidation if it was not registered at Companies House pursuant to section 395 of the 1985 Companies Act or section 860(7) of the 2006 Companies Act.
- It is theoretically possible that a collateral giver might have had the legal capacity under its constituting documents to enter into title transfer collateral arrangements but not pledge arrangements before it became insolvent. This is, however, unlikely.
- The title transfer documentation would be defective as it would need different provisions to be a security interest or pledge.
- A negative pledge is an undertaking by a borrower in a loan agreement that it will not give security to any of its lenders. If title transfer collateral is recharacterised as a pledge or security interest it would undoubtedly breach any negative pledge given by an insolvent collateral giver to a lender. This would then allow that lender to accelerate its loan to the collateral giver and demand repayment. A negative pledge can also appear in bond documentation.

Recharacterisation would, of course, defeat the purpose of using a title transfer collateral arrangement to avoid cumbersome pledge formalities and restrictions on use. Generally speaking, the recharacterised arrangement would not satisfy the necessary formalities and restrictions for security interests and therefore would be void or unenforceable.

The gradual implementation of the Collateral Directive is removing this risk across Europe in those countries which have adopted it. However, recharacterisation still remains a risk in some countries outside the EU (e.g. in Kuwait).

CONFLICT OF LAWS RULES

Conflict of laws (also known as private international law) concern the discordance between the laws of one country and another applied to the same subject matter.

One of the most difficult areas for global financial institutions operating across borders is determining which jurisdiction's laws apply to which part of a collateral arrangement. This includes the creation/perfection of collateral, priority between claimants in an insolvency and enforceability of the collateral arrangement. Not only are the choice of law rules potentially difficult to apply within a single jurisdiction, but your counterparty's jurisdiction might choose to interpret them differently, meaning that the same question (e.g. whose law governs perfection in a particular case?) could be answered differently by courts in the other jurisdiction.

In addition, the law applying to collateral assets may not necessarily be the same law as the law governing the place (*lex situs*) where the assets are located. Since bonds and cash are most commonly taken as collateral, it is not unknown for these assets to be subject to a different governing law to that of their *lex situs*. Indeed with some assets (e.g. bearer bonds in a definitive form), the *lex situs* may change during the life of the collateral arrangement as ownership changes. Finally, not all jurisdictions' conflict of laws rules necessarily apply the concept of *lex situs* when determining which governing law applies to the location of collateral assets. So it's all a bit of a minefield.

Conflict of laws rules are rather old fashioned in this context. Where they apply to bonds, they presuppose that a bond exists as a certificate in the hands of the collateral giver. They deal inadequately with bonds held in dematerialised form in modern electronic clearing systems and/or through a chain of custodians.

A single bond could, for instance, be deemed to be located where its issuer has its head office or where the bond register is kept or where the bond itself is kept.

In the US, this conflict of laws situation has been simplified by the adoption of revised Article 8 of the Uniform Commercial Code (the "UCC") which provides that the location of a party's interest in securities held through a custodian (referred to as a "securities intermediary" in the UCC) is the place where the custodian holds the account of such party.

THE PRIMA RULE

In Europe, the situation has been somewhat eased by Article 9(2) of the 1998 European Union Settlement Finality Directive where the approach adopted is the PRIMA, i.e. the place of the relevant intermediary approach. This is where your ownership rights in bond collateral are deemed to be legally located in a clearing system. Here the word "intermediary" means custodian.

Not only is PRIMA practically desirable, it also has a sound technical basis. The *lex situs* principle was developed to determine the law governing the perfection of interests in real property and other tangible assets by looking to the law of the place where the assets are physically located. Therefore with an office building in London its *lex situs* would be English law. However, interests in bonds held in clearing systems are evidenced by book entries and are intangible, which means, by definition, that they are not located anywhere. As far as most clearing systems are concerned the only place at which there exists any evidence of the collateral taker's interest in the bonds is on the books of its immediate intermediary or custodian. Further up the chain, the interests of the collateral taker's custodian and that custodian's sub-custodian are reflected in book entries, but the collateral taker itself is not recorded at all. So, when trying to determine the *lex situs* of the collateral taker's interest in the bonds, it makes sense to look to the location of its immediate intermediary or custodian. This ensures that the collateral taker obtains a clear legal title to his bond collateral under the laws of a single jurisdiction.

Example

You make a collateral call on your counterparty and he offers to meet it with Austrian government bonds which are Eligible Credit Support under the English Law CSA between you. He delivers these bonds to your account at Euroclear. In Euroclear's books you are recorded as the legal owner of those Austrian government bonds. Euroclear then decides that it prefers to transfer these bonds to its German sub-custodian and does so. In the German sub-custodian's books Euroclear is shown as the legal owner of those Austrian government bonds and not you. The German sub custodian then decides that it wishes to transfer these bonds to its Austrian sub-custodian and does so. In the Austrian sub-custodian's books the German sub-custodian is recorded as the legal owner of those Austrian government bonds, not Euroclear and not you. Therefore, as far as you are concerned, the only place that you are recorded as the legal owner of those bonds is in the books of your immediate custodian, Euroclear, under the laws of Belgium – and that is the PRIMA rule.

The certainty of PRIMA has been adopted by statute in Belgium, Luxembourg and the USA. It is also favoured by the Collateral Directive, of which more later.

On 19 May 1998, the European Parliament and Council adopted the Settlement Finality Directive (the "SFD") which had to be implemented in all European Member States by 11 December 1999.

Article 9(2) of the SFD closely follows the PRIMA principle. However, the scope of the provision is qualified by the definition of collateral security in Article 2(m) which led to two views. Under one view – the narrow view – Article 9(2) would only eliminate this aspect of legal risk for certain collateral takers, viz:

- **central banks of Member States;**
- **the European Central Bank; and**
- **liquidity providers to an EU payment or securities settlement system to which the SFD applies (e.g. clearing houses or investment exchanges).**

Under the other view – the broad view – Article 9(2) would eliminate this aspect of legal risk for all participants in an EU settlement system. Article 9, therefore, establishes a conflicts of laws rule for EU Member States as to the location of bonds held indirectly.

OTHER LEGAL ISSUES

Governing law

It is possible to have an ISDA Collateral Document governed by a different law than the one in the related ISDA Master Agreement. This is the case between English law and New York law documents, but you should take specific legal advice on this if you want other governing laws to apply.

Example

I was working for a UK bank when an Australian bank asked to put a CSA in place with the ISDA Master Agreement the parties had signed in 1993. That Agreement was under New York Law but they did not want to put a New York Law CSA in place with it because they were unfamiliar with New York Law. Nor did they want to change the governing law of the Master Agreement to English Law. Nobody on either side knew why the original Agreement was governed by New York Law as all the negotiators involved had left the respective banks long before. Because these documents are composed under the common law codes of England and the State of New York, it was possible to have the Master Agreement governed by New York Law and the CSA governed by English Law.

Preference rules

Under the preference rules of some jurisdictions, deliveries of top-up collateral made by a party because of collateral calls during a specific period before insolvency (typically called a suspect or preference period) may be invalidated by a liquidator. He would consider that the bankrupt party was preferring its counterparty over other creditors by making collateral transfers during this period. Preference periods are typically three or six months before insolvency depending upon the country. If successful this would require the collateral taker to return the collateral to the liquidator of an insolvent collateral giver.

Moreover, when daily collateral movements have occurred over say, a six-month suspect period, a large portion of the collateral held by the collateral taker could be subject to avoidance in this way, with potentially serious consequences for the collateral taker (and possibly for its own creditors).

Where the collateral arrangement is not itself a preference, it should not make deliveries of top-up collateral voidable as a preference during a suspect period.

Upshot of these challenges in Europe

Given all these challenges it is no wonder that the ISDA Collateral Law Reform Group lobbied for change with the following objectives:

- rules and procedures for implementing and maintaining a collateral arrangement to be simple, clear and cost-effective;
- cumbersome formalities such as registration, notification, filing and similar requirements to be abolished;
- a collateral taker to be free to deal with the collateral until it needs to return it. Third parties receiving such collateral from the collateral taker should receive clean legal title to the collateral whether or not they have notice of the collateral giver's original interest;
- a giver of pledge collateral (a pledgor) to be protected from the insolvency of the taker of that collateral (the pledgee);
- the law governing the creation and priority of the collateral arrangement to be the law chosen by the parties;
- where no law has been chosen by the parties, the governing law to be the law of the place where the collateral is held, collateral held through a custodian being deemed held where the custodian maintains the account, register or other official record for such collateral;
- the legal nature of a party's holding of securities in a clearing system to be clarified;
- collateral arrangements to be protected from the challenges of third parties;

- top-up deliveries of collateral under mark-to-market collateral arrangements to be protected from avoidance under preference and similar insolvency rules.

The European Commission and the European Central Bank both supported a more harmonised collateral regime for Europe, and collateral featured as a high priority point in the Action Plan agreed by EU Finance Ministers in May 1999. In September 1999, the EU established a consultative Forum Group to study the issue further. From this initiative developed the European Directive on Financial Collateral Arrangements.

The European Directive on Financial Collateral Arrangements (2002/47/EC)

This Directive, which was approved in June 2002, builds upon the 1998 Settlement Finality Directive and seeks to provide a uniform legal framework across the EU for taking collateral.

It only deals with cash and securities collateral (bonds or shares) regardless of whether they were provided under a pledge, title transfer document or a repo.

The Directive's main objectives are:

- to ensure simple, effective regimes for creating title transfer or pledge collateral. With pledge collateral, notification to and acknowledgment by a custodian and the holding of cash or securities in segregated accounts are the only requirements. The sale of collateral does not need a public announcement or waiting period;
- to provide limited protection from insolvency laws where these are hostile to effective realisation of collateral, close-out netting, top-up margining and collateral substitution;
- to extend PRIMA across the EU;
- to reduce administrative burdens in creating, using or enforcing collateral;
- to permit re-use of pledge collateral;
- to prohibit title transfer arrangements being recharacterised as pledges.

The Directive is divided into 13 Articles and has been positively received by the market because it allows collateral takers to simplify their documentation and due diligence procedures except in the areas of legal capacity and authority, insolvency and tax.

All 27 EU states have implemented the Directive and it has also been implemented in Norway, Gibraltar and Iceland. Because the Directive can be implemented in various ways in each country and each country can make choices about its scope some initial analysis of each country's position is necessary upon implementation.

Amending Directive to the Collateral Directive and the Settlement Finality Directive

In December 2006 the EU Commission presented an Evaluation Report on the Collateral Directive to the European Parliament and European Council. The report concluded that overall the member states had adequately implemented the Collateral Directive although there was some controversy as to whether this was the case in Poland. Ultimately Poland passed legislation which fixed this problem with effect from 20 July 2011. In addition respondents generally found that since the implementation of the Directive it had become easier to use collateral in the European market and that processes for doing so had also become more efficient.

In April 2008 the EU Commission decided to amend the Settlement Finality Directive ("SFD") and the Collateral Directive, to bring both Directives in line with market and regulatory developments in the post-trading area.

On 6 May 2009, the European Parliament and Council adopted Directive 2009/44/EC (the "Amending Directive") that amends both Directives. Member states had until 30 December 2010 to adopt and publish their implementing measures, which are to apply from no later than 30 June 2011. In the UK they applied from 6 April 2011.

Key changes made by the Amending Directive include:

- **Introducing the concept of interoperable systems into the SFD. Since 1998, the post-trading environment has changed considerably and systems that operated separately and nationally have often become linked (interoperable) and international. The Amending Directive makes changes to ensure interoperable systems (i.e. clearing, settlement or payment systems linked to each other) are brought within its scope.**
- **Bringing credit claims into the scope of the Collateral Directive. The Amending Directive adds credit claims (i.e. loans made by credit institutions) to the collateral types eligible for the Collateral Directive's protections but does not allow a collateral taker to reuse them. The inclusion of credit claims as a form of collateral could lower funding costs for credit institutions and perhaps encourage them to lend more. The Eurosystem has since 2007 accepted credit claims as collateral in its credit operations. Certain EU countries (such as Luxembourg) already include credit claims in the scope of their implementation of the Collateral Directive, meaning that implementation of the Amending Directive will put relevant UK entities on a level playing field in this respect.**

Other issues dealt with by the Amending Directive as far as the Collateral Directive is concerned were as follows:

1 Meaning of "possession"

The Financial Collateral Regulations (No.2) Regulations 2003 (the "2003 Regulations") require that, for a security interest to constitute a financial collateral arrangement, the relevant collateral be within the possession or control of the collateral taker. Recent case law (*Gray* v *G-T-P Group* (2010) EWHC 1772 Ch) has indicated that "possession" was not relevant for intangible assets and required a high level of "control", including the legal right to stop a collateral provider from dealing with the relevant assets before enforcement – which would be generally inconsistent with an English floating charge. Under the new regulations, "possession" will now include the case where cash or financial instruments have been credited to an account held by or on behalf of the collateral taker, and provided that the collateral provider's rights in such collateral are limited to the substitution of collateral with new collateral of the same or greater value or the return of surplus collateral. Therefore floating charges are now brought more clearly within the ambit of the Collateral Directive's protections.

The amendment also clarifies the treatment of security structures where the collateral taker is acting as custodian for the collateral provider (e.g. in prime brokerage arrangements).

2 Collateral substitution

Historically there has been concern that repo transactions, which operate on the basis of an outright sale for legal purposes, could be recharacterised as a floating charge if the repo seller did not need the buyer's consent to substitute the repoed securities. In the worst case the potential downside was significant, in that a recharacterised transaction would be void against the repo seller's liquidator for lack of registration.

This downside is mitigated if the "floating charge" qualifies as a security financial collateral arrangement under the Collateral Directive because such arrangements are exempt from registration. The Financial Collateral Regulations expressly state that substitution rights do not stop a security interest from being an eligible financial collateral arrangement which is exempt from the registration requirement. However, in a shortcoming in UK implementation, substitution in this case was defined as the right to substitute identical assets (i.e. "equivalent financial collateral"), making the exemption pointless. The new regulations amend the position to protect transactions that contain a right to substitute assets of the same or greater value.

3 Conflicts of laws

The new regulations provide that the English courts will not recognise or enforce orders of a foreign court or foreign insolvency proceedings where they would not have been permitted under the relevant parts of the Financial Collateral Regulations.

ISDA COLLATERAL LEGAL OPINIONS

To date ISDA has commissioned and issued collateral legal opinions for 45 countries. When relying on a netting or collateral opinion from ISDA you should ensure that your counterparty is a type of entity covered by the opinion.

It is vitally important to understand and apply the findings of the ISDA legal opinions in such areas as the creation and perfection of security rights, asset ownership rights, law governing the collateral, registration, enforceability, insolvency netting, set-off, choice of law issues and the use of third party custodians/sub-custodians. While the Collateral Directive may have streamlined many of these issues in the European Union, this is not the case in some countries outside it.

The current position with completed ISDA collateral opinions is shown in Annex 3.

HAGUE CONVENTION ON INDIRECTLY HELD SECURITIES

The Hague Conference on International Private Law has also worked on collateral but in a global context. Its main aims are to adopt a Convention on the law for ownership rights in securities held in clearing systems (often called "intermediated securities") and to harmonise laws around the world where the perfection or completion of security interest or title transfer collateral involves a number of jurisdictions. In short, it aims to resolve the question on which law applies in cross-border securities transactions and where a securities account is actually held in an intermediary. For this purpose it actually rejected the PRIMA rule and determined that:

- **the account holder and relevant intermediary may choose in the account agreement the law to govern the issues under the Convention; and**
- **this choice will be respected under the Hague Convention provided that the chosen law is of a place where the relevant intermediary has an office that is involved in the maintenance of securities accounts (a "qualifying office").**

The first step in this process is to look to the law expressly agreed between the account holder and its immediate (relevant) intermediary in the account agreement. If this is silent on the matter but the parties have expressly agreed on the law to govern the account agreement, then that governing law shall govern the issues under the Convention.

The second step is to apply the "qualifying office" test. Article 4(2) contains a "black list" of activities, each of which by itself is not sufficient to constitute maintenance of securities accounts. Where this rule does not provide a result, and a written account agreement exists which "expressly and unambiguously" states that the relevant intermediary entered into the account agreement through a particular office, the applicable law is the law of the location of that office, provided the "qualifying office" test is fulfilled (Article 5(1)).

Articles 5(2) and (3) provide a fallback where Article 5(1) provides no answer. Under these provisions, the applicable law is determined with reference to the place of incorporation or organisation of the relevant intermediary or its principal place of business.

Another issue involves the question of the territorial unit of a multi-unit state like Canada or Australia. Article 12 indicates that the applicable law can be the law of a territorial unit stated in the account agreement provided that the relevant intermediary has a qualifying office somewhere in that multi-unit state.

The Convention was approved at a special Diplomatic Session of the Hague Conference in December 2002. Switzerland and Mauritius have ratified the Convention, while it has been signed (but not ratified) by the USA. In addition, the European Commission recommended in July 2006 that its member states sign the Convention but then withdrew its recommendation in March 2009. No EU member state has yet signed the Convention, which needs to be signed and ratified by 3 Hague Member States (of which there are currently 65).

GENEVA SECURITIES CONVENTION

In 2002 Unidroit (the International Institute for the Unification of Private Law) started a negotiation process with a view to harmonising important substantive law aspects of intermediated securities. The purpose is to achieve a further step towards legal integration of securities markets that consist not only in identifying the applicable law, but also in harmonising some parts of the legislation of the signatory States. These negotiations eventually reached the adoption (after seven years), in October 2009, of the Unidroit Convention on Substantive Rules for intermediated securities, also known as the Geneva Securities Convention.

Unidroit was established in Rome in 1926 as part of the League of Nations and has developed into an intergovernmental organisation that studies private international law and commercial law with a view to modernising, harmonising and co-ordinating it among member states (of which there are currently 61).

Like the Hague Securities Convention, the Geneva Securities Convention only deals with book entry or dematerialised securities. It aims to provide a basic legal framework for holding intermediated securities.

The Convention is divided into the following seven Chapters:

Chapter I **Definitions, Sphere of Application and Interpretation**
Chapter II **Rights of the Account Holder** – these are rights to intermediated securities
Chapter III **Transfer of Intermediated Securities**

Chapter IV	**Integrity of the Intermediated Holding System** – including upon the intermediary's insolvency
Chapter V	**Special Provisions in Relation to Collateral Transactions**
Chapter VI	**Transitional Provision** – on Priority, i.e. pre-existing interests with priority in a Contracting State conditionally retain their priority before the date the Convention comes into force in that state
Chapter VII	**Final Provisions** – mostly administrative formalities.

In particular, on the subject of holding securities with an intermediary, the Convention:

- describes the rights arising from the credit of securities to a securities account;
- establishes different methods to transfer securities and to establish a security or other interest therein;
- clarifies the rules regarding the irrevocability of instructions to make book entries and the finality of the resulting book entries;
- establishes a priority ranking among competing interests with respect to securities;
- protects the innocent ("good faith") purchaser of securities from adverse claims;
- sets out the rights of the account holder and the responsibilities of the intermediary in the event of insolvency;
- establishes a regime for loss allocation; and
- defines the legal relationship between collateral providers and collateral takers where securities are provided as collateral.

The following matters are worth highlighting from Chapters IV and V.

Chapter IV

Article 30

Set off

> As between an account holder that holds intermediated securities for its own account and the issuer of those securities, the fact that the account holder holds the securities through an intermediary or intermediaries shall not of itself, in any insolvency proceeding in relation to the issuer, preclude the existence or prevent the exercise of any rights of set-off which would have existed and been exercisable if the account holder had held the securities otherwise than through an intermediary.

Chapter V

Article 33

Enforcement

1 On the occurrence of an enforcement event:

(a) the collateral taker may realise the collateral securities delivered under a security collateral agreement by:

(i) selling them and applying the net proceeds of sale in or towards the discharge of the relevant obligations; or

(ii) appropriating the collateral securities as the collateral taker's own property and setting off their value against, or applying their value in or towards the discharge of, the relevant obligations, provided that the collateral agreement provides for realisation in this manner and specifies the basis on which collateral securities are to be valued for this purpose; or

(b) a close-out netting provision may be operated.

2 If an enforcement event occurs while any obligation of the collateral taker to deliver equivalent collateral under a collateral agreement remains outstanding, that obligation and the relevant obligations may be the subject of a close-out netting provision.

3 Collateral securities may be realised, and a close-out netting provision may be operated, under this Article:

(a) subject to any contrary provision of the collateral agreement, without any requirement that:

(i) prior notice of the intention to realise or operate the close-out netting provision shall have been given;

(ii) the terms of the realisation or the operation of the close-out netting provision be approved by any court, public officer or other person; or

(iii) the realisation be conducted by public auction or in any other prescribed manner or the close-out netting provision be operated in any prescribed manner; and

(b) notwithstanding the commencement or continuation of an insolvency proceeding in relation to the collateral provider or the collateral taker.

Article 34

Right to use collateral securities

1 If and to the extent that the terms of a security collateral agreement so provide, the collateral taker shall have the right to use and dispose of the collateral securities as if it were the owner of them (a "right of use").

Article 35

Requirements of non-Convention law relating to enforcement

Articles 33 and 34 do not affect any requirement of the non-Convention law to the effect that the realisation or valuation of collateral securities or the calculation of any obligations must be conducted in a commercially reasonable manner.

Article 36

Top-up or substitution of collateral

1 If a collateral agreement includes:

(a) an obligation to deliver additional collateral securities:

(i) in order to take account of changes in the value of the collateral delivered under the collateral agreement or in the amount of the relevant obligations;

(ii) in order to take account of any circumstances giving rise to an increase in the credit risk incurred by the collateral taker as determined by reference to objective criteria relating to the creditworthiness, financial performance or financial condition of the collateral provider or other person by whom the relevant obligations are owed; or

(iii) to the extent permitted by the non-Convention law, in any other circumstances specified in the collateral agreement; or

(b) a right to withdraw collateral securities or other assets on delivering collateral securities or other assets of substantially the same value, the delivery of securities or other assets as described in sub-paragraphs (a) and (b) shall not be treated as invalid, reversed or declared void solely on the basis that they are delivered during a prescribed period before, or on the day of but before, the commencement of an insolvency proceeding in relation to the collateral provider, or after the relevant obligations have been incurred.

2 A Contracting State may declare that paragraph 1(a)(ii) shall not apply.

Article 37

Certain insolvency provisions disapplied

If Article 36 does not apply, a collateral agreement or the delivery of collateral securities under such agreement shall not be treated as invalid, reversed or declared void solely on the basis that the agreement is entered into or the collateral securities are delivered during a prescribed period before, or on the day of but before, the commencement of an insolvency proceeding in relation to the collateral provider.

Article 38

Declarations in relation to Chapter V

1 A Contracting State may declare that this Chapter shall not apply.

2 A Contracting State may declare that this Chapter shall not apply:

(a) in relation to collateral agreements entered into by natural persons or other persons falling within such categories as may be specified in the declaration;

(b) in relation to intermediated securities that are not permitted to be traded on an exchange or regulated market;

(c) in relation to collateral agreements that relate to relevant obligations falling within such categories as may be specified in the declaration.

While the drafters of the Convention tried to produce a neutral text, the overall approach taken in the Hague Securities Convention was more influenced by US (e.g. Article 33(1) and (3)) rather than European securities laws. Some commentators regard this as the reason why few countries have signed up to these Conventions.

So far only Bangladesh has signed the Geneva Securities Convention although more member states are expected to sign when an official commentary on the Convention is published by Unidroit.

COLLATERALISATION AND CENTRAL CLEARING COUNTERPARTIES (CCPS)

Talk about clearing OTC derivatives is not new. It was proposed as far back as 1993 but was neither adopted by the industry nor required by regulators. Therefore the industry enjoyed self-regulation until the credit crunch. This let the major players control the business and maximise their profit margins.

Following President Obama's signing of the Dodd-Frank Act into law on 21 July 2010, OTC derivatives will be divided into standardised derivatives that can be executed on trading platforms (to be known as "Swap Execution Facilities") and cleared through exchanges or clearing houses, and structured derivatives that cannot. US regulators had an initial deadline of 15th July 2011 to define into law the scope of "standardised derivatives" and all other matters under the Dodd-Frank Act. This was extended to 31 December 2011 due to the Act's complexity. It has again been extended, probably until the second or third quarter of 2012. A similar debate is going on in Europe on "eligible derivatives".

This move to clearing plain vanilla derivatives arises from the credit crunch and the collapse of Bear Stearns, Lehman Brothers and the rescue of AIG. Regulators want to avoid another failure of a big derivatives dealer. Clearing houses can reduce counterparty credit risk and systemic risk (i.e. the collapse of a market through the too close interconnection of trading relationships). Clearing houses reduce credit risk by standing in the middle of trades. There is, of course, the remote risk that the clearing house could collapse. However, clearing houses are owned by major financial institutions that contribute capital and market players collateralise their trades through initial and variation margin. If one clearing house member defaults, the others cover the loss.

At present investment banks are sending draft documentation to their clients which is often voluminous. Apart from the usual compliance and onboarding documentation, clients are being sent clearing agreements, give-up agreements, deeds of assignment and an ISDA Master Agreement (for the purpose of calculating damages for uncleared, terminated transactions).

This documentation is not fully developed and its final shape may be many months away partly because Europe has until the end of 2012 to finalise its modus operandi for clearing OTC derivatives via CCPs.

However, what we can deduce from the current LCH Clearnet ("LCH") draft documentation is that there will be a Non-Clearing ISDA Master Agreement between the client and the SwapClear clearing member (the "SCM") and a Clearing ISDA Master Agreement is deemed to be created on identical terms among LCH, the SCM and the Client.

Any existing English law or New York law ISDA Credit Support Annex is switched off and replaced by the relevant template shown in Annex 1 of the LCH Clearing Agreement. A separate CSA for the Clearing ISDA is not executed. Zero Thresholds and Minimum Transfer Amounts would apply to both parties. There is no pass through of Distributions and interest on cash collateral: alternative payments are agreed instead.

Where a SCM commits a default the remedies are porting (i.e. transferring) all deals to another SCM or closing them out.

Porting

If LCH considers that the SCM will become unable to meet its obligations it may issue the SCM with a default notice declaring a Clearing Default.

If beforehand the Client has entered into mirror or back-up arrangements with another SCM, porting takes place by transferring the open contracts and the collateral balance (the "Margin Account Balance") to that other SCM.

Otherwise, a Clearing Default causes the transactions between the defaulting SCM and the Client to be closed out immediately and the Client's Margin Account Balance with the defaulting SCM is written down. The Close-Out Amount is the LCH valuation, i.e. zero. A Clearing Default prevails over all other Events of Default and Termination Events under the Clearing ISDA.

Next, identical transactions are automatically created between the Receiving SCM and the Client, and the Client's Margin Account Balance with the Receiving SCM is written up to its correct level. There will need to be a Non-Clearing ISDA between the Receiving SCM and the Client.

Close-out

Where porting does not or cannot take place (e.g. there is no other SCM or a Back Up SwapClear Member declines to act as such), the defaulting SCM's open positions are closed out. The rest of the process is as follows:

- **The SCM and Client positions are closed out at by LCH according to LCH Valuation Methodology.**
- **The SCM discharges its liabilities to LCH against the margin held.**
- **The SCM's Credit Support Balance is set off against the Close-out Amount.**
- **At that stage LCH will pay over the remaining Margin Account Balance to the Client under the terms of a Deed of Assignment previously executed among the SCM, LCH and the Client. Normally there will be surplus collateral over risk exposure where clearing houses like LCH are involved.**
- **The amount received is used to discharge the SCM's obligations to the Client.**

It is likely that some further refinement will be needed in the "brave new world" of OTC derivatives clearing and collateralisation and its documentation. Indeed it could be said that the documentation will only be finalised when the rules are finalised.

US PERSPECTIVE BY CHRISTIAN JOHNSON

INTRODUCTION

In contrast to Europe, US laws governing the pledging of collateral have been historically stable and generally uniform across the various states. The State of New York, in particular, has developed a sophisticated set of statutory and judicial rules that govern the pledging of collateral. These rules provide a predictable and stable legal environment that enforce the rights of parties under security agreements, such as the ISDA Credit Support Annex, that are governed by New York law.

Even given this stability, however, parties should be aware that in the United States, the pledging of collateral and the enforcement of a party's rights under a security agreement are governed by statute and are therefore strictly enforced and construed. Failure to follow the statutory requirements can render a secured party's rights in collateral unenforceable. This discussion only outlines the general concepts that a party should understand before entering into a security agreement. Parties should consult US legal counsel as they enter into security agreements governed by US law.

This part of Chapter 3 discusses the legal issues (and any uncertainties) affecting the pledging of collateral to secure obligations under the ISDA Master Agreement and the New York Law CSA in the United States. We will assume that both the ISDA Master Agreement and the New York Law CSA are governed by the laws of the State of New York.

In this discussion, the party giving the collateral is called the Pledgor and the party receiving the collateral is called the Secured Party (as such terms are used in the New York Law CSA). We will further assume that only US dollar cash collateral or US government treasury securities are being pledged and that all collateral is held in the State of New York.

Much of the early documentation for pledging collateral to secure obligations under the ISDA Master Agreement was drafted using New York law. In addition, the collateral pledged was typically US dollar cash collateral or US government treasury securities, both of which were generally held in New York. Both US and foreign parties have become comfortable pledging collateral in the United States. Many major US dealers have been entering into security agreements with US and foreign counterparties on a regular basis since the late 1980s.

The early security agreements governing the pledging of collateral to secure obligations under ISDA Master Agreements were non-standard agreements that were developed by each dealer. This often led to serious and protracted negotiations as parties attempted to reconcile the differences between their security agreement's respective terms. By 1994, ISDA introduced the New York Law CSA which has done much to standardise the documentation process. Today, virtually all parties doing business in the United States use the New York Law CSA to pledge collateral to secure obligations under an ISDA Master Agreement.

There are several legal factors that need to be considered when completing collateral documentation in the United States. These are:

- **the enforcement of the choice of New York law;**
- **the creation and perfection of a security interest under New York law;**

- the enforcement of a secured party's rights under the collateral agreement;
- other issues involved in pledging collateral under New York law.

ENFORCEMENT OF NEW YORK CHOICE OF LAW

The New York Law CSA is not a freestanding agreement, but rather supplements and forms a part of the ISDA Master Agreement. Accordingly, the New York Law CSA is governed by the law designated by the parties to govern the ISDA Master Agreement. This is almost always New York law if the New York Law CSA is chosen.

When entering into a New York Law CSA, both the US and non-US parties anticipate that a New York court would enforce the selection of New York law, regardless of whether either party is organised in New York.

New York statutory law is unusual in that it expressly provides that the choice of New York law in a contract will be enforced. The only caveat is that the aggregate amount of obligations arising out of the contract is not less than US$250,000 (N.Y. General Obligation Law §5-1401(1)). It is generally assumed that it would be sufficient that the notional amount of any OTC derivative transaction entered into must exceed US$250,000 as opposed to the net mark-to-market amount.

New York law also expressly agrees to enforce New York as the forum for litigation "for which a choice of New York has been made" (NY General Obligation Law §5-1402(1)). However, it must involve an obligation arising out of a transaction covering not less than US$1,000,000. Again, it is generally assumed that it would be sufficient for the notional amount of any OTC derivative transaction entered into to exceed US$1,000,000 as opposed to the net mark-to-market amount.

SECURITY INTEREST CREATION AND PERFECTION

In the United States, OTC derivative market participants almost always take collateral by taking a security interest as opposed to title transfer. As with many jurisdictions, in order for a secured party to enforce its rights with respect to a security interest under New York law, the security interest must first attach and then be perfected. An unperfected security interest is still enforceable against the debtor but would be subordinated to other perfected lienholders.

In the United States, generally every state, including New York, has adopted a version of the Uniform Commercial Code ("UCC") (relevant extracts of which may be found in Annex 4) that governs the attachment and perfection of a security interest in collateral. Article 9 governs how a secured party first attaches and perfects a security interest in collateral, and second how it can exercise its rights with respect to that collateral (see N.Y.U.C.C. Article 9).

As parties begin to hold and transfer securities through large multi-tiered financial intermediaries by electronic book entry, New York law has recognised that older rules based on certificated securities held and transferred directly by the parties have become outmoded. Now, for example, a party may own a US Treasury Security that is held in book entry form on the account of the party's bank in the Federal Reserve System. When a party pledges that security to another, the pledgor will instruct its bank to transfer the security to the secured party. The pledgor's bank will then notify the Federal Reserve to move the security from its account to the Federal Reserve account of the secured party's bank.

New York law has been amended to recognise that such transfers by the parties through various financial intermediaries have the same effect as if the parties had transferred certificated securities between themselves (see N.Y.U.C.C. Article 8). For example, New York law recognises that a party giving instructions to its financial intermediary (generally referred to as a securities intermediary) to transfer the treasury security is sufficient to constitute a transfer to its counterparty for the purposes of creating a security interest by a security agreement.

Attachment and perfection

Under New York law, for a security interest to attach, there generally must be (1) a written security agreement, (2) the pledgor must have rights in the collateral pledged, and (3) the secured party must give the pledgor value. Once the security interest has attached to the collateral, then the secured party may exercise its rights against the pledgor with respect to the collateral.

For a party to exercise its rights against third parties, however, the security interest must also be perfected. This typically requires the secured party either expressly or indirectly to give third parties notice that the security interest has attached. With respect to cash and securities collateral, New York law requires the secured party to have possession (either directly or through an intermediary) of the collateral and it cannot be perfected by notice.

These general rules, however, are pre-empted by Federal law with respect to the attachment and perfection of security interests in US government treasury securities. These rules are set forth in Federal regulations, commonly referred to as the "Trades Regulations" (13 C.F.R. Part 357). The attachment and perfection of similar types of book entry collateral such as securities issued by Federal National Mortgage Association ("Fannie Mae") or the Federal Home Loan Mortgage Corporation ("Freddie Mac") are also governed by Federal rules.

The Trades Regulations, however, do not create a new method for attaching and perfecting a security interest in US government treasury securities. Instead they specify that the attachment and perfection are governed by the securities intermediary's jurisdiction. In the case of the New York Law CSA, this jurisdiction will generally be New York because the parties almost always require that collateral be held in New York.

A securities intermediary is an entity that, in the ordinary course of business, maintains securities accounts for others. For example, a large custodial bank (e.g. Bank of New York Mellon or JPMorgan Chase) maintains a securities account at the Federal Reserve Bank of New York. In that account, the Federal Reserve Bank of New York acts as a securities intermediary as it holds book entry US treasury securities on behalf of literally thousands of different parties.

Once the parties have entered into the New York Law CSA and the pledgor has pledged collateral to the secured party and transferred US government treasury securities to the secured party through a securities intermediary, the secured party will have an attached and perfected security interest in the collateral held in the security intermediary's account.

Under New York law, fluctuations in the amount to be secured under the New York Law CSA should not affect the validity of the secured party's security interest in the collateral. New York law provides that collateral may secure future obligations and that fluctuations in the amount owing will not affect the security interest.

Federal Deposit Insurance Act requirements

In dealing with US parties that are subject to the Federal Deposit Insurance Act (such as banks that hold insured deposits), foreign counterparties should be aware that there are certain additional requirements that must be met.

Generally, to establish a security interest that would be enforceable against the Federal Deposit Insurance Corporation (the "FDIC"), the security interest must be (i) in writing, (ii) executed contemporaneously with the transaction, (iii) approved by the bank's board of directors, and (iv) an official record of the bank (12 U.S.C. §1823(e)).

It would appear easy to fail any of these requirements considering how OTC derivative documentation is often negotiated. However, the FDIC has provided several safe harbours for qualified financial contracts (i.e. OTC derivatives) to meet these requirements. For example, a Confirmation will generally be considered to meet the writing requirement. In addition, a party may rely on corporate resolutions provided by the bank to meet the board of directors' approval requirement. Finally, the non-bank party may meet the official record requirement by providing copies of its own records documenting the transactions (FDIC, Statement of Policy on Qualified Financial Contracts, 1989).

In another policy statement, the FDIC has stated that it will not seek to void an otherwise enforceable security interest based on the "contemporaneous" requirement (FDIC, Statement of Policy Regarding Treatment of Security Interests After Appointment of the FDIC as Conservator or Receiver, 1993).

EXERCISING RIGHTS UNDER THE SECURITY AGREEMENT

New York and US bankruptcy law provide strong statutory protections that permit a secured party to dispose of or liquidate collateral pledged to it upon the occurrence of an event of default under the security agreement. There are additional issues, however, that a secured party needs to take into account depending upon whether the pledgor is solvent or insolvent.

Solvent pledgors

The most straightforward (but probably most uncommon) situation involves a solvent pledgor who defaults under the terms of the ISDA Master Agreement (and/or the corresponding credit support document). New York law permits the secured party to dispose of the collateral to satisfy the pledgor's obligation to it under the ISDA Master Agreement (N.Y.U.C.C. §9-610(a)). A requirement of the secured party is that the disposition or liquidation of the collateral must be done in a commercially reasonable manner (N.Y.U.C.C. §9-610(b)).

Assuming that the collateral comprises such items as US treasury securities or similar types of collateral that are traded on a recognised market, the secured party does not even need to notify the pledgor of the disposition. However, the secured party has a duty to return any proceeds to the pledgor that exceed the amount owed to it (N.Y.U.C.C. §9-615). The secured party may even retain the collateral provided that it complies with certain procedural safeguards set forth in the statute (N.Y.U.C.C. §9-620 and 9-621).

The secured party should always be aware, however, that the pledgor has the right to redeem the collateral by meeting in full its obligations to the secured party before the secured party has disposed of or liquidated the collateral (N.Y.U.C.C. §9-623).

Insolvent pledgors

Historically, there has been great concern about the secured party's rights under New York and US bankruptcy law to exercise its rights under a security agreement with an insolvent pledgor. Fortunately these concerns have largely been eliminated in the United States by statutory changes to the US Bankruptcy Code and banking insolvency law.

Resolution of these issues, however, was complicated by the number of different bankruptcy and insolvency law regimes in the United States. Most insolvent or bankrupt corporations in the United States are governed by the US Bankruptcy Code. The US Bankruptcy Code is Federal law and governs those bankrupt corporations subject to it regardless of where they are located. If the pledgor is a financial institution with federally insured deposits, the insolvent institution will probably be governed by the Federal Deposit Insurance Act ("FDIA"), as amended by the Financial Institutions Reform, Recovery and Enforcement Act of 1989 ("FIRREA").

Although most counterparties will be governed by the US Bankruptcy Code or the FDIA, broker dealers, insurance companies, and quasi-government agencies such as the Federal National Mortgage Association or the Federal Home Loan Banks, all have their own statutory insolvency regimes and regulators. This discussion, however, will only focus on those pledgors that are subject to either the US Bankruptcy Code or banking insolvency law.

Before the statutory changes discussed above, parties were concerned about several issues. Secured parties were concerned that a court would not permit a party to terminate all Transactions under the ISDA Master Agreement upon the occurrence of the insolvency or enforce the close out and other netting provisions of the Agreement. They were also worried that they would be subject to the automatic stay under the US Bankruptcy Code and its statutory equivalents under the banking insolvency law and thus be unable to realise the collateral. Such restrictions would delay the ability of the secured party to exercise self-help remedies such as set-off and the liquidation of collateral pledged to secure the now insolvent party's obligations.

To fully understand a secured party's rights, it is necessary to discuss and compare how a secured party's rights differ depending upon whether the pledgor is subject to the US Bankruptcy Code or banking insolvency law.

The US Bankruptcy Code has special rules dealing with a bankrupt pledgor that has entered into a "swap agreement" with a "swap participant". The US Bankruptcy Code defines a swap participant as "an entity that, at the time before the filing of the petition, has an outstanding swap agreement with the debtor" (11 U.S.C. §101(53C)). A swap agreement is broadly defined to include the majority of OTC derivative transactions and any master agreement governing these transactions (11 U.S.C. §101(53B)).

In spite of the changes made to the bankruptcy and banking insolvency issues in the 1990s, there were still some uncertainties that needed to be clarified. Fortunately, these were resolved in 2005, when Congress passed the Bankruptcy Abuse Prevention and Consumer Protection Act of 2005 (the "2005 Legislation").

An important concern prior to 2005 was whether the definitions of "swap agreement" found in the US Bankruptcy Code and in FDIA were too narrow. Some participants were worried that equity derivatives and credit derivatives would not fall under the phrase "any other similar agreement" as defined in the relevant statutes. If these transactions were not considered to meet the definition of swap agreement, equity derivatives and credit derivatives would not qualify for the special safe harbour provisions in the relevant statutes.

The 2005 Legislation addressed these concerns by including "an equity index or equity swap, option, future, or forward agreement" in the definition of swap agreement. The definition is also expanded by adding "a total return, credit spread or credit swap, option, future, or forward agreement" to the definition of a swap agreement.

In the 2005 Legislation, Congress also clarified its legislative intent with respect to the interpretation of the phrase "any other similar agreement" language in the current statute. New language clarified that the phrase was to be forward looking to include certain other transactions that have not yet been developed by the industry.

Another important change in the 2005 Legislation was to clarify that the existence of non-qualifying transactions under the same swap agreement does not disqualify the other qualifying transactions from the safe harbours and other protections provided in the statutes.

Upon the filing of a bankruptcy petition, the automatic stay under Section 362 of the US Bankruptcy Code generally stays the secured party of a bankrupt pledgor from exercising the legal rights and remedies in its collateral agreement. The automatic stay ordinarily remains in effect until the case is dismissed, completed or the judge grants relief. Because of the automatic stay, a swap participant would normally be prevented, without the safe harbour referred to below, from exercising any of the self-help remedies found in the collateral agreement, such as foreclosing on collateral.

The US Bankruptcy Code, however, provides a specific exemption from the automatic stay for swap agreements (11 U.S.C. §362(b)(17)). This exemption also permits a swap participant to liquidate any collateral or margin held to secure the bankrupt pledgor's obligations under a swap agreement, just as the secured party could have done had the pledgor been solvent. The exemption permits a swap participant to net any amounts that the bankrupt pledgor owes to it against any amounts that the swap participant owes to the bankrupt pledgor under the ISDA Master Agreement.

There was also concern that a secured party could not terminate the ISDA Master Agreement without the bankruptcy court's permission even though the Agreement provides that a party may terminate it upon the bankruptcy or insolvency of its counterparty. The US Bankruptcy Code, however, now permits a swap participant to exercise its rights under the ISDA Master Agreement to terminate it and any underlying Transactions upon the bankruptcy of its counterparty (11 U.S.C. §560).

Secured parties were concerned about limitations upon their close-out netting rights under the ISDA Master Agreement, resulting in the possibility of a bankruptcy trustee "cherry-picking" among the various OTC derivative transactions between the secured party and its bankrupt pledgor.

Cherry-picking occurs when a bankruptcy trustee can terminate individual transactions for which the bankrupt pledgor was out-of-the-money (i.e. had payment obligations to the secured party) and keep those transactions for which the bankrupt pledgor was in-the-money (i.e. was entitled to payments from the secured party).

Congress resolved the cherry-picking concern by first permitting the secured party to terminate all outstanding Transactions under the ISDA Master Agreement upon the bankruptcy of the pledgor. Section 560 of the US Bankruptcy Code also allows close-out netting. Close-out netting permits the secured party to net together any amounts payable under all of the Transactions to be terminated under the ISDA Master Agreement.

Debtors subject to banking insolvency laws

Debtors that are financial institutions that take federally insured deposits such as banks and savings institutions are not subject to the insolvency rules in the US Bankruptcy Code. Instead, they are subject to insolvency rules found in the Federal Deposit Insurance Act ("FDIA"), as amended by the Financial Institutions Reform, Recovery and Enforcement Act of 1989 ("FIRREA").

Many of the same concerns that worried secured parties dealing with pledgors subject to the US Bankruptcy Code were still a concern in dealing with pledgors that are subject to the FDIA and FIRREA. Similar to the changes made to the US Bankruptcy Code, Congress has now resolved concerns around the rights of a secured party to exercise its rights under a security agreement with an insolvent financial institution subject to FDIA.

FDIA, as amended by FIRREA, now provides similar protections for secured parties that have entered into a "swap agreement" with the pledgor. "Swap agreement" is defined in a manner similar to the US Bankruptcy Code definition and is broadened to include the majority of typical OTC derivative transactions and any master agreement governing them (12 U.S.C. §1821(e)(8)(D)(iv)).

Under the FDIA, the secured party will generally have the right to terminate the ISDA Master Agreement upon the appointment of a receiver (and under certain circumstances upon the appointment of a conservator). Upon a permitted termination of the ISDA Master Agreement, the secured party will have the right to exercise its rights under the New York Law CSA with respect to such termination including its close-out netting rights (12 U.S.C. §1821(e)(8)(a)).

Under the FDIA's general rules, a creditor of an insolvent financial institution is generally precluded from terminating the ISDA Master Agreement and underlying transactions solely because of the financial institution's insolvency. The FDIA, however, provides that a swap agreement can be terminated under certain circumstances depending upon whether the Federal Deposit Insurance Corporation ("FDIC") is appointed as a receiver or a conservator of the insolvent financial institution.

The secured party of an insolvent financial institution can terminate the swap agreement upon the appointment of the FDIC as a receiver one day after such appointment is made (12 U.S.C. §1821(e)(8)(D)(vii)). As a receiver, the FDIC has the power to liquidate (but not operate) the financial institution and wind up its affairs.

In contrast, if the FDIC is appointed as conservator of the insolvent financial institution, the secured party will not have the right to terminate all Transactions under the ISDA Master Agreement because of the insolvency of the financial institution. The FDIC, as conservator, has the right to operate the financial institution as a going concern. The FDIC essentially steps into the shoes of the now insolvent pledgor. To terminate the ISDA Master Agreement upon appointment of the FDIC as a conservator, an Event of Default (other than an insolvency) or a Termination Event would have to occur.

Upon a permitted termination of all Transactions, the FDIA must recognise the close out netting rights under the Agreement. This permits the secured party to net any amounts that it owes the pledgor under the Agreement with any amounts owing to the secured party (12 U.S.C. §1821(e)(8)(A)(iii)).

Under general insolvency rules, the FDIC has the right to repudiate the contracts of an insolvent financial institution. This could result in the FDIC cherry-picking by selectively terminating or transferring the disadvantageous contracts and maintaining the advantageous ones. The FDIA, however, provides that if the FDIC is going to transfer any swap agreements, it must transfer all the swap agreements of a creditor to the same party if it is going to transfer any (12 U.S.C. §1821(e)(3)(C)). The FDIC also may not selectively repudiate or terminate any individual transaction or contract under an ISDA Master Agreement that the insolvent financial institution had with its counterparty; rather, it must terminate all underlying transactions at once if it intends to terminate any individual transaction (12 U.S.C. §1821(e)(8)(D)(vii)).

Secured parties have also worried in the past that the FDIC may try to avoid certain payments made before the insolvency of the financial institution as a preferential payment. Such payments, however, may not be avoided unless "the transferee had actual intent to hinder, delay, or defraud such institution" (12 U.S.C. §1821(e)(8)(c)). This should protect the vast majority of payments made in the normal course of business under the ISDA Master Agreement.

It is possible that the New York Banking Law may apply to the insolvency of a pledgor. These rules generally parallel those described above under FDIA. Generally, however, an insolvency that would involve the New York Banking Law would also involve FDIC and the rules discussed above with respect to the FDIA. Although it is possible that the New York Banking Law may apply alone, it is more likely that this would occur with a New York branch of a non-US bank that does not have deposits insured by the FDIC, a situation beyond the scope of this discussion.

FDICIA

In addition to the statutory provisions favouring secured parties under both FDIA and the US Bankruptcy Code, the US Congress has enacted additional statutory provisions as part of the Federal Deposit Insurance Corporation Improvement Act of 1991 ("FDICIA") to enforce close-out netting. Under FDICIA, netting rights are enforced regardless of whether they would be enforced under the US Bankruptcy Code or the FDIA provided that both parties are "financial institutions" as defined in FDICIA. Although the FDICIA netting rules originally applied only to netting contracts governed by state law (such as the laws of the State of New York), the rules are now applicable to netting contracts governed by both US and non-US law.

The definition of "financial institution" includes not only financial institutions that accept federally insured deposits, but also "a broker or dealer, a depository financial institution, a futures commission merchant, or any other financial institution as determined by the Board of Governors of the Federal Reserve System" (12 U.S.C. §4402(9)). Under Federal Reserve Board regulations, a financial institution also includes large parties that meet quantitative and qualitative tests that generally describe the characteristics of a dealer in the OTC derivatives space. The financial institution, however, does not need to be chartered or organised under US Federal or state law in order to benefit from FDICIA.

The qualitative test requires that a party "engage in financial contracts as a counterparty on both sides in one or more financial markets". The quantitative test measures the volume of a party's activity in the OTC derivatives markets. If a party has entered into financial contracts totalling at least US$1 billion in outstanding notional principal amount, it will meet the quantitative test. It will also satisfy the test if it can demonstrate that it has financial contracts with gross mark-to-market positions of at least US$100 million. Financial contracts include securities contracts, commodity contracts, forward contracts, repurchase agreements, swap agreements, and any similar agreement as defined in the FDIA (12 U.S.C. §1821(e)(8)(D)(i)).

OTHER ISSUES

Substitution

Frequently, a pledgor will discover that it has pledged collateral that it now requires for other uses and wants to substitute that collateral with different collateral. Secured parties have been concerned that providing for such substitution may affect the attachment and perfection of their security interests. However, the official comments to New York's U.C.C. indicate that such substitution should not affect the secured party's rights in the collateral (see Official Comment 7 to U.C.C. §8-106).

Care of collateral

A secured party under New York law generally has a duty of reasonable care with respect to the collateral that it holds from the pledgor (N.Y.U.C.C. §9-207). Generally, such a duty would require that the secured party keep the collateral identifiable which would restrict the secured party from commingling it with other collateral or property. However, if the collateral is considered to be "fungible collateral" there is no such duty. The market generally considers cash and US treasury securities to be fungible collateral.

Rehypothecation

As explained above, Section 6(c) of the New York Law CSA permits what is commonly referred to as rehypothecation or "reuse rights". This permits a dealer to rehypothecate or "reuse" for its own purposes the posted collateral, subject to the obligation to return the collateral once the pledgor has satisfied all its obligations under the ISDA Master Agreement. Dealers will repo this collateral or may even repledge it as security for their own obligations.

There are two issues with respect to rehypothecation. The first is whether a secured party risks losing its security interest if it rehypothecates the collateral. The second is whether the pledgor faces any risk in permitting the secured party to rehypothecate the collateral that it has pledged.

There is some concern that a secured party may be required actually to maintain possession or control of collateral pledged to it at all times. By rehypothecating the collateral, there may be an argument that the secured party no longer controls that collateral. It is generally believed, however, that the New York statutes do not require such continuous control in order for the secured party to maintain its security interest, only that the secured party was in possession of the pledged collateral when the collateral was initially pledged. (That being said, however, the analysis may be more complicated in the unlikely event that the collateral involves certificated securities.)

There has also been some concern that rehypothecation potentially represents a new risk for a pledgor. By agreeing to rehypothecation, there is the possibility that the secured party could become insolvent and therefore be unable to return the posted collateral after the pledgor has met its payment obligations. The pledgor could possibly end up having met its contractual payment obligations under a transaction, yet not have the collateral returned to it because it was no longer in the secured party's possession. This is because a pledgor only has a contractual right to the return of the collateral if it agrees to rehypothecation.

The pledgor, however, is probably protected against this possibility by its set-off rights. If the secured party became insolvent, the pledgor would set off the amount that it owes the secured party against the collateral held by the secured party. The Schedule to the 1992 ISDA Master Agreement, the main text of the 2002 ISDA Master Agreement and the New York Law CSA generally give the pledgor such a set-off right. This contractual right of set-off should be recognised under applicable US state, banking and bankruptcy law. The pledgor also has a set-off right under the New York set-off statute (N.Y. Debt & Cred. Law §151) or under common law.

The set-off right, however, would not fully protect the pledgor in the event that it had overcollateralised its obligation to the secured party. The set-off would only protect it up to the amount owing to the secured party. The pledgor would probably be a general creditor with respect to any excess collateral. (For a detailed discussion of this issue, see ISDA, *Independent Amounts* (1 March 2010), available at www.isda.org.)

Capacity to pledge collateral

As with European documentation, it is important that the US party has the legal capacity to enter into OTC derivative transactions and provide collateral. Where a US entity is concerned, however, there is no precedent under New York law where a party has been found to lack this legal capacity. Unfortunately there are no statutory protections against *ultra vires* actions in this area as are found in English law as discussed above. In contrast to England, US parties generally have not suggested or pushed for such legislation in the United States.

Generally, US dealers (whether they are a bank or non-bank entity) take the position that such capacity is understood and such powers are part of its business as a dealer. A foreign party can generally eliminate such concerns, however, by requesting that the US party deliver a secretary's certificate that certifies that its board of directors has approved such actions.

A foreign party may want to be more vigilant, however, when dealing with non-dealers such as government entities, pension plans and others that are governed by special statutory rules and regulations. For example, it was suggested by some in the Orange County repo litigation that the Orange County government might have lacked legal capacity to engage in such sophisticated transactions.

Cash collateral pledged and held outside the State of New York

Because most OTC derivative activity has been centred in New York, non-US parties have become comfortable posting collateral to New York counterparties who hold it in New York. There are, however, several large dealers whose home offices are not located in New York and who may insist on holding cash collateral in a state outside of New York. However, holding cash collateral outside New York should not change the result for a secured party with a security interest.

As discussed above, to obtain and exercise rights with respect to a security interest in collateral, the UCC provides that a security interest must first "attach" and then be "perfected". Once the security interest has attached to the collateral, then the secured party may exercise its rights against the pledgor with respect to that collateral. For a party to exercise its rights against third parties, however, the security interest must also be perfected. For cash and securities, this requires the secured party to have "control" over the pledged collateral.

NY UCC §1-105 provides that the parties generally can designate that the New York UCC will govern their rights and duties with respect to pledged collateral. However, Section 1-105 provides that the conflict of law rules found in NY UCC §9-304 will govern the perfection and priority of a security interest in a deposit account, regardless of the agreement of the parties.

NY UCC §9-304 provides that "the local law of a bank's jurisdiction governs perfection, the effect of perfection or nonperfection, and the priority of a security interest in a deposit account maintained with that bank". NY UCC 9-304(b) determines the secured bank's jurisdiction for the purpose of perfection. If the parties select New York as the bank's jurisdiction, then New York law would govern perfection of the security interest in the deposit account.

If the cash collateral is being held in a New York bank, the secured party perfects its security interest in cash by control as set out in UCC §9-314. Under UCC § 9-314, control is established by the amount being deposited in a deposit account controlled by the secured party (see UCC §9-104). Prior to the 1999 revisions effective in 2001, courts had held that a party could not take a security interest in a deposit under the UCC; instead it could be taken under common law. The 1999 revisions, however, provide that a secured party may expressly take a security interest in a deposit account under the NY UCC. The New York Law CSA presumes that perfection of the security interest in the cash will be done through deposit accounts controlled by the secured party. For example, the New York Law CSA provides in its Paragraph 13 that transfers of cash will be made by wire transfers and held in deposit accounts.

If the Cash Collateral is held in a deposit account in a state other than New York, the same perfection rules apply assuming that that state has a UCC section that conforms with NY UCC§9-314 and 9-104. (The parties will need to look at 9-304(b) to determine the secured party's jurisdiction.) Most states have a code section conforming to NY UCC §9-313, including California, Illinois and North Carolina. This means that even if the cash is held outside of New York, a secured party would still have a perfected security interest in the cash collateral provided that it was held in a deposit account.

The parties can also agree that even if the cash collateral is held outside the State of New York, the parties can agree under Section §9-304(b) that the New York UCC will govern the perfection of the cash collateral in those deposit accounts. Again, California, Illinois and North Carolina all have a conforming Code section to NY UCC §9-304(b) that would provide that such a designation could be made.

OTHER ENFORCEMENT CONCERNS

Non-US parties are often concerned about dealing with the non-NewYork head office of a US counterparty. There are several large US dealers with their head offices located outside of New York as well as a few large foreign banks with US branches outside New York. Non-US parties may be concerned about whether the close-out netting provisions found in the ISDA Master Agreement will be enforced in the event of an insolvency of these US dealers.

Initially, non-US parties should remember that FDICIA (as discussed above) will always enforce close-out netting between "financial institutions" under the ISDA Master Agreement, provided that the Agreement is governed by US Federal or state law. Even if the ISDA Master Agreement is not governed by US Federal or state law, FDICIA now includes Agreements governed by non-US law such as English law. In addition, as discussed above, the financial institutions themselves do not need to be chartered under US Federal or state law to qualify as a financial institution; they only need to meet the definition in order to benefit from FDICIA.

There should be little concern about a US dealer that is a national bank, even if its home office is outside of New York. A national bank is organised under the laws of the United States and is regulated by the Office of the Comptroller of the Currency. The netting protections found in FIRREA will ensure that close-out netting provisions (as discussed above) will be enforced.

There should also be little concern about a US dealer that is a state chartered bank or an insured depository institution (i.e. the bank accepts deposits insured by the Federal Deposit Insurance Corporation). The netting protections found in FIRREA (as discussed above) will ensure that close-out netting provisions will be enforced for an insured depository institution.

There are two situations that may be more problematic. The first is a state chartered bank that is not an insured depository institution or that is not chartered under New York state law. The second is a foreign bank that has a US branch located outside of New York. The first concern is that such institutions would not be subject to the netting protection provisions of either FIRREA or the US Bankruptcy Code. Most state banking laws (other than those of New York) do not have express provisions that protect netting for a state chartered bank or for a US branch of a foreign bank. Because of this, there may be some concern that a state banking authority may engage in ringfencing in the event that the bank or branch became insolvent.

This may be less problematic than it appears, however. First, assuming that both parties are financial institutions and the ISDA is governed by New York law, they would still be subject to the netting protection provisions of FDICIA. As explained above, even if the ISDA Master Agreement is not governed by US Federal or state law, legislation passed by Congress expands FDICIA's reach by including ISDA Master Agreements governed by non-US law.

Second, there is no authority or precedent that a state banking authority would engage in ringfencing in the event of such an insolvency. This is still an issue that many state banking authorities (unlike New York's) have never had to address.

Finally, I am unaware of any OTC derivatives dealer that is a state chartered bank that is not an insured depository or is not chartered under New York state law. There are also few if any US branches of foreign banks that are not licensed in New York and many of these probably have some kind of an office or branch in New York that they could utilise for these particular trading relationships.

DODD-FRANK CHANGES

Passage of the Dodd-Frank Wall Street Reform and Consumer Protection Act (the "Act") has brought, and will bring, enormous changes to the collateralisation of OTC derivatives. The most controversial aspect of the Act requires that OTC derivatives that are capable of being cleared through an exchange or derivative clearing organisation, must be cleared, subject to certain exemptions. The Act also imposes additional collateralisation and collateral segregation requirements on those derivatives that are not clearable.

The collateral derivative provisions of the Act generally become effective 360 days after its enactment (in this case by 15 July 2011). The effective date of these provisons have, however, been extended into 2012. Prior to the effective date, the Commodity Futures Trading Commission (the "CFTC") and the Securities and Exchange Commission are drafting the detailed regulations to implement the Act's legislative provisions. The practical details of implementation of the Act are dependent upon the form that these regulations will take. The CFTC and SEC will issue these regulations in draft and then will finalise them after a comment period in each case.

Section 323 of the Act provides that it is mandatory to clear an OTC derivative that can be cleared. When an OTC derivative is cleared, the trade is transformed from a bilateral transaction between a dealer and its counterparty, into two trades. One trade will be between the customer and the clearinghouse. The other trade will be between the dealer and the clearinghouse.

For example, assume that the parties want to enter into a plain vanilla interest rate swap that is required to be cleared. Party A wants to pay a fixed rate and Party B wants to pay a floating rate. The parties will first agree between themselves the terms of the trade just as if the trade was not to be cleared. At that point, the trade will be "given up" to the clearinghouse. Instead of a bilateral trade between the parties, the trade will be entered into by each party with the clearinghouse. For example, Party A will pay fixed and received floating from the clearinghouse. Party B will pay floating and receive fixed from the clearinghouse. The key advantage of the cleared trade is that the parties now do not have credit risk on each other, but instead have credit risk on the clearinghouse. A detailed discussion of the clearing process is beyond the scope of this chapter.

The CFTC will make a determination upon application by a central counterparty (i.e. a clearinghouse) to clear a particular type of transaction. The Act provides a variety of factors in section 323 as to whether a particular type of transaction should be cleared. The CFTC has issued final rules interpreting those statutory factors. (See Process for Review of Swaps for Mandatory Clearing, 17 CFR Parts 39 and 140, 76 F.R. No. 211, 26 July 2011, at 44464.)

If a transaction is required to be cleared, both parties have to post margin similar to the margin posting that is done for exchange traded derivatives. This consists of initial margin and variation margin. A party will be required to post initial margin when a transaction is executed. Initial margin is essentially a cushion or buffer that is required to be posted in order to ensure that sufficient collateral is always posted. It overcollateralises the risk exposure. The initial margin functional equivalent under ISDA documentation is the Independent Amount.

Variation Margin is the functional equivalent of the Credit Support Balance under the CSA. For cleared transactions, however, the pledging threshold will always be zero. Both the initial margin and the variation margin will be determined by the clearinghouse. Unlike bilateral trades, however, there will be little, if any, opportunity for a party to dispute the margin calculations provided by the clearinghouse.

If an OTC derivative is required to be cleared, whether ISDA documentation will continue to be required will depend upon whether the clearinghouse is operating under an agency model or a principal model. A complete discussion of the two models is beyond the scope of this chapter. However, generally the principal model, currently used by LCH. Clearnet, for example, outside the US relies upon an amended form of the ISDA Master Agreement Schedule. The agency model, to be utilised for example by the Chicago Mercantile Exchange, instead relies on documentation similar to what is utilised for exchange traded derivatives: a clearing agreement between the customer and its clearing broker (technically referred to as a futures commission merchant), and an OTC derivative addendum to that agreement to take into account technical differences between exchange traded derivatives and OTC derivatives.

The Act also made important changes to OTC derivatives that are not required to be cleared. These are transactions that either have not been approved for clearing by the CFTC or are exempted from clearing. The statutory exemption provides that an eligible end user is not required to clear an otherwise clearable OTC derivative provided that he is: (i) not a financial entity; (ii) only uses swaps to "hedge or mitigate" commercial risk; and (iii) must notify the CFTC how he generally meets his financial obligations relating to non-cleared swaps. The proposed regulations will eventually interpret and provide more detail on these requirements.

A financial entity is defined as an entity that is: (i) a swap dealer; (ii) a major swap participant; (iii) a Commodity pool; (iv) a private fund (section 202 of the Investment Advisers Act of 1940); (v) an employee benefit plan; (vi) engaged in activities that are (a) in the business of banking or (b) are of a financial nature (section 4(k) of the Bank Holding Company Act of 1956). A party is not considered to be a financial entity if it is a bank, savings association, farm credit system institution, or credit union with less than US$10 billion in assets.

Although a transaction may not be required to be cleared, section 731 of the Act provides the CFTC and the SEC with the authority to impose margin requirements on non-cleared trades. In other words, the parties will continue to trade on a bilateral basis, but the pledging threshold requirements negotiated under the Credit Support Annex will be replaced by margin requirements determined by the CFTC or the SEC.

It is not clear whether an end user will be subject to these margining requirements in the event that it elects not to clear an otherwise clearable trade under the exemption described above. Although the statute does not address this particular requirement, in a letter from Senators Lincoln and Dodd to Congressmen Frank and Peterson, the Senators stated the following:

> **The legislation does not authorize the regulators to impose margin on end users, those exempt entities that use swaps to hedge or mitigate commercial risk... . Congress clearly stated in this bill that the margin and capital requirements are not to be imposed on end users, nor can the regulators require clearing for end user trades.**

(A full version of the letter is available at http://agriculture.house.gov/pdf/letters/HouseSenateEndUserLetter.pdf.) It is unclear, however, whether such legislative history will be binding upon the regulators or the court with respect to interpreting this particular provision.

The final key collateral requirement deals with the segregation of initial margin held by a swap dealer for a non-cleared transaction. Section 724 provides that an end user may only require a swap dealer to segregate "initial margin" through a third party custodian. Variation margin, however, is not required to be segregated. ISDA is currently drafting standardised segregation provisions that can be incorporated into a CSA to meet this requirement.

One concern that has been voiced is whether the imposition of these collateral requirements would trigger illegality provisions under the ISDA documentation. For example, if a CSA had pledging thresholds that did not otherwise meet the regulatory margin requirements, there might be an argument that the transaction was illegal. The Act, however, provides that the imposition of requirements under the Act will not result in such an illegality. The following is a provision that could be added to the ISDA Master Agreement Schedule to clarify this issue:

Dodd-Frank. The parties agree that, for the avoidance of doubt, for purposes of Section 5(b)(i) of the Agreement and any Transaction hereunder, "any applicable law" shall include the Dodd-Frank Wall Street Reform and Consumer Protection Act of 2010 (the "Dodd-Frank Act"), any rules and regulations promulgated thereunder or in connection with implementation thereof, and any similar law or regulation, without regard to Section 739 of the Dodd-Frank Act or any similar legal certainty provision in any legislation enacted, or rule or regulation promulgated, on or after the Trade Date, and the consequences specified herein and in the relevant Confirmation shall apply. Furthermore, nothing in Section 22(a)(5) of the Commodity Exchange Act, as amended by the Dodd-Frank Act, shall amend the terms of any Transaction hereunder relating to a Termination Event, force majeure, illegality, increased cost, regulatory change, or similar event based upon or arising from the enactment of the Dodd-Frank Act, any requirement thereunder or any amendment made thereby. The parties specifically reserve the right to terminate, renegotiate, modify, amend or supplement any Transaction in accordance with the terms thereof.

4

Credit issues relating to collateral

INTRODUCTION

Collateral is primarily a credit risk mitigation technique. It lessens a party's concerns about its counterparty's creditworthiness by securing its risk exposure with liquid assets.

Credit risk reduction techniques include payment netting, guarantees, letters of credit, credit default swaps, close-out netting under master agreements, set-off or not trading with the counterparty at all. Other credit risk mitigation techniques include the use of covenant protections such as financial covenants and rating agency downgrade clauses and the use of break clauses inserted in either the master agreement or individual trade confirmations giving the opportunity to reduce the tenor of certain trades.

In this chapter credit risk is defined as the probability of a counterparty defaulting on its future payment or delivery obligations.

As stated in Chapter 1, taking collateral is no substitute for a full risk analysis of your counterparty and it does not eliminate credit risk all the time because market rates and prices are moving all the time. Taking collateral considerably improves your rate of recovery if your counterparty defaults or goes bankrupt. However, as we also pointed out this improvement in counterparty credit risk could be offset by possible legal, documentation and operational risks. In addition, collateral has no bearing on your counterparty's default probability or credit rating.

So, collateral lessens risk exposure because it can be offset if the counterparty defaults on its obligations in a portfolio of Transactions. Collateral is also convenient. It is not as capital intensive as a Triple A special purpose vehicle; it does not involve the cumbersome procedures of early termination provisions; or involve third parties providing guarantees.

As far as collateral management is concerned, a credit department is likely to concern itself with the following matters:

- establishment of collateral management risk guidelines;
- establishment of parameters for Independent Amount, Threshold and Minimum Transfer Amount levels often using formal credit ratings to formulate an appropriate matrix;
- scope of products to be collateralised and location of collateral calling branches;
- establishment of a haircut methodology;
- establishing choice of eligible collateral for the institution;
- establishing collateral parameters for certain categories of counterparties;
- processing of collateralised trading line applications where special considerations apply (e.g. hedge funds);
- considering policy exceptions requested by counterparties;

- considering the impact of the following risks:
  - Issuer or Position Risk;
  - Delivery Risk;
  - Custodian Risk;
  - Legal Risk;
  - Market Risk;
  - Concentration Risk;
  - Correlation Risk;
  - Liquidity Risk;
  - Liquidation Risk;
  - Operational Risk;
  - Foreign Exchange Risk.

ESTABLISHMENT OF COLLATERAL MANAGEMENT RISK GUIDELINES

When it is proposed to establish a collateral management unit and periodically thereafter, the credit department will be involved in formulating risk guidelines for the institution's collateralised OTC derivatives business and for reviewing and updating them. This is achieved through discussions with the collateral management unit who would usually propose what they want, taking into account the day-to-day practicalities of collateral management itself.

First and foremost, the credit department will be concerned with the frequency of marking to market or revaluing the OTC derivative risk exposure and valuing any collateral already held. Ideally the credit department would want this done every business day (this is favoured by regulators), so that collateral can be called for and transferred either on the same day (e.g. for cash), or within one to three Local Business Days for bonds (unless both parties have Euroclear or Clearstream accounts when it is quicker). This limits the time during which the institution's risk exposure is uncovered to a one to three Local Business Day timescale. It also avoids the danger of "stale prices" where illiquid bond collateral is taken and up to date prices are in short supply.

Collateralisation, therefore, takes into account not only current risk exposure but also potential future risk exposure between mark-to-market and collateral transfer dates.

Second, the credit department will want to determine the likely timescale for realising its collateral upon a counterparty's default or insolvency. In the table in Chapter 2 (see page 31), we saw that it was possible for a 14-day period to elapse before bond collateral could be realised. Please note that this did include a period where a dispute had arisen.

Credit officers are, therefore, interested both in the volatilities of risk exposure and collateral valuations. They seek to protect against these through the respective use of initial margin (called Independent Amounts in most ISDA Collateral Documents) and haircuts (discounts on collateral value).

INITIAL MARGIN

Initial margin is collateral which may be offered up front by one or both parties to the collateral agreement. Normally initial margin is required from the weaker of the two parties. For example, a well-rated bank is very unlikely to put up initial margin for its own OTC derivative liabilities. A small hedge fund would typically be required to do so. Occasionally, a letter of credit or guarantee is offered to cover the initial margin requirement but more normally cash collateral is taken. This could be a fixed sum such as US$ 5 million or a small percentage of the notional amount of individual transactions based upon their maturity plus an add on for volatility. Initial margin acts as a form of overcollateralisation for OTC derivative risk exposure.

As mentioned above, ISDA covers initial margin under the term Independent Amount. Confusingly, this term can mean initial margin taken at the start of a collateral relationship and not counted in the collateral balance (e.g. a good faith deposit from a new counterparty) or a sum taken later in the relationship and which is counted in it. The situation is much clearer in the *2001 ISDA Margin Provisions* where initial margin is called Lock-Up Margin and the other sort of margin (top-up collateral) is called Additional Margin Amount. There is more on this in Chapter 5 on page 185.

Independent Amounts are sometimes taken to reflect the possible increase in Exposure that may occur between Valuation Dates due to volatility in mark-to-market values or between the time collateral is called for and actually delivered.

HAIRCUTS

While initial margin tries to deal with the volatility of risk exposure, "haircuts" deal with the volatility of collateral price movements between the time the collateral is called and its receipt.

Bond collateral is normally valued using bid prices from a major automated price information service like Reuters or Bloomberg.

A haircut is a discount applied to the value of your collateral to cover the worst expected price movements over the mark-to-market frequency period and a holding period if collateral needs to be liquidated following a default. It provides a cushion of additional value to the collateral taker. Typical haircuts are 0% for cash and between 1% and 5% for government securities of up to 10 years' remaining maturity. Corporate bonds often attract a 5–10% haircut depending upon tenor; equities up to 40%. These ranges assume that bonds are issued by highly rated and frequent issuers and assuming daily valuations are available.

Haircuts can, in disaster scenarios, be very inaccurate. Witness the 1998 Russian debt crisis where the value of Russian government bonds fell 80% in value in a week. No institution had a haircut of that level for them.

A haircut, being a discount on your security value, means that more collateral has to be given to cover the risk exposure. This is why some people talk about "overcollateralisation" in this context. For example with a 5% haircut, 105% of the bond value needs to be given to cover the risk exposure. The longer the bond's maturity or the more volatile the collateral price movements, the higher the haircut should be. Some banks apply a 10% haircut to government bonds where the residual maturity exceeds 10 years. Tenors should be measured in residual maturities and not original maturities because prices are based upon a bond's residual maturity. Institutions should review their haircut percentages every 6–12 months to assess whether they are still reasonable. This was largely neglected before the 2008 financial crisis, but there is much more focus on it now.

Haircuts provide an extra cushion to protect collateral value between Valuation Dates or during a liquidation period. They are highly correlated to the tenor and price volatility of bond collateral.

Haircuts should not be adjusted for counterparty risk because they only relate to the collateral. You do not have a lower collateral haircut because your counterparty is JPMorgan Chase rather than a hedge fund. This is another reason why you need to perform a thorough analysis of your counterparty's creditworthiness.

THRESHOLDS

A Threshold is the unsecured risk exposure you are prepared to allow your counterparty or receive from him before either of you can call for collateral. This could be a fixed money sum or it might be linked to a credit ratings table. Thresholds are an important factor in operating your collateral policy.

The credit department will decide an appropriate level of Threshold for your counterparty either on a credit ratings basis or individually in certain cases. Figure 2.3 in Chapter 2 gives examples of both. If you are concerned about the counterparty's credit quality you would probably want to apply a low or zero Threshold to them.

Many banks are interested in the regulatory capital savings possibilities of collateral. To maximise these they propose a zero Threshold each way with their counterparties. This can sometimes be resisted by counterparties that cannot obtain such savings (e.g. corporates).

In the United States historically Thresholds have been much higher than in Europe.

MINIMUM TRANSFER AMOUNTS

The credit department is likely to be only marginally involved in setting Minimum Transfer Amounts that are needed to avoid costly transfers of small amounts of collateral. At least initially Operations or Collateral Management will set appropriate levels for this. Minimum Transfer Amounts vary from US$50,000 to US$1 million. However, a credit department will be involved initially if it is decided to link Minimum Transfer Amounts to formal credit ratings as in Figure 2.3 in Chapter 2. Otherwise the credit department is only likely to be interested where the Minimum Transfer Amount is the control mechanism for the level of unsecured risk exposure (i.e. where there is a zero Threshold). In these circumstances, it would focus on the combined level of the Threshold and Minimum Transfer Amount.

For example, assume that the Threshold is US$10 million and the Minimum Transfer Amount is US$1 million. Your counterparty effectively does not need to transfer collateral until your risk exposure on them reaches US$11,000,001.

ELIGIBLE COLLATERAL

When you think about it, collateral is in great demand. Apart from collateralising OTC derivative risk exposure it is needed in the following circumstances:

- for repos and securities lending which are both collateralised products;
- in Euroclear it is normal for all credit lines to be secured;
- the Target Euro payments system uses high-quality collateral to secure all intra day payments.

This means that collateral could theoretically become a scarce resource. A highly restrictive collateral policy (cash and G7 government securities only) may be good for gaining regulatory capital savings, but could be bad for diversification and might push up collateral prices if everyone is chasing the same collateral types. Back in 1995 some G7 governments were redeeming bond issues and not replacing them. Of course, following the credit crunch there is no shortage of government bonds in circulation although most collateral takers prefer them to be AAA/Aaa rated.

A typical example of a cash and government bond mix of collateral that might appear in Paragraph 11 of an English Law CSA is set out in Table 4.1. Many smaller banks and institutions new to collateralisation will only offer cash as collateral in the first instance because it is easiest to value and transfer. However, where they do expand the range of their eligible collateral they will need to have good collateral management systems and understand the collateral types well in order to avoid adding collateral risk to their counterparty credit risk!

In all cases collateral should only be accepted where there is a high degree of legal certainty about the collateral taker's ability to enforce the collateral agreement and realise the collateral if a counterparty defaults or becomes insolvent.

Table 4.1 **Example of eligible collateral from the English Law CSA**

	Party A	Party B	Valuation percentage
(A) cash in an Eligible Currency	X	X	100
(B) negotiable debt obligations issued by the Government of the United States of America, the United Kingdom or Germany having a remaining maturity of not more than 1 year	X	X	99
(C) negotiable debt obligations issued by the Government of the United States of America, the United Kingdom or Germany having a remaining maturity of more than 1 year but not more than 5 years	X	X	97
(C) negotiable debt obligations issued by the Government of the United States of America, the United Kingdom or Germany having a remaining maturity of more than 5 years but not more than 10 years	X	X	95
(D) negotiable debt obligations issued by the Government of the United States of America, the United Kingdom or Germany having a remaining maturity of more than 10 years	X	X	90

SCOPE OF COLLATERALISATION

As taking collateral has become a more established credit risk mitigation technique, credit departments have been willing to extend the range of OTC derivative risk exposure they want covered by eligible collateral. They also want to cover all branches through which they can value collateral and risk exposure through automatic feeds.

The scope for doing this will depend upon the sophistication of their own and their counterparties' systems. Products typically proposed for collateralisation are:

- interest rate swaps and options;
- cross currency swaps;
- forward rate agreements;
- commodity derivatives;
- equity derivatives;
- bond options;
- credit derivatives;
- foreign exchange;
- currency options.

If you are entering a collateralised relationship with a counterparty, it is better to go the whole hog. Excluding some transactions from the collateral arrangements leaves unsecured risk exposure and in a close-out situation it may be difficult to co-ordinate partial collateralisation with close-out netting for all transactions. In the past, separate ISDA Master Agreements for collateralised and uncollateralised transactions were the only solution but now parties often prefer to amend the definition of Exposure in its fourth line by replacing the word "Transactions" by the term "Collateralised Transactions" (which is also defined) and with its scope usually set out in an Appendix. There is an example of this on pages 238–40. The result is that only agreed Transactions are collateralised.

As mentioned in Chapter 1, it is also common to exclude spot FX from Collateralised Transactions in view of their very short shelf life (i.e. two business days).

ESTABLISHING A POLICY FOR ELIGIBLE COLLATERAL

The credit department will liaise closely with the Collateral Management Unit on this and, in the early days of its involvement, may limit eligible collateral to Euro, US Dollar or Sterling cash and G10 government securities rated AA or above. It will also set the haircuts for these. Eventually these requirements may be relaxed and other kinds of collateral accepted if the business case for doing so is very convincing. However, since the 2008 credit crunch the range of collateral taken has narrowed with a definite "flight to quality".

SPECIAL COUNTERPARTIES

Credit departments often have to consider what special provisions might need to apply to certain counterparties. Typically these are:

- sovereigns;
- supranational entities;
- hedge funds.

SOVEREIGNS

Generally speaking a sovereign entity especially in Europe may well insist upon the following:

- a Threshold of Infinity for itself where it has a Triple A rating;
- this entails one-way collateralisation from their counterparty. This is achieved through the sovereign's Threshold of Infinity. You can also add a simple statement that the collateral agreement is one-way in the Elections and Variables paragraph of an ISDA Collateral Document (see page 235 for an example of such wording);
- Specified Conditions (see pages 285 and 332–3 for an explanation of this term) if an ISDA English Law Credit Support Deed or New York Law CSA is used for the non-sovereign counterparty.

SUPRANATIONAL ENTITIES

Supranational entities include such bodies as the European Bank for Reconstruction and Development, the European Central Bank and the World Bank. Again, these are Triple A rated and may require the same Threshold of Infinity and one-way collateral in their favour. Alternatively, if they accept two-way collateralisation they might propose a very high Threshold for themselves (e.g. US$150 million), making it unlikely that they would ever have to post collateral.

Supranationals often have strict negotiation policies with collateral documents and rarely concede much to their counterparties.

HEDGE FUNDS

Hedge funds are at the other end of the credit spectrum. There are numerous types of hedge funds that reflect different investment styles, product lines and geographic regions. They often use complex computer investment programs and strategies to enhance returns on their investments. They make frequent use of leverage, are virtually always unrated, usually based offshore and lightly regulated (although regulation is increasing on them in the USA and Europe). Consequently, banks will only ever deal with them on a collateralised basis.

Credit officers are concerned about the management and performance of the hedge fund and will usually require Additional Termination Events in the ISDA Master Agreement in respect of:

- **a Minimum Net Asset Value to be maintained at all times; and/or**
- **maximum permitted declines in Net Asset Value or Net Asset Value per share measured over agreed periods of time (typically no more than a 15% decline over a 1 month period; 25% over 3 months; or 35% over 12 months);**
- **resignation of key investment managers; and**
- **failure to provide monthly Net Asset Value figures by an agreed deadline.**

ISDA Master Agreement Schedules and Credit Support Annexes involving hedge funds are often intensively negotiated by both parties. Hedge funds are usually very sophisticated and thorough negotiators and often employ major law firms for this purpose.

Credit departments typically want to apply initial margin requirements and low Thresholds to hedge funds. They will also usually require external legal opinions on a hedge fund's legal capacity to enter into OTC derivatives transactions that are collateralised and, as with many other counterparty types, will also want to ensure that close-out netting and collateral realisation are easily enforceable in the hedge fund's jurisdiction of incorporation.

The largest hedge funds may well refuse to pay for legal opinions on their legal capacity to transact and collateralise and the bank may well need to pay for these itself. Where they are incorporated in major benign tax havens like the Cayman Islands or the British Virgin Islands such legal opinions are often deemed unnecessary if their fund prospectuses and investment management agreements clearly state their legal capacity and authority to enter into OTC derivatives transactions.

OTHER DUTIES

As well as setting policy, credit departments process applications for dealing lines as well as evaluating concessions sought by counterparties from the collateral documentation negotiation policy they have issued. Typically these concessions relate to the level of initial margin and Threshold, the nature of acceptable collateral and the frequency of marking to market.

RISKS

It is, of course, a credit issue whether or not collateral is taken. However, badly chosen collateral gives rise to unacceptable levels of price risk, liquidity risk, operational risk and legal uncertainty.

Taking collateral is, therefore, not risk free and credit departments will typically be aware of the following risks for any particular counterparty:

Issuer risk

This is the risk that the issuer of the bond used as collateral will default during the life of the collateral arrangement. The credit department will evaluate the likelihood of this happening. As regards the bond collateral it will apply a haircut to the bond value that it considers appropriate taking into account the bond's remaining life until its maturity. This will increase recovery at least in part because the risk exposure will be overcollateralised. However, in an insolvency, bond prices, for instance, will probably plummet and full recovery may well not be possible. This risk can sometimes be mitigated by "the right of substitution" which may be negotiated. It can be agreed that if a bond falls below a certain pre-determined credit rating or if more than a certain percentage of an issue is held as collateral, then the affected collateral will be substituted for collateral meeting the required conditions to be eligible collateral under the agreement.

Delivery risk

This is simply the risk that the cash or bond collateral is not delivered within the agreed deadline following a collateral call. This could lead to an Event of Default and close-out of all Transactions under the ISDA Master Agreement.

Custodian risk

If bond collateral is taken under an ISDA English Law Credit Support Deed or a New York Law CSA it might be placed with a custodian for safekeeping. In the respective Paragraphs 13 of those two collateral agreements, parties can include certain criteria that the custodian has to fulfil before bond collateral can be placed with it. These criteria typically include:

- minimum credit rating or level of assets held;
- minimum level of share capital and reserves;
- limitations on jurisdictions where collateral may be held;
- the custodian (if it is one of the parties to the collateral agreement) is not a Defaulting Party nor subject to an unsecured Specified Condition.

Custodian risk typically takes three forms, viz:

1 The custodian becomes insolvent. To mitigate this risk, apart from pre-vetting the custodian, it is also important to know if the custodian would commingle your bonds with the same bonds owned by its other custody clients. If so, it may prove difficult to reclaim your collateral held in the custodian's insolvency because your precise collateral may be difficult to identify. You may prefer your collateral to be held in segregated accounts which, in theory at least, should make it easier to identify and therefore to reclaim it. The market is currently moving in this direction with Independent Amounts. Or

2 The custodian deposits the bond collateral with another (probably foreign) sub-custodian and that sub-custodian becomes insolvent. The custodian might do this, for example, if it is a custodian in Country A and it is holding bonds issued in Country B that it considers could be administered more effectively if deposited with a sub-custodian in Country B. Or

3 A party agrees that instead of pledging or transferring collateral to it, its counterparty can hold the collateral on its behalf in a segregated account. It might do this if it was new to collateralisation and had made no arrangements to hold collateral either in-house or with an external custodian. In other words, it allows its counterparty to hold its collateral in its own custody. Despite the level of trust it may have for its counterparty this is rarely a good idea because, despite a promise to hold the collateral in a segregated account, the counterparty could withdraw it, pledge it elsewhere and then go bust. In that case the original party would only rank as a general, unsecured creditor.

Legal risk

This risk arises from a failure to agree on the interpretation of a legal document or such a document being unfit for purpose or because of difficulty in enforcing a legal agreement when a default occurs.

Legal risk can also arise where legal due diligence both with respect to the counterparty's legal capacity to enter into OTC derivatives transactions and the collateral agreement's enforceability has not been completed properly. This is a serious risk and can invalidate the whole collateral arrangement.

First of all, it is important to verify that the ISDA Master Agreement is legally enforceable in the counterparty's jurisdiction of incorporation and that its close-out netting mechanism is positively recognised there.

Second, any ISDA commissioned or self-commissioned legal opinion on the enforceability of collateral in that country should also be carefully studied and the effect of any limitations, reservations or exceptions on the type of collateral that can be taken should be evaluated by the Legal Department and reported to the credit department where significant. For instance, if bonds issued by a particular government can only be accepted as collateral if held offshore, this should be advised to the credit department who will need to make this a condition to be observed in agreeing to accept this type of collateral.

These ISDA opinions do not cover all types of entities and if the counterparty falls into an uncovered category the credit department will probably request that an external legal opinion is commissioned which would be paid for by the trading desk (if they agree). The information in such an opinion would need to be closely followed.

Legal risk also arises if collateral perfection formalities are not performed promptly and in the form required. The penalties can be severe and could include invalidation of the collateral arrangement. If that happened when the counterparty became insolvent it would have serious consequences for collateral realisation.

Market risk

Market risk is also called price risk and rate risk and affects both risk exposure and collateral value calculations. A movement in market rates could cause a temporary or permanent loss in value in a Transaction which is why collateral is taken. In turn the market or price risk of the collateral is primarily alleviated by the haircuts applied to the collateral type. This is normally calculated based on historic volatility plus an add-on to cover unforeseen circumstances and coupled with the frequency of the valuation periods (i.e. daily marking to market is preferred).

Concentration risk

Concentration risk arises where large amounts of the same bond issue are taken as collateral by an institution from a number of its counterparties with the unintended effect that the institution finds itself relying upon that collateral too much and holding too much of that bond issue. Much depends on the size of an issue, but most institutions now apply a single issue concentration limit of 5–10% of the total issue size. Clearly, if these instruments are highly volatile, low maximum concentration limits and high haircuts are advisable.

These limits are meant to protect against the effects of a collapse in the bond's price and avoid a prolonged sale of the collateral.

Concentration risk can also arise with sectors, currencies, maturities and even with custodians (i.e. if too much collateral is being held in one location).

Correlation risk

There is also the question of correlation (something corresponding to something else). Bond collateral correlates to its issuer.

In the case of collateral management the primary correlation concern is any direct or indirect link between the collateral's value and the creditworthiness of the counterparty itself. Clearly the higher the correlation between the two, the less value that can be ascribed to the collateral offered. In extreme cases this could totally negate the value of the collateral.

Any collateral whose value is highly or perfectly correlated to the creditworthiness of your counterparty should not be accepted or, if taken, be subject to low maximum concentration limits and high haircuts. In particular, bonds issued by your counterparty itself are not acceptable collateral because this represents collateralising their OTC derivative risk exposure with their own credit risk. Caution should also be exercised in accepting bond collateral in markets where your counterparty is known to be heavily exposed, as a sector downturn in that market could well adversely affect your counterparty too.

So collateral that is highly positively correlated to the fortunes of your counterparty should only be carefully accepted; so should collateral that is negatively correlated to their risk exposure. Negative correlation occurs where the collateral value decreases as the risk exposure increases usually in the same market. This can arise from a high degree of correlation between Treasury rates that might apply to the bond collateral and market interest rates that would apply to the risk exposure. A general increase in rates could cause the risk exposure to rise rapidly while the bond collateral value falls (because it will be at a less favourable fixed rate).

No correlation between the collateral and the underlying risk exposure is best of all. Weak correlation is next best.

Liquidity risk

This is connected with market risk and is specifically the risk that bond collateral realisations will be reduced and a loss made because of prevailing bid-offer spreads in the market, especially where this is due to a lot of bond collateral being sold in a short time. This risk is increased if illiquid bond collateral or very large tranches of even a well-rated issue or conversely "odd lots" (i.e. usually small, non-standard, amounts) are taken.

Liquidation risk

This is the risk that collateral realisations may be delayed by events in the market and an opportune selling window may be missed. Banks take account of this risk in the period they estimate for collateral realisations which underpins their collateral credit policy (see the table in Chapter 2 on page 31).

Operational risk

ISDA usefully defines operational risk as "the risk of direct or indirect loss resulting from inadequate or failed internal processes, people and systems and from external events". This clearly would embrace missed collateral calls, failed deliveries, computer breakdown, human error or fraud, force majeure and impractical and prejudicial provisions in collateral documentation.

Foreign exchange risk

For a small bank or company new to collateralisation of its OTC derivative risk exposure, it is best to take collateral (whether cash or bonds) in the same currency as the risk exposure in order to avoid foreign exchange risk or mismatch risk. Where the two parties to the collateral agreement are in the same country or in the Eurozone this should be possible. Otherwise, it is likely that at least one party will need to bear this risk. Large banks with global portfolios of collateralised OTC derivative risk exposure habitually accept foreign exchange risk.

The above risks highlight the need to have a well diversified, liquid collateral portfolio. This is happening as more market players become familiar with collateral types and the haircuts to apply to them. Of course, a well diversified portfolio is better protected against the effects of economic downturns.

THE BASEL II CAPITAL ACCORD

The treatment of collateral for capital allocation purposes for underlying risks falls under Pillar 1 – Minimum Capital Requirement of the Basel II Capital Accord.

The eligibility of collateral for regulatory capital relief depends upon banks fulfilling certain minimum requirements:

- The collateral taker must have clear legal rights over the collateral and be able to liquidate it following the collateral giver's default or insolvency.
- The collateral taker must have taken all steps to perfect its legal rights over the collateral.

- Positive legal opinions on the collateral's enforceability must have been obtained from the relevant jurisdictions. These must be updated at least annually.
- The collateral arrangements must be properly documented with a clear procedure laid down for liquidation.
- There must be a low correlation between the collateral giver's credit quality and the value of the collateral.
- Robust risk management and collateral management systems must be in place.
- Frequent revaluation of collateral (ideally daily) is required.
- There must be disclosure on how collateral is reused.

The Basel II Accord proposes two standardised treatments of collateralised transactions, viz:

- the simple approach; or
- the comprehensive approach.

The simple approach is likely to be used by banks with relatively few collateralised transactions. Taking of eligible collateral substitutes the collateral issuer's risk weighting for that of the collateral giver, subject to a floor of 20% (which may be reduced to 10% if certain other conditions are fulfilled).

Partial collateralisation will also be recognised in the simple approach. It will, however, entail higher capital requirements for collateralised transactions than the more sophisticated comprehensive approach.

Under the Basel II Accord haircut levels are supposed to be reviewed quarterly. Under the comprehensive approach, haircuts are applied to the collateral value to protect against price volatility. After that the residual risks of the collateralised position are given a further haircut to cover the volatility of the underlying OTC derivative risk exposure and any foreign exchange conversion risk. Against this, some recognition is given for diversification achieved in a bank's collateral portfolio. Partial collateralisation will also be recognised in this approach.

Banks must choose one approach to cover all their collateralised transactions. Under both approaches eligible collateral may include:

- cash;
- gold bullion;
- sovereign debt rated above BB–;
- corporate debt rated above BBB–;
- equities comprised in major stock indices;
- equities traded on major exchanges;
- certain collective investment scheme assets.

Supervisors may permit banks to estimate their own haircuts, but this will be limited to those banks that received supervisory approval for using their own internal market price and foreign exchange volatility models. A 10-business day holding period is the benchmark for haircuts in the internal model method.

Table 4.2 shows the standard haircuts that are based upon this 10-business day holding period, daily marking to market and collateral calls.

Table 4.2 **Basel Committee standardised supervisory haircuts**

Type	Up to 1 year	1–5 years	Over 5 years
Sovereigns			
AAA/AA–	0.5%	2%	4%
A+/BBB–	1%	3%	6%
BB+ to BB–	15%	15%	15%
Other issuers			
AAA/AA	1%	4%	8%
A/BBB	2%	6%	12%
BB	N/A	N/A	N/A
Other assets			
Cash	0%		
Main equity index shares	15%		
Other quoted shares	25%		

A contingent credit risk factor is included to cover correlation risk where there is a risk of joint default under both the collateral and the underlying OTC derivatives transaction(s).

POSITION OF COLLATERALISATION UNDER BASEL III

In September 2010 the Basel Committee on Banking Supervision announced the rules that will govern the capital and liquidity levels or buffers that banks must carry in future. Basel III sets a new core Tier I capital ratio of 7% (up from 2% under Basel II) including a capital conservation buffer of 2.5% to help absorb losses during periods of financial and economic stress. Banks whose capital falls within the buffer zone will have restrictions imposed on them on paying dividends and discretionary bonuses. The new rules will be phased in from January 2013 until January 2019. The total capital ratio requirement remains at 8% and so does not need to be phased in. The difference between the total capital requirement and the Tier 1 requirement, i.e. 1%, can be met by Tier 2 and higher forms of capital. Supervisors can also impose a discretionary surcharge on systemically important institutions, i.e. the market's major players.

There is also a countercyclical capital buffer of up to 2.5% of common equity or other fully loss absorbing capital to cover rapid credit growth that regulators consider would cause system-wide risk and a downturn. This buffer can be released at that time and would effectively be an addition to the capital conservation buffer.

In December 2010 the Committee published *Basel III: A global regulatory framework for more resilient banks and banking systems*. In it the Committee said it was strengthening standards for collateral management and initial margining. It stated that banks with large and illiquid derivative risk exposures to a counterparty would have to apply longer margining periods in order to determine regulatory capital requirements. Higher standards have also been adopted to strengthen collateral risk management practices. The Committee's specific requirements and expectations on this for banks applying the internal model method are set out on pages 40, 42–45 of the Framework.

One issue is where a counterparty's credit rating is downgraded. Often this triggers a call for more collateral to be posted. Basel III states that if cash or high-quality debt collateral is already posted, no additional Liquidity Coverage Ratio is required, but if other collateral is used a 20% collateral surcharge will apply.

It also recommends that a review of the counterparty credit risk management process must take place at regular intervals (at least once a year).

There is also a focus on banks managing their liquidity flows to minimise the risk of a liquidity crunch in financial crises. Accordingly, banks will need to maintain capital in the form of liquid assets sufficient to cover their operations for 30 days in times of significant stress under a Liquidity Cover Ratio. Banks will also have to ensure they have access to funding that will remain fixed and stable for a period of one year under a Net Stable Funding Ratio rather than relying on short-term funding arrangements that may disappear in a financial crisis.

The Committee has stated that its liquidity requirements will be introduced in two stages: the 30-day liquidity requirement will be introduced on 1 January 2015 and the one-year funding requirement will be introduced by 1 January 2018.

The Committee's revised supervisory haircut table is shown in Table 4.3. Only banks and other issuers are shown. Haircuts for securitisation exposures are higher and are included in the table in the Framework document but are not shown here.

Table 4.3 **Basel III standardised supervisory haircuts (December 2010)**

Type	Up to 1 year	1–5 years	Over 5 years
Sovereigns			
AAA/AA–	0.5%	2%	4%
A+/BBB–	1%	3%	6%
BB+ to BB–	15%	15%	15%
Other issuers			
AAA/AA	1%	4%	8%
A/BBB	2%	6%	12%
BB	N/A	N/A	N/A
Other assets			
Cash	0%		
Main equity index shares	15%		
Other quoted shares	25%		

Source: Basel Committee on Banking Supervision, Basel II: A global regulatory framework for more resilient banks and banking systems (December 2010)

These haircuts assume daily marking to market and collateralisation and a 10-business day holding period.

THE FUTURE

There is a growing trend among institutions towards considering the integration of their collateral and credit risk management systems.

In a book like this, it is easy to see collateral management as the centre of the universe. In fact if you view it in the context of global credit risk platforms, netting engines and data warehouses, it becomes a small but, nonetheless, important part of an institution's overall risk and information systems.

Historically, within banks, products like repo, foreign exchange, swaps, commodities trading and options have been developed by individual (or independent!) specialists or fiefdoms. This is the so-called "silo" approach. Sometimes the credit risk management system has not been well integrated with the collateral management system in relation to the product base with the result that trading lines might have been recorded as fully utilised when in fact they are wholly or partly collateralised and there was headroom for further trading both in individual countries and globally.

This situation arose because banks developed systems for these various products over time so that each tended to operate in semi-isolation from the others. It has, of course, been a challenge to integrate product trade data into a collateral management system but now some banks are looking to extend collateralisation across more products and to bolster their risk management systems in the process.

It is not too difficult to imagine that eventually banks will need to merge their various departments and desks where product collateralisation is taking place into one global margining centre. This will particularly help in identifying areas where collateral is required and the preferred types needed and areas where surplus assets are available for reuse. Automated systems can be designed to pair off likely matches and optimise the use of surplus cash or bonds where they are most needed. It will also assist in the development of firm-wide collateral reporting. This is already happening with the most sophisticated players.

However, even in this brave new world, risk could still be lurking. For instance, there may be occasions where it would be better to close out deals rather than take ever-increasing amounts of collateral. Moreover, a collateral manager might create unwanted concentrations of bond collateral while channelling such assets where they are most needed – an example of efficiency actually increasing risk in a collateralised portfolio.

The collateral juggernaut is rolling along the highways of more sophisticated settlement netting and cross-product collateralisation. Such a journey will both reduce risks and spawn new ones.

5

The ISDA Credit Support Annex under English Law

Paragraph by paragraph analysis

Glossary of terms in Paragraph 10

Examples of Paragraph 11 provisions

This chapter sets out a paragraph by paragraph interpretation of the English Law CSA. After Paragraph 11 (the Elections and Variables Paragraph), the remainder of the chapter focuses on common and rare amendments seen in the market. Chapter 6, written by Christian Johnson on the New York Law CSA, takes a similar approach.

(Bilateral Form - Transfer)[1] **(ISDA Agreements Subject to English Law)[2]**

1 This document is not intended to create a charge or other security interest over the assets transferred under its terms. Persons intending to establish a collateral arrangement based on the creation of a charge or other security interest should consider using the ISDA Credit Support Deed (English law) or the ISDA Credit Support Annex (New York law), as appropriate.

2 This Credit Support Annex has been prepared for use with ISDA Master Agreements subject to English law. Users should consult their legal advisers as to the proper use and effect of this form and the arrangements it contemplates. In particular, users should consult their legal advisers if they wish to have the Credit Support Annex made subject to a governing law other than English law or to have the Credit Support Annex subject to a different governing law than that governing the rest of the ISDA Master Agreement (e.g., English law for the Credit Support Annex and New York law for the rest of the ISDA Master Agreement).

PARAGRAPH BY PARAGRAPH ANALYSIS

Headings and footnotes

1 The English Law CSA, in its standard form, is a bilateral title transfer document meaning that collateral given under it passes fully into the legal ownership of the collateral taker. Footnote 1 stresses that it is not a pledge or a security interest document and if parties want to achieve that position they must use either the ISDA Credit Support Deed (English law) or the New York Law CSA.

2 This document is an English Law CSA and it is recommended that specific legal advice is necessary if it is to be subject to any other governing law. Indeed this extends in Footnote 2 to governing law mixing arrangements, for example English law for the Credit Support Annex and New York law for the rest of the ISDA Master Agreement. However, in practice, such a combination of these particular governing laws in these documents has not proved a problem and, in any case, is quite rare. In particular, now that the US FDICIA netting provisions have been extended under the 2005 legislation to bilateral netting agreements governed by laws other than New York, it has become even more uncommon.

ISDA®

International Swaps and Derivatives Association, Inc.

CREDIT SUPPORT ANNEX

to the Schedule to the

ISDA Master Agreement

dated as of ……………………………………

between

…………………………………….. and ……………………………………..
("Party A") **("Party B")**

Introduction

The English Law CSA is the ISDA Collateral Document negotiated most often in Europe.

It was published by ISDA in late 1995 and was quickly taken up by the market. This is the only version of the English Law CSA: there is no 2002 version. Because of this, however, it is advisable to add certain conforming amendments to the English Law CSA if it is to be used with the 2002 ISDA Master Agreement as discussed on page 129.

Under the English Law CSA the collateral giver (the Transferor) transfers full legal title to and ownership of the collateral to the collateral taker (the Transferee) who is obliged to transfer back equivalent collateral (subject to its Threshold and Minimum Transfer Amount) when the risk exposure that it has on the Transferor is removed or reduced and on maturity of all Transactions under the Master Agreement.

The CSA is divided into 11 paragraphs. Paragraph 11 is like the ISDA Master Agreement Schedule where the parties provide certain required information and provisions are amended or added to through negotiation. First of all when you see the word "Paragraph" in this document it means a paragraph of the CSA. When you see the word "Section" it refers to a Section of the ISDA Master Agreement.

Dating and nomenclature

The English Law CSA will be dated as of the same date as the ISDA Master Agreement. It is normal to date the Agreement as of the date of the first trade between the parties, even if it is not signed until several months later. This is based on US practice where the words "as of" mean "with effect from" a specified date. Since the Annex forms part of the Agreement Schedule (see commentary on preamble below) it is dated as of the same date as the Agreement even if the Agreement was signed 10 years ago. If one of the parties has changed its name during that period you can quote their present name and add "formerly known as" in brackets.

The parties next enter their full legal names in the spaces provided.

This Annex supplements, forms part of, and is subject to, the ISDA Master Agreement referred to above and is part of its Schedule. For the purposes of this Agreement, including, without limitation, Sections 1(c), 2(a), 5 and 6, the credit support arrangements set out in this Annex constitute a Transaction (for which this Annex constitutes the Confirmation).

Preamble

Much is going on in these four lines of text.

The great poet and critic Samuel Taylor Coleridge (1772–1834) said that because of all the inconsistencies in the plays of Shakespeare, when reading them people needed to "suspend disbelief". We need to do that here.

Technically the Annex is described as part of the ISDA Master Agreement Schedule and, like its supplements, forms part of and is subject to the Master Agreement itself.

It is not a Credit Support Document like the New York CSA or the English Law Deed. Because of this, a default under the English Law CSA is not a Credit Support Default under the ISDA Master Agreement. Instead, a party will need to look to other provisions as discussed below.

By reference, the single agreement concept of Section 1(c) of the Agreement is reinforced here. This concept stops a liquidator from cherry-picking (i.e. making payments under those Transactions profitable to his insolvent client and refusing to pay on those unprofitable to it but insisting that you as Non-defaulting Party make your payments under those Transactions). Section 1(c) of the Agreement prevents this by effectively collapsing all the Transactions into a single net termination payment due to one party or the other.

What happens in the CSA is that the collateral held under it is transformed into an additional Transaction in the normal course of business. How do I know this? Well in the preamble it says: "the credit support arrangements set out in this Annex constitute a Transaction". This is a technical matter and has no day-to-day effect. Following a default it is transformed again into an Unpaid Amount as we shall see in Paragraph 6, so that it can interact with the close-out netting mechanism of Section 6(e) of the Agreement. Then, of course, it is not a technical matter but a real part of the termination process.

Therefore the CSA relies on the close-out netting provisions of Section 6(e) of the Agreement and is closely interlinked with it. It cannot be enforced separately from the close-out procedure under the ISDA Master Agreement.

The effect of close-out netting, of course, is to produce a single net payment requirement for all terminated Transactions rather than multiple early termination payments for each Transaction between the parties.

The Annex is stated to be the Confirmation for the so-called Transaction, which is technically correct but no actual Confirmation is sent out. It is just a mechanism for legitimising the collateral balance being reclassified as a Transaction because in the world of ISDA documentation every Transaction needs a Confirmation.

The references to the Sections of the Agreement are as follows:

- Section 1(c) Single Agreement;
- Section 2(a) Payments in the normal course of business and when an event intervenes potentially leading to close-out;
- Section 5 The Agreement's Events of Default and Termination Events;
- Section 6 The close-out netting mechanism.

Paragraph 1. Interpretation

Capitalised terms not otherwise defined in this Annex or elsewhere in this Agreement have the meanings specified pursuant to Paragraph 10, and all references in this Annex to Paragraphs are to Paragraphs of this Annex. In the event of any inconsistency between this Annex and the other provisions of this Schedule, this Annex will prevail, and in the event of any inconsistency between Paragraph 11 and the other provisions of this Annex, Paragraph 11 will prevail. For the avoidance of doubt, references to "transfer" in this Annex mean, in relation to cash, payment and, in relation to other assets, delivery.

Paragraph 1. Interpretation

Paragraph 1 states that if there is any inconsistency between the Annex and the other provisions of the ISDA Schedule the Annex will prevail. However, Paragraph 11 (the Elections and Variables paragraph) will prevail if it clashes with the other provisions of the Annex.

Paragraph 1 also clarifies certain basic matters, for example that the term "transfer" embraces the payment of cash and the delivery of securities and other assets as appropriate.

Paragraph 2. Credit Support Obligations

(a) ***Delivery Amount.*** Subject to Paragraphs 3 and 4, upon a demand made by the Transferee on or promptly following a Valuation Date, if the Delivery Amount for that Valuation Date equals or exceeds the Transferor's Minimum Transfer Amount, then the Transferor will transfer to the Transferee Eligible Credit Support having a Value as of the date of transfer at least equal to the applicable Delivery Amount (rounded pursuant to Paragraph 11(b)(iii)(D)). Unless otherwise specified in Paragraph 11(b), the "Delivery Amount" applicable to the Transferor for any Valuation Date will equal the amount by which:

(i) the Credit Support Amount

exceeds

(ii) the Value as of that Valuation Date of the Transferor's Credit Support Balance (adjusted to include any prior Delivery Amount and to exclude any prior Return Amount, the transfer of which, in either case, has not yet been completed and for which the relevant Settlement Day falls on or after such Valuation Date).

Paragraph 2. Credit Support Obligations

Essentially this Paragraph concerns collateral calls and returns and how they are calculated.

Basically the Transferee compares his risk exposure to the collateral he already holds and calls for more, returns any surplus, if asked, or does nothing depending upon his calculations after taking into account Independent Amounts, Thresholds and/or Minimum Transfer Amounts.

In Paragraph 2(a) the collateral taker (the Transferee) can call for collateral from the collateral giver (the Transferor) where his OTC derivatives risk exposure on the Transferor is greater than the Transferor's Minimum Transfer Amount after deducting its Threshold. These are both considered in collateral calls.

The calculation of exposure of the Credit Support Amount will take into account:

- the net mark-to-market valuation of all Transactions under the Agreements plus or minus;
- the net Independent Amounts between the parties (see page 185 for an explanation of this term); and
- any Threshold (see page 80 for an explanation of this term) applicable to the Transferor.

When called upon and assuming there is no dispute, the Transferor will transfer the requested amount of collateral (the "Delivery Amount") to the Transferee. Any transfers already in transit for previous collateral calls but not yet received are also taken into account in the calculation of the Delivery Amount.

(b) ***Return Amount.*** Subject to Paragraphs 3 and 4, upon a demand made by the Transferor on or promptly following a Valuation Date, if the Return Amount for that Valuation Date equals or exceeds the Transferee's Minimum Transfer Amount, then the Transferee will transfer to the Transferor Equivalent Credit Support specified by the Transferor in that demand having a Value as of the date of transfer as close as practicable to the applicable Return Amount (rounded pursuant to Paragraph 11(b)(iii)(D)) and the Credit Support Balance will, upon such transfer, be reduced accordingly. Unless otherwise specified in Paragraph 11(b), the "Return Amount" applicable to the Transferee for any Valuation Date will equal the amount by which:

(i) the Value as of that Valuation Date of the Transferor's Credit Support Balance (adjusted to include any prior Delivery Amount and to exclude any prior Return Amount, the transfer of which, in either case, has not yet been completed and for which the relevant Settlement Day falls on or after such Valuation Date)

exceeds

(ii) the Credit Support Amount.

Paragraph 2(b) covers the position where the Transferee holds surplus collateral which it must return to the Transferor if it is above the Transferee's Minimum Transfer Amount after deducting its Threshold and the Transferor calls for the return of the collateral. Please note that if the Transferor fails to make a call, the Transferee is not obliged to transfer the collateral or point this out to the Transferor. However, if a third party Valuation Agent is involved this, of course, will not arise, assuming the Valuation Agent is managing the relationship properly.

To recap, a Return Amount arises where the value of the collateral held by the Transferee is greater than its risk exposure on the Transferor and is above the Transferee's agreed Minimum Transfer Amount and Threshold.

Again with a Return Amount any collateral already in transit but not yet received will be taken into account in calculating the collateral amount to be returned.

Of course, where the Transferee's risk exposure on the Transferor reduces to zero (assuming no Independent Amount applies), the Transferee will return all collateral he holds to the Transferor because provision will normally be made for this in market standard Minimum Transfer Amount wording in Paragraph 11(b)(iii)(C) – see page 197.

Let us take some simple examples.

Imagine that you are Bank A and are trading with Bank B. You each have a Threshold of EUR1,000,000 and a Minimum Transfer Amount of EUR100,000.

You look at your daily exposure report and see that from yesterday your total risk exposure on Bank B is EUR1,050,000. Can you make a collateral call on them? No. This is because when you deduct the Threshold (EUR1,000,000) from the risk exposure (EUR1,050,000) you are left with EUR50,000 which is below the Minimum Transfer Amount.

The following day your total risk exposure on them has increased to EUR2,550,000. Can you make a call on them now? Yes.

For how much? You claim the excess over the Threshold, i.e. EUR1,550,000, which gives you unsecured risk exposure of EUR1,000,000 again. Under the English Law CSA, a party is entitled to claim the surplus over the Threshold provided it is more than the Minimum Transfer Amount.

Paragraph 3. Transfers, Calculations and Exchanges

(a) ***Transfers.*** All transfers under this Annex of any Eligible Credit Support, Equivalent Credit Support, Interest Amount or Equivalent Distributions shall be made in accordance with the instructions of the Transferee or Transferor, as applicable, and shall be made:

(i) in the case of cash, by transfer into one or more bank accounts specified by the recipient;

(ii) in the case of certificated securities which cannot or which the parties have agreed will not be delivered by book-entry, by delivery in appropriate physical form to the recipient or its account accompanied by any duly executed instruments of transfer, transfer tax stamps and any other documents necessary to constitute a legally valid transfer of the transferring party's legal and beneficial title to the recipient; and

(iii) in the case of securities which the parties have agreed will be delivered by book-entry, by the giving of written instructions (including, for the avoidance of doubt, instructions given by telex, facsimile transmission or electronic messaging system) to the relevant depository institution or other entity specified by the recipient, together with a written copy of the instructions to the recipient, sufficient, if complied with, to result in a legally effective transfer of the transferring party's legal and beneficial title to the recipient.

Subject to Paragraph 4 and unless otherwise specified, if a demand for the transfer of Eligible Credit Support or Equivalent Credit Support is received by the Notification Time, then the relevant transfer will be made not later than the close of business on the Settlement Day relating to the date such demand is received; if a demand is received after the Notification Time, then the relevant transfer will be made not later than the close of business on the Settlement Day relating to the day after the date such demand is received.

(b) ***Calculations.*** All calculations of Value and Exposure for purposes of Paragraphs 2 and 4(a) will be made by the relevant Valuation Agent as of the relevant Valuation Time. The Valuation Agent will notify each party (or the other party, if the Valuation Agent is a party) of its calculations not later than the Notification Time on the Local Business Day following the applicable Valuation Date (or, in the case of Paragraph 4(a), following the date of calculation).

Paragraph 3. Transfers, Calculations and Exchanges

All transfers are to be made in accordance with the instructions of the Transferor or Transferee. Paragraph 3(a) states how transfers will be made under the Annex for cash and securities in book entry and certificate form, viz:

(a) with cash, this is by transfer to the recipient's nominated bank account(s);

(b) with bond certificates, this will involve physical delivery to the recipient or its account together with all necessary transfer documentation which will vest legal ownership of the bonds in the recipient with full title guarantee;

(c) with book entry or dematerialised bonds, this entails the transferring party giving written instructions in a choice of media to the recipient's central securities depository system (e.g. Euroclear or Clearstream) where he holds his account. A copy of such instructions (which must be sufficient to transfer legal ownership of the bonds with full title guarantee) must be sent to the recipient.

It also provides through the definition of Settlement Day in Paragraph 10 that each transfer of eligible collateral (a) in form of cash will be made on the next Local Business Day and (b) in the form of bonds will be made on the number of days after demand customary for settlement through the agreed clearing system or otherwise in the relevant local market. This is adjusted if the demand is made after the Notification Time agreed in Paragraph 11(c)(iv) when collateral delivery will take place one Local Business Day later. This Settlement Day definition was intended to be sufficiently flexible to cover various settlement periods for different types of bonds in different international and European domestic markets and settlement systems where different settlement timescales apply.

Things are much more streamlined under the New York Law CSA where US Dollars are the only cash collateral and can be easily wired within one Local Business Day and US Treasuries and Fannie Mae and Freddie Mac notes are held in electronic book entry form and settle in T+1.

Paragraph 3(b) provides for the calculation of risk exposure and the value of collateral held to be made by the relevant Valuation Agent stated in Paragraph 11 for the purposes of calculating Delivery Amounts and Return Amounts both in the normal course of business and in disputes. The Valuation Agent will notify its calculations to the other party (or to both parties if it is a third party) by the deadline (Notification Time) on the Local Business Day after it makes its calculations.

(c) ***Exchanges.***

(i) Unless otherwise specified in Paragraph 11, the Transferor may on any Local Business Day by notice inform the Transferee that it wishes to transfer to the Transferee Eligible Credit Support specified in that notice (the "New Credit Support") in exchange for certain Eligible Credit Support (the "Original Credit Support") specified in that notice comprised in the Transferor's Credit Support Balance.

(ii) If the Transferee notifies the Transferor that it has consented to the proposed exchange, (A) the Transferor will be obliged to transfer the New Credit Support to the Transferee on the first Settlement Day following the date on which it receives notice (which may be oral telephonic notice) from the Transferee of its consent and (B) the Transferee will be obliged to transfer to the Transferor Equivalent Credit Support in respect of the Original Credit Support not later than the Settlement Day following the date on which the Transferee receives the New Credit Support, unless otherwise specified in Paragraph 11(d) (the "Exchange Date"); *provided* that the Transferee will only be obliged to transfer Equivalent Credit Support with a Value as of the date of transfer as close as practicable to, but in any event not more than, the Value of the New Credit Support as of that date.

Paragraph 3(c)

Paragraph 3(c) is about changes or substitutions of collateral. Whenever you see the word "exchange" in the English law CSA it means substitution.

(i) Unless forbidden in Paragraph 11, the Transferor (the collateral giver) may request by notice to the Transferee (the collateral taker) a substitution of part or all of the collateral it has already transferred to the collateral taker in exchange for new collateral acceptable to the collateral taker. This would relate to bond collateral.

(ii) If the collateral taker consents to this then the collateral giver must transfer the new collateral to him on the first trade settlement date thereafter. After it has received the new collateral, the collateral taker must start the process of returning the original collateral which has been substituted no later than the trade settlement date after he has received the new collateral from the collateral giver. This will usually be the following Local Business Day. In any case on the transfer date the collateral must be worth the same or nearly the same and in no circumstances is he obliged to retransfer original collateral worth more than the new collateral. The consent point was important at least under English law because if the Transferee were not completely free to consent or not he could have been deemed by a court not to be the true owner of the collateral and this could have led to the title transfer nature of the English Law CSA being recharacterised as a security interest or pledge which could fail for lack of registration if it were deemed to be a floating charge in a liquidation situation (refer to the discussion of this point in Chapter 3, page 40).

This risk has, of course, been neutralised by the Collateral Directive in those countries that have adopted it. But there is another risk here.

The Transferor's potential credit risk on the Transferee increases during the short period when the Transferee holds both the old and new collateral. If he goes bankrupt in that short window then the Transferor can only rank as an unsecured creditor in his liquidation. The market knows this risk and accepts it because it regards it as remote. The failure of Lehman Brothers, however, highlighted that parties need to be vigilant to avoid having the Transferee holding more collateral than entitled.

Please note that technically under the English Law CSA an exchange is a sale of New Credit Support to the Transferee coupled with a sale of Equivalent Credit Support (i.e. the Original Credit Support) back to the Transferor. As both legs of the exchange are a "sale" this precludes any recharacterisation challenge.

Paragraph 4. Dispute Resolution

(a) ***Disputed Calculations or Valuations*** . If a party (a "Disputing Party") reasonably disputes (I) the Valuation Agent's calculation of a Delivery Amount or a Return Amount or (II) the Value of any transfer of Eligible Credit Support or Equivalent Credit Support, then:

(1) the Disputing Party will notify the other party and the Valuation Agent (if the Valuation Agent is not the other party) not later than the close of business on the Local Business Day following, in the case of (I) above, the date that the demand is received under Paragraph 2 or, in the case of (II) above, the date of transfer;

(2) in the case of (I) above, the appropriate party will transfer the undisputed amount to the other party not later than the close of business on the Settlement Day following the date that the demand is received under Paragraph 2;

(3) the parties will consult with each other in an attempt to resolve the dispute; and

Paragraph 4. Dispute Resolution

(a) If a party disputes the Valuation Agent's calculation of risk exposure or the value of collateral held, Paragraph 4 provides a framework for resolving the dispute if it cannot be settled informally. Most disputes are settled informally since many disputes involve reconciling the outstanding trades between the parties or other straightforward errors.

Collateral disputes always relate to these two matters and the calculation of risk exposure is the more common kind of dispute. Disputes may also arise over the valuation of collateral if not very liquid securities are being transferred.

Please note in Paragraph 4(a) the Disputing Party has to observe a standard of reasonableness in starting a dispute with its counterparty.

The steps are outlined in Paragraph 4(a)(1)–(4) and involve:

(1) A requirement for the Disputing Party to notify its counterparty that it wishes to dispute the risk exposure calculation or collateral valuation no later than the close of business on the Local Business Day after either the date the collateral call notice is received or the date the collateral transfer has been made. This covers the situation where a collateral call has been made; the collateral transferred; and then the Transferor realising he has made a big mistake. The Disputing Party will almost always be the party called upon to transfer collateral. The Valuation Agent will typically be the non-disputing party.

(2) In the case of disputes over risk exposure calculation for collateral calls, the Disputing Party agrees to transfer the undisputed amount to the other party no later than the close of business on the trade settlement date following the date he receives the collateral call notice from the Valuation Agent.

(3) The parties will attempt to resolve the dispute by the deadline stated in Paragraph 11(e)(i) – the Resolution Time.

(4) if they fail to resolve the dispute by the Resolution Time, then:

(i) in the case of a dispute involving a Delivery Amount or Return Amount, unless otherwise specified in Paragraph 11(e), the Valuation Agent will recalculate the Exposure and the Value as of the Recalculation Date by:

(A) utilising any calculations of that part of the Exposure attributable to the Transactions that the parties have agreed are not in dispute;

(B) calculating that part of the Exposure attributable to the Transactions in dispute by seeking four actual quotations at mid-market from Reference Market-makers for purposes of calculating Market Quotation, and taking the arithmetic average of those obtained; *provided* that if four quotations are not available for a particular Transaction, then fewer than four quotations may be used for that Transaction, and if no quotations are available for a particular Transaction, then the Valuation Agent's original calculations will be used for the Transaction; and

(C) utilising the procedures specified in Paragraph 11(e)(ii) for calculating the Value, if disputed, of the outstanding Credit Support Balance;

(ii) in the case of a dispute involving the Value of any transfer of Eligible Credit Support or Equivalent Credit Support, the Valuation Agent will recalculate the Value as of the date of transfer pursuant to Paragraph 11(e)(ii).

Following a recalculation pursuant to this Paragraph, the Valuation Agent will notify each party (or the other party, if the Valuation Agent is a party) as soon as possible but in any event not later than the Notification Time on the Local Business Day following the Resolution Time. The appropriate party will, upon demand following such notice given by the Valuation Agent or a resolution pursuant to (3) above and subject to Paragraph 3(a), make the appropriate transfer.

(4) If they fail then:

(i) (A) if the dispute involves the amount of collateral called for, the Valuation Agent will recalculate his figures for risk exposure and collateral value (including any haircut) by reusing any calculation of the undisputed part of the risk exposure if he can isolate it.

(B) It will then approach four Reference Market-makers for mid-market quotations (i.e. the average of the bid and offer prices of the Transactions concerned). Provided four quotations are received the arithmetic mean of these quotations is used. To this is added the risk exposure calculation that is not in dispute. However, fewer than four quotations may be used in the recalculation of risk exposure but if no quotations are available for a particular Transaction then the Valuation Agent's original calculation will be used for that Transaction because it is the only reasonable thing to do in the circumstances. This provision highlights the control enjoyed by the Valuation Agent in these disputes.

The effort of having to get the quotations will often shorten the dispute process. Depending upon the size of the dispute, many parties will be unwilling to disclose their trades to third parties simply to resolve a small dispute over Exposure. If the Valuation Agent, however, is unwilling to move forward with the quotations then that will limit its ability to compel a Disputing Party to transfer additional collateral.

(C) The Valuation Agent will also follow the method stated in Paragraph 11(e)(ii) for calculating the value of collateral held. This method has to be stated in Paragraph 11(e)(ii) or the dispute resolution provisions will not work. There is no fallback.

(ii) The Valuation Agent will directly home in on what it says in Paragraph 11(e)(ii) where the dispute solely involves the value of collateral held.

When all the recalculations have been done the Valuation Agent will notify the other party of the revised figures not later than the deadline (Notification Time) on the Local Business Day after the Resolution Time (i.e. the dispute resolution deadline agreed in Paragraph 11(e)(i)).

Once all is agreed a revised collateral call notice is sent and the necessary collateral transfer is made. But what happens if it is not made?

(b) ***No Event of Default.*** The failure by a party to make a transfer of any amount which is the subject of a dispute to which Paragraph 4(a) applies will not constitute an Event of Default for as long as the procedures set out in this Paragraph 4 are being carried out. For the avoidance of doubt, upon completion of those procedures, Section 5(a)(i) of this Agreement will apply to any failure by a party to make a transfer required under the final sentence of Paragraph 4(a) on the relevant due date.

(b) Paragraph 4(b) clarifies that failure to transfer a disputed amount does not constitute an Event of Default under the Agreement while the dispute resolution process is being carried out. However, when the process is ended and the transfer is still not made then Section 5(a)(i) of the Master Agreement – Failure to Pay or Deliver – comes into play and an Event of Default will be called if the transfer is not made within three Local Business Days with a 1992 Agreement or one Local Business Day with a 2002 Agreement following notice to the party who has failed to transfer the collateral. This assumes the standard grace periods apply in these Agreements. This is another way in which the CSA links into the ISDA Master Agreement.

It is worth reiterating, as discussed above, that the relevant Event of Default is Section 5(a)(i) and not the Credit Support Default found in Section 5(a)(iii) since the English Law CSA is not a Credit Support Document but rather a Transaction.

An ISDA Working Group is currently working on finalising Dispute Resolution Procedures for the market (see pages 418–23 for more details).

Paragraph 5. Transfer of Title, No Security Interest, Distributions and Interest Amount

(a) ***Transfer of Title.*** Each party agrees that all right, title and interest in and to any Eligible Credit Support, Equivalent Credit Support, Equivalent Distributions or Interest Amount which it transfers to the other party under the terms of this Annex shall vest in the recipient free and clear of any liens, claims, charges or encumbrances or any other interest of the transferring party or of any third person (other than a lien routinely imposed on all securities in a relevant clearance system).

(b) ***No Security Interest.*** Nothing in this Annex is intended to create or does create in favour of either party any mortgage, charge, lien, pledge, encumbrance or other security interest in any cash or other property transferred by one party to the other party under the terms of this Annex.

(c) ***Distributions and Interest Amount.***

(i) ***Distributions.*** The Transferee will transfer to the Transferor not later than the Settlement Day following each Distributions Date cash, securities or other property of the same type, nominal value, description and amount as the relevant Distributions ("Equivalent Distributions") to the extent that a Delivery Amount would not be created or increased by the transfer, as calculated by the Valuation Agent (and the date of calculation will be deemed a Valuation Date for this purpose).

Paragraph 5. Transfer of Title, No Security Interest, Distributions and Interest Amount

Paragraph 5(a) clearly states that each party when making transfers under the Annex thereby transfers outright legal ownership to the collateral concerned or any distributions or interest on it to the other party free of all encumbrances except for any liens (charges to cover custody fees) routinely imposed on all bonds by clearing systems.

Paragraph 5(b) expressly states that no security interest of any kind is being created over collateral transferred between the parties under the Annex.

(c)(i) A guiding principle of collateral arrangements is that the collateral giver should not be disadvantaged by them. While ownership of the collateral clearly passes to the collateral taker it is anticipated that at some point the collateral taker will be obliged to return the collateral to the collateral giver, for example when risk exposure moves in favour of the collateral giver or when the Transactions covered by the collateral mature.

During this period coupons will be paid on bonds to the Transferee (the collateral taker) because he will be registered as their owner in the bond issuer's books.

The market convention is then for the Transferee to make a separate payment to the Transferor equivalent to 100% of the coupon payment received from the bond issuer. This is what is stipulated in Paragraph 5(c)(i).

This payment is known in the market as a "manufactured dividend". However, such payments are not made if they give rise to creating or increasing a collateral call. In these circumstances they will remain part of the collateral balance held by the collateral taker. With a bond, part of its price is represented by the accrued interest on it. When that interest is paid, its price falls. If the payment of a manufactured dividend by the Transferee to the Transferor immediately results in a collateral call for this reason, the transfer of the manufactured dividend is not made.

Where, for tax purposes, a collateral taker is reluctant or concerned about doing this, parties provide for this in Paragraph 11(h) and arrange a substitution of the bond before the coupon payment date for one where no coupon is due for a while.

Please note that when collateral transfers or income flows from the collateral taker to the collateral giver, it is preceded by the word "Equivalent" as here in "Equivalent Distributions".

(ii) ***Interest Amount.*** Unless otherwise specified in Paragraph 11(f)(iii), the Transferee will transfer to the Transferor at the times specified in Paragraph 11(f)(ii) the relevant Interest Amount to the extent that a Delivery Amount would not be created or increased by the transfer, as calculated by the Valuation Agent (and the date of calculation will be deemed a Valuation Date for this purpose).

(c)(ii) Interest Amount is the interest payable by the collateral taker on cash deposits he holds as collateral from the collateral giver. The frequency at which cash interest is paid over to the collateral giver is stated in Paragraph 11(f)(ii). It is usually monthly. Again it will not be paid over if it creates or increases a collateral call and will continue to be held as part of the collateral taker's collateral balance in those circumstances. Given current interest rates, it would have to be a huge amount of interest to make this happen.

Typically such interest is paid in arrears on the first, second or third Local Business Day of the month depending upon a party's operational capability.

Paragraph 6. Default

If an Early Termination Date is designated or deemed to occur as a result of an Event of Default in relation to a party, an amount equal to the Value of the Credit Support Balance, determined as though the Early Termination Date were a Valuation Date, will be deemed to be an Unpaid Amount due to the Transferor (which may or may not be the Defaulting Party) for purposes of Section 6(e). For the avoidance of doubt, if Market Quotation is the applicable payment measure for purposes of Section 6(e), then the Market Quotation determined under Section 6(e) in relation to the Transaction constituted by this Annex will be deemed to be zero, and, if Loss is the applicable payment measure for purposes of Section 6(e), then the Loss determined under Section 6(e) in relation to the Transaction will be limited to the Unpaid Amount representing the Value of the Credit Support Balance.

Paragraph 6. Default

Much is also going on in these few lines and, once again, as with the preamble to the CSA, you need to suspend disbelief.

This is a technical Paragraph but very important. First of all in a close-out situation under the Master Agreement the date on which termination calculations are made (the Early Termination Date) will be treated as if it were Valuation Date here. The collateral previously transferred by the collateral giver to the collateral taker becomes an Unpaid Amount under the early termination provisions of Section 6(e) of the Master Agreement.

Close-out involves the netting off of the termination values of all Transactions under the Master Agreement and bringing Unpaid Amounts into the close-out calculations.

The collateral balance held by the collateral taker, which was previously a Transaction, is now deemed to be an Unpaid Amount owing to the collateral giver (who could be but need not be the Defaulting Party). The Master Agreement operates irrespective of whether the Transferee is the Defaulting Party or the Non-defaulting Party.

The Unpaid Amount needs to be valued.

In Part 1(f) of the 1992 Master Agreement Schedule the payment measure for calculating termination payments is chosen. Market Quotation involves obtaining close-out quotations for Transactions from up to four leading dealers, if possible, and taking the arithmetic mean of the two remaining quotations after discarding the highest and lowest. Loss is a more subjective measure and is the Non-defaulting Party's good faith calculation of its losses and costs minus its gains.

Here there is no need to obtain four quotations on the likely value of the collateral (cash is most commonly taken) and so Market Quotation is discarded as inappropriate. It will be considered to be zero which is no help at all in calculating the Unpaid Amount's value. Loss is fallen back on to value the Unpaid Amount requested by the Non-defaulting Party. However, Loss is calculated as 100% of the collateral's market value and any haircuts previously applied are ignored.

This process is another way in which the CSA links into the ISDA Master Agreement.

You will notice here that you have the terms "Market Quotation" and "Loss" that are used in the 1992 version of the ISDA Master Agreement. However, many people are nowadays entering into the 2002 version of the Agreement and there is only the 1995 version of the English Law CSA. How can they harmonise Close-out Amount which is the sole payment measure in the 2002 Agreement with Market Quotation and Loss which appear in the CSA?

Well there are four possible solutions:

- They could have signed up to the ISDA's 2002 ISDA Master Agreement Protocol which closed on 1 June 2004: 287 market players signed up to this Protocol.
- They could have entered into the Amendment Agreement published by ISDA in May 2003 that updated the English Law CSA's Dispute Resolution and Default provisions and definition of Exposure in this way.
- They can import that wording into Paragraph 11(h) of their CSA and agree it there.
- They can include a 2002 ISDA Master Agreement Protocol provision into their 2002 ISDA Schedule.

The following is the typical wording for such a provision:

> *2002 Master Agreement Protocol.* The parties agree that the definitions and provisions contained in Annexes 1 to 16 and Section 6 of the 2002 Master Agreement Protocol published by the International Swaps and Derivatives Association, Inc. on 15th July, 2003 are incorporated into and apply to this Agreement.

Annex 15 of the Protocol contains the necessary wording for the English Law CSA.

A common amendment to Paragraph 6 is to extend it beyond Events of Default to Termination Events involving close-out of all Affected Transactions. An example of such wording can be seen on page 237.

Paragraph 7. Representation

Each party represents to the other party (which representation will be deemed to be repeated as of each date on which it transfers Eligible Credit Support, Equivalent Credit Support or Equivalent Distributions) that it is the sole owner of or otherwise has the right to transfer all Eligible Credit Support, Equivalent Credit Support or Equivalent Distributions it transfers to the other party under this Annex, free and clear of any security interest, lien, encumbrance or other restriction (other than a lien routinely imposed on all securities in a relevant clearance system).

Paragraph 7. Representation

This is a representation that each transferring party confirms to the other that it is the sole legal owner of or has the sole right to transfer the relevant collateral and distributions on it. It repeats that transfers are free of encumbrances in a similar manner to Paragraph 5(a).

Paragraph 8. Expenses

Each party will pay its own costs and expenses (including any stamp, transfer or similar transaction tax or duty payable on any transfer it is required to make under this Annex) in connection with performing its obligations under this Annex, and neither party will be liable for any such costs and expenses incurred by the other party.

Paragraph 8. Expenses

This is a simple statement that each party will pay its own expenses (including any stamp or transfer taxes) relating to its performance obligations under the English Law CSA and will not be liable for any costs or expenses incurred by its counterparty.

Paragraph 9. Miscellaneous

(a) ***Default Interest.*** Other than in the case of an amount which is the subject of a dispute under Paragraph 4(a), if a Transferee fails to make, when due, any transfer of Equivalent Credit Support, Equivalent Distributions or the Interest Amount, it will be obliged to pay the Transferor (to the extent permitted under applicable law) an amount equal to interest at the Default Rate multiplied by the Value on the relevant Valuation Date of the items of property that were required to be transferred, from (and including) the date that the Equivalent Credit Support, Equivalent Distributions or Interest Amount were required to be transferred to (but excluding) the date of transfer of the Equivalent Credit Support, Equivalent Distributions or Interest Amount. This interest will be calculated on the basis of daily compounding and the actual number of days elapsed.

(b) ***Good Faith and Commercially Reasonable Manner.*** Performance of all obligations under this Annex, including, but not limited to, all calculations, valuations and determinations made by either party, will be made in good faith and in a commercially reasonable manner.

(c) ***Demands and Notices.*** All demands and notices given by a party under this Annex will be given as specified in Section 12 of this Agreement.

(d) ***Specifications of Certain Matters.*** Anything referred to in this Annex as being specified in Paragraph 11 also may be specified in one or more Confirmations or other documents and this Annex will be construed accordingly.

Paragraph 9. Miscellaneous

This contains a number of protective boilerplate provisions.

(a) Paragraph 9(a) states that the Transferee will pay default interest to the Transferor for any overdue return of collateral or overdue payment of interest on cash collateral or manufactured dividends on bonds. This default interest is calculated at the Default Rate (1% over the Transferor's cost of funds to paraphrase the Master Agreement's definition of this term). The default interest period includes the date on which such return or payment was due to but excluding the date on which it is actually made (in accordance with the normal practice in the OTC derivatives markets). It will also be subject to daily compounding.

(b) Each party must perform all its obligations under the English Law CSA in good faith and in a commercially reasonable manner. This level of care is also set for a Calculation Agent under the various sets of ISDA's general and product Definitions booklets.

(c) All demands and notices under the English Law CSA will be given in one of the traditional or electronic means stated in Section 12 of the Master Agreement.

(d) This tucked-away provision enables any matters referred to in a Confirmation or other document that could alternatively be stated in the English Law CSA's Paragraph 11 to be interpreted as being a provision of the English Law CSA itself. If any such use of a Confirmation is made it should state that the provision will survive the maturity of the Transaction which is the subject of the Confirmation. However, there could be monitoring problems with this.

Paragraph 10. Definitions

As used in this Annex:

"Base Currency" means the currency specified as such in Paragraph 11(a)(i).

"Base Currency Equivalent" means, with respect to an amount on a Valuation Date, in the case of an amount denominated in the Base Currency, such Base Currency amount and, in the case of an amount denominated in a currency other than the Base Currency (the "Other Currency"), the amount of Base Currency required to purchase such amount of the Other Currency at the spot exchange rate determined by the Valuation Agent for value on such Valuation Date.

"Credit Support Amount" means, with respect to a Transferor on a Valuation Date, (i) the Transferee's Exposure plus (ii) all Independent Amounts applicable to the Transferor, if any, minus (iii) all Independent Amounts applicable to the Transferee, if any, minus (iv) the Transferor's Threshold; *provided, however,* that the Credit Support Amount will be deemed to be zero whenever the calculation of Credit Support Amount yields a number less than zero.

"Credit Support Balance" means, with respect to a Transferor on a Valuation Date, the aggregate of all Eligible Credit Support that has been transferred to or received by the Transferee under this Annex, together with any Distributions and all proceeds of any such Eligible Credit Support or Distributions, as reduced pursuant to Paragraph 2(b), 3(c)(ii) or 6. Any Equivalent Distributions or Interest Amount (or portion of either) not transferred pursuant to Paragraph 5(c)(i) or (ii) will form part of the Credit Support Balance.

"Delivery Amount" has the meaning specified in Paragraph 2(a).

"Disputing Party" has the meaning specified in Paragraph 4.

"Distributions" means, with respect to any Eligible Credit Support comprised in the Credit Support Balance consisting of securities, all principal, interest and other payments and distributions of cash or other property to which a holder of securities of the same type, nominal value, description and amount as such Eligible Credit Support would be entitled from time to time.

"Distributions Date" means, with respect to any Eligible Credit Support comprised in the Credit Support Balance other than cash, each date on which a holder of such Eligible Credit Support is entitled to receive Distributions or, if that date is not a Local Business Day, the next following Local Business Day.

Paragraph 10. Definitions

With, no doubt, a big government health warning from lawyers, I set out below a simplified glossary of all terms in a bilateral English Law CSA.

GLOSSARY OF TERMS IN PARAGRAPH 10

Base Currency	The currency into which risk exposure and collateral already held is converted to calculate if a collateral call needs to be made.
Base Currency Equivalent	If collateral is denominated in another currency, the amount in the Base Currency needed to buy the other currency at the spot rate of exchange so as to convert it into the Base Currency.
Credit Support Amount	The net risk exposure the collateral taker has on the collateral giver and which needs to be collateralised.
Credit Support Balance	The actual amount of collateral held at any one time by the collateral taker.
Delivery Amount	The amount of collateral the collateral giver needs to deliver if he agrees with a collateral call from the collateral taker.
Disputing Party	A party who disputes the other party's calculation of Transaction values in determining risk exposure and/or the value of any collateral held or to be returned.
Distributions	Periodic payments of interest or dividends on bonds or shares by their issuers to their holders.
Distributions Date	The date upon which holders of bonds or shares are entitled to receive interest or dividends from their issuers.

"Eligible Credit Support" means, with respect to a party, the items, if any, specified as such for that party in Paragraph 11(b)(ii) including, in relation to any securities, if applicable, the proceeds of any redemption in whole or in part of such securities by the relevant issuer.

"Eligible Currency" means each currency specified as such in Paragraph 11(a)(ii), if such currency is freely available.

"Equivalent Credit Support" means, in relation to any Eligible Credit Support comprised in the Credit Support Balance, Eligible Credit Support of the same type, nominal value, description and amount as that Eligible Credit Support.

"Equivalent Distributions" has the meaning specified in Paragraph 5(c)(i).

"Exchange Date" has the meaning specified in Paragraph 11(d).

"Exposure" means, with respect to a party on a Valuation Date and subject to Paragraph 4 in the case of a dispute, the amount, if any, that would be payable to that party by the other party (expressed as a positive number) or by that party to the other party (expressed as a negative number) pursuant to Section 6(e)(ii)(1) of this Agreement if all Transactions (other than the Transaction constituted by this Annex) were being terminated as of the relevant Valuation Time, on the basis that (i) that party is not the Affected Party and (ii) the Base Currency is the Termination Currency; *provided* that Market Quotations will be determined by the Valuation Agent on behalf of that party using its estimates at mid-market of the amounts that would be paid for Replacement Transactions (as that term is defined in the definition of "Market Quotation").

"Independent Amount" means, with respect to a party, the Base Currency Equivalent of the amount specified as such for that party in Paragraph 11 (b)(iii)(A); if no amount is specified, zero.

"Interest Amount" means, with respect to an Interest Period, the aggregate sum of the Base Currency Equivalents of the amounts of interest determined for each relevant currency and calculated for each day in that Interest Period on the principal amount of the portion of the Credit Support Balance comprised of cash in such currency, determined by the Valuation Agent for each such day as follows:

(x) the amount of cash in such currency on that day; multiplied by

(y) the relevant Interest Rate in effect for that day; divided by

(z) 360 (or, in the case of pounds sterling, 365).

Eligible Credit Support	The collateral types and maturities agreed by the parties that can be transferred under the English Law CSA.
Eligible Currency	The agreed currency or currencies for cash collateral transferred under the English Law CSA.
Equivalent Credit Support	The collateral the collateral taker is obliged to return to the collateral giver when its risk exposure on the collateral giver reduces or when the collateral taker agrees a substitution. The returned collateral must be of the same issuer, class, type and issue but need not be the identically numbered bonds or shares originally received.
Equivalent Distributions	The separate payment or manufactured dividend the collateral taker makes to the collateral giver equal to 100% of the interest or dividend he has received from the bond or share issuer.
Exchange Date	The deadline for the collateral taker to return designated previously delivered collateral to the collateral giver following an agreed substitution.
Exposure	The estimated replacement value of all Transactions (using mid market quotations from dealers) so as to calculate risk exposure. The calculation is made as if the Transactions were being closed out on the basis described in the definition.
Independent Amount	A confusing term meaning either the equivalent of initial margin taken at the start of a collateral relationship and not counted in risk exposure calculations, or a sum taken later in the relationship and which is counted in the risk exposure calculations.
Interest Amount	The aggregate sum of interest due on cash collateral including its conversion into the Base Currency Equivalent where cash collateral interest is due in various currencies.

"Interest Period" means the period from (and including) the last Local Business Day on which an Interest Amount was transferred (or, if no Interest Amount has yet been transferred, the Local Business Day on which Eligible Credit Support or Equivalent Credit Support in the form of cash was transferred to or received by the Transferee) to (but excluding) the Local Business Day on which the current Interest Amount is transferred.

"Interest Rate" means, with respect to an Eligible Currency, the rate specified in Paragraph 11(f)(i) for that currency.

"Local Business Day", unless otherwise specified in Paragraph 11(h), means:

(i) in relation to a transfer of cash or other property (other than securities) under this Annex, a day on which commercial banks are open for business (including dealings in foreign exchange and foreign currency deposits) in the place where the relevant account is located and, if different, in the principal financial centre, if any, of the currency of such payment;

(ii) in relation to a transfer of securities under this Annex, a day on which the clearance system agreed between the parties for delivery of the securities is open for the acceptance and execution of settlement instructions or, if delivery of the securities is contemplated by other means, a day on which commercial banks are open for business (including dealings in foreign exchange and foreign currency deposits) in the place(s) agreed between the parties for this purpose;

(iii) in relation to a valuation under this Annex, a day on which commercial banks are open for business (including dealings in foreign exchange and foreign currency deposits) in the place of location of the Valuation Agent and in the place(s) agreed between the parties for this purpose; and

(iv) in relation to any notice or other communication under this Annex, a day on which commercial banks are open for business (including dealings in foreign exchange and foreign currency deposits) in the place specified in the address for notice most recently provided by the recipient.

"Minimum Transfer Amount" means, with respect to a party, the amount specified as such for that party in Paragraph 11(b)(iii)(C); if no amount is specified, zero.

"New Credit Support" has the meaning specified in Paragraph 3(c)(i).

"Notification Time" has the meaning specified in Paragraph 11(c)(iv).

Interest Period	Basically the period from the date when interest was last paid on cash collateral to the date on which it is next due to be paid.
Interest Rate	The particular benchmark interest rate (e.g. EONIA, Fed Funds) which the parties agree shall be paid on cash deposited as collateral. It may include a spread.
Local Business Day	A business day for commercial banks in the location required for the valuation of Transactions and collateral under the English Law CSA. With securities transfers it is a business day for securities clearance systems.
Minimum Transfer Amount	The agreed minimum level that the Credit Support Amount must reach after taking account of any Threshold before a party is obliged to deliver or return collateral.
New Credit Support	Where agreed by the collateral taker, collateral transferred by the collateral giver in substitution for other collateral already held by the collateral taker.
Notification Time	The agreed deadline for making a collateral call.

"Recalculation Date" means the Valuation Date that gives rise to the dispute under Paragraph 4; *provided, however,* that if a subsequent Valuation Date occurs under Paragraph 2 prior to the resolution of the dispute, then the ***"Recalculation Date"*** means the most recent Valuation Date under Paragraph 2.

"Resolution Time" has the meaning specified in Paragraph 11(e)(i).

"Return Amount" has the meaning specified in Paragraph 2(b).

"Settlement Day" means, in relation to a date, (i) with respect to a transfer of cash or other property (other than securities), the next Local Business Day and (ii) with respect to a transfer of securities, the first Local Business Day after such date on which settlement of a trade in the relevant securities, if effected on such date, would have been settled in accordance with customary practice when settling through the clearance system agreed between the parties for delivery of such securities or, otherwise, on the market in which such securities are principally traded (or, in either case, if there is no such customary practice, on the first Local Business Day after such date on which it is reasonably practicable to deliver such securities).

"Threshold" means, with respect to a party, the Base Currency Equivalent of the amount specified as such for that party in Paragraph 11(b)(iii)(B); if no amount is specified, zero.

"Transferee" means, in relation to each Valuation Date, the party in respect of which Exposure is a positive number and, in relation to a Credit Support Balance, the party which, subject to this Annex, owes such Credit Support Balance or, as the case may be, the Value of such Credit Support Balance to the other party.

"Transferor" means, in relation to a Transferee, the other party.

"Valuation Agent" has the meaning specified in Paragraph 11(c)(i).

"Valuation Date" means each date specified in or otherwise determined pursuant to Paragraph 11(c)(ii).

"Valuation Percentage" means, for any item of Eligible Credit Support, the percentage specified in Paragraph 11(b)(ii).

Recalculation Date	In a dispute, the date or dates upon which recalculation of Transaction and collateral values are made.
Resolution Time	The agreed deadline for resolving disputes.
Return Amount	The collateral amount to be returned by the collateral taker to the collateral giver because it is surplus to the collateral taker's risk exposure on the collateral giver.
Settlement Day	For cash collateral transfers, the following Local Business Day. For securities collateral, the next Local Business Day when transfer of such securities can be completed in their normal settlement cycle.
Threshold	The unsecured risk exposure each party allows the other. Collateral may only be called or returned where the risk exposure exceeds the relevant party's Threshold and Minimum Transfer Amount.
Transferee	The collateral taker.
Transferor	The collateral giver.
Valuation Agent	Either each party to the English Law CSA performing their own valuations of Transactions and collateral and making calls as appropriate, or a third party doing this for them both. For example, a Transferor would be the Valuation Agent if it were making a demand for a return of collateral.
Valuation Date	The Local Business Day upon which risk exposure calculations and collateral valuations are made to determine if a collateral call is needed.
Valuation Percentage	The remaining value of collateral expressed in percentage terms after the agreed haircut has been deducted.

"Valuation Time" has the meaning specified in Paragraph 11(c)(iii).

"Value" means, for any Valuation Date or other date for which Value is calculated, and subject to Paragraph 4 in the case of a dispute, with respect to:

(i) Eligible Credit Support comprised in a Credit Support Balance that is:

(A) an amount of cash, the Base Currency Equivalent of such amount multiplied by the applicable Valuation Percentage, if any; and

(B) a security, the Base Currency Equivalent of the bid price obtained by the Valuation Agent multiplied by the applicable Valuation Percentage, if any; and

(ii) items that are comprised in a Credit Support Balance and are not Eligible Credit Support, zero.

Valuation Time	The reference time as at which calculations for collateral calls are made. They are normally based on prices at the close of business on the Local Business Day before the Valuation Date.
Value	The agreed valuation bases in Paragraph 11(e) of the English Law CSA for cash and securities collateral required to value collateral in the normal course of business or in a dispute.

Paragraph 11. Elections and Variables

(a) ***Base Currency and Eligible Currency.***

(i) "Base Currency" means United States Dollars unless otherwise specified here:

……………………………………………………

(ii) "Eligible Currency" means the Base Currency and each other currency specified here:

…………………………………………………

…………………………………………………

(b) ***Credit Support Obligations.***

(i) ***Delivery Amount, Return Amount and Credit Support Amount.***

(A) ***"Delivery Amount"*** has the meaning specified in Paragraph 2(a), unless otherwise specified here: ……………………………………………

(B) ***"Return Amount"*** has the meaning specified in Paragraph 2(b), unless otherwise specified here: …………………………………………..

(C) ***"Credit Support Amount"*** has the meaning specified in Paragraph 10, unless otherwise specified here: ……………………………………………

Paragraph 11. Elections and Variables

This is the Elections and Variables paragraph where the parties make choices for operating the collateralised relationship between them. Paragraph 11 is the equivalent of the ISDA Master Agreement Schedule.

An explanation of the Paragraph 11 provisions follows.

For the purpose of illustrating market practice on various choices made in Paragraph 11, I have reviewed many versions of Paragraph 11 to the English Law CSA used by various dealers and sophisticated end users that I consider to be a reasonable cross-section of the documentation seen in the market. Examples of wording used for Paragraph 11 provisions follows the general explanation.

Base Currency

The Base Currency is the currency into which the collateral value and the risk exposure are converted in order to determine if a collateral call is needed. It is often the same as the Termination Currency stated in the ISDA Schedule. This is the expectation in the definition of Exposure in Paragraph 10. This is necessary if collateral, for example, is in a currency other than a Base Currency. Under the New York law CSA, there are no references to a Base Currency since that document presupposes that only US dollar collateral will be pledged.

Eligible Currency

These are the currencies the parties are willing to accept as cash collateral.

Delivery Amount/Return Amount

If you change the definition of either of these you must change the other because they are mirror images of each other.

Credit Support Amount

Unless amended, the Credit Support Amount is the risk exposure that needs to be collateralised on a Valuation Date. This definition is normally only amended if you are dealing with a hedge fund counterparty when any Independent Amounts transferred by the Transferee are ignored so that the entire focus is on its gross risk exposure on the hedge fund Transferor. An example of this wording is shown on page 169.

However, the Credit Support Amount is deemed to be zero whenever its calculation would yield a negative number.

(ii) ***Eligible Credit Support***. The following items will qualify as ***"Eligible Credit Support"*** for the party specified:

		Party A	Party B	Valuation Percentage
(A)	cash in an Eligible Currency	[ ]	[ ]	[ ]%
(B)	negotiable debt obligations issued by the Government of [ ] having an original maturity at issuance of not more than one year	[ ]	[ ]	[ ]%
(C)	negotiable debt obligations issue by the Government of [ ] having an original maturity at issuance of more than one year but not more than 10 years	[ ]	[ ]	[ ]%
(D)	negotiable debt obligation issued by the Government of [ ] having an original maturity at issuance of more than 10 years	[ ]	[ ]	[ ]%
(E)	other:	[ ]	[ ]	[ ]%

Eligible Credit Support

If only cash is taken as Eligible Credit Support it alone will be shown in the table.

However, it is more normal to include bonds as well and I reproduce the sample table (Table 4.1) from the previous chapter as Table 5.1.

Table 5.1 **Example of eligible collateral from the English Law CSA**

Year	Party A	Party B	Valuation percentage
(A) cash in an Eligible Currency	X	X	100
(B) negotiable debt obligations issued by the Government of the United States of America, the United Kingdom or Germany having a remaining maturity of not more than 1 year	X	X	99
(C) negotiable debt obligations issued by the Government of the United States of America, the United Kingdom or Germany having a remaining maturity of more than 1 year but not more than 5 years	X	X	97
(C) negotiable debt obligations issued by the Government of the United States of America, the United Kingdom or Germany having a remaining maturity of more than 5 years but not more than 10 years	X	X	95
(D) negotiable debt obligations issued by the Government of the United States of America, the United Kingdom or Germany having a remaining maturity of more than 10 years	X	X	90

Here the Eligible Credit Support includes securities issued by the governments of the United States of America, United Kingdom and Germany. Clearly other countries are possible such as Austria, Belgium, Canada, France, Italy, Swizerland and the Netherlands. This list is not exhaustive. In other jurisdictions (e.g. South Africa) you would need to obtain or review the ISDA collateral legal opinion for that country to check how robust its legal regime is in respect of taking and enforcing collateral and whether securities collateral has to be held offshore or with a particular depository.

There is sometimes confusion over the terms Valuation Percentage and "haircut". Haircuts are discounts applied to the value of collateral. Therefore a 2% haircut will result in a 98% Valuation Percentage for the collateral concerned.

Please note that most market players amend "having an original maturity at issuance of" to "having a remaining maturity of" in their templates so that focus of the bond haircutting is on the bond's residual life.

No haircut is normally applied to Cash and so its Valuation Percentage is usually 100%.

Reviewing a cross section of English Law CSAs, the Valuation Percentages of G7 government securities were in the following range:

Residual term	Valuation percentage range
Up to 1 year	98–100%
Over 1 year but less than 5 years	95–97%
Over 5 years but less than 10 years	94–95%
Over 10 years	90%

Some market players put an upward limit on the last residual term of 20 or 30 years.

The most aggressive Valuation Percentages I saw were:

Residual term	Valuation percentage
Up to 1 year	100%
Over 1 year but less than 10 years	98%
Over 10 years	97%

In addition where bonds are concerned, parties sometimes quote the unique ICAD codes for certain bonds so that it is clear that the bond concerned is agreed to be Eligible Credit Support under the Annex. The word ICAD means ISDA Collateral Asset Definition and these codes may be found in the *ISDA Collateral Asset Definitions* which were published in June 2003, and are available on the ISDA website. The ICADs have not been updated by ISDA since publication.

Here is an example of such wording:

(i) **Eligible Credit Support. Eligible Credit Support applicable to Party A and Party B, shall consist of those assets identified by the ICAD codes listed below, as such ICAD codes are defined in the ISDA Collateral Asset Definitions (First Edition – June 2003), *provided however*, that such items listed in "(E)" through "(Q)" must be rated AAA by Moody's and Aaa by S&P.**

	ICAD Code	Remaining term to maturity of one 1 year or under	Remaining term to maturity of more than 1 year up to and including 5 years	Remaining term to maturity of more than 5 years up to and including 10 years	Remaining term to maturity of more than 10 years and up to and including 30 years
(A)	US-CASH	100%	N/A	N/A	N/A
(B)	EU-CASH	100%	N/A	N/A	N/A
(C)	CA-CASH	100%	N/A	N/A	N/A
(D)	GB-CASH	100%	N/A	N/A	N/A
(E)	US-TBILL	99%	N/A	N/A	N/A
(F)	US-TNOTE	99%	98%	97%	N/A
(G)	US-TBOND	99%	98%	97%	95%
(H)	FR-BTF	99%	N/A	N/A	N/A
(I)	FR-BTAN	99%	98%	N/A	N/A
(J)	FR-OAT	99%	98%	97%	95%
(K)	DE-BOND	99%	98%	97%	95%
(L)	DE-NOTE2	99%	98%	N/A	N/A
(M)	DE-NOTE5.5	99%	98%	97%	N/A
(N)	NL-BOND	99%	N/A	N/A	N/A
(O)	NL-BILL	99%	98%	97%	N/A
(P)	SE-GOVT	99%	98%	97%	95%
(Q)	GB-GLT	99%	N/A	N/A	N/A

The purpose of quoting an ICAD code is to ensure that you receive exactly the bond you expected to receive. A problem arose with US Treasuries when inflation-linked bonds were transferred as collateral when the Transferee was expecting to receive straight bonds. Quoting an ICAD code avoids this problem.

Before this you saw and even today you might see the following wording at the end of the Eligible Credit Support table:

> **Provided, however, that any debt obligations issued by the US Treasury Department which has a coupon or a redemption amount which is determined by reference to an inflation index shall not qualify as Eligible Credit Support. For the avoidance of doubt, Treasury Inflation Protected Securities shall not quality as Eligible Credit Support.**

Finally you occasionally see general wording for other Eligible Credit Support e.g.

Such other Eligible Credit Support as the parties may from time to time agree in writing as being acceptable.	To be agreed by the parties on a case by case basis.

The problem with this is that there is a risk that the collateral may be approved at the wrong level, for example by a Front Office trader rather than a Credit, Collateral and Legal Department. In order to avoid this risk and any uncertainty, I think it best not to include such a provision. Specific additional Eligible Credit Support can always be stated in a subsequent Amendment Agreement.

(iii) ***Thresholds.***

(A) ***"Independent Amount"*** means with respect to Party A: ………………………………
"Independent Amount" means with respect to Party B: ………………………………

(B) ***"Threshold"*** means with respect to Party A: ………………………………………
"Threshold" means with respect to Party B: ………………………………………

(C) ***"Minimum Transfer Amount"*** means with respect to Party A: …………………………
"Minimum Transfer Amount" means with respect to Party B: …………………………

(iii) Thresholds

Independent Amount

Independent Amount is a confusing term in the English Law CSA. It can mean initial margin taken at the start of a collateral relationship and not counted in the collateral balance or a sum taken later in the relationship and that is counted in it (although technically it could also be taken at the beginning as well).

It is taken to address the estimated volatility of a particular Transaction; the time gap between a collateral call and the delivery of the collateral itself (e.g. with emerging markets bonds which can take up to 14 days to settle); or in relation to credit concerns relating to one or both parties. Independent Amount can be a fixed monetary amount or be expressed as a formula (e.g. as a percentage of the Transaction's notional amount) or even based upon low credit ratings. If an Independent Amount is not stated it is deemed to be zero.

Independent Amounts overcollateralise derivatives risk exposure. A problem arose with the Lehman Brothers' insolvency in that Independent Amounts posted to Lehmans and reused by them proved not to be recoverable by Pledgors in many cases. That was because the receivers of that collateral could offset it against their own risk exposure on Lehmans. In fact under the New York Law CSA the Pledgor only has a contractual right to the return of collateral if it agrees for it to be reused by the Secured Party. In this case, the Pledgor would become an unsecured creditor with respect to the return of its own collateral from Lehmans. This led ISDA to produce a White Paper that proposes isolating Independent Amounts through segregation from other collateral and the possible use of pledge and custody type arrangements for such Independent Amounts. The market is considering the White Paper proposals as there are operational challenges in each case. There is more on this subject on pages 413–18.

Threshold

Threshold is the unsecured risk exposure a party is willing to tolerate before it calls for collateral from its counterparty.

A Threshold can be a fixed monetary amount but it is also often linked to a credit ratings table. If a Threshold is not stated it is deemed to be zero.

Banks often propose zero Thresholds both ways with other banks so that they each might benefit from regulatory capital savings on their trading book risk.

Minimum Transfer Amount

Minimum Transfer Amounts should prevent costly transfers of "nuisance" amounts of collateral. They are often linked to a credit ratings table. If a Minimum Transfer Amount is not stated it is deemed to be zero.

Because the use of a Minimum Transfer Amount only establishes a "floor", it does not stop the delivery of uneven amounts of Eligible Credit Support or Equivalent Credit Support. Applying a rounding convention overcomes this.

(D) ***Rounding.*** The Delivery Amount and the Return Amount will be rounded [down to the nearest integral multiple of ..../up and down to the nearest integral multiple of ...., respectively[3]].

(c) ***Valuation and Timing.***

(i) ***"Valuation Agent"*** means, for purposes of Paragraphs 2 and 4, the party making the demand under Paragraph 2, and, for purposes of Paragraph 5(c), the Transferee, as applicable, unless otherwise specified here: ……………………………………………………………

(ii) ***"Valuation Date"*** means: ………………………………………………………………………

Rounding

Parties usually select one of the following options: (i) round the Delivery Amount and Return Amount down to the nearest integral multiple stated (e.g. US$10,000) or (ii) round the Delivery Amount up and the Return Amount down to the nearest integral multiple stated. If no rounding convention is stated, then the Delivery Amount and the Return Amount will not be rounded.

Parties would not normally state that both Delivery and Return Amounts are to be rounded up as this could leave a Transferee undercollateralised by nearly up to the agreed integral multiple (typically US$10,000).

Most common is to round the Delivery Amount up and the Return Amount down.

Valuation Agent

The Valuation Agent calculates the Delivery Amount and the Return Amount and reports these calculations to the other party so that they can fulfil their obligations under Paragraph 2 of the Annex.

The parties may name one of themselves as the Valuation Agent. If no Valuation Agent is stated here then the party calling for the collateral (the Transferee) under Paragraph 2(a) is the Valuation Agent. The Transferee is also the Valuation Agent for transferring Distributions or Interest Amounts under Paragraph 5(c). The Transferor would be the Valuation Agent if it were calling for a Return Amount under Paragraph 2(b) because he knows how much he will call for.

Valuation Date

Valuation Date states the frequency at which risk exposure and collateral are revalued under the ISDA Master Agreement and CSA.

This item must be completed as there is no ISDA fallback position here.

Valuation on every Local Business Day is the most common choice among major players and is favoured by regulators. Any other frequency would probably require credit approval.

(iii) ***"Valuation Time"*** means:

[ ] the close of business in the place of location of the Valuation Agent on the Valuation Date or date of calculation, as applicable;

[ ] the close of business on the Local Business Day immediately preceding the Valuation Date or date of calculation, as applicable;

provided that the calculations of Value and Exposure will, as far as practicable, be made as of approximately the same time on the same date.

(iv) ***"Notification Time"*** means 1:00 p.m., London time, on a Local Business Day, unless otherwise specified here: ……………………………………………………………………

(d) ***Exchange Date. "Exchange Date"*** has the meaning specified in Paragraph 3(c)(ii), unless otherwise specified here: ……………………………………………………………………

Valuation Time

The Valuation Time is the time as at which the Valuation Agent calculates Exposure and the value of collateral held to determine if a Delivery Amount or Return Amount call is needed. The Valuation Agent will also factor in any Distributions or Interest Amounts due to the Transferor at the Valuation Time.

The parties have two main choices, viz:

1 **as at the close of business on the Valuation Date or the date of calculation for Paragraph 5(c) payments to the Transferor; or**

2 **as at the close of business on the Local Business Day immediately before the Valuation Date or the date of calculation for Paragraph 5(c) payments to the Transferor.**

Once they have made their choice, the Annex stipulates that the calculation of risk exposure and collateral values has to be made as of approximately the same time on the selected date.

A Valuation Time as at the close of business on the Local Business Day immediately before the Valuation Date is the most common choice because collateral management units are then working from reports of risk exposure and collateral values as at the close of the previous business day when they come into work in the morning.

Notification Time

This is the time by which, among other things, (1) the Valuation Agent must notify the other party of its calculations under Paragraph 3(b) on the Local Business Day following a Valuation Date and (2) a party must make a demand for a transfer of Eligible Credit Support or Equivalent Credit Support (i.e. a collateral call) so that the other party makes the appropriate transfer not later than the close of business on the next Local Business Day. If a demand for a transfer is made after the Notification Time then the transfer can be made up to the close of business on the second Local Business Day following the day on which the demand was made. Such transfers are subject to the absence of any dispute.

The Notification Time is stated to mean 1.00 p.m. London time on the appropriate Local Business Day unless the parties agree otherwise.

Exchange Date

This concerns collateral substitutions.

Most parties choose Paragraph 3(c)(ii)to apply. However, this is sometimes amended to reduce the time period in which the Transferee must return Equivalent Credit Support after receiving New Credit Support (see pages 242–3).

(e) ***Dispute Resolution.***

(i) ***"Resolution Time"*** means 1:00 p.m., London time, on the Local Business Day following the date on which the notice is given that gives rise to a dispute under Paragraph 4, unless otherwise specified here: ………………………………………………

(ii) ***Value.*** For the purpose of Paragraphs 4(a)(4)(i)(C) and 4(a)(4)(ii), the Value of the outstanding Credit Support Balance or of any transfer of Eligible Credit Support or Equivalent Credit Support, as the case may be, will be calculated as follows: ………………………………..

(iii) ***Alternative.*** The provisions of Paragraph 4 will apply, unless an alternative dispute resolution procedure is specified here: ………………………………………………………………………

(e) Dispute Resolution

Resolution Time

The Resolution Time is the deadline for the parties to resolve their dispute under Paragraph 4. If they fail the Valuation Agent makes certain recalculations under Paragraph 4(a)(4)(i).

Value

Paragraph 4 requires that the parties provide a means for the Valuation Agent to recalculate the Value of the outstanding Credit Support Balance and the Value of any collateral transfer in a dispute. If this provision is not completed, the Valuation Agent will be unable to resolve such disputes. This provision must therefore be completed.

The simplest Value provision where only cash collateral is involved is:

(ii) **The Value of Cash will be the face value thereof multiplied by the applicable Valuation Percentage.**

The most common method for valuing bond collateral is to obtain two or three bid quotations from leading dealers and take their arithmetic mean. Please see page 219 for the sample wording.

Alternative

This provision enables the parties to adopt a different dispute resolution procedure to that contained in Paragraph 4. Normally parties adopt Paragraph 4 but there are other alternatives which are discussed on pages 223–5. In addition ISDA is working on finalising Collateral Dispute Resolution Procedures for the whole market and this is discussed on pages 418–23.

(f) ***Distributions and Interest Amount.***

(i) ***Interest Rate.*** The "Interest Rate" in relation to each Eligible Currency specified below will be:

Eligible Currency	*Interest Rate*
……………………………………	……………………………………
……………………………………	……………………………………
……………………………………	……………………………………

(ii) ***Transfer of Interest Amount.*** The transfer of the Interest Amount will be made on the last Local Business Day of each calendar month and on any Local Business Day that a Return Amount consisting wholly or partly of cash is transferred to the Transferor pursuant to Paragraph 2(b), unless otherwise specified here: ……………………………………

(iii) ***Alternative to Interest Amount.*** The provisions of Paragraph 5(c)(ii) will apply, unless otherwise specified here: ……………………………………………………………

(g) ***Addresses for Transfers.***

Party A: ……………………………………………………………………………………………
………

Party B: ……………………………………………………………………………………………
………

(h) ***Other Provisions.***

(f) Distributions and Interest Amount

Interest Rate

The Interest Rate is the interest which will be paid on the cash collateral received from the Transferor flat or minus a spread. It will reflect the frequency of the Valuation Dates. If these are daily and Euro cash is the collateral, EONIA (Euro Overnight Index Average) could be used; if weekly or monthly EURIBOR might be an option.

This section must be completed as there is no ISDA fallback.

Transfer of Interest Amount

As long as the Transferee does not become undercollateralised by transferring an Interest Amount, Paragraph 11(f)(ii) proposes that interest on cash collateral is transferred to the Transferor on the last Local Business Day of each month and on any Local Business Day when a cash Return Amount is due to the Transferor.

Whether this payment structure is acceptable will depend upon the parties' operational systems. Many parties prefer such interest transfers to take place on the second Local Business Day of the following calendar month because they can spend the first Local Business Day of that month checking calculations and preparing the necessary electronic transfers.

Alternative to Interest Amount

This provision affords the Transferee, with the Transferor's agreement, the opportunity to invest part of the cash collateral in other instruments rather than just paying over an agreed interest return. This is rarely agreed.

(g) Addresses for Transfers

This must be completed if collateral transfers and interest payments and Distributions are to be correctly routed to the recipient.

Parties often issue separate payment instructions to each other in this respect.

(h) Other Provisions

Paragraph 11(h) is similar to Part 5 of the ISDA Master Agreement Schedule – a place where other provisions may be inserted.

(a) ***Base Currency and Eligible Currency.***

(i) "Base Currency" means United States Dollars unless otherwise specified here:

……………………………………………………

(ii) "Eligible Currency" means the Base Currency and each other currency specified here:

……………………………………………………

……………………………………………………

EXAMPLES OF PARAGRAPH 11 PROVISIONS

(a) Base Currency and Eligible Currency

Euro and United States Dollars are the most common currencies specified as the Base Currency. I have also seen Sterling and even Japanese Yen. The Base Currency is the currency into which the collateral values and the risk exposure are converted in order to determine if a collateral call is needed. If the underlying risk exposure is in Euro, then the Euro should be the Base Currency.

Eligible Currency is the currency or currencies the parties agree are acceptable for cash collateral under the English Law CSA.

The Eligible Currency is sometimes just limited to cash collateral denominated in the Base Currency. The Base Currency is always included to which may be added one or two other mainstream currencies depending upon the range of collateral which a party to an English Law CSA will accept.

It is possible that if you have a Japanese counterparty they may wish you to take Japanese Yen; if you have an Australian counterparty they may want you to take Australian Dollar cash collateral; if you have a Scandinavian counterparty they may want you to take kroner cash collateral. You need to ask your collateral management unit if they have any use for these currencies or if they have the operational capacity to accept certain types of cash collateral.

Where a counterparty like a supranational does not want cash collateral at all because it will only accept G7 government bonds as collateral, for example, they may state "None" in "Eligible urrency" after deleting reference to the Base Currency. Others will just leave the Base Currency but offer a miserably low interest rate on it to discourage it being offered as collateral.

(b) ***Credit Support Obligations.***

(i) ***Delivery Amount, Return Amount and Credit Support Amount.***

(A) ***"Delivery Amount"*** has the meaning specified in Paragraph 2(a), unless otherwise specified here: ……………………………………………

(B) ***"Return Amount"*** has the meaning specified in Paragraph 2(b), unless otherwise specified here: ……………………………………………

(C) ***"Credit Support Amount"*** has the meaning specified in Paragraph 10, unless otherwise specified here: ……………………………………………

(b) (i) Credit Support Obligations

Most often (A), (B) and (C) remain unaltered, but should you make any changes to (A) Delivery Amount, it is vital to make corresponding changes to (B) Return Amount because they are mirror images of each other. One example I saw was as follows:

> (A) "Delivery Amount" has the meaning specified in Paragraph 2(a) except that the words "Paragraph 11(b)(iii)(D)" in the penultimate line shall be amended to read "Paragraph 11(b)(iv)".
>
> (B) "Return Amount" has the meaning specified in Paragraph 2(b) except that the words "Paragraph 11(b)(iii)(D)" in the fifth line shall be amended to read "Paragraph 11(b)(iv)".

However, this was merely a revised cross reference because they preferred to show Rounding in that manner.

(C) This is the Transferee's net risk exposure on the Transferor. It is the risk exposure that needs to be collateralised.

Credit Support Amount first appears in Paragraph 2 (Delivery Amounts and Return Amounts). The calculation of exposure in the Credit Support Amount will take into account:

- the net mark-to-market valuation of all Transactions under the Agreement plus or minus;
- the net Independent Amounts between the parties; and
- any Threshold.

Normally in Paragraph 11 the definition of Credit Support Amount is not changed but quite often with hedge fund counterparties, the following wording will be used instead in Paragraph 11(b)(i)(C):

> (C) "Credit Support Amount" means, for any Valuation Date (i) the Transferee's Exposure for that Valuation Date plus (ii) the aggregate of all Independent Amounts applicable to the Transferor, if any, minus (iii) the Transferor's Threshold; provided, however, that (x) in the case where the sum of the Independent Amounts applicable to the Transferor exceeds zero, the Credit Support Amount will not be less than the sum of all Independent Amounts applicable to the Transferor and (y) in all other cases, the Credit Support Amount will be deemed to be zero whenever the calculation of Credit Support Amount yields an amount less than zero.

The purpose of this amendment is to eliminate the subtraction of Independent Amounts applying to the Transferee from the calculation of Credit Support Amount and therefore focuses on the Transferee's gross risk exposure on the Transferor. This would leave the calculation of Credit Support Amount to the following:

- **The Transferee's Exposure**
  plus
- **all Independent Amounts applicable to the Transferor**
  minus
- **the Transferor's Threshold.**

This could result in both parties holding Eligible Credit Support at the same time. The Transferor will hold collateral taken for the Transferee's Independent Amount (which has been ignored here) while the Transferee will hold collateral from the Transferor following the taking of an Independent Amount and a Delivery Amount under a collateral call. Both sides are therefore fully collateralised.

A further amendment is usually made in the Other Provisions section of Paragraph 11, viz:

> **Additions to Paragraph 2. The following subparagraph (c) is hereby added to Paragraph 2 of this Annex:**
>
> ***No offset*. On any Valuation Date, if either (i) each party is required to make a transfer under Paragraph 2(a) or (ii) each party is required to make a transfer under Paragraph 2(b), then the amounts of those obligations will not offset each other.**

This prohibition on offset seeks to ensure that collateral held by the Transferee is not offset against collateral it gives to a Transferor as support for its Independent Amount following price or rate movements in order to avoid undercollateralisation.

Appendix B to the *User's Guide to the ISDA Credit Support Documents under English Law* gives a useful worked example of why this is important. Its example is based upon the ISDA English Law Credit Support Deed but it can be adapted for the English Law Credit Support Annex as follows:

> **On a Valuation Date Party A makes a collateral call on Party B who transfers EUR50 as a Delivery Amount to cover Party A's risk exposure on Party B. On the same Valuation Date Party A transfers EUR10 to Party B in connection with an Independent Amount applying to it for a new deal under the Annex.**

On a later Valuation Date:

> **The value of the collateral held by Party B for Party A's Independent Amount has reduced to EUR9 while the risk exposure of Party A on Party B has increased to EUR70.**

If these obligations were offset Party B would transfer EUR19 to Party A which would leave both parties undercollateralised by EUR1, i.e. Party A would have total collateral of EUR69 (50 + 19) against a risk exposure of

EUR70 on Party B. Party B would have collateral of EUR9 for Party A's Independent Amount of EUR10.

If these obligations cannot be offset as per the prohibition above, Party A would transfer EUR1 to Party B and Party B would transfer EUR20 to Party A. Both would then be fully collateralised.

This is particularly important where dealing with hedge funds as no bank would want to be undercollateralised with them.

(ii) ***Eligible Credit Support***. The following items will qualify as ***"Eligible Credit Support"*** for the party specified:

		Party A	Party B	Valuation Percentage
(A)	cash in an Eligible Currency	[ ]	[ ]	[ ]%
(B)	negotiable debt obligations issued by the Government of [ ] having an original maturity at issuance of not more than one year	[ ]	[ ]	[ ]%
(C)	negotiable debt obligations issue by the Government of [ ] having an original maturity at issuance of more than one year but not more than 10 years	[ ]	[ ]	[ ]%
(D)	negotiable debt obligation issued by the Government of [ ] having an original maturity at issuance of more than 10 years	[ ]	[ ]	[ ]%
(E)	other:	[ ]	[ ]	[ ]%

(b) (ii) Eligible Credit Support

If only cash is taken as Eligible Credit Support it alone will be shown in the table. However, it is more normal to include bonds as well and I now reproduce the sample table (Table 4.1) from the previous chapter as Table 5.2.

Table 5.2

Example of eligible collateral from the English Law CSA

Year	Party A	Party B	Valuation percentage
(A) cash in an Eligible Currency	X	X	100
(B) negotiable debt obligations issued by the Government of the United States of America, the United Kingdom or Germany having a remaining maturity of not more than 1 year	X	X	99
(C) negotiable debt obligations issued by the Government of the United States of America, the United Kingdom or Germany having a remaining maturity of more than 1 year but not more than 5 years	X	X	97
(C) negotiable debt obligations issued by the Government of the United States of America, the United Kingdom or Germany having a remaining maturity of more than 5 years but not more than 10 years	X	X	95
(D) negotiable debt obligations issued by the Government of the United States of America, the United Kingdom or Germany having a remaining maturity of more than 10 years	X	X	90

Here the Eligible Credit Support includes bonds issued by the governments of the US, the UK and Germany. Clearly, other countries are possible such as Austria, Belgium, Canada, France, Italy, Japan, the Netherlands and Switzerland. This list is not exhaustive.

In a bilateral English Law CSA both boxes (for Party A and Party B) would be checked and the appropriate Valuation Percentage, determined by the credit department, entered alongside.

No haircut is normally applied to Cash and so its Valuation Percentage is invariably 100%.

Reviewing a cross-section of English Law CSAs, the Valuation Percentages of G7 government securities were in the range as follows:

Residual term	Valuation percentage range
Up to 1 year	98–100
Over 1 year but less than 5 years	95–97
Over 5 years but less than 10 years	94–95
Over 10 years	90

Some market players put an upward limit on the last residual term of 20 or 30 years.

The most aggressive Valuation Percentages I saw are as follows:

Residual term	Valuation percentage
Up to 1 year	100
Over 1 year but less than 10 years	98
Over 10 years	97

This is less common since the credit crunch.

Sometimes you see further qualifications as to what counts as eligible bond collateral, for example:

> Negotiable Debt Obligations must be denominated in the domestic currency of the issuing country.
>
> Negotiable Debt Obligations must be rated by Moody's Investors Service Inc., or any successor thereto ("Moody's"), and/or Standard and Poor's Rating Group (a division of McGraw-Hill, Inc.), or any successor thereto ("S&P"), Aa1/AA+ or higher.
>
> For the avoidance of doubt, where Negotiable Debt Obligations are rated by only one of the above relevant rating agencies, the rating applied will be based on the rating of that agency.
>
> Where the ratings of the relevant agencies differ with respect to the same Negotiable Debt Obligation, the lower of the ratings shall apply.
>
> If at any time the Negotiable Debt Obligations fail (or cease) to be rated by at least one of the above agencies then such Negotiable Debt Obligations shall not be considered Eligible Credit Support.
>
> Both parties agree that the Negotiable Debt Obligations set out above will only constitute Eligible Credit Support provided that they are able to be cleared through Euroclear and/or Clearstream (or any successor thereto).

Highly rated corporate bonds may also be accepted as Eligible Credit Support and usually Valuation Percentages will be lower and other conditions more onerous. An example of this is shown in Table 5.3.

Table 5.3

Corporate Bonds, as defined below, with a long term rating of Aaa by Moody's, or AAA by S&P, as defined below having a residual time to maturity of:	Not more than 5 years More than 5 years < 10 years More than 10 years	95% 92% 90%
Corporate Bonds with a long term rating of Aa1 to Aa3 by Moody's or AA+ to AA– by S&P having a residual time to maturity of:	Not more than 5 years More than 5 years < 10 years More than 10 years	92% 89% 87%
Corporate Bonds with a long term rating of A1 to A3 by Moody's or A+ to A– by S&P having a residual time to maturity of:	Not more than 5 years More than 5 years < 10 years More than 10 years	87% 86% 84%
Corporate Bonds with a long term rating of Baa1 to Baa2 by Moody's or BBB+ to BBB by S&P having a residual time to maturity of:	Not more than 5 years More than 5 years < 10 years More than 10 years	84% 83% 80%

Concentration limits with respect to Eligible Credit Support

(i) The nominal amount of each relevant series of Corporate Bonds as comprised in the Credit Support Balance shall not exceed 20 per cent of the total aggregate nominal amount in issue from time to time outstanding of that relevant series of Corporate Bonds;

(ii) Corporate Bonds of any one issuer comprised in the Credit Support Balance shall not exceed 20 per cent of the total Value of the Credit Support Balance;

(iii) Without prejudice to Paragraph 11(c)(ii), in the event that the senior unsecured unsubordinated debt obligations ratings of Corporate Bonds as comprised in the Credit Support Balance, fall below Aa3, A3 or Baa2 by Moody's, respectively, or AA–, A– or BBB by S&P, respectively, the Transferee shall have the right to demand the Transferor to exchange the relevant downgraded Corporate Bonds with other Corporate Bonds which fits the correct rating criteria.

Additional Definitions

"Corporate Bonds" shall mean any debt securities issued by any U.S. or Eurozone Corporation (as defined below) which:

(a) is in the form of Senior Unsubordinated bonds or notes;

is denominated and payable by its terms solely in the lawful currency of the United States of America or Eurozone state, as applicable;

- is repayable in an amount equal to its outstanding principal balance;

- is not repayable in an amount determined by reference to any formula or index;
- is not subject to any contingency with respect to repayment;
- bears simple interest at either a fixed or floating rate that is paid on a periodic basis and computed on a benchmark interest rate plus or minus a spread, if any;
- is transferable to any third party without any restriction (provided that restrictions that provide for eligibility for resale pursuant to Rule 144A or Regulation S promulgated under the United States Securities Act of 1933, as amended, shall not be considered restrictions);
- clears through the Depository Trust Company (or its successor) or Euroclear (or its successor), as applicable;
- is part of an issue having an aggregate outstanding principal balance of not less than US$100,000,000.00 or EUR100,000,000.00;
- such securities of any one US or Eurozone Corporation shall comprise no more than US$50,000,000 or EUR50,000,000 as applicable, of the Credit Support Balance posted by, or on behalf of, the Transferor held by, or on behalf of, the Transferee if such bonds have a long term rating of Aaa (by Moody's) and AAA (by S&P) and shall comprise no more than US$10,000,000 or EUR10,000,000 as applicable of the Credit Support Balance posted by, or on behalf of, the Transferor held by, or on behalf of, the Transferee if such bonds have a lower long term rating than Aaa (by Moody's) or AAA (by S&P);
- is not issued by a financial institution or insurance company in general nor Party A nor Party B or any of its affiliates in particular. For the avoidance of doubt, Corporate Bonds shall not consist of any debt issued by any Holding Company;
- for the purposes hereof "U.S. Corporation" means a corporation (which is not a special purpose vehicle, howsoever described) organised and existing under the laws of one of the 50 states comprising the United States of America;
- for the purposes hereof "Eurozone Corporation" means a corporation (which is not a special purpose vehicle, howsoever described) organised and existing under the laws of one of the following countries: Austria, Belgium, Denmark, Finland, France, Germany, Italy, Netherlands, Sweden, and United Kingdom.

You occasionally see general wording for other Eligible Credit Support, for example:

Such other Eligible Credit Support as the parties may from time to time agree in writing as being acceptable.	To be agreed by the parties on a case by case basis.

The slight danger here is that the wording in the boxes might potentially allow traders in each party's Front Offices to agree collateral which might not be acceptable to the Credit Department or the Collateral Management Unit. While this risk is remote in a well run organisation it is conceivable that it might happen. This is why I am not in favour of such a vague provision. The appropriate people on each side should always agree what is Eligible Credit Support for them and I would not include such a provision but rather add any new type of collateral to the CSA via an Amendment Agreement.

Ineligible Credit Support

It is quite common nowadays to include language under the table dealing with bond collateral previously delivered becoming Ineligible Credit Support and what to do about it. The following is an example of such wording:

> If any of above debt obligations held by the Transferee as Credit Support Balance cease to satisfy the credit rating requirements for Eligible Credit Support, such affected debt obligations ("Affected Credit Support") shall no longer constitute Eligible Credit Support and accordingly their Value shall be zero. The Transferor shall promptly notify the Transferee of such adverse rating event. Accordingly, the Transferee shall be entitled to make a demand for the transfer of Eligible Credit Support pursuant to Paragraph 2(a). The Transferee shall, on the first Local Business Day following receipt of such new Eligible Credit Support and subject to the condition precedent that there is then no Delivery Amount applicable to the Transferor, transfer to the Transferor Affected Credit Support of the same type, nominal value, description and amount as that Affected Credit Support.

OR

> (iii) Substitution of Eligible Credit Support. In the event that the Moody's and/or S&P rating assigned to securities transferred to and held by a party as Eligible Credit Support ("Affected Credit Support") fall below the minimum rating requirements

imposed under the definition of "Eligible Credit Support" herein following the date of such transfer, that party shall be entitled to demand (by written or telephonic notice) the further transfer to it of Eligible Credit Support in equal value to and in exchange for Affected Credit Support, and the other party shall be obliged to make such transfer on the first Settlement Day following the date on which it receives such notice. The other party will only be obligated to return the Affected Credit Support after receiving the substitute Eligible Credit Support.

OR

(i) Ineligible Credit Support. If at any time any Eligible Credit Support which has been transferred pursuant to Paragraph 2(a) ceases to qualify as Eligible Credit Support ("Ineligible Credit Support") while there still exist other types of Eligible Credit Support as set out in the table above, the Transferee shall, upon demand by the Transferor, transfer to the Transferor Equivalent Ineligible Credit Support having the same total nominal value as the Ineligible Credit Support comprised in the Transferor's Credit Support Balance. The Transferee's obligation to transfer such Equivalent Ineligible Credit Support is subject to the condition precedent that there is then no Delivery Amount applicable to the Transferor, or no Delivery Amount would be created by the transfer of such Equivalent Ineligible Credit Support, as determined by the Transferee.

"Equivalent Ineligible Credit Support" means in relation to any Ineligible Credit Support, either the Ineligible Credit Support itself or Ineligible Credit Support of the same type, nominal value, description and amount as that Ineligible Credit Support.

Very occasionally where only one government's bonds are taken as Eligible Credit Support, the potential ineligibility question might be dealt with by additional wording to the above as follows:

For the avoidance of doubt, in the event that, at any given time, all items listed as Eligible Credit Support in the table above cease to qualify as Eligible Credit Support, the parties will agree to new items to be accepted as Eligible Credit Support along with any Valuation Percentage(s) applicable thereto. If applicable, the Transferor shall, in accordance with subsection (i) above, transfer to the Transferee such new Eligible Credit Support in accordance with Paragraph 2(a).

Pending agreement between the parties as to new items of acceptable Eligible Credit Support, a failure by the Transferor to transfer under Paragraph 2(a) shall not constitute an Event of Default.

If, after 5 (five) calendar days from the date upon which all items listed as Eligible Credit Support in the table above cease to qualify as Eligible Credit Support, the parties have failed to agree on new Eligible Credit Support, such failure to agree shall constitute an Additional Termination Event*. For the purpose of the foregoing Additional Termination Event the Transferor shall be the Affected Party and the notice requirement in Section 6(b)(i) of the Agreement shall not apply. Instead the Transferee shall refer to the occurrence of this Additional Termination Event in its notice to the Transferor designating an Early Termination Date pursuant to Section 6(b)(iv) of the Agreement.

**An Additional Termination Event would need to be inserted in Part 1(g) of a 2002 ISDA Schedule possibly using the following wording*:

(g) Additional Termination Event as it is described in Paragraph 11(b)(ii) of the CSA will apply to Party B who will be the sole Affected Party** for the purposes of the Additional Termination Event therein specified.

*** This would normally be used with a one-way CSA.*

Sometimes at the end of the Eligible Credit Support table the following wording will be added:

Notwithstanding the foregoing, the Valuation Percentage with respect to all Eligible Credit Support shall be deemed to be 100% with respect to a Valuation Date which is an Early Termination Date designated or deemed to have occurred as a result of an Event of Default.

The purpose of this is to emphasise that in a close-out situation collateral will be valued at its market value and all haircuts will be ignored. Variations of this wording may be found on pages 237–8.

Bank standby Letters of Credit

Companies in the oil and gas or energy sectors typically do not wish to tie up their cash as collateral and often do not have a portfolio of government bonds they can offer for this purpose.

Energy companies therefore often offer bank standby letters of credit as Eligible Credit Support and they would have a 100% Valuation Percentage unless they were due to expire shortly.

Typical wording for this is:

Eligible Credit Support. On any date, Letter of Credit as defined in Paragraph 11(h)(i) below (Valuation Percentage: 100% of the amount of the Letter of Credit unless a Letter of Credit Default shall have occurred with respect to such Letter of Credit in which case the Valuation Percentage shall be zero) will qualify as "Eligible Credit Support" for Party B.

Quite extensive provisions can appear for Letters of Credit in Paragraph 11(h) of the CSA. They normally cover the following matters:

- Definition of a Letter of Credit;
- Definition of Value for Letters of Credit;
- Procedure for drawings under the Letter of Credit;
- Transfer language;
- Minimum rating/ratings for a Letter of Credit Issuer;
- Letter of Credit Defaults.

The example shown below represents comprehensive wording for this type of collateral and it would normally appear in Paragraph 11(h) of the CSA:

Letters of Credit – Definitions

(i) Letter of Credit means an irrevocable, transferable, standby letter of credit denominated in the Base Currency or an Eligible Currency issued by a financial institution acceptable to the other Party with a Credit Rating at the time of issue of at least AA by S&P or Aa2 by Moody's, in a form acceptable to the Transferee.

(ii) Transfer means, with respect to Eligible Credit Support or Equivalent Credit Support in the form of Letters of Credit meeting the criteria set out in Paragraph 11(b)(ii):

(1) for the purposes of Paragraph 2(a), by delivery of a duly executed Letter of Credit or duly executed amendment to such Letter of Credit (extending the term or increasing the amount available to the Transferee thereunder) by the Transferor or issuer of the Letter of Credit to the Transferee at the address specified in the Notices Section of this Agreement;

(2) for the purposes of Paragraph 2(b), by return of an outstanding Letter of Credit or delivery of a duly executed amendment to the Letter of Credit in form and substance acceptable to the Transferee (reducing the amount available to the Transferee thereunder), by the Transferor or the issuer of the Letter of Credit to the Transferee at the Transferee's address specified in the Notices Section of this Agreement.

If:

(1) the Credit Support Balance comprises or includes a Letter of Credit (the "specified Letter of Credit");

(2) the Transferor of such Credit Support Balance duly demands a Return Amount;

(3) the Transferor does not deliver by 1:00 p.m. on the first Local Business Day following such demand an amendment to the specified Letter of Credit to reduce the amount available to the Transferee which is in form and substance satisfactory to the Transferee; and

(4) the Value of the specified Letter of Credit exceeds the sum of the Return Amount minus the Value of all Equivalent Credit Support (that is not the specified Letter of Credit) Transferred to meet the relevant demand,

then the Transferee shall not be obliged to return the specified Letter of Credit to the Transferor.

(iii) Value means, with respect to Eligible Credit Support in the form of Letters of Credit, the Base Currency Equivalent of the stated amount (undrawn portion) of any Letter of Credit multiplied by the Valuation Percentage.

(iv) Letter of Credit Default means, with respect to an outstanding Letter of Credit, the occurrence of any of the following events:

(1) the issuer of such Letter of Credit failing to maintain a Credit Rating of at least AA by S&P or Aa2 by Moody's;

(2) the issuer of the Letter of Credit failing to comply with or perform its obligations under such Letter of Credit if such failure shall be continuing after the lapse of any applicable grace period;

(3) the issuer of such Letter of Credit disaffirming, disclaiming, repudiating or rejecting, in whole or in part, or challenging the validity of, such Letter of Credit;

(4) the issuer of such Letter of Credit fails to ensure the renewal or replacement of the Letter of Credit to the Transferee at least twenty (20) Local Business Days prior to the expiration of such Letter of Credit;

(5) such Letter of Credit expiring or terminating, or failing or ceasing to be in full force and effect at any time during the term of this Agreement, in any such case without replacement; or

(6) any event analogous to an event specified in Section 5(a)(vii) of the Agreement shall occur with respect to the issuer of such Letter of Credit,

provided, however, that no Letter of Credit Default shall occur in any event with respect to a Letter of Credit after the time such Letter of Credit is required to be cancelled or returned to the Transferor in accordance with the terms of this Annex.

(v) Letters of Credit – Other Provisions

(1) Default. For the purposes of Paragraph 6:

(aa) the Value of Eligible Credit Support comprised of a Letter of Credit shall be excluded from the calculation of the Value of the Credit Support Balance; and

(bb) in respect of any Letter of Credit, to the extent that the Transferee draws under such Letter of Credit, the Transferee may apply any proceeds of such drawing against any amount payable to it as a result of a Termination Event, an Event of Default or an Early Termination Date and exercise any other applicable rights it may have in respect of such proceeds.

(2) Requirements for Letters of Credit.

A Letter of Credit shall provide that the Transferee may draw upon the Letter of Credit in one or more drawings in an aggregate amount (up to the face amount for which the Letter of Credit has been issued) that is equal to all amounts that are due and payable by the Transferor but have not been paid to the Transferee within the time allowed for such payments under this Agreement (including any related notice or grace period or both). A Letter of Credit shall provide that a drawing be made on the Letter of Credit upon submission to the issuer thereof of one or more documents specifying the amounts due and payable to the Transferee in accordance with specific requirements of the Letter of Credit.

(3) Drawing. If:

(aa) an Event of Default or Termination Event has occurred and is continuing with respect to a Transferor of an outstanding Letter of Credit; or

(bb) an Early Termination Date is designated or deemed to occur as a result of an Event of Default or Termination Event with respect to a Transferor of an outstanding Letter of Credit; or (cc) the Transferor of an outstanding Letter of Credit shall fail to pay or deliver, when due, any amount payable by it under the Agreement and such failure is continuing; or

(dd) a Letter of Credit Default has occurred and is continuing with respect to a Letter of Credit comprised in a party's Credit Support Balance,

then the Transferee may draw on the entire or part of the undrawn portion of any outstanding Letter of Credit upon submission to the issuer thereof of one or more documents specifying the amounts due and payable to the Transferee in accordance with the specific requirements of the Letter of Credit. The Transferor shall remain liable for any amounts due and payable to the Transferee and remaining unpaid after the application of the amounts so drawn by the Transferee.

(4) Other

(a) Notwithstanding Paragraph 8, in all cases, the costs and expenses (including, but not limited to the reasonable costs, expenses and attorney's fees of the Transferee) of establishing, renewing, substituting, cancelling, increasing and reducing the amount of (as the case may be) one or more Letters of Credit shall be borne by the Transferor.

(b) Notwithstanding any other provision of this Annex, any Letter of Credit Default that occurs with respect to a Letter of Credit comprised in the Transferor's Credit Support Balance and is not cured by the Transferor in accordance with the terms of this Annex shall constitute an Event of Default with respect to the Transferor under Section 5(a)(iii) of this Agreement.

(c) For the avoidance of doubt and notwithstanding that the Value of Eligible Credit Support comprised of a Letter of Credit shall be excluded from the calculation of the Value of the Credit Support Balance for the purpose of Paragraph 6, the amount of any drawing of a Letter of Credit shall constitute Eligible Credit Support and shall be comprised in the Credit Support Balance of the Letter of Credit's Transferor.

Clause (iv)4 of this wording on page 181 highlights the importance of monitoring when the standby Letter of Credit is due to expire so that it can be renewed in good time. Quite often in energy companies two people are each responsible for such monitoring.

(iii) ***Thresholds.***

(A) ***"Independent Amount"*** means with respect to Party A: ………………………………
"Independent Amount" means with respect to Party B: ………………………………

(iii) Thresholds

(A) Independent Amount

As mentioned previously, Independent Amounts can be an initial amount deposited by a less creditworthy party with its counterparty before any trading takes place. It might be a blocked deposit upon which interest is paid outside the collateral arrangements. In this case it is excluded from the Exposure calculations upon which any collateral call is based. Alternatively, it can be a sum which is callable after trading has occurred and may affect either party, possibly as a result of a credit ratings downgrade. This type of Independent Amount will be included in the calculation of Exposure for collateral call purposes.

An Independent Amount may be a fixed money sum or a percentage of the notional amount of an individual Transaction or Transactions. This is usually graduated according to the maturity of the individual Transaction. It aims to protect against volatility of Transaction values between Valuation Dates. Independent Amounts are typically lower for Transactions involving fixed income derivatives than those for equity or credit derivatives.

The effect of an Independent Amount is to increase the Credit Support Amount due by a Transferor and to reduce the Credit Support Amount due by a Transferee.

Independent Amount may not apply to either party in which case it is stated as follows:

> (A) "Independent Amount" means with respect to Party A: Zero
> "Independent Amount" means with respect to Party B: Zero

OR

> (A) "Independent Amount" will not apply to Party A or Party B unless otherwise specified in a Confirmation.

Alternatively, where it is ratings linked you may see a provision like the following:

> (A) "Independent Amount" means with respect to Party A: US$10 million if the Rating assigned to such party by S&P is BB+ or lower or by Moody's Ba1 or lower, and otherwise zero.
>
> "Independent Amount" means with respect to Party B: US$10 million if the Rating assigned to such party by S&P is BB+ or lower or by Moody's Ba1 or lower, and otherwise zero.

OR

> "Independent Amount" means with respect to Party A and to Party B:

(i) On any date when such party or, in the case of Party B, its Credit Support Provider shall not be "Below Investment Grade" then Nil with respect to such party, and (ii) on any date when Party A or Party B's Credit Support Provider is "Below Investment Grade" the amount equal to the fair market value of 5% of Exposure with respect to such party.

For the purposes of this Agreement, "Below Investment Grade" means; (a) the rating classification assigned to any long-term unsecured unsubordinated debt securities of Party A or Party B's Credit Support Provider by (i) Moody's Investors Service, Inc. ("Moody's") shall be Ba1 or below, (ii) Standard & Poor's Ratings Group ("S&P") shall be BB+ or below, or (iii) Fitch Ratings ("Fitch") shall be BB+ or below, or (b) all outstanding long-term unsecured unsubordinated debt securities of Party A or Party B's Credit Support Provider shall fail (or cease) to be rated by at least one of Moody's, S&P or Fitch. In the event of a split rating classification by these rating agencies, the rating classification shall be the lowest rating classification.

Where the parties wish to refer to Independent Amounts in Confirmations linked to individual Transactions you might see the following wording:

(A) "Independent Amount" means with respect to Party B only: the aggregate sum of each of the amounts specified in any Confirmation governed by the Agreement as an "Independent Amount" (for the purpose of this definition, each an "Individual Independent Amount"), provided that, in respect of the Individual Independent Amount set out in the Confirmation relating to any given Transaction, such Individual Independent Amount shall not be taken into account in calculating the Independent Amount after such Transaction has expired.

Sometimes in hedge fund Credit Support Annexes you find Independent Amounts linked to falls in Net Asset Value rather than credit ratings as in the following example:

(A) "Independent Amount" for Party B means, with respect to each Transaction the greater of (i) zero, (ii) any amount specified in a Confirmation for a Transaction; and (iii) if the Net Asset Value ("NAV") (as defined in the Schedule to the Master Agreement dated as of the date hereof between Party A and Party B) of Party B declines by more than [ ]% from the NAV at a time 12 months prior to the date of any such determination, an amount equal to [ ]% of the Notional Amount.

The credit department will decide on the appropriate level of Net Asset Value decline and percentage of the Notional Amount. It is possible to include monthly and quarterly NAV declines as well as annually measured ones.

With collateralisation of equity derivative transactions for a less creditworthy counterparty, I have seen the following wording for Independent Amount:

> "Independent Amount" means with respect to Party B: the aggregate of (i) 50,000 GBP and (ii) 10% of the amount produced by multiplying the Number of Shares by the Initial Price for each Transaction entered into between parties.

Finally, with corporate counterparties, the term Independent Amount is sometimes abandoned in favour of Initial Margin and in one example this was defined as follows:

> Calculation of Initial Margin
>
> Initial Margin for any Valuation Date means, the aggregate of (1) with respect to interest rate swap Transactions only, the estimated Value at Risk (as specified below) of all outstanding interest rate swap Transactions as of that Valuation Date, and (2) with respect to all other Collateralised Transactions, the percentage of the notional that is specified by Party A in the relevant Confirmation to that Collateralised Transaction.
>
> The estimated Value at Risk shall be calculated by Party A, (in accordance with its standard practices for making such a calculation) for a two week time period within a 95% confidence level.

Such wording, however, is rare.

If an Independent Amount is not stated it is deemed to be zero.

(B) ***"Threshold"*** means with respect to Party A: ……………………………………………….
"Threshold" means with respect to Party B: ……..……………………………………….

(B) Threshold

The Threshold is the level of unsecured risk exposure each party is content to allow the other before any collateral is called. This unsecured risk exposure will be increased by any Minimum Transfer Amount applying to the parties.

Generally speaking Thresholds are recorded either as a monetary amount (or zero) or in the form of a credit ratings matrix. An example of the first is:

> (B) "Threshold" means with respect to Party A: US$10 million
> "Threshold" means with respect to Party B: US$5 million

An example of the second kind is:

> (B) "Threshold" means the amounts determined on the basis of the lower ratings assigned by either Standard & Poor's Ratings Group ("S&P"), a division of McGraw-Hill, Inc. or Moody's Investor Services, Inc. ("Moody's") to the long term, unsecured and unsubordinated debt of Party B; provided that if (x) Party B has no such ratings or (y) an Event of Default has occurred and is continuing, the Threshold with respect to the relevant party shall be zero:

S&P Rating	Moody's Rating	Threshold (US$ million)
AAA	Aaa	
AA+	Aa1	
AA	Aa2	
AA–	Aa3	
A+	A1	
A	A2	
A–	A3	
BBB+	Baa1	
BBB	Baa2	
BBB–	Baa3	
BB+	Ba1	
BB	Ba2	
BB– and below	Ba3 and below	

Again the credit function would supply the necessary figures.

In this example there are a few more default triggers where the Threshold could fall to zero:

> "Threshold" means, with respect to Party A EUR 5 million and in respect of Party B, EUR 1 million unless an Event of Default, Credit Event Upon Merger, or Additional Termination Event has occurred and is continuing, then the Threshold with respect to the Defaulting Party or the Affected Party shall be zero.

Here is an example of a rather conservative linkage to a ratings table:

(B) "*Threshold*" means in the case of Party A and Party B, the amount determined on the basis of the lower of the Ratings in the table set forth below, provided however that if (i) a party has no Rating or (ii) an Event of Default has occurred and is continuing with respect to such party, such party's Threshold shall be zero.

S&P Rating	Moody's Rating	Threshold (US$ million)
AAA to AA	Aaa to Aa2	8
AA–	Aa3	5
A+	A1	3
A and A–	A2 and A3	1
BBB+ and below	Baa1 and below	Zero

The English Law CSA can be made unilateral by assigning a Threshold of Infinity to one of the parties. Where the credit quality differential between the parties is broad, this can look quite stark:

(B) "Threshold" means with respect to Party A: Infinity
"Threshold" means with respect to Party B: Zero

You will also recall (see page 157) that a zero Threshold is not only used where a counterparty is considered a weak credit risk but also to maximise regulatory capital savings because collateral is callable all the sooner where there is a zero Threshold. In fact, the lower the Threshold and Minimum Transfer Amount, the lower the capital that needs to be set aside by financial institutions to cover trading book risk. This in turn could have a beneficial effect on the pricing of Transactions.

If a Threshold is not stated it is deemed to be zero.

(C) ***"Minimum Transfer Amount"*** means with respect to Party A: ……………………………
"Minimum Transfer Amount" means with respect to Party B: ……………………………

(C) Minimum Transfer Amount

Minimum Transfer Amounts are designed to prevent costly transfers of low or "nuisance" amounts of collateral. Occasionally you see a Minimum Transfer Amount of zero which if combined with a zero Threshold means that you do not wish to take any unsecured risk on your counterparty.

Normally, the Minimum Transfer Amount is expressed in a fixed monetary sum (e.g. US$50,000) or linked to a credit ratings matrix as in the following example:

> **"Minimum Transfer Amount" means with respect to Party A and Party B, the amount determined on the basis of the lower of the Long Term Debt Ratings in the table set forth below; provided however that if (i) a party has no Long Term Debt Ratings or (ii) an Event of Default has occurred and is continuing with respect to such party, such party's Minimum Transfer Amount shall be zero.**

S&P Rating	Moody's Rating	Minimum Transfer Amount
AAA to A–	Aaa to A3	US$500,000
BBB+ to BB	Baa1 to Ba2	US$100,000
BB– and below	Ba3 and below	US$50,000

From my experience, Minimum Transfer Amounts tend to be larger in the US than in Europe.

A common amendment is to include a zero Minimum Transfer Amount if a party suffers an Event of Default:

> **(C) "Minimum Transfer Amount" means, with respect to a party, US$100,000; provided, that if an Event of Default has occurred and is continuing, the Minimum Transfer Amount with respect to such party shall be zero.**

Sometimes the Minimum Transfer Amount can shift with a decline in formal credit ratings, for example:

> **"Minimum Transfer Amount" means with respect to Party A: US$100,000 unless the Rating assigned to such party by S&P is BB+ or lower or by Moody's is Ba1 or lower, in which case the Minimum Transfer Amount means US$10,000.**

A common amendment relates to the situation where a party's risk exposure on the other party is, or is deemed to be, zero in which case it is often stated that the Minimum Transfer Amount will also be zero. The Transferor will want to call for the return of his collateral and in those circumstances the Transferee's Minimum Transfer Amount will fall to zero so that the Transferor's collateral is not trapped by a high Minimum Transfer Amount:

(C) "Minimum Transfer Amount" means, with respect to each party, US$1 million; provided that (i) if an Event of Default has occurred and is continuing with respect to a party, or (ii) for the purpose of the calculation of the Return Amount where a party's Credit Support Amount is, or is deemed to be, zero, the Minimum Transfer Amount with respect to that party shall be zero and Rounding shall not apply.

OR

Notwithstanding the provisions of Paragraph 11(iii)(C), when the Credit Support Amount with respect to a party on a Valuation Date is zero, the Minimum Transfer Amount with respect to both parties shall be zero.

OR

Notwithstanding the provisions of Paragraph 11(iii)(C), when the Credit Support Amount with respect to a Transferor on a Valuation Date is zero, then for the purposes of any Return Amount due to such Transferor the Minimum Transfer Amount with respect to the Transferee shall be zero.

Where the Minimum Transfer Amount is not stated it is deemed to be zero.

You often see credit rating matrices covering Independent Amount, Thresholds and Minimum Transfer. Such matrices normally define the ratings as a new subparagraph (E) along the following lines:

(E) "Rating" means the rating issued by either Moody's Investor Services (Moody's) or Standard and Poor's Rating Group, a division of McGraw-Hill, Inc. (S&P) in respect of either party's long-term, unsecured and unsubordinated debt securities.

Because the Minimum Transfer Amount only establishes a floor for transfers it does not avoid transfers of uneven amounts of collateral. Applying a rounding convention overcomes this.

(D) ***Rounding.*** The Delivery Amount and the Return Amount will be rounded [down to the nearest integral multiple of ..../up and down to the nearest integral multiple of ...., respectively[3]].

(D) Rounding

One of the following options is usually selected:

- **round the Delivery and Return Amount down to the nearest integral multiple specified; or**
- **round the Delivery Amount up and the Return Amount down to the nearest integral multiple specified (this is the more common choice).**

If no rounding convention is stated, then the Delivery Amount and the Return Amount will not be rounded.

You would not normally state that both Delivery and Return Amounts are to be rounded up as this could leave a Transferee undercollateralised after transferring a Return Amount.

A rounding convention can be used as an alternative to stating a Minimum Transfer Amount. Appendix B of *The User's Guide to the ISDA Credit Support Documents under English Law* (page 70) gives an example of this.

A typical example of a rounding provision is:

> **(D) Rounding. The Delivery Amount and the Return Amount will be rounded up and down respectively to the nearest integral multiple of US$10,000.**

Very occasionally you might see:

> **(D) Rounding. The Delivery Amount and the Return Amount will not be rounded.**

This should be resisted where bond collateral is taken as this is often transferred in round amounts.

(c) ***Valuation and Timing.***

(i) ***"Valuation Agent"*** means, for purposes of Paragraphs 2 and 4, the party making the demand under Paragraph 2, and, for purposes of Paragraph 5(c), the Transferee, as applicable, unless otherwise specified here: ……………………………………………………………

(c) Valuation and Timing

(i) Valuation Agent

The Valuation Agent calculates the Delivery Amount and the Return Amount and reports these calculations to the Transferor and Transferee so that they can fulfil their obligations under Paragraph 2 of the English Law CSA.

It does this by calculating:

- the Exposure;
- the value of posted collateral;
- the Credit Support Amount; and
- the Delivery or Return Amounts,

all as of the Valuation Time (see below).

The parties may agree one of themselves or a third party as the Valuation Agent. If no Valuation Agent is stated here, then the party calling for the collateral (the Transferee) under Paragraph 2(a) is the Valuation Agent. The Transferee is also the Valuation Agent for transferring Distributions or Interest Amounts under Paragraph 5(c). The Transferor would be the Valuation Agent if it were calling for a Return Amount under Paragraph 2(b). In all cases each of these will best know the amount he needs to call or transfer.

The standard wording is most commonly used.

However, sometimes alternative provision is made where the Valuation Agent suffers an actual or Potential Event of Default:

> (i) "Valuation Agent" means, for purposes of Paragraphs 2 and 4, the party making demand under Paragraph 2, and, for purposes of Paragraph 5(c), the Transferee, as applicable, unless there has occurred and is continuing any Event of Default or Potential Event of Default with respect to a party, in which case the other party shall be the Valuation Agent.

OR a little more comprehensively:

> (i) "Valuation Agent" means, for purposes of Paragraphs 2 and 4, the party making demand under Paragraph 2, and, for purposes of Paragraph 5(c), the Transferee, as applicable, provided that in the case of an Event of Default or Termination Event the Non-defaulting Party or, as the case may be, if there is one Affected Party, then the party which is not the Affected Party shall be the Valuation Agent. If there are two Affected Parties, then both parties shall be joint Valuation Agent.

A variation on this theme allows for the appointment of a third party Valuation Agent instead of the other party:

(i) "Valuation Agent" means, for purposes of Paragraphs 2 and 4, the party making the demand under Paragraph 2, and for purposes of Exchanges and Distributions under Paragraph 3(c) and Paragraph 5(c) respectively, the Transferee, as applicable, unless an Event of Default or Potential Event of Default has occurred and is continuing with respect to such party, or an Early Termination Date has been designated in connection with any such event with respect to such party. In any such event the other party shall be the Valuation Agent or may appoint a third party selected by it as Valuation Agent.

Sometimes parties object to the inclusion of Potential Events of Default because even if they were responsible for one, they consider they would not lose their skillset to be a Valuation Agent. However, the other party is likely to be uncomfortable about this and the argument does not usually succeed.

Occasionally, a large bank will insist when dealing with a much weaker counterparty that it alone should be the Valuation Agent. Then you would see the following wording:

"Valuation Agent" means, for the purposes of Paragraphs 2 and 4, Party A.

Where the counterparty has a little more bargaining power you might see:

(i) "Valuation Agent" means Party A and any Value shall be subject to the agreement of both parties.

I have seen an example of a split Valuation Agent for risk exposure and collateral as follows:

(i) "Valuation Agent" means (1) for the purpose of the Credit Support Amount: Party A and Party B and (2) for the purpose of valuation of the Credit Support Balance: Euroclear Bank NV/SA.

Finally you might see a commitment for a Valuation Agent to provide Exposure valuations such as the following:

... In addition, Party A commits to provide Party B with calculations of Exposure on each Valuation Date.

(ii) ***"Valuation Date"*** means: ……………………………………………………………………

(ii) Valuation Date

This item must be completed as there is no ISDA fallback position here.

Valuation Date states the frequency at which risk exposure and collateral are revalued under the ISDA Master Agreement and English Law CSA. On each Valuation Date, the Valuation Agent must calculate and advise the other party/parties of the following:

- **the Exposure;**
- **the Value of the Transferor's Credit Support Balance (if any);**
- **the Credit Support Amount;**
- **the Delivery Amount (if any); and**
- **the Return Amount (if any),**

all as at the Valuation Time (see below).

A number of frequencies are, of course, possible (e.g. daily, weekly, monthly or on a particular day of each week or month).

The most common is:

> **(ii) "Valuation Date" means any Local Business Day.**

This allows for daily risk exposure and collateral valuation and is favoured by regulators. Sometimes parties like to specify cities too, for example:

> **(ii) "Valuation Date" means: Each Local Business Day in Frankfurt am Main and London.**

In this case, this would normally be where each party is located.

This arrangement can, on occasion, become quite complicated:

> **(ii) "Valuation Date" means: the first London, Frankfurt and Amsterdam Business Day on or immediately following each 15th of the month, and any other London, Frankfurt and Amsterdam Business Day designated as an additional Valuation Date by Party A or Party B provided that any Delivery Amount or Return Amount, as the case may be, calculated on such additional Valuation Date shall be in excess of EUR 10 million.**

A somewhat too flexible arrangement could be:

> **(ii) "Valuation Date" means any Local Business Day selected by a Party.**

This is only acceptable if both parties can react operationally within the same timescale.

In a one-way CSA the Transferee may insist on something similar as follows:

> **(ii) "Valuation Date" means any day which the Transferee elects shall be designated a Valuation Date (which designation shall be effected by the making of an applicable demand under Paragraph 2(a)).**

Looking at less frequent Valuation Dates I have come across the following:

> (ii) "Valuation Date" means each Wednesday following the Trade Date and in the case of the Termination Date or such earlier date as may be agreed that same day if that is a Wednesday or otherwise the next following Wednesday.

OR

> (ii) "Valuation Date" means the third Local Business Day of a calendar week or if such day is not a Local Business Day the next following Local Business Day of each calendar week or such other Local Business Day as Party A or Party B may select.

OR

> (ii) "Valuation Date" means the first Local Business Day of each calendar month and any other Local Business Day selected by a Party, provided, that for the avoidance of doubt, Party A and Party B agree that the same modus operandi will apply to such other Valuation Date as would apply to a Valuation Date on the first Local Business Day of each calendar month.

OR

> (ii) "Valuation Date" means any Local Business Day in relation to which either party has designated a Valuation Date by giving the other party at least one Local Business Day's prior notice.

OR the *pièce de résistance*:

> (ii) "Valuation Date" means (a) the Trade Date of each Transaction, if either party has an Independent Amount greater than zero for that Transaction, (b) a day not more than once per calendar week or if such day is not a Local Business Day then the immediately preceding Local Business Day and (c) any other Local Business Day designated as a "Valuation Date" by notice given by one party to the other no later than the Notification Time on the Local Business Day before the Valuation Date so designated.

So a great deal of flexibility is possible here provided it suits both parties.

Nowadays most parties want every Local Business Day to be the Valuation Date. Any Valuation Date with less frequency (e.g. weekly, monthly) is likely to need special credit approval that will depend on the counterparty's creditworthiness. While this might be acceptable with a Triple A supranational it would not be with a hedge fund.

(iii) ***"Valuation Time"*** means:

[ ] the close of business in the place of location of the Valuation Agent on the Valuation Date or date of calculation, as applicable;

[ ] the close of business on the Local Business Day immediately preceding the Valuation Date or date of calculation, as applicable;

provided that the calculations of Value and Exposure will, as far as practicable, be made as of approximately the same time on the same date.

(iii) Valuation Time

The Valuation Time is the time at which the Valuation Agent calculates Exposure and the value of collateral held to determine if a Delivery Amount or Return Amount call is needed. The Valuation Agent will also factor in any Distributions or Interest Amounts due to the Transferor at the Valuation Time.

The parties have two main choices, viz:

1 **as at the close of business on the Valuation Date or the date of calculation for Paragraph 5(c) payments to the Transferor; or**

2 **as at the close of business on the Local Business Day immediately before the Valuation Date or the date of calculation for Paragraph 5(c) payments to the Transferor.**

They can, of course, choose another means for deciding the Valuation Time by amending this sub-paragraph but that is rare.

Once they have made their choice, the Annex stipulates that the calculation of risk exposure and collateral values has to be made approximately at the same time on the selected date. This is to avoid major discrepancies in the calculations.

You would have to have excellent real time operational systems to select the first option.

A Valuation Time as at the close of business on the Local Business Day immediately preceding the Valuation Date is the most common choice because collateral management units are then working from reports of exposure and collateral values as at the close of the previous business day when they come into work in the morning.

Where there is doubt that a counterparty does not actually value its positions in this way, it might be appropriate to use the following wording:

> **"Valuation Time" means for the calculation of Value and Exposure:**
>
> **(A) for purposes other than those described in Paragraph 6 (*Default*), a point in time on the Local Business Day immediately preceding the Valuation Date or date of calculation, as applicable, as determined by the Valuation Agent; and**
>
> **(B) for the purpose of Paragraph 6 (*Default*), a point in time on the Valuation Date as determined by the Valuation Agent.**

(iv) ***"Notification Time"*** means 1:00 p.m., London time, on a Local Business Day, unless otherwise specified here: ……………………………………………………………..

(iv) Notification Time

This is the time by which, among other things, (1) the Valuation Agent must notify its counterparty of its calculations under Paragraph 3(b) on the Local Business Day following a Valuation Date and (2) a party must make a demand for a transfer of collateral so that its counterparty makes the appropriate transfer not later than the close of business on the next Local Business Day. If a demand for a transfer is made after the Notification Time, then the transfer does not have to be made until the close of business on the second Local Business Day following the day on which the demand was made.

A classic example of this is as follows:

> "Notification Time" means by 1:00 p.m., London time, on a Local Business Day. Notwithstanding Paragraph 3(a) of the Credit Support Annex, if a request for transfer is made by the Notification Time, then the relevant transfer shall be made not later than the close of business on the next Local Business Day or, if such request is received after the Notification Time, then such transfer shall be made not later than the close of business on the second Local Business Day following demand.

Such transfers are subject to the absence of a dispute and no condition precedent being unfulfilled in Section 2(a)(iii) of the ISDA Master Agreement.

The Notification Time in the template is specified as 1.00 p.m. London time on the appropriate Local Business Day unless the parties agree otherwise.

Sometimes parties arrange for the Notification Time for the Valuation Agent's risk exposure calculations to be earlier than the Notification Time for collateral calls (at least where a third party acts as the Valuation Agent). In these circumstances, a party receiving notice of the Valuation Agent's calculations will be able to make a collateral call on the same day for a transfer to be made on the next Local Business Day.

The latest Notification Time I have seen is 4.00 p.m. London Time, which makes me wonder how it can take a Valuation Agent nearly all day to work out if it needs to make a collateral call. In my experience a late Notification Time indicates poor operational systems.

The one exception to a collateral transfer on the following Local Business Day is with US$ cash where I have seen the following language:

> (iv) "Notification Time" means 9:00 a.m. New York time on the Valuation Date provided, however, that, notwithstanding Paragraph 3(a), (x) with regard to Transfers of Eligible Credit Support in the form of US$ cash, if a request for delivery or return is made by the Notification Time, then the relevant Transfer shall be made not later than the close of business on the day on which such a request is received, or if such day is not a Local Business Day or if such request is made after the Notification Time, not later than the close of business on the next Local Business Day and (y) with regard to Transfers of other forms of Eligible Credit Support or posted credit support, the relevant Transfer shall be made in accordance with Paragraph 3(a).

(d) ***Exchange Date. "Exchange Date"*** has the meaning specified in Paragraph 3(c)(ii), unless otherwise specified here: ……………………………………………………………………….

(d) Exchange Date

In Paragraph 3(c) the Transferor can notify the Transferee that it wishes to substitute New Credit Support for particular collateral (Original Credit Support) that it previously transferred to the Transferee. This collateral would be bond collateral.

In England in the past it was advisable for the Transferee to consent to the substitution to avoid any recharacterisation risk, but following the implementation of the Collateral Directive this is no longer an issue. However, the Transferee may have sold, lent or repoed out the bonds and it may be inconvenient for him to retrieve them because of his counterparty's substitution request. Therefore he should have the right not to consent for commercial reasons.

Assuming that consent is forthcoming the Transferor must then transfer the New Credit Support on the first Settlement Day after the Transferee's consent.

When received, the Transferee must retransfer the Original Credit Support to the Transferor no later than the Settlement Day after the Local Business Day he received the New Credit Support.

However, parties can agree to vary this timescale where the securities have a longer settlement cycle or to reduce it (see pages 242–3).

Sometimes an Exchange Notification Time is included as follows:

(d) Exchanges

(i) For the purposes of Paragraph 3(c) notice must be given by the "Exchange Notification Time" which will be 1:00 p.m. London time, on a Local Business Day failing which the relevant notice will be deemed to have been received on the following Local Business Day.

(ii) "Exchange Date" has the meaning specified in Paragraph 3(c)(ii).

In one-way CSAs where only cash is Eligible Credit Support or only one type of bond collateral is acceptable you might see a ban on substitutions as follows:

(d) Exchanges: Paragraph 3(c) shall not apply.

However, this is rare.

Occasionally, to reduce the number of potential substitution requests, wording is inserted stating that the value of the substitution must exceed the Transferor's Minimum Transfer Amount:

"Exchange Date" has the meaning specified in Paragraph 3(c)(ii). The following shall be inserted at the end of Paragraph 3(c)(ii) "and provided, further however, that any such request to exchange Eligible Credit Support must seek the exchange of Eligible Credit Support in an amount in excess of the Transferor's Minimum Transfer Amount".

Sometimes counterparties are concerned about withholding tax risks if they hold bond collateral over a Distributions Date and so seek to substitute their Original Credit Support with New Credit Support where a coupon or dividend is not due imminently.

It was important at least under English law that they do not have an automatic right to do this but must once again obtain the Transferee's consent.

An example of such wording is the following:

(iv) Paragraph 3(c) is amended by adding the following as Paragraph 3(c)(iii):

(iii) (1) Unless otherwise specified in Paragraph 11, the Transferee, may, on any Local Business Day, by notice, request the Transferor, to transfer to the Transferee by the Exchange Notification Time, certain New Credit Support, specified in the notice in exchange for certain Original Credit Support specified in that notice comprised in the Transferor's Credit Support Balance. If the Transferor consents to the Transferee's request (such consent not to be unreasonably withheld) the Transferor will be obliged to transfer to the Transferee the New Credit Support by the Exchange Notification Time on the date and having such Value and in the manner specified in the notice to the Transferor and the Transferee will be obliged to transfer to the Transferor Equivalent Credit Support in respect of the Original Credit Support promptly upon receiving such New Credit Support, but in any event not later than the close of business on the next Local Business Day thereafter; provided that the Transferee will only be obliged to transfer Equivalent Credit Support with a Value as at the date of transfer as close as practicable to, but in any event not more than, the Value of the New Credit Support as of that date.

For the purposes of this subparagraph (c)(iii)(1), the definitions of New Credit Support and Original Credit Support are amended accordingly to refer to the Eligible Credit Support specified in the Transferee's notice described above.

(2) Any New Credit Support specified in the Transferee's notice shall have a Distributions Date of not less than thirty (30) days after the date upon which it is delivered to the Transferee; and

(3) All calculations of Value will be made by the Valuation Agent as of the relevant Valuation Time.

This type of provision is likely to be placed in the Other Provisions section of Paragraph 11, i.e. Paragraph 11(h).

(e) ***Dispute Resolution.***

(i) ***"Resolution Time"*** means 1:00 p.m., London time, on the Local Business Day following the date on which the notice is given that gives rise to a dispute under Paragraph 4, unless otherwise specified here: ……………………………………………

(e) Dispute Resolution

(i) Resolution Time

The Resolution Time is the deadline for the parties to resolve their dispute under Paragraph 4. If they fail, the Valuation Agent makes certain recalculations under Paragraph 4(a)(4)(i).

The fallback dispute Resolution Time is 1.00 p.m. London time on the Local Business Day after the date notice is given that gives rise to a dispute under Paragraph 4, although this wording is sometimes changed to "the date on which notice of dispute is given under Paragraph 4" to avoid confusion with the Valuation Agent's notice of Exposure or collateral valuation.

The latest Resolution Time I have seen is 3.00 p.m. London time.

Currently ISDA's Collateral Initiatives Working Group is working on a Convention, Market Polling Procedure and a Protocol so that the market may have a more standardised procedure available to it to resolve disputes.

(ii) ***Value.*** For the purpose of Paragraphs 4(a)(4)(i)(C) and 4(a)(4)(ii), the Value of the outstanding Credit Support Balance or of any transfer of Eligible Credit Support or Equivalent Credit Support, as the case may be, will be calculated as follows: ……………………………..

(ii) Value

This provision must be completed because there is no ISDA fallback and, without it, the Valuation Agent cannot resolve the dispute because he will be unable to value the outstanding collateral or the transfer in dispute.

The most simple Value provision where only cash collateral is involved is:

> (ii) The Value of Cash will be the face value thereof multiplied by the applicable Valuation Percentage.

Where there is a one-way CSA, you might see:

> (ii) Value. For the purpose of Paragraphs 4(a)(4)(i)(C) and 4(a)(4)(ii), the Value of the outstanding Credit Support Balance or of any transfer of Eligible Credit Support or Equivalent Credit Support, as the case may be, will be calculated by the Valuation Agent.

I have also seen "by the Transferee".

The most common method for valuing securities collateral is to obtain three bid quotations from leading dealers, for example:

> (ii) Value. For the purpose of Paragraphs 4(a)(4)(i)(C) and 4(a)(4)(ii), the Value of the outstanding Credit Support Balance or of any transfer of Eligible Credit Support or Equivalent Credit Support, as the case may be, will be calculated as follows: disputes over value will be resolved by the Valuation Agent seeking three bid quotations as of the relevant Valuation Date or date of transfer from parties that regularly act as dealers in the securities or other property in question. The value will be the arithmetic mean of the quotations received by the Valuation Agent multiplied by the applicable Valuation Percentage.

If such quotations are not available you sometimes see reference back to the previous Local Business Day when such quotations were available, viz:

> The mean of the bid prices quoted on such date by any three principal market makers in the securities or property in question, or if three quotations are not available, the mean of three such prices as of the immediate preceding day on which such quotations were available, multiplied by the applicable Valuation Percentage, if any.

A variation on this takes account of accrued interest too, for example:

> a security, (i) either (x) the Base Currency Equivalent of the arithmetic mean of the closing bid prices quoted on the relevant date of three nationally recognised principal market makers (which may include an Affiliate of Party A) for such security chosen by the Valuation Agent or (y) if no quotations are available from such principal market makers on the relevant date, the Base Currency

Equivalent of the arithmetic mean of the closing bid prices on the next preceding date, plus (ii) the Base Currency Equivalent of the accrued interest on such security (except to the extent transferred to a party pursuant to any applicable provision of this Agreement or included in the applicable price referred to in (i) of this provision).

Sometimes parties select mid-market quotations:

(ii) Value. For the purpose of Paragraphs 4(a)(4)(i)(C) and 4(a)(4)(ii), the Value of the outstanding Credit Support Balance or of any transfer of Eligible Credit Support or Equivalent Credit Support, as the case may be, will be calculated as follows: Disputes over Value will be resolved by the Valuation Agent seeking three mid-market quotations as of the relevant Valuation Date or date of Transfer from parties that regularly act as dealers in the securities or other property in question. The Value will be the arithmetic mean of the quotations received by the Valuation Agent.

However, most market players prefer bid quotations because these are a dealer's buying prices.

Things can sometimes get rather pernickety:

Each party shall name a market maker that regularly acts as dealer in the securities. If the party which is not the Valuation Agent does not name a market maker within 30 minutes of such a request from the Valuation Agent, the Valuation Agent shall choose a second market maker and will ask each market maker for a bid quotation as of the relevant Valuation Date or date of transfer and shall calculate the Value according to the procedures set out in section (B) of the Definition of Value in Paragraph 10 using instead the arithmetic average of the bid quotations obtained from each market maker.

Or just all embracing and comprehensive:

the Value for negotiable debt obligations and treasuries,

(x) the closing bid prices quoted on the relevant date (plus accrued interest if not reflected in such closing bid prices) which appears on the display of Bloomberg Financial Markets Commodities News (or its successor) published by Bloomberg L.P. or such other financial information provider reasonably chosen by the Valuation Agent multiplied by the applicable Valuation Percentage, or

(y) if no quotations are available pursuant to (x) above, the arithmetic mean of the closing bid prices quoted on the relevant date of three recognised principal market makers for such security chosen by the Valuation Agent (plus accrued interest if not reflected in such closing bid prices) multiplied by the applicable Valuation Percentage; or

(z) if no quotations are available from such principal market makers on the relevant date, the arithmetic mean of the closing bid prices on the next preceding date (plus accrued interest if not reflected in such closing bid prices) multiplied by the applicable Valuation Percentage.

(iii) ***Alternative.*** The provisions of Paragraph 4 will apply, unless an alternative dispute resolution procedure is specified here: ……………………………………………………………………

(iii) Alternative

This provision enables the parties to adopt a different dispute resolution procedure to that contained in Paragraph 4. Normally parties adopt Paragraph 4.

Where Alternative is involved it can be just to clarify matters:

> (iii) Alternative. The provisions of Paragraph 4 will apply, unless an alternative dispute resolution procedure is specified here: The provisions of Paragraph 4 will apply, except to the following extent: (A) pending the resolution of a dispute, Transfer of the undisputed Value of Eligible Credit Support involved in the relevant demand will be due as provided in Paragraph 4 if the demand is given by the Notification Time, but will be due on the second Local Business Day after the demand if the demand is given after the Notification Time; and (B) the Disputing Party need not comply with the provisions of Paragraph 4(a)(2) if the amount to be Transferred does not exceed the Disputing Party's Minimum Transfer Amount.

Sometimes parties seek to resolve disputes by the use of a tolerance amount as in the following example:

> (iii) Alternative. The provisions of Paragraph 4 will apply provided that in the case of (I) therein, (A) if the difference between (i) the Delivery Amount or a Return Amount calculated by the Valuation Agent and (ii) the Delivery Amount or Return Amount calculated by the Disputing Party (the "Difference") is Euro 5,000,000 or less, the appropriate party will transfer the undisputed amount plus one half of the Difference to the other party – in full settlement of the dispute – not later than the close of business on the Settlement Day following the date the demand is received under Paragraph 2 (and the parties waive any further recourse to the rights enumerated in Paragraph 4 with respect to such dispute); or (B) if the Difference is greater than Euro 5,000,000, the appropriate party will transfer the undisputed amount to the other party not later than the close of business on the Settlement Day following the date the demand is received under Paragraph 2 and the parties will seek a resolution of the dispute in accordance with the remaining provisions of Paragraph 4.

Another variation concerns the failure of a Valuation Agent to notify its recalculations to a Disputing Party which can lead to the following circumstances:

> Paragraph 4(a) of this Credit Support Annex shall be amended by the insertion of the following additional paragraph after the last paragraph thereof:
>
> "If the Valuation Agent fails to notify the Disputing Party of its recalculation pursuant to this Paragraph by the Notification Time on the Local Business Day following the Resolution Time, then the Disputing Party may:

(i) notify the other party and the Valuation Agent (if the Valuation Agent is not the other party) of the failure (and of the appointment of a Replacement Valuation Agent, where the Disputing Party makes an appointment in accordance with (iv) below) not later than the Notification Time on the second Local Business Day following the Resolution Time; and/or

(ii) in the case of a dispute involving a Delivery Amount or Return Amount, unless otherwise specified in Paragraph 11(e), recalculate the Exposure and the Value as of the Recalculation Date in accordance with Paragraph 4(a)(4)(i)(A)–(C); and/or

(iii) in the case of a dispute involving the Value of any transfer of Eligible Credit Support or Equivalent Credit Support, recalculate the Value as of the date of transfer pursuant to Paragraph 11(e)(ii); and/or

(iv) appoint a replacement Valuation Agent (the "Replacement Valuation Agent") to perform (ii) and (iii) above.

Following a recalculation, the Disputing Party or the Replacement Valuation Agent will notify each party (or the other party, if the Valuation Agent is a party) of the recalculation as soon as possible, but in any event not later than the third Local Business Day following the Resolution Time. The appropriate party will upon demand following such notice, make the appropriate transfer."

Paragraph 4(b) of this Credit Support Annex shall be amended by the replacement of the final sentence thereof with the following:

For the avoidance of doubt, upon completion of those procedures, Section 5(a)(i) of this Agreement will apply to any failure by a party to make a transfer required under either the sub-paragraph in Paragraph 4(a) that commences with "Following a recalculation pursuant to this Paragraph", or the penultimate sentence of Paragraph (4) (as applicable) on the relevant due date.

(f) ***Distributions and Interest Amount.***

(i) ***Interest Rate.*** The "Interest Rate" in relation to each Eligible Currency specified below will be:

Eligible Currency	***Interest Rate***
....	....
....	....
....	....

(f) Distributions and Interest Amount

(i) Interest Rate

The Interest Rate is the interest which will be paid by the Transferee on the cash collateral received from the Transferor plus or minus a spread. It will reflect the frequency of the Valuation Dates. If these are daily and euro cash collateral is involved, EONIA (Euro Overnight Index Average) could be used; if weekly or monthly EURIBOR might be an option.

This section must be completed as there is no ISDA fallback.

If parties are concerned about potential withholding tax liabilities, they might apply a zero interest rate if this affected them both. This is rare, however, and may be done for other reasons.

Unlike the New York Law CSA where only US$ cash collateral is involved, the English Law CSA caters for EU and non-EU currencies and provides for interest in different currencies to be converted into the Base Currency. Interest is calculated on an Actual/360 or Actual/365 basis depending upon the convention for the particular currency.

A typical example is:

(i) Interest Rate. The "Interest Rate" in relation to each Eligible Currency specified below will be:

Eligible Currency	Interest Rate
EUR	EONIA as defined below
US$	US$-Federal Funds-H.15 as defined below
GPB	SONIA as defined below

The "*Interest Rate*" will be the US Federal Funds H.15. "US Federal Funds H.15" means that the rate for any day will be the rate set forth in H.15 (519) for that day opposite the caption "Federal Funds Effective" as such rate is displayed on Reuters Page FEDFUNDS1. If on any day such rate does not appear on Reuters Page FEDFUNDS1 *or* in the event of such page not being available on ReutersUSONFFE= *or* is not yet published in H.15 (519) the rate for that day will be the rate set forth in H.15 Daily Update, or such other recognised electronic source used for the purpose of displaying such rate, for that day opposite the caption "Federal Funds Effective". If on any day such rate does not appear on the Reuters Page FEDFUNDS1 or ReutersUSONFFE= or is not yet published in H.15 (519) or H.15 Daily Update or another recognised electronic source, the rate for that day will be the rate agreed between the parties.

With respect to the Euro:

The "*Interest Rate*" will be "EONIA". "EONIA" means, for any day, the reference rate to the overnight rate as calculated by the European Central Bank and appearing on the REUTERS page EONIA on the first TARGET Settlement Day following that day. For the purposes of this provision, TARGET Settlement Day means any day on which the Trans-European Automated Real-Time Gross Settlement Express Transfer (TARGET) System is open. If such rate does not appear on the Reuters Page EONIA on any day, the rate for that day will be the rate agreed between the Parties.

With respect to Sterling:

The "*Interest Rate*" will be "SONIA". "SONIA" means, for any day, the reference rate equal to the overnight rate as calculated by the Wholesale Market Brokers Association which appears on the Reuters Page SONIA under the heading "Sterling Overnight Index" as of 9.00 a.m., London time, on the first London Banking Day following that day. If such rate does not appear on the Reuters Page SONIA on any day, the rate for that day will be the rate agreed between the Parties.

For the avoidance of doubt, the Interest Amount will be calculated on a daily, non-compounded basis.

The last sentence is useful as disagreements have occurred over whether interest is compounded or not.

Interest Rates, as mentioned above can sometimes be quoted minus a spread as in the following example:

Eligible Currency	Interest Rate	Spread basis points	Designated maturity
US$	US$-LIBOR-BBA	minus 12.5	1 week
EURO	EURO-LIBOR-BBA	minus 12.5	1 week

Negative spreads can be used by some counterparties (e.g. supranationals) as a disincentive. They would be sending a message that they do not want to receive cash collateral (i.e. they only want G7 government bond collateral possibly).

Sometimes, the Interest Rate can be split for cash collateral deposited for the whole of an Interest Period:

(i) Interest Rate. The "Interest Rate" in relation to each Eligible Currency specified below will be determined on the following basis:

Eligible Currency	Rate Source	Spread
EURO	EONIA	Zero

Provided, however, any amount of Eligible Currency that constitutes part of the Credit Support Balance for the entire Interest Period, "Interest Rate" in relation to each such Eligible Currency in the type specified below will be determined on the following basis:

Eligible Currency	Rate Source	Spread
EURO	EURIBOR	–.25

Sometimes parties prefer not to have interest amounts in different currencies converted into the Base Currency but for them to be paid separately in their respective currencies. The English Law CSA can be amended to cater for this in Paragraph 11(h) using wording along the following lines:

(a) The definition of "Interest Amount" shall be deleted and replaced with the following:

"Interest Amount" means, with respect to an Interest Period and each portion of the Credit Support Balance comprised of cash in an Eligible Currency, the sum of the amounts of interest determined for each day in that Interest Period by the Valuation Agent as follows:

(x) the amount of such currency comprised in the Credit Support Balance at the close of business for general dealings in the relevant currency on such day (or, if such day is not a Local Business Day, on the immediately preceding Local Business Day); multiplied by

(y) the relevant Interest Rate; divided by

(z) 360 (or in the case of Pounds Sterling, 365).

OR more plainly:

The definition of "Interest Rate" is amended by deletion of the words "the aggregate sum of the Base Currency Equivalents of" with the intention that the amount of interest payable on the principal amount of the portion of the Credit Support Balance comprised of cash will be payable in the currency in which such cash is denominated and not in the Base Currency.

It might be useful to mention here the question of default interest where a Transferee fails to pay Distributions of Interest Amounts or Return Amounts on time. Essentially, what happens here is that default interest under Paragraph 9(a) of the Annex is calculated using the Default Rate (i.e. 1% over the payee's cost of funds) of Section 9(h) of the 2002 ISDA Master Agreement on an Actual/Actual day count fraction basis. It is subject to daily compounding.

Of course, where cash collateral is not to be tken, Paragraphs 11(f)(i)–(iii) are disapplied.

(ii) ***Transfer of Interest Amount.*** The transfer of the Interest Amount will be made on the last Local Business Day of each calendar month and on any Local Business Day that a Return Amount consisting wholly or partly of cash is transferred to the Transferor pursuant to Paragraph 2(b), unless otherwise specified here: ……………………………………

(ii) Transfer of Interest Amount

As long as the Transferee does not become undercollateralised by transferring an Interest Amount, Paragraph 11(f)(ii) proposes that interest on cash collateral is transferred to the Transferee on the last Local Business Day of each month and on any Local Business Day when a cash Return Amount is transferred to the Transferor.

Whether this payment structure is acceptable will depend upon the parties' operational systems. Many parties prefer such interest transfers to take place on the second Local Business Day of the succeeding calendar month because they can spend the first Local Business Day of that month checking calculations and preparing the necessary electronic transfers.

There are not a large number of variations on this theme but sometimes you see that the interest transfer date must be a Local Business Day in the cities where both parties are located.

Finally, some parties propose that the Interest Amount be added to the Credit Support Balance and not paid over. Where this is agreed you might see the following wording:

> (ii) **Transfer of Interest Amount. The Interest Amount in relation to each currency comprised in the Credit Support Balance for each Interest Period will be credited to the Credit Support Balance on the second Local Business Day following the end of each calendar month.**

As regards payments of securities interest or dividends to the Transferor this is dealt with under Paragraph 5(c)(i) of the Annex (see page 123).

(iii) ***Alternative to Interest Amount.*** The provisions of Paragraph 5(c)(ii) will apply, unless otherwise specified here: ………………………………………………………………

(iii) Alternative to Interest Amount

This provision affords the Transferee, with the Transferor's agreement, the opportunity to invest part of the cash collateral in other instruments, rather than just paying over an agreed interest return. It is rarely used. Some parties amend the provision to clarify that interest is to be compounded where this is required, for example:

> (iii) For the avoidance of doubt the Interest Amount will be computed for each Interest Period on a compounded basis.

OR

> (iii) Alternative to Interest Amount. The provisions of Paragraph 5(c)(ii) will apply, provided however, that the Interest Amount will compound on each TARGET Settlement Day, i.e. for Euro cash collateral.

(g) ***Addresses for Transfers.***

Party A: ....
....

Party B: ....
....

(h) ***Other Provisions.***

(g) Addresses for Transfers

This must be completed if collateral transfers and interest payments and Distributions are to be correctly routed to the recipient. Sometimes these details are spelt out by currency for cash and securities and sometimes a general statement is made as follows:

> Addresses for Transfers.
>
> Party A: As set forth in notices to Party B pursuant to Paragraph 3(b).
>
> Party B: As set forth in notices to Party A pursuant to Paragraph 3(b).

Parties often issue separate payment instructions to each other in this respect.

(h) Other provisions

Paragraph 11(h) is similar to Part 5 of the ISDA Master Agreement Schedule – a place where other provisions may be inserted. Virtually anything could potentially be included here, but my review of English Law CSAs has found that the following provisions feature quite regularly:

- one-way agreements;
- Paragraph 6 amendments;
- Valuation Percentage at close-out;
- Exposure and Collateralised Transactions;
- Exchanges (substitutions);
- Notices;
- Miscellaneous.

(i) One-way agreements

Apart from a Threshold of Infinity for one party, the standard bilateral English Law CSA can be amended to make it unilateral by using the following wording or similar:

> For the purposes of this Annex Party A is the Transferee and Party B the Transferor.

OR

> One-Way Collateral Agreement. Notwithstanding anything in this Agreement to the contrary, Transferee shall mean Party B and Transferor shall mean Party A in all circumstances in this Annex. This Annex provides for one-way transfer of Credit Support from Party A to Party B.

OR

Agreement as to Single Transferee and Transferor. Party A and Party B agree that, notwithstanding anything to the contrary in the recital to this Annex, Paragraph 2 or the definitions in Paragraph 10, (a) the term "Transferee" as used in this Annex means only Party A, (b) the term "Transferor" as used in this Annex means only Party B, (c) only Party B makes the representation in Paragraph 7 and (d) only Party B will be required to make Transfers of Eligible Credit Support hereunder.

OR

Party A and Party B agree that notwithstanding anything to the contrary set out within this Annex, Party A is under no obligation to make any transfer under this Annex in support of any Transactions under the ISDA Master Agreement. Party B will make any and all transfers required under this Annex in support of any Transactions undertaken under the ISDA Master Agreement. All references in this Annex to the "Transferor" will be to Party B and all corresponding references to the "Transferee" will be to Party A.

Party A will not at any time be expected to make any transfers to Party B save where Party A is under an obligation to Party B to deliver a Return Amount or make an exchange of Equivalent Credit Support in respect of New Credit Support transferred by Party B.

(It is not advisable to make Minimum Transfer Amounts infinite.)

(ii) Paragraph 6 amendments

When you use a 1995 English Law CSA with a 2002 Master Agreement without amendment you are intermixing the payment measures of Market Quotation and Loss under the 1992 ISDA Master Agreement with the single payment measure of Close-Out Amount under the 2002 Agreement.

The most common amendment for this in Paragraph 11(h) of the CSA is:

The terms of Paragraph 6 of the Annex are amended to read in their entirety as follows:

"If an Early Termination Date is designated or deemed to occur as a result of an Event of Default in relation to a party, an amount equal to the Value of the Credit Support Balance, determined as though the Early Termination Date were a Valuation Date, will be deemed to be an Unpaid Amount due to the Transferor (which may or may not be the Defaulting Party) for purposes of Section 6(e). For the avoidance of doubt, the Close-out Amount determined under Section 6(e) in relation to the Transaction constituted by this Annex will be deemed to be zero. For purposes of this Paragraph 6, the Value of the Credit Support Balance shall be determined on the basis that the Valuation Percentage applicable to each item of Eligible Credit Support is 100%."

This wording is part of the ISDA Form of Amendment to the English Law Annex issued by ISDA in May 2003.

There is another amendment you often see in the market in this connection. It is becoming more common to extend Paragraph 6 to Termination Events that close out all Affected Transactions.

This can be done as follows:

Paragraph 6. Default.

Paragraph 6 shall be amended by the insertion of: (i) in the first line after the words "Event of Default" the words "or a Termination Event resulting in the termination of all (but not less than all) Transactions"; and (ii) in the fourth line after the words "Defaulting Party" the words "or the Affected Party as the case may be".

(iii) Valuation Percentage at close-out

As we know, during the collateralised relationship, securities collateral is subject to a haircut or a discount to its face value. However, it would be unfair for this to apply in a close-out situation. Parties, therefore, regularly amend the Annex to provide for realisation of securities collateral at 100% of market value. This is also based on the common law principle that a creditor is not entitled to receive more than 100% of what he is owed from the collateral he holds and must account to the debtor for any surplus.

The amendment can be made in the following or similar wording:

Paragraph 6 is amended by inserting the following at the end thereof:

"Notwithstanding anything to the contrary provided in Paragraph 11(b)(ii) or elsewhere in this Annex, the applicable Valuation Percentage for the purpose of determining the Value of Eligible Credit Support included within the Credit Support Balance shall, for the purpose of this Paragraph 6, be 100%."

OR

The definition of "Valuation Percentage" in Paragraph 10 is amended by the addition of the following at the end of the definition:

"except that, for the purposes of Paragraph 6, Valuation Percentage for each item of Eligible Credit Support is 100%."

That is a very common form of this amendment.

OR

(i) Paragraph 6. Default.

For the purposes of determining the Credit Support Balance pursuant to Paragraph 6 the definition of Value in Paragraph 10 shall be amended by deleting the words "...multiplied by the applicable Valuation Percentage, if any..." from subsections (i)(A) and (B).

OR

"Paragraph 6"

Add at the end of the definition of Value in Paragraph 10 the following:

"provided that for a Valuation Date which is an Early Termination Date designated or deemed to have occurred as a result of an Event of Default, the Valuation Percentage shall be deemed to be 100%."

OR

Amendment to Paragraph 10. The definition of "Value" in Paragraph 10 is amended by adding at the end thereof the following:

"provided that, for a Valuation Date that is an Early Termination Date designated or deemed to have occurred as a result of an Event of Default or a Termination Event in respect of which all Transactions are Affected Transactions, the Valuation Percentage for all Eligible Credit Support comprised in the Credit Support Balance shall be 100%."

(iv) Exposure and Collateralised Transactions

Exposure is the estimated value of all Transactions (using mid-market quotations from dealers) in calculating risk exposure. The calculation is made as if the Transactions were being closed out.

While you cannot include collateralised and uncollateralised Transactions under the same Agreement in a close-out situation, it is possible to apply collateralisation to particular Transactions in such circumstances.

This can be achieved by amending the term "Exposure" to refer only to "Collateralised Transactions" so that the Credit Support Amount only represents net risk exposure of the Transferee on the Transferor in relation to such Collateralised Transactions. In this way, the single agreement concept is not vitiated.

Relevant wording for this could be:

Definitions. The following amendments shall be made to Paragraph 10.

(a) The following definition shall be added:

"Collateralised Transaction" means any Transaction designated as such in a relevant Confirmation or specified in the Appendix to this Annex. For the avoidance of doubt, the Transaction constituted by this Annex is not a Collateralised Transaction.

(b) The definition of "Exposure" shall be amended to replace the words "Transactions (other than the Transaction constituted by this Annex)" in the fourth line with the words "Collateralised Transactions".

Another way to specify Collateralised Transactions is to list them as products in an Appendix sometimes with the relevant Offices of each party through which they can be traded. Whether this is possible will depend upon the valuation feeds and systems of the two parties.

An example of such an Appendix is as follows:

APPENDIX

COLLATERALISED TRANSACTIONS

Each type of Transaction nominated in sub-clauses (1), (2) and (3) below, in relation to which the parties are acting through relevant Offices (as listed in the relevant sub-clause) and each Transaction specified in sub-clause (4) below is a Collateralised Transaction:

(1) Any Transaction which is a:
interest rate swap transaction
currency swap transaction
cross-currency interest rate swap transaction
interest rate cap, collar or floor transaction
swaption transaction
forward rate transaction (FRA)
bond option transaction
equity derivative transaction
credit derivative transaction

For the purposes of this sub-clause (1) the relevant Office(s) of Party A is (are):

For the purposes of this sub-clause (1) the relevant Office(s) of Party B is (are):

(2) Any forward foreign exchange transaction (whether deliverable or non-deliverable) in relation to which each party is acting through one of its Offices specified below:

For the purpose of this sub-clause (2) the relevant Office(s) of Party A is (are):

For the purposes of this sub-clause (2) the relevant Office(s) of Party B is (are):

(3) For the purpose of this sub-clause (3) any currency option transaction in relation to which each party is acting through one of its Offices specified below:

For the purpose of this sub-clause (3) the relevant Office(s) of Party A is (are):

For the purposes of this sub-clause (3) the relevant Office(s) of Party B is (are):

For the avoidance of doubt: with respect to sub-clauses (1), (2) and (3) of this Appendix, the following types of Transactions are not Collateralised Transactions:
Spot foreign exchange transactions
Commodity derivative transactions
Any other type of transaction not listed above.

With very risky counterparties you might seek to include spot foreign exchange transactions but as they are very short-dated, i.e. settlement after two Local Business Days, it is often not considered worth it.

Sometimes Offices are not specified but only products, as in the following example:

Transactions

The definition of "Exposure" in Paragraph 10 shall be amended by adding the following sentence at the end thereof:

"For purpose of this definition, the term "Transaction" will only cover the following transactions: any rate swap transaction, basis swap, forward rate transaction, bond option, interest rate option, cap transaction, floor transaction, collar transaction, cross-currency rate swap transaction (including any option with respect to any of these transactions), Equity Swap Transactions, Index Transactions, Share Transactions, Index Basket Transactions, Share Basket Transactions, Basket Option Transactions, and any Option Transaction as defined in the 2002 Equity Derivatives Definitions."

This is, of course, subject to operational capability and confirmation that your collateral legal opinion covers all these products in the jurisdiction(s) concerned.

Where there is an imbalance in parties' systems to collateralise a particular product, I have seen the following example relating to currency options where they are excluded until the other party catches up:

> The definition of "Exposure" contained in Paragraph 10 of this Annex is hereby amended by the addition of the following after "Market Quotation" on the last line thereof:
>
> "; and provided further that, during such time as either Party A or Party B is unable for operational reasons to automatically integrate exposures resulting from foreign exchange option transactions with exposures resulting from other Transactions, the Market Quotation or Loss with respect to all Transactions which constitute foreign exchange option transactions shall be deemed to be zero for the purposes of the determination of "Exposure"."

Sometimes parties like to clarify that uncollateralised Transactions shall not form part of the Credit Support Amount for close-out purposes, for example:

> Insert the following sentence at the end of this definition: [i.e. "Exposure"]
>
> "For the avoidance of doubt, solely for the purposes of the calculation of Exposure hereunder, the amount payable pursuant to Section 6(e)(ii)(1) in respect of Transactions which are not Collateralised Transactions shall be deemed to be zero (but without prejudice to payment or delivery obligations under the Transaction constituted by this Annex)."

There are also a couple of amendments which I have seen relating to the proviso at the end of the Exposure definition. In a very one-way CSA I have seen:

> The definition of "Exposure" shall be amended by deleting the proviso at the end.

In another, a more reasonable provision, viz:

> The definition of "Exposure" in Paragraph 10 shall be amended by adding the words "in accordance with generally accepted industry standard" on line 7 after the words "the Valuation Agent on behalf of that party".

(v) Exchanges (substitutions)

As mentioned before, in order to be on the safe side and formerly to avoid recharacterisation risk, it was considered best to avoid any amendments which gave the Transferor an automatic right of substitution without consent. This is less of a problem now following the implementation of the Collateral Directive in England.

Nonetheless you might see this amendment:

> *Exchanges*. The words "which consent will not be unreasonably withheld" are inserted at the end of the first line of Paragraph 3(c)(ii).

Where you still see it, one relatively common amendment requires the Transferee to use its best endeavours to return the equivalent of the Original Credit Support on the same Local Business Day as it receives the New Credit Support:

Exchanges:

Paragraph 3(c)(ii) will be amended by inserting the following after the words "Original Credit Support" in line five "...promptly upon receipt of the New Credit Support (and if practicable on the day of such receipt) and in any case not later...".

Sometimes parties propose a sequence of deadlines as in the following example:

Exchange Date.

Paragraph 3(c)(ii) is hereby substituted in its entirety with the following:

"(ii) If the Transferee notifies the Transferor that it has consented to the proposed exchange:

(A) the Transferor will be obliged to transfer the New Credit Support to the Transferee:

(1) on the Settlement Day following the date on which it receives notice (which may be oral telephonic notice) from the Transferee of its consent if it receives such notice before 1:00 p.m. London time on such date; and

(2) on the second Settlement Day following the date on which it receives such notice if it receives such notice at or after 1:00 p.m. London time on such date; and

(B) the Transferee will be obliged to transfer to the Transferor Equivalent Credit Support in respect of the Original Credit Support not later than:

(1) the date on which the Transferee receives the New Credit Support if it receives such New Credit Support before 5:00 p.m. London time on such date and the Equivalent Credit Support is in US Dollars; and

(2) the Settlement Day following the date on which the Transferee receives the New Credit Support if it receives such New Credit Support at or after 5:00 p.m. London time on such date or the Equivalent Credit Support is in Euros;

provided that the Transferee will only be obliged to transfer Equivalent Credit Support with a Value as of the date of transfer as close as practicable to, but in any event not more than, the Value of the New Credit Support as of that date."

Where Original Credit Support becomes downgraded, a Transferee may well wish to have the right to request the Transferor to substitute New Credit Support of the requisite rating to restore the status quo, as in the following examples:

Exchange of Eligible Credit Support in the event that the issuer of the Government debt obligations is downgraded. If the rating assigned by S&P or Moody's to the negotiable debt obligations held as Eligible Credit Support falls below the minimum rating requirements imposed under the definition of Eligible Credit Support (the Affected Credit Support), then the party that holds the Affected Credit Support shall be entitled to demand by written notice the further transfer to it of substitute Eligible Credit Support (of equal value) in exchange for the Affected Credit Support. The party obligated to provide such substitute Credit Support shall make such transfer on the first Local Business Day following the date on which it receives such notice. The other party will only be obligated to return the Affected Credit Support after receiving the substitute Eligible Credit Support.

OR

If at any time the Ratings assigned by S&P and Moody's to any Eligible Credit Support comprising the Credit Support Balance fall below AA– or Aa3, respectively (the "Downgraded Credit Support"), the Transferee may by notice in writing to the Transferor require the Transferor to provide a request to exchange the Downgraded Credit Support for New Credit Support (such New Credit Support having a Rating assigned by S&P and/or Moody's of at least AA– or Aaa3, respectively), in accordance with the provisions of Paragraph 3(c)(i) of the Credit Support Annex, within five Local Business Days of receipt of such notice.

Substitutions can arise for a number of reasons:

- because the Transferor needs it to fulfil an obligation to a third party;
- because the collateral has become ineligible or has been downgraded;
- because the Transferor does not wish to receive a manufactured dividend from the Transferee for tax reasons.

An example of wording for a substitution for tax reasons is:

> The parties agree that if a coupon date occurs in relation to an item of Eligible Credit Support, the Transferor will have the right to take the necessary steps in order to exchange this item of Eligible Credit Support before the coupon date in the manner provided for in Paragraph 3(c).

A similar situation might arise if a change in tax regulations occurs:

> Taxes. If at any time there occurs a change in taxation in relation to any Eligible Credit Support which has a negative impact on the Transferor or Transferee, the Transferee shall have the right (i) to refuse to accept a transfer of any securities by the Transferor and/or (ii) to insist on the immediate substitution of any securities already held by the Transferee as Eligible Credit Support.

Exchanges or substitutions of cash in different currencies are relatively rare.

(vi) Notices

Paragraph 11(h) often starts with a section where the parties provide details of where any notices or demands between them should be sent.

Other notice type provisions include the following:

> (ii) Notices. Notwithstanding Section 12 of the Agreement, any communication by a party ("X") to the other party ("Y") requesting Eligible Credit Support to be transferred pursuant to Paragraph 3 of this Annex may be given via facsimile at the times specified in this Agreement and during normal business hours in the city in which Y is located on any Local Business Day. Any such facsimile will be deemed received and effective when actually received.

> (iii) Sharing of Information. The parties hereto agree that a party shall prepare written statements identifying the Transactions included in the calculation of Exposure hereunder (1) at the Notification Time upon making a demand under Paragraph 2, or (2) immediately upon reasonable request by the other party. These statements shall list the Transactions according to their types, their currency and their maturity date.

> (iv) Confidentiality. Any statement required to be delivered by a party pursuant to Paragraph 11(h)(iii) above may contain information which the party receiving such statements shall use on a confidential basis.

(vii) Miscellaneous

Among the interesting provisions I have seen are the following:

Additional Representations

> **Additional Representations. Each party hereby represents to the other (which representation will be deemed to be repeated as of each date on which it, as Transferor, transfers Eligible Credit Support) that**
>
> **(A) no consent, approval or other authorization of any governmental authority or regulatory body is required in connection with the transfer of Eligible Credit Support; and**
>
> **(B) Transferor hereby represents to Transferee (which representation will be deemed to be repeated as of each date on which it, as Transferor, Transfers Eligible Credit Support) that its assets on such date exceed its liabilities.**

How anyone can be entirely sure of (B) unless they are Group Accountant beats me.

Sharing of Information

> **Sharing of Information. The parties hereto agree that they shall make their best efforts to send, upon request, written statements listing the Transactions included in the calculation of Exposure hereunder, according to their deal number, currency, notional amount, type, value date and maturity date.**

However, this could impose an onerous obligation on the collateral management department especially if counterparty information requests are frequent.

Moreover, giving undertakings on a best efforts basis should be avoided as this implies quite a high standard of conduct. For example, in the case of *IBM United Kingdom Ltd* v *Rockware Glass Ltd* [1980] FSR 335, a best endeavours clause (which is arguably similar to a best efforts clause) was described as one in which the obligor should take "all those steps in their power which are capable of producing the desired results … being steps which a prudent, determined and reasonable [obligee], acting in his own interests and desiring to achieve that result, would take". It may not always be possible for the collateral management team to comply with this requirement due to operational error or lack of time. Any obligation to provide such information should be subject to the caveat that failure to provide it should not constitute an Event of Default. However, I would recommend that it be resisted for the reasons given in these two paragraphs.

No Specific Performance

> **No Specific Performance. Each party agrees that in relation to legal proceedings it will not seek specific performance of the other party's obligations to transfer Eligible Credit Support, Equivalent Credit Support, Interest Amounts or Equivalent Distributions, but without prejudice to any other rights it may have.**

While this emphasises that cash damages are the only compensation under the ISDA Master Agreement, it is not essential to include it.

Transfer Timing

An extension of the delivery period for a Delivery or a Return Amount:

> Transfer Timing. The final paragraph of Paragraph 3(a) shall be deleted and replaced with the following:
>
> "Subject to Paragraph 4 and unless otherwise specified, if a demand for the transfer of Eligible Credit Support or Equivalent Credit Support is received by the Notification Time, then the relevant transfer will be made not later than the close of business on the second Local Business Day relating to the date such demand is received; if a demand is received after the Notification Time, then the relevant transfer will be made not later than the close of business on the third Local Business Day relating to the day after the date such demand is received."

This should only be granted where the securities collateral concerned has a longer settlement cycle. However, as drafted, it would allow either party two to three Local Business Days to transfer cash collateral!

It is becoming more common to define Local Business Day in Paragraph 11(h), for example:

> "Local Business Day" means, notwithstanding the definition in Paragraph 10, for the purposes of the definitions of "Valuation Date", "Valuation Time", "Notification Time" and "Resolution Time", a day on which commercial banks are open for business (including dealings in foreign exchange and foreign currency deposits) in London and Madrid.

It is also possible to define FX Local Business Day and even Gold Business Day (e.g. for collateral gold bullion transactions).

Final Returns

The following is a common addition in Paragraph 11(h):

> Final Returns
>
> When no amounts are or may become payable by the Transferor with respect to any obligations under the Agreement (except for any potential liability under Section 2(d) of the Agreement), the Transferee will transfer to the Transferor Equivalent Credit Support having a Value as close as practicable to the Credit Support Balance. For this purpose the Valuation Percentage for any item of the Credit Support Balance shall be 100% and the Minimum Transfer Amount and Rounding amount shall both be deemed to be zero.

OR

> When no amounts are or may become payable by the Transferor with respect to any obligations under the Agreement (except for any potential liability under Section 2(d) of the Agreement), the Transferee will transfer to the Transferor Equivalent Credit Support with respect to the Credit Support Balance.

Final Returns concern final returns of collateral when neither party has any risk exposure on the other. It is normal to have either this provision or the following wording often added to Minimum Transfer Amount:

> Notwithstanding the provisions of Paragraph 11(iii)(C), when the Credit Support Amount with respect to a party on a Valuation Date is zero, the Minimum Transfer Amount with respect to both parties shall be zero.

You do not normally include both.

Interest Amount and withholding tax

A provision relating to withholding tax may be included:

> For the avoidance of doubt, where any Distribution or Interest Amount occurs, the interest and other payments and distributions of cash or other property that the holder of the same type, nominal value, description and amount of such Eligible Credit Support is entitled to, shall be deemed to be such amount free and clear of any deduction or withholding for or on account of any Tax.

With Italian counterparties the following acknowledgement is sometimes made:

> Party A and Party B acknowledge that any transfer of Eligible Credit Support pursuant to this Annex would constitute a pegno irregolare if this Annex was governed by Italian law.

This is because in Italy a *pegno irregolare* (irregular pledge) is classified as a type of security interest under Article 1851 of the Italian Civil Code although it essentially acts as a transfer of title document.

In connection with Hong Kong, the definition of Local Business Day is modified to take into account, inter alia, some stormy weather.

> The "." at the end of sub-clause (iv) of the definition of "Local Business Day" in Paragraph 10 is hereby deleted, and the following proviso is hereby inserted at the end of the definition of "Local Business Day" as aforesaid (and applying in respect of all sub-clauses thereof):

> provided that where Hong Kong is the or a relevant location for the purposes of the definition of "Local Business Day", none of the following shall be deemed to be a Local Business Day in Hong Kong:

(a) Any Saturday; and/or

(b) Any day upon which any Adverse Weather Condition is issued or raised (as appropriate), on or before 11:00 a.m. and (a) not lowered or withdrawn at or before 12:00 noon or (b) if so lowered or withdrawn subsequently issued or raised before 2:30 p.m. on that day.

For purposes hereof, "Adverse Weather Condition" means a black rainstorm warning and/or No. 8 or greater typhoon signal in Hong Kong.

A potential example of real life impacting upon the markets!

Finally with unsophisticated counterparties no detail is too small to check in operating the collateral arrangement:

All payments to be made under this Agreement shall be effected through the CHAPS settlement system and unless expressly agreed in writing by both parties, payment by cheque shall not constitute a valid payment.

Table 5.4 summarises the ISDA fallbacks for Paragraph 11 and the provisions that must be completed for the English Law CSA to be operative.

Table 5.4 **ISDA fallbacks in the English law CSA**

If no choice is made the following apply by default:	
Provision	**Fallback**
Base Currency	US Dollars
Eligible Currency	Base Currency
Independent Amount	Zero
Threshold	Zero
Minimum Transfer Amount	Zero
Rounding	No rounding
Valuation Agent	The party making demand under Paragraph 2 and the Transferee for Paragraph 5 payments
Exchange Date	The Settlement Date following the Transferee's receipt of New Credit Support
Resolution Time	1.00 p.m. London time on the Local Business Day after the day the dispute notice was issued
Alternative	Paragraph 4 dispute resolution procedures apply
Transfer of Interest	Last Local Business Day of a calendar month and any Local Business Day when a cash Return Amount is transferred to the Transferor
Alternative to Interest Amount	Paragraph 5(c)(ii) and Paragraph 10 definition of Interest Amount applies

Provisions which must be completed as there is no fallback are as follows:

- Eligible Credit Support;
- Valuation Date;
- Valuation Time;
- Notification Time;
- Value;
- Interest Rate;
- Addresses for Transfers.

Amendment Agreements

In many instances, parties may have entered into an ISDA Master Agreement several years before they decide to collateralise their respective trading portfolios by entering into an English Law CSA.

To facilitate this they can either just enter into such an English Law CSA or do so via an Amendment Agreement that adds the Annex to the Schedule of the ISDA Master Agreement.

An example of such an Amendment Agreement may be found in Appendix A of the *User's Guide to the ISDA Credit Support Documents under English Law*.

6

The New York Law Credit Support Annex

Paragraph by paragraph analysis

Glossary of terms in Paragraph 12

Examples of Paragraph 13 provisions

Comparison of the New York Law CSA with the English Law CSA

This Chapter provides a paragraph by paragraph analysis of the New York Law CSA, including its Paragraph 13 (the Elections and Variables paragraph) that is individually negotiated by the parties. Terms capitalised in this Chapter have the same meaning as used in the New York Law CSA and the ISDA Master Agreement. The discussion of Paragraph 13 also provides common and unusual amendments seen in the market. Chapter 5 written by Paul Harding on the English Law CSA takes a similar approach.

(Bilateral Form) (ISDA Agreements Subject to New York Law Only)

PARAGRAPH BY PARAGRAPH ANALYSIS

Headings

The New York Law CSA, in its standard form, is a bilateral pledge agreement. In contrast to the English Law CSA, the Pledgor grants a security interest in the pledged collateral to the Secured Party as opposed to an actual transfer in legal ownership of the pledged collateral. It is important to appreciate that although the two different forms of CSA share a common structure and vocabulary, the basis for a party's legal rights to liquidate the collateral is completely different.

This document was drafted to be governed by New York law and it is recommended that specific legal advice be taken if it is to be subject to any other governing law.

ISDA®

International Swaps and Derivatives Association, Inc.

CREDIT SUPPORT ANNEX

to the Schedule to the

……………………………………………………………………………………

dated as of ………………………

between

…………………………………………………… and ……………………………………………………

("Party A") ("Party B")

Dating and Nomenclature

The New York Law CSA will typically be dated as of the same date as the ISDA Master Agreement. It is market practice to date the ISDA Master Agreement as of the date of the first trade between the parties even if it is not signed until several months later. This is based on US practice where the words "as of" mean "with effect from" a specified date. Since the New York Law CSA forms part of the Agreement Schedule (see commentary on its preamble below) it is dated as of the same date as the Agreement.

The parties enter their full legal names in the spaces provided.

This Annex supplements, forms part of, and is subject to, the above-referenced Agreement, is part of its Schedule and is a Credit Support Document under this Agreement with respect to each party.

Preamble

Technically the New York Law CSA is described as part of the ISDA Master Agreement and like it supplements, forms part of and is subject to the ISDA Master Agreement itself. It is not a standalone document like the ISDA Credit Support Deed (English law) but is part of the ISDA Master Agreement Schedule and considered to be a Credit Support Document under the ISDA Master Agreement, and in this sense is somewhat hybrid in nature. This is in contrast to the English Law CSA that is characterised under English law as a Transaction that is confirmed with a Confirmation and not as a Credit Support Document.

The single agreement concept of Section 1(c) of the ISDA Master Agreement is reinforced here. This concept prevents a bankruptcy court or receiver from cherry-picking (i.e. making payments under those Transactions favourable to his insolvent client and refusing to pay on those unprofitable to it). Section 1(c) of the Agreement prevents this by effectively collapsing all the Transactions into a single net termination payment due to one party or the other.

Accordingly, the parties agree as follows:—

Paragraph 1. Interpretation

(a) ***Definitions and Inconsistency.*** Capitalized terms not otherwise defined herein or elsewhere in this Agreement have the meanings specified pursuant to Paragraph 12, and all references in this Annex to Paragraphs are to Paragraphs of this Annex. In the event of any inconsistency between this Annex and the other provisions of this Schedule, this Annex will prevail, and in the event of any inconsistency between Paragraph 13 and the other provisions of this Annex, Paragraph 13 will prevail.

(b) ***Secured Party and Pledgor.*** All references in this Annex to the "Secured Party" will be to either party when acting in that capacity and all corresponding references to the "Pledgor" will be to the other party when acting in that capacity; *provided, however*, that if Other Posted Support is held by a party to this Annex, all references herein to that party as the Secured Party with respect to that Other Posted Support will be to that party as the beneficiary thereof and will not subject that support or that party as the beneficiary thereof to provisions of law generally relating to security interests and secured parties.

Paragraph 1. Interpretation

(a) Definitions and Inconsistency. This clause clarifies that any capitalised terms not defined in the ISDA Master Agreement or Schedule will have the meaning given to the term in Paragraph 12 of the New York CSA. The clause further clarifies that any references to a particular paragraph are references to paragraphs in the New York Law CSA. Finally, it states that if there is any inconsistency between the Annex and the other provisions of the ISDA Schedule, the New York Law CSA will prevail. However, Paragraph 13 (the Elections and Variables paragraph) will prevail if it is inconsistent with the other provisions of the New York Law CSA.

(b) Under the New York Law CSA, drafted as a bilateral pledging document, either party may at times be the Secured Party or the Pledgor depending on which party is exposed to the other. A party pledging collateral (or receiving collateral that is being returned) is referred to as the Pledgor. A party receiving pledged collateral (or holding or returning collateral to the Pledgor) is referred as the Secured Party. In respect of Other Posted Support the Secured Party will be considered to hold it as a beneficiary rather than as a pledgee (i.e. secured party).

Paragraph 2. Security Interest

Each party, as the Pledgor, hereby pledges to the other party, as the Secured Party, as security for its Obligations, and grants to the Secured Party a first priority continuing security interest in, lien on and right of Set-off against all Posted Collateral Transferred to or received by the Secured Party hereunder. Upon the Transfer by the Secured Party to the Pledgor of Posted Collateral, the security interest and lien granted hereunder on that Posted Collateral will be released immediately and, to the extent possible, without any further action by either party.

Paragraph 2. Security Interest

Paragraph 2, governed by the New York Uniform Commercial Code (the "UCC"), is typically referred to as the granting clause. Here the Pledgor grants a security interest in (or a lien on) the property that is pledged to the Secured Party. Here, the Pledgor is obligated to grant "a first priority continuing security interest" to the Secured Party. Under the New York UCC, this means that the Secured Party generally has a claim to the pledged collateral superior to any other creditor provided that the Secured Party perfects its rights in the pledge. Assuming that the Pledgor is pledging Cash or US Treasury securities, the security interest in the pledged collateral is perfected by the Secured Party taking possession (although not ownership) of the pledged collateral. See Chapter 3 (pages 58–9) for a discussion of the attachment and perfection of a security interest in Posted Collateral under the UCC.

The Secured Party also agrees in the paragraph that, in the event the Secured Party returns the Posted Collateral to the Pledgor, its security interest in the collateral is automatically released. Because attachment and perfection of Posted Collateral such as Cash and securities is normally done by possession, surrender of such possession will also normally release the Secured Party's lien on the surrendered collateral under the UCC.

Paragraph 3. Credit Support Obligations

(a) ***Delivery Amount.*** Subject to Paragraphs 4 and 5, upon a demand made by the Secured Party on or promptly following a Valuation Date, if the Delivery Amount for that Valuation Date equals or exceeds the Pledgor's Minimum Transfer Amount, then the Pledgor will Transfer to the Secured Party Eligible Credit Support having a Value as of the date of Transfer at least equal to the applicable Delivery Amount (rounded pursuant to Paragraph 13). Unless otherwise specified in Paragraph 13, the ***"Delivery Amount"*** applicable to the Pledgor for any Valuation Date will equal the amount by which:

(i) the Credit Support Amount

exceeds

(ii) the Value as of that Valuation Date of all Posted Credit Support held by the Secured Party.

(b) ***Return Amount.*** Subject to Paragraphs 4 and 5, upon a demand made by the Pledgor on or promptly following a Valuation Date, if the Return Amount for that Valuation Date equals or exceeds the Secured Party's Minimum Transfer Amount, then the Secured Party will Transfer to the Pledgor Posted Credit Support specified by the Pledgor in that demand having a Value as of the date of Transfer as close as practicable to the applicable Return Amount (rounded pursuant to Paragraph 13). Unless otherwise specified in Paragraph 13, the ***"Return Amount"*** applicable to the Secured Party for any Valuation Date will equal the amount by which:

(i) the Value as of that Valuation Date of all Posted Credit Support held by the Secured Party

exceeds

(ii) the Credit Support Amount.

"Credit Support Amount" means, unless otherwise specified in Paragraph 13, for any Valuation Date (i) the Secured Party's Exposure for that Valuation Date plus (ii) the aggregate of all Independent Amounts applicable to the Pledgor, if any, minus (iii) all Independent Amounts applicable to the Secured Party, if any, minus (iv) the Pledgor's Threshold; *provided, however*, that the Credit Support Amount will be deemed to be zero whenever the calculation of Credit Support Amount yields a number less than zero.

Paragraph 3. Credit Support Obligations

This Paragraph concerns collateral calls and returns and how they are calculated.

Basically the Secured Party compares his risk exposure to the Pledgor with the collateral that he holds and calls for additional collateral, returns any excess collateral to the Pledgor, or does nothing depending upon the calculations after taking into account Independent Amounts, Thresholds, Minimum Transfer Amounts and/or rounding.

In Paragraph 3(a) the Secured Party can call for collateral when the Credit Support Amount exceeds the value of any Posted Collateral (i.e. pledged collateral). This is referred to as the Delivery Amount. When called upon and assuming there is no dispute, the Pledgor will transfer the requested Delivery Amount of collateral to the Secured Party. However, the amount of the call must still be greater than the Pledgor's Minimum Transfer Amount after deducting its Threshold (see pages 80–1 for explanations of these terms).

In Paragraph 3(b), the Pledgor can request that collateral be returned in an amount equal to the value of any Posted Collateral less the Credit Support Amount. The Secured Party's amount of collateral requested to be returned must be greater than the Minimum Transfer Amount. Please note that if the Pledgor fails to make a call, the Secured Party is not obliged to transfer the collateral or advise the Pledgor. However, if a third party Valuation Agent is involved, this should not arise if the Valuation Agent is properly managing the relationship.

The Credit Support Amount is determined by first calculating the Secured Party's Exposure as of the Valuation Date. The Secured Party's Exposure is equal to the amount that would be owed to the Secured Party if the Agreement were terminated on the Valuation Date, using a mid-market calculation. See the discussion of the definition of Exposure below. The Independent Amount (see page 323 for an explanation of this term) for the Pledgor is added to the amount of Exposure and the Independent Amount for the Secured Party is subtracted. Finally, the Pledgor's Threshold is subtracted.

Example of the calculation of a Delivery Amount (without Independent Amounts)

Assume the following facts for this calculation. Party A calculates an Exposure of US$25 million (in other words, assuming that Party B were to default, Party A would be entitled to an early termination payment from Party B of US$25 million). Party B has a Threshold Amount of US$4 million. The parties have agreed to a Minimum Transfer Amount of US$250,000 and rounding of US$10,000. There are no Independent Amounts agreed to between the parties. Party B has previously transferred US$11 million of collateral to Party A.

The Credit Support Amount would be calculated as follows:

Exposure	US$25 million
Less Pledgor's Threshold	US$4 million
Credit Support Amount	US$21 million

The Delivery Amount is equal to the Credit Support Amount of US$21 million less the amount of collateral previously pledged of US$11 million for a Delivery Amount to be delivered to Party A by Party B equal to US$10 million.

Example of the calculation of a Return Amount (without Independent Amounts)

Assume the following facts for this calculation. Party A calculates an Exposure of US$25 million (in other words, assuming that Party B were to default, Party A would be entitled to an early termination payment from Party B of US$25 million). Party B has a Threshold Amount of US$4 million. The parties have agreed to a Minimum Transfer Amount of US$250,000 and rounding of US$10,000. There are no Independent Amounts agreed to between the parties. Party B has previously transferred US$30 million of collateral to Party A.

The Credit Support Amount would be calculated as follows:

Exposure	US$25 million
Less Pledgor's Threshold	US$4 million
Credit Support Amount	US$21 million

The Return Amount is equal to the Credit Support Amount of US$21 million less the amount of collateral pledged of US$30 million for a Return Amount to be delivered by Party A to Party B equal to US$9 million.

Paragraph 4. Conditions Precedent, Transfer Timing, Calculations and Substitutions

(a) ***Conditions Precedent.*** Each Transfer obligation of the Pledgor under Paragraphs 3 and 5 and of the Secured Party under Paragraphs 3, 4(d)(ii), 5 and 6(d) is subject to the conditions precedent that:

(i) no Event of Default, Potential Event of Default or Specified Condition has occurred and is continuing with respect to the other party; and

(ii) no Early Termination Date for which any unsatisfied payment obligations exist has occurred or been designated as the result of an Event of Default or Specified Condition with respect to the other party.

(b) ***Transfer Timing.*** Subject to Paragraphs 4(a) and 5 and unless otherwise specified, if a demand for the Transfer of Eligible Credit Support or Posted Credit Support is made by the Notification Time, then the relevant Transfer will be made not later than the close of business on the next Local Business Day; if a demand is made after the Notification Time, then the relevant Transfer will be made not later than the close of business on the second Local Business Day thereafter.

Paragraph 4. Conditions Precedent, Transfer Timing, Calculations and Substitutions

Paragraph 4(a)–(b)

Under Paragraph 4(a)(i), a party is not obligated to transfer collateral that it would otherwise be required to transfer under the New York Law CSA if

- an Event of Default,
- Potential Event of Default or
- a Specified Condition

has occurred with respect to the other party. This protects a party from having to transfer collateral to a counterparty that is in difficulty. This provision may have the effect of one of the two parties being either under or overcollateralised. During the Lehman Brothers bankruptcy, this clause was first triggered when the guarantor of the Lehman Brothers trading entity (its parent) declared bankruptcy on 15 September 2008. At that point, a counterparty of the Lehman Brothers trading entity had the right to stop pledging. (See page 285 for a discussion of Specified Conditions.)

Paragraph 4(a)(ii) provides that neither party is obligated to transfer collateral after the designation of an Early Termination Date, regardless of who designated the Early Termination Date, why it was designated or when the termination payment is due. Presumably this is because the parties will soon be making the early termination payment. If a party is concerned about being exposed during that period, the Early Termination Date should occur as soon as possible after the party gives the termination notice.

Under the general rule of Paragraph 4(b), a party is required to deliver collateral by the close of business on the next Local Business Day if it receives notice by the Notification Time. If it receives a call for collateral after the Notification Time, it is required to deliver collateral by the close of business on the second Local Business Day. It is relatively common for parties to provide for same day transfer of collateral if the collateral call is made by the Notification Time. However, this time may need to be extended if the parties are operating in different time zones.

It is unclear in the New York Law CSA what is meant by "close of business". Presumably, this would be close of business for banks and other financial institutions in the jurisdiction of the party calling for the collateral transfer.

(c) ***Calculations.*** All calculations of Value and Exposure for purposes of Paragraphs 3 and 6(d) will be made by the Valuation Agent as of the Valuation Time. The Valuation Agent will notify each party (or the other party, if the Valuation Agent is a party) of its calculations not later than the Notification Time on the Local Business Day following the applicable Valuation Date (or in the case of Paragraph 6(d), following the date of calculation).

(d) ***Substitutions.***

(i) Unless otherwise specified in Paragraph 13, upon notice to the Secured Party specifying the items of Posted Credit Support to be exchanged, the Pledgor may, on any Local Business Day, Transfer to the Secured Party substitute Eligible Credit Support (the "Substitute Credit Support"); and

(ii) subject to Paragraph 4(a), the Secured Party will Transfer to the Pledgor the items of Posted Credit Support specified by the Pledgor in its notice not later than the Local Business Day following the date on which the Secured Party receives the Substitute Credit Support, unless otherwise specified in Paragraph 13 (the "Substitution Date"); *provided* that the Secured Party will only be obligated to Transfer Posted Credit Support with a Value as of the date of Transfer of that Posted Credit Support equal to the Value as of that date of the Substitute Credit Support.

Paragraph 4(c)–(d)

Paragraph 4(c) requires the Valuation Agent to make the calculations of Value and Exposure as of the Valuation Time (typically the Local Business Day preceding the Valuation Date). It is generally more efficient to make the required calculations if they are based on mark-to-market calculations at the close of business on the previous day and previously published quotations of the Value of collateral. The Valuation Agent will notify the other party of its calculations not later than the Notification Time on the Local Business Day following the Valuation Date or in respect of payments of interest on bonds or cash on the date of calculation itself.

Paragraph 4(d) provides the Pledgor with the opportunity to substitute Eligible Collateral for collateral that it had previously posted to the Secured Party. A Pledgor may want to substitute collateral in the event that the previously pledged collateral is needed for a new purpose by the Pledgor.

The Secured Party must agree to such a substitution unless Paragraph 13 requires the Pledgor to obtain the Secured Party's consent for the substitution. A Secured Party may require consent in order to avoid situations where the Pledgor becomes a nuisance by making too many substitutions of Eligible Collateral. Although the Secured Party is not necessarily in a weaker position after a substitution, frequent substitutions of collateral by the Pledgor can prove to be a time-consuming nuisance for the Secured Party's back office and will involve transfer costs.

The Secured Party is not required to transfer the previously Posted Collateral to the Pledgor until it has received the substitute collateral. The Secured Party is obligated to transfer the previously Posted Collateral on the Local Business Day following receipt of the substitute collateral and then only in an amount that does not exceed the Value of the Substitute Credit Support. Parties may agree to same day substitution of Posted Collateral.

Paragraph 5. Dispute Resolution

If a party (a "Disputing Party") disputes (I) the Valuation Agent's calculation of a Delivery Amount or a Return Amount or (II) the Value of any Transfer of Eligible Credit Support or Posted Credit Support, then (1) the Disputing Party will notify the other party and the Valuation Agent (if the Valuation Agent is not the other party) not later than the close of business on the Local Business Day following (X) the date that the demand is made under Paragraph 3 in the case of (I) above or (Y) the date of Transfer in the case of (II) above, (2) subject to Paragraph 4(a), the appropriate party will Transfer the undisputed amount to the other party not later than the close of business on the Local Business Day following (X) the date that the demand is made under Paragraph 3 in the case of (I) above or (Y) the date of Transfer in the case of (II) above, (3) the parties will consult with each other in an attempt to resolve the dispute and (4) if they fail to resolve the dispute by the Resolution Time, then:

(i) In the case of a dispute involving a Delivery Amount or Return Amount, unless otherwise specified in Paragraph 13, the Valuation Agent will recalculate the Exposure and the Value as of the Recalculation Date by:

(A) utilizing any calculations of Exposure for the Transactions (or Swap Transactions) that the parties have agreed are not in dispute;

(B) calculating the Exposure for the Transactions (or Swap Transactions) in dispute by seeking four actual quotations at mid-market from Reference Market-makers for purposes of calculating Market Quotation, and taking the arithmetic average of those obtained; *provided* that if four quotations are not available for a particular Transaction (or Swap Transaction), then fewer than four quotations may be used for that Transaction (or Swap Transaction); and if no quotations are available for a particular Transaction (or Swap Transaction), then the Valuation Agent's original calculations will be used for that Transaction (or Swap Transaction); and

(C) utilizing the procedures specified in Paragraph 13 for calculating the Value, if disputed, of Posted Credit Support.

(ii) In the case of a dispute involving the Value of any Transfer of Eligible Credit Support or Posted Credit Support, the Valuation Agent will recalculate the Value as of the date of Transfer pursuant to Paragraph 13.

Paragraph 5. Dispute Resolution

If a party disputes the Valuation Agent's calculation of Exposure or the Value of the Posted Collateral, Paragraph 5 provides a framework for resolving the dispute if it cannot be settled informally.

The dispute resolution provisions are important because as long as a disputing party complies with the provisions, it will not be in default under the Credit Support Annex if it disputes the calculation and does not make the disputed transfer.

Collateral disputes *always* relate to these two matters and the calculation of Exposure is the most common kind of dispute. Parties often disagree on the calculation of Exposure if the underlying Transactions are illiquid or otherwise difficult to value.

Disputes may also arise over the valuation of collateral if illiquid securities that are difficult to value are being pledged.

The steps are outlined in Paragraph 5(a)(i) and (ii) and involve:

1 A requirement for the Disputing Party (i) if it wishes to dispute the calculation of risk exposure, to notify its counterparty or the third party Valuation Agent (if any) by the close of business on the Local Business Day after the date the collateral call notice is received, or (ii) if it wishes to dispute the calculation of the value of the collateral transferred, to notify the third party Valuation Agent on the date that the collateral transfer has been made.

2 the Disputing Party agrees to transfer the undisputed amount to the other party no later than (i) in the case of disputes over risk exposure, by the close of business on the Local Business Day after the collateral call is made, or (ii) in the case of disputes over the valuation of collateral, the date the collateral is transferred.

3 The parties will attempt to resolve the dispute by the deadline nominated in Paragraph 13(f)(i) – the Resolution Time.

4 If they fail then:

(i) (A) If the dispute involves the amount of collateral called for, the Valuation Agent will recalculate his figures by reusing any calculation of the amount of Exposure not in dispute.

(B) It will then approach four Reference Market-makers for mid-market quotations (i.e. the average of the bid and offer prices of the Transactions concerned). Provided four quotations are received the arithmetic average of these quotations is used. To this is added the Exposure calculation which is not in dispute. However, fewer than four quotations may be used in the recalculation of Exposure if four quotations are not available to calculate the amount for a particular Transaction. If

Following a recalculation pursuant to this Paragraph, the Valuation Agent will notify each party (or the other party, if the Valuation Agent is a party) not later than the Notification Time on the Local Business Day following the Resolution Time. The appropriate party will, upon demand following that notice by the Valuation Agent or a resolution pursuant to (3) above and subject to Paragraphs 4(a) and 4(b), make the appropriate Transfer.

no quotations are available, then the Valuation Agent's original calculation will be used for that Transaction. Because this Exposure calculation is important only for purposes of collateral transfer and not for early termination, this should be a reasonable approach although it could lead to under or overcollateralisation.

Although this method helps provide legal certainty, it can be cumbersome to go out and get four quotations. Although the Credit Support Annex contemplates that this process could be done in a 24-hour period, it conceivably could take much longer. By soliciting quotations, the Valuation Agent also discloses the particular terms of a Transaction to competitors.

(C) The Valuation Agent will also follow the method specified in Paragraph 13(f)(ii) for calculating the value of collateral held. A method has to be specified in Paragraph 13(f)(ii) or the dispute resolution provisions with respect to the calculations of Value become inoperative. There is no fallback.

(ii) The Valuation Agent will directly focus on Paragraph 13(f)(ii) where the dispute solely involves the Value of collateral held.

When all the recalculations have been done the Valuation Agent will notify each party (if it is a third party) and the other party (if it is not) of the revised figures not later than the deadline (Notification Time) on the Local Business Day after the Resolution Time (i.e. the dispute resolution deadline agreed in the New York Law CSA).

Once the amount of Exposure and the Value of collateral has been agreed, a revised collateral call notice is sent and the necessary collateral transfer is made. The plain language suggests that the revised amount should be transferred on the same day to the non-disputing party. It could also be argued that the transfer should be made on the following Local Business Day based on the transfer rules discussed above.

It should also be noted that the dispute may become moot as the Exposure changes due to a change in market conditions or the fair market value of the Posted Collateral fluctuates.

At this point, the disputing party must make the transfer of the amount in the revised collateral call notice or it will be default under the Credit Support Annex. The non-disputing party could then exercise its rights and remedies under Paragraph 8 of the Credit Support Annex.

Paragraph 6. Holding and Using Posted Collateral

(a) ***Care of Posted Collateral.*** Without limiting the Secured Party's rights under Paragraph 6(c), the Secured Party will exercise reasonable care to assure the safe custody of all Posted Collateral to the extent required by applicable law, and in any event the Secured Party will be deemed to have exercised reasonable care if it exercises at least the same degree of care as it would exercise with respect to its own property. Except as specified in the preceding sentence, the Secured Party will have no duty with respect to Posted Collateral, including, without limitation, any duty to collect any Distributions, or enforce or preserve any rights pertaining thereto.

(b) ***Eligibility to Hold Posted Collateral; Custodians.***

(i) ***General.*** Subject to the satisfaction of any conditions specified in Paragraph 13 for holding Posted Collateral, the Secured Party will be entitled to hold Posted Collateral or to appoint an agent (a "Custodian") to hold Posted Collateral for the Secured Party. Upon notice by the Secured Party to the Pledgor of the appointment of a Custodian, the Pledgor's obligations to make any Transfer will be discharged by making the Transfer to that Custodian. The holding of Posted Collateral by a Custodian will be deemed to be the holding of that Posted Collateral by the Secured Party for which the Custodian is acting.

(ii) ***Failure to Satisfy Conditions.*** If the Secured Party or its Custodian fails to satisfy any conditions for holding Posted Collateral, then upon a demand made by the Pledgor, the Secured Party will, not later than five Local Business Days after the demand, Transfer or cause its Custodian to Transfer all Posted Collateral held by it to a Custodian that satisfies those conditions or to the Secured Party if it satisfies those conditions.

(iii) ***Liability.*** The Secured Party will be liable for the acts or omissions of its Custodian to the same extent that the Secured Party would be liable hereunder for its own acts or omissions.

Paragraph 6. Holding and using Posted Collateral

Paragraph 6(a)–(b)

Paragraph 6(a) generally imposes the same duty of care on the Secured Party with respect to holding the pledged collateral as is imposed through the New York UCC §9-207 (see Annex 4). The Secured Party will be deemed to have met that duty if it uses the same care that it would have used in holding its own property. It is also important to note that Secured Party has no duty to collect distributions or to enforce or preserve any rights that the Pledgor has in the Posted Collateral.

Paragraph 6(b)(i) provides that a Secured Party may hold the Posted Collateral itself provided that it meets any eligibility conditions specified in Paragraph 13(g) designated by the parties. The Secured Party may also designate an agent to hold the Posted Collateral. Although the agent is defined in paragraph 6(b) as a "Custodian", it is important to understand that the Credit Support Annex itself refers to the Custodian as an agent and the Custodian is acting as an agent and at the direction of the Secured Party. It is not acting as an escrow agent on behalf of the two parties nor would it have any fiduciary duties to the Pledgor. If the Pledgor desired to create such a relationship, the parties would need to create some kind of control agreement or custodial agreement similar to the triparty custodial agreements sometimes used with repos.

The holding of Posted Collateral by a Custodian is considered equivalent to the Secured Party holding it himself.

If a party or a Custodian fails to satisfy the specified requirements, Paragraph 6(b)(ii) provides a Pledgor with the right to require the Secured Party to transfer the Posted Collateral (within 5 Local Business Days of a demand by the Pledgor) to a custodian which meets the eligibility tests of Paragraph 13(g)(i) or to the Secured Party (if it meets those tests).

Paragraph 6(b)(iii) is merely a reflection of agency law that requires a party to be liable for the actions of its agent. This also provides some comfort to the Pledgor in that it will always have recourse against the Secured Party regardless of whether it was the Secured Party or the Custodian that breached its duties of care with respect to holding the Posted Collateral.

(c) ***Use of Posted Collateral.*** Unless otherwise specified in Paragraph 13 and without limiting the rights and obligations of the parties under Paragraphs 3, 4(d)(ii), 5, 6(d) and 8, if the Secured Party is not a Defaulting Party or an Affected Party with respect to a Specified Condition and no Early Termination Date has occurred or been designated as the result of an Event of Default or Specified Condition with respect to the Secured Party, then the Secured Party will, notwithstanding Section 9-207 of the New York Uniform Commercial Code, have the right to:

(i) sell, pledge, rehypothecate, assign, invest, use, commingle or otherwise dispose of, or otherwise use in its business any Posted Collateral it holds, free from any claim or right of any nature whatsoever of the Pledgor, including any equity or right of redemption by the Pledgor; and

(ii) register any Posted Collateral in the name of the Secured Party, its Custodian or a nominee for either.

For purposes of the obligation to Transfer Eligible Credit Support or Posted Credit Support pursuant to Paragraphs 3 and 5 and any rights or remedies authorized under this Agreement, the Secured Party will be deemed to continue to hold all Posted Collateral and to receive Distributions made thereon, regardless of whether the Secured Party has exercised any rights with respect to any Posted Collateral pursuant to (i) or (ii) above.

Paragraph 6(c)

Paragraph 6(c) grants to the Secured Party what is commonly referred to as "use" or "rehypothecation" rights to the Posted Collateral. To restrict these rights, the parties would need to specify in Paragraph 13 that Paragraph 6(c) did not apply. In addition, these rights do not apply if an Event of Default or Specified Condition had occurred with respect to the Secured Party. Rehypothecation rights are often heavily negotiated. For a discussion of the legal effects of rehypothecation, see Chapter 3, at page 66.

Although it may have reused the Posted Collateral, this sub-paragraph makes it clear that the Secured Party is still regarded as the holder of the Posted Collateral and the recipient of Distributions even if it has used its sale and rehypothecation rights under this sub-paragraph.

(d) ***Distributions and Interest Amount.***

(i) ***Distributions.*** Subject to Paragraph 4(a), if the Secured Party receives or is deemed to receive Distributions on a Local Business Day, it will Transfer to the Pledgor not later than the following Local Business Day any Distributions it receives or is deemed to receive to the extent that a Delivery Amount would not be created or increased by that Transfer, as calculated by the Valuation Agent (and the date of calculation will be deemed to be a Valuation Date for this purpose).

(ii) ***Interest Amount.*** Unless otherwise specified in Paragraph 13 and subject to Paragraph 4(a), in lieu of any interest, dividends or other amounts paid or deemed to have been paid with respect to Posted Collateral in the form of Cash (all of which may be retained by the Secured Party), the Secured Party will Transfer to the Pledgor at the times specified in Paragraph 13 the Interest Amount to the extent that a Delivery Amount would not be created or increased by that Transfer, as calculated by the Valuation Agent (and the date of calculation will be deemed to be a Valuation Date for this purpose). The Interest Amount or portion thereof not Transferred pursuant to this Paragraph will constitute Posted Collateral in the form of Cash and will be subject to the security interest granted under Paragraph 2.

Paragraph 6(d)

The general rule under Paragraph 6(d)(i) is that Distributions (such as principal or interest payments on Posted Collateral) are to be passed through to the Pledgor and are not treated as the property or income of the Secured Party. This rule preserves the rights of the Pledgor, as the owner of the Posted Collateral, to any Distributions made with respect to such Posted Collateral. Such transfer of a Distribution is not required to be passed through to the Pledgor if it would create a Delivery Amount (i.e. a collateral call) because the value of the Posted Collateral held by the Secured Party would decrease due to the transfer of the Distribution to the Pledgor. In this case the amount of the Distribution is retained and forms part of the Posted Collateral.

Paragraph 6(d)(ii) sets forth whether and how the Secured Party will pay interest on Cash that is Posted Collateral. The assumption behind the paragraph is that the Secured Party will at the minimum invest the Cash in federal funds or a similar investment during the period that it holds the Cash. In lieu of paying over the actual interest earned, this section provides that the Secured Party will pay the Pledgor a fixed amount based upon an interest rate formula set out by the parties in Paragraph 13 (typically Fed Funds (Effective)).

Where a Delivery Amount would arise from the transfer of the Interest Amount to the Pledgor, the Secured Party is entitled to retain the Interest Amount as part of the Posted Collateral which will also be subject to the New York Law CSA's security interest.

Paragraph 7. Events of Default

For purposes of Section 5(a)(iii)(1) of this Agreement, an Event of Default will exist with respect to a party if:

(i) that party fails (or fails to cause its Custodian) to make, when due, any Transfer of Eligible Collateral, Posted Collateral or the Interest Amount, as applicable, required to be made by it and that failure continues for two Local Business Days after notice of that failure is given to that party;

(ii) that party fails to comply with any restriction or prohibition specified in this Annex with respect to any of the rights specified in Paragraph 6(c) and that failure continues for five Local Business Days after notice of that failure is given to that party; or

(iii) that party fails to comply with or perform any agreement or obligation other than those specified in Paragraphs 7(i) and 7(ii) and that failure continues for 30 days after notice of that failure is given to that party.

Paragraph 7. Events of Default

Under section 5(a)(iii)(1) of the ISDA Master Agreement, it is an Event of Default where one occurs under a Credit Support Document. Paragraph 7 sets forth what constitutes an Event of Default under the New York Law CSA for purposes of Section 5(a)(iii)(1).

In particular, it is an Event of Default under Paragraph 7(a)(i) if a party fails to make a required Transfer of collateral or interest on cash collateral and such failure continues for two Local Business Days after notice. Many parties are now requesting that the cure period for the failure to make a Transfer be reduced to one Local Business Day.

It is also an Event of Default under Paragraph 7(a)(ii) if a party fails to comply with any restrictions on reuse of collateral five Local Business Days after notice of such failure. Presumably this would occur if a Secured Party were to rehypothecate the Posted Collateral even though it was not permitted to do so under the Annex.

Finally, it is an Event of Default under Paragraph 7(a)(iii) if a party fails to perform any other obligation under the Credit Support Annex that remains unremedied 30 days after notice. One example could be a failure to properly safeguard Posted Collateral. Another may be a failure to use a Custodian to hold Posted Collateral if the Secured Party is ineligible to do so.

Paragraph 8. Certain Rights and Remedies

(a) ***Secured Party's Rights and Remedies.*** If at any time (1) an Event of Default or Specified Condition with respect to the Pledgor has occurred and is continuing or (2) an Early Termination Date has occurred or been designated as the result of an Event of Default or Specified Condition with respect to the Pledgor, then, unless the Pledgor has paid in full all of its Obligations that are then due, the Secured Party may exercise one or more of the following rights and remedies:

(i) all rights and remedies available to a secured party under applicable law with respect to Posted Collateral held by the Secured Party;

(ii) any other rights and remedies available to the Secured Party under the terms of Other Posted Support, if any;

(iii) the right to Set-off any amounts payable by the Pledgor with respect to any Obligations against any Posted Collateral or the Cash equivalent of any Posted Collateral held by the Secured Party (or any obligation of the Secured Party to Transfer that Posted Collateral); and

(iv) the right to liquidate any Posted Collateral held by the Secured Party through one or more public or private sales or other dispositions with such notice, if any, as may be required under applicable law, free from any claim or right of any nature whatsoever of the Pledgor, including any equity or right of redemption by the Pledgor (with the Secured Party having the right to purchase any or all of the Posted Collateral to be sold) and to apply the proceeds (or the Cash equivalent thereof) from the liquidation of the Posted Collateral to any amounts payable by the Pledgor with respect to any Obligations in that order as the Secured Party may elect.

Each party acknowledges and agrees that Posted Collateral in the form of securities may decline speedily in value and is of a type customarily sold on a recognized market, and, accordingly, the Pledgor is not entitled to prior notice of any sale of that Posted Collateral by the Secured Party, except any notice that is required under applicable law and cannot be waived.

Paragraph 8. Certain Rights and Remedies

Paragraph 8a

Paragraph 8(a) provides important rights and remedies to the Secured Party. It is first important to note that the Secured Party has the right to exercise its rights and remedies under the New York Law CSA (and under applicable law) upon the occurrence of an Event of Default or a Specified Condition (certain Termination Events designated in Paragraph 13) regardless of whether an Early Termination Date has occurred. It is important to note also that the occurrence of a Termination Event or the designation of an Early Termination Date under the ISDA Master Agreement because of a Termination Event will not provide a right or remedy under the New York Law CSA unless it was designated as a Specified Condition.

The term Specified Condition is not specifically defined in Paragraph 12 of the New York Law CSA. Its terms of reference are instead specified in Paragraph 13(d). These are typically the Termination Events or Additional Termination Events which appear in the ISDA Master Agreement Schedule. If a Specified Condition applies to a party, that party cannot call for collateral, substitute it or receive Distributions or interest on collateral posted by it. There is also no reason why the parties could not agree to add additional Specified Conditions beyond those generally designated.

The idea behind this limitation is that the parties did not want to give the Secured Party (also a non-Affected Party) the right to liquidate collateral based only upon the occurrence of a Termination Event that was not listed as a Specified Condition. Assuming that the Affected Party was still solvent, it could make the early termination payment and then be entitled to the return of its Posted Collateral. In the event the Affected Party failed to make the early termination payment, the Secured Party would then have the right to give notice of a payment default under Section 5(a)(i), and then, after the cure period had expired, would declare an Event of Default. At that point, the non-Affected Party would have the right to liquidate the Posted Collateral and apply the proceeds against the early termination amount.

The rights and remedies under Paragraph 8(a) for the Secured Party are:

- any rights or remedies it has under applicable law, maximising the possibilities for action for the Secured Party;
- any rights and remedies under the terms of Other Posted Support such as a letter of credit or surety bond (relatively uncommon types of Eligible Collateral);
- the right to set off any amounts payable by the Pledgor under the ISDA Master Agreement against any Posted Collateral held by the Secured Party; and
- the right to liquidate Posted Collateral, for example through public or private sales or a sale to itself free from any claim from the Pledgor and without any claim unless required by law.

The proceeds of the liquidation of Posted Collateral will be applied by the Secured Party in any order it sees fit against the Pledgor's Obligations to it.

In the final paragraph it is acknowledged that time is of the essence in liquidating securities collateral and therefore the Pledgor is not entitled to notice of such a sale by the Secured Party unless the law requires this.

(b) ***Pledgor's Rights and Remedies.*** If at any time an Early Termination Date has occurred or been designated as the result of an Event of Default or Specified Condition with respect to the Secured Party, then (except in the case of an Early Termination Date relating to less than all Transactions (or Swap Transactions) where the Secured Party has paid in full all of its obligations that are then due under Section 6(e) of this Agreement):

(i) the Pledgor may exercise all rights and remedies available to a pledgor under applicable law with respect to Posted Collateral held by the Secured Party;

(ii) the Pledgor may exercise any other rights and remedies available to the Pledgor under the terms of Other Posted Support, if any;

(iii) the Secured Party will be obligated immediately to Transfer all Posted Collateral and the Interest Amount to the Pledgor; and

(iv) to the extent that Posted Collateral or the Interest Amount is not so Transferred pursuant to (iii) above, the Pledgor may:

(A) Set-off any amounts payable by the Pledgor with respect to any Obligations against any Posted Collateral or the Cash equivalent of any Posted Collateral held by the Secured Party (or any obligation of the Secured Party to Transfer that Posted Collateral); and

(B) to the extent that the Pledgor does not Set-off under (iv)(A) above, withhold payment of any remaining amounts payable by the Pledgor with respect to any Obligations, up to the Value of any remaining Posted Collateral held by the Secured Party, until that Posted Collateral is Transferred to the Pledgor.

Paragraph 8(b)

Paragraph 8(b) is important to the Pledgor who, although "out of the money" with respect to its Transactions with the Secured Party, may still be the Non-defaulting Party or non-Affected Party. In contrast with Paragraph 8(a), the Pledgor cannot exercise its rights and remedies until after an Early Termination Date has been designated upon the occurrence of an Event of Default or Specified Condition with respect to the Secured Party.

The idea behind this limitation is that the parties did not want to give a non-Affected Party the right to liquidate collateral based only upon the occurrence of an Early Termination Event that was not listed as a Specified Condition. Assuming that the Affected Party was still solvent, it could make the early termination payment and then be entitled to the return of its Posted Collateral. In the event the Affected Party failed to make the early termination payment, the non-Affected Party would then have the right to give notice of a payment default, and then, after the cure period had expired, would declare an Event of Default. At that point, the Non-Affected Party would have the right to liquidate the Posted Collateral and apply the proceeds against the Early Termination Amount.

The rights and remedies under Paragraph 8(b) for the Pledgor are:

- any rights or remedies it has under applicable law;
- any rights and remedies under the terms of Other Posted Support such as a letter of credit or surety bond (relatively uncommon types of Eligible Collateral);
- the right to the return of all Posted Collateral and interest on cash collateral from the Secured Party (this presupposes, of course, that the Pledgor would pay off its Obligations to the Secured Party before the Secured Party returned the Posted Collateral). This may be unrealistic to rely upon, however, if the Secured Party is in trouble financially;
- to the extent that the Posted Collateral is not returned, the right to set off any amounts payable by the Pledgor under the ISDA Master Agreement against any Posted Collateral held by the Secured Party; and
- to the extent that the Pledgor does not exercise its set off rights, the right to withhold residual early termination payments until the Posted Collateral is returned.

Because the Pledgor does not have a "lien" on the Posted Collateral that it has pledged to the Secured Party, the Pledgor would be only an unsecured creditor with respect to its right to the return of any Posted Collateral upon the insolvency of a Secured Party. It will generally be easier to exercise its set off rights rather than petition the bankruptcy court for the return of its Posted Collateral.

(c) ***Deficiencies and Excess Proceeds.*** The Secured Party will Transfer to the Pledgor any proceeds and Posted Credit Support remaining after liquidation, Set-off and/or application under Paragraphs 8(a) and 8(b) after satisfaction in full of all amounts payable by the Pledgor with respect to any Obligations; the Pledgor in all events will remain liable for any amounts remaining unpaid after any liquidation, Set-off and/or application under Paragraphs 8(a) and 8(b).

(d) ***Final Returns.*** When no amounts are or thereafter may become payable by the Pledgor with respect to any Obligations (except for any potential liability under Section 2(d) of this Agreement), the Secured Party will Transfer to the Pledgor all Posted Credit Support and the Interest Amount, if any.

Paragraph 8(c) and (d)

Paragraph 8(c) generally restates a Pledgor's rights under the UCC to any surplus Posted Credit Support after the Secured Party has received its full early termination payment. It also restates a Secured Party's right to further pursue the Pledgor for payment in the event that the Posted Collateral is insufficient to satisfy the Pledgor's Obligations to the Secured Party.

In Paragraph 8(d) the Pledgor is entitled to the return of any Posted Collateral and any interest payable on cash collateral upon the Pledgor's satisfaction of all of its payment obligations to the Secured Party. Any potential liability to withholding tax is ignored in these circumstances.

Paragraph 9. Representations

Each party represents to the other party (which representations will be deemed to be repeated as of each date on which it, as the Pledgor, Transfers Eligible Collateral) that:

(i) it has the power to grant a security interest in and lien on any Eligible Collateral it Transfers as the Pledgor and has taken all necessary actions to authorize the granting of that security interest and lien;

(ii) it is the sole owner of or otherwise has the right to Transfer all Eligible Collateral it Transfers to the Secured Party hereunder, free and clear of any security interest, lien, encumbrance or other restrictions other than the security interest and lien granted under Paragraph 2;

(iii) upon the Transfer of any Eligible Collateral to the Secured Party under the terms of this Annex, the Secured Party will have a valid and perfected first priority security interest therein (assuming that any central clearing corporation or any third-party financial intermediary or other entity not within the control of the Pledgor involved in the Transfer of that Eligible Collateral gives the notices and takes the action required of it under applicable law for perfection of that interest); and

(iv) the performance by it of its obligations under this Annex will not result in the creation of any security interest, lien or other encumbrance on any Posted Collateral other than the security interest and lien granted under Paragraph 2.

Paragraph 9. Representations

These representations serve the same purpose (and are deemed repeated each time Eligible Collateral is Transferred) as the representations made in Section 3 of the ISDA Master Agreement. A breach of any of the representations set forth in Paragraph 9 would constitute a misrepresentation and thus an Event of Default under Section 5(a)(iv) of the ISDA Master Agreement, permitting the Secured Party to terminate all Transactions under it. The Misrepresentation Event of Default found in Section 5(a)(iv) expressly includes any misrepresentation made in a Credit Support Document. These representations are relatively straightforward and are rarely, if ever, amended by the parties.

Paragraph 10. Expenses

(a) ***General.*** Except as otherwise provided in Paragraphs 10(b) and 10(c), each party will pay its own costs and expenses in connection with performing its obligations under this Annex and neither party will be liable for any costs and expenses incurred by the other party in connection herewith.

(b) ***Posted Credit Support.*** The Pledgor will promptly pay when due all taxes, assessments or charges of any nature that are imposed with respect to Posted Credit Support held by the Secured Party upon becoming aware of the same, regardless of whether any portion of that Posted Credit Support is subsequently disposed of under Paragraph 6(c), except for those taxes, assessments and charges that result from the exercise of the Secured Party's rights under Paragraph 6(c).

(c) ***Liquidation/Application of Posted Credit Support.*** All reasonable costs and expenses incurred by or on behalf of the Secured Party or the Pledgor in connection with the liquidation and/or application of any Posted Credit Support under Paragraph 8 will be payable, on demand and pursuant to the Expenses Section of this Agreement, by the Defaulting Party or, if there is no Defaulting Party, equally by the parties.

Paragraph 10. Expenses

Paragraph 10(a) is a simple statement that each party will pay its own expenses relating to its performance of its obligations under the New York Law CSA and will not be liable for any costs or expenses incurred by the other party.

Paragraph 10(b) clarifies that the Pledgor will be liable for taxes and other assessments with respect to the Posted Collateral, except for those taxes and assessments resulting from the Secured Party exercising its "use" rights under Paragraph 6(c).

When a Non-defaulting Party exercises its enforcement rights under Paragraph 8 all reasonable costs and expenses shall be borne by the Defaulting Party, or if there is none, by the parties equally.

Paragraph 11. Miscellaneous

(a) ***Default Interest.*** A Secured Party that fails to make, when due, any Transfer of Posted Collateral or the Interest Amount will be obligated to pay the Pledgor (to the extent permitted under applicable law) an amount equal to interest at the Default Rate multiplied by the Value of the items of property that were required to be Transferred, from (and including) the date that Posted Collateral or Interest Amount was required to be Transferred to (but excluding) the date of Transfer of that Posted Collateral or Interest Amount. This interest will be calculated on the basis of daily compounding and the actual number of days elapsed.

(b) ***Further Assurances.*** Promptly following a demand made by a party, the other party will execute, deliver, file and record any financing statement, specific assignment or other document and take any other action that may be necessary or desirable and reasonably requested by that party to create, preserve, perfect or validate any security interest or lien granted under Paragraph 2, to enable that party to exercise or enforce its rights under this Annex with respect to Posted Credit Support or an Interest Amount or to effect or document a release of a security interest on Posted Collateral or an Interest Amount.

(c) ***Further Protection.*** The Pledgor will promptly give notice to the Secured Party of, and defend against, any suit, action, proceeding or lien that involves Posted Credit Support Transferred by the Pledgor or that could adversely affect the security interest and lien granted by it under Paragraph 2, unless that suit, action, proceeding or lien results from the exercise of the Secured Party's rights under Paragraph 6(c).

(d) ***Good Faith and Commercially Reasonable Manner.*** Performance of all obligations under this Annex, including, but not limited to, all calculations, valuations and determinations made by either party, will be made in good faith and in a commercially reasonable manner.

(e) ***Demands and Notices.*** All demands and notices made by a party under this Annex will be made as specified in the Notices Section of this Agreement, except as otherwise provided in Paragraph 13.

(f) ***Specifications of Certain Matters.*** Anything referred to in this Annex as being specified in Paragraph 13 also may be specified in one or more Confirmations or other documents and this Annex will be construed accordingly.

Paragraph 11. Miscellaneous

Consistent with Section 2(e) of the ISDA Master Agreement, a Secured Party must pay interest at the Default Rate (i.e. 1% over the Pledgor's cost of funds) on the value of any Posted Collateral or Interest Amount on any cash collateral not transferred on the due date under the New York Law CSA. Paragraph 11 clarifies that the Default Interest accrued will be compounded daily from and including the due date to the day before the Transfer is actually made.

Paragraph 11(b) first obligates the Pledgor to co-operate with the Secured Party in the event that the Secured Party is having difficulty attaching, perfecting or enforcing its security interest in the Posted Collateral. The failure of the Pledgor to co-operate would constitute an Event of Default under Paragraph 7(iii).

Paragraph 11(b) then obligates the Secured Party to co-operate with the Pledgor in order to enable the Pledgor to obtain the release of a security interest in the Posted Collateral or an Interest Amount. The failure of the Pledgor to co-operate would also constitute an Event of Default under Paragraph 7(iii) because the New York Law CSA is a Credit Support Document for the Secured Party as well as for the Pledgor.

Paragraph 11(c) is helpful to the Secured Party in that it requires the Pledgor to defend any third party claims against the Posted Collateral. Again, failure to assist the Secured Party in such defence would constitute an Event of Default. However, there is no such obligation on the Pledgor where such legal action arises from the Secured Party's reuse of the Posted Collateral.

Paragraph 11(d) restates a party's obligations to act in good faith and in a commercially reasonable manner under the New York Law CSA.

Although Paragraph 11(e) is a mundane boilerplate provision, it is critical that a party understands how to make demands and give notice in order to ensure that it can exercise its rights and remedies under the New York Law CSA promptly. Parties should be sure to understand how to give notice properly in order to ensure that notice and cure periods are triggered promptly and effectively under this provision.

Paragraph 11(f) points out that the terms of the New York Law CSA can be amended through a Confirmation as well as through a formal amendment to the New York Law CSA itself.

Paragraph 12. Definitions
As used in this Annex:—

"Cash" means the lawful currency of the United States of America.

"Credit Support Amount" has the meaning specified in Paragraph 3.

"Custodian" has the meaning specified in Paragraphs 6(b)(i) and 13.

"Delivery Amount" has the meaning specified in Paragraph 3(a).

"Disputing Party" has the meaning specified in Paragraph 5.

"Distributions" means with respect to Posted Collateral other than Cash, all principal, interest and other payments and distributions of cash or other property with respect thereto, regardless of whether the Secured Party has disposed of that Posted Collateral under Paragraph 6(c). Distributions will not include any item of property acquired by the Secured Party upon any disposition or liquidation of Posted Collateral or, with respect to any Posted Collateral in the form of Cash, any distributions on that collateral, unless otherwise specified herein.

"Eligible Collateral" means, with respect to a party, the items, if any, specified as such for that party in Paragraph 13.

"Eligible Credit Support" means Eligible Collateral and Other Eligible Support.

Paragraph 12. Definitions

The following is a simplified glossary of all terms in the New York Law CSA.

GLOSSARY OF TERMS IN PARAGRAPH 12

Cash	Cash is always defined in the New York Law CSA to be US dollars.
Credit Support Amount	See annotation in Paragraph 3.
Custodian	See annotation in Paragraph 6(b).
Delivery Amount	See annotation in Paragraph 3.
Disputing Party	A party who disputes the other party's calculation of Transaction values in determining risk exposure and/or the value of any collateral held or to be returned.
Distributions	Distributions include any transfers of principal, interest or any other distributions made with respect to Posted Collateral except cash collateral.
Eligible Collateral	The types of collateral and their maturities that can be pledged by the Pledgor.
Eligible Credit Support	This includes Eligible Collateral and any other credit support designated by the parties such as letters of credit.

"Exposure" means for any Valuation Date or other date for which Exposure is calculated and subject to Paragraph 5 in the case of a dispute, the amount, if any, that would be payable to a party that is the Secured Party by the other party (expressed as a positive number) or by a party that is the Secured Party to the other party (expressed as a negative number) pursuant to Section 6(e)(ii)(2)(A) of this Agreement as if all Transactions (or Swap Transactions) were being terminated as of the relevant Valuation Time; *provided* that Market Quotation will be determined by the Valuation Agent using its estimates at mid-market of the amounts that would be paid for Replacement Transactions (as that term is defined in the definition of "Market Quotation").

"Independent Amount" means, with respect to a party, the amount specified as such for that party in Paragraph 13; if no amount is specified, zero.

"Interest Amount" means, with respect to an Interest Period, the aggregate sum of the amounts of interest calculated for each day in that Interest Period on the principal amount of Posted Collateral in the form of Cash held by the Secured Party on that day, determined by the Secured Party for each such day as follows:

(x) the amount of that Cash on that day; multiplied by

(y) the Interest Rate in effect for that day; divided by

(z) 360.

"Interest Period" means the period from (and including) the last Local Business Day on which an Interest Amount was Transferred (or, if no Interest Amount has yet been Transferred, the Local Business Day on which Posted Collateral in the form of Cash was Transferred to or received by the Secured Party) to (but excluding) the Local Business Day on which the current Interest Amount is to be Transferred.

"Interest Rate" means the rate specified in Paragraph 13.

Exposure	The estimated termination value of all Transactions so as to calculate risk exposure. The calculation is made as if the Transactions were being closed out as of the Valuation Time at mid-market values.
Independent Amount	A term meaning either initial margin taken at the start of a collateral relationship and not counted in risk exposure calculations or a sum taken later in the relationship and which is counted in the risk exposure calculations.
Interest Amount	The aggregate sum of interest due on Cash collateral. The interest accrued during the interest period is not compounded (unless provided for in an amendment in Paragraph 13).
Interest Period	The period from and including the date when interest was last paid on Cash collateral to but excluding the date on which it is next due to be paid.
Interest Rate	The particular benchmark interest rate (e.g. Federal Funds (Effective)). In agreements involving US parties, it is typically based on Federal Funds (Effective). It may also include a spread.

"Local Business Day", unless otherwise specified in Paragraph 13, has the meaning specified in the Definitions Section of this Agreement, except that references to a payment in clause (b) thereof will be deemed to include a Transfer under this Annex.

"Minimum Transfer Amount" means, with respect to a party, the amount specified as such for that party in Paragraph 13; if no amount is specified, zero.

"Notification Time" has the meaning specified in Paragraph 13.

"Obligations" means, with respect to a party, all present and future obligations of that party under this Agreement and any additional obligations specified for that party in Paragraph 13.

"Other Eligible Support" means, with respect to a party, the items, if any, specified as such for that party in Paragraph 13.

"Other Posted Support" means all Other Eligible Support Transferred to the Secured Party that remains in effect for the benefit of that Secured Party.

"Pledgor" means either party, when that party (i) receives a demand for or is required to Transfer Eligible Credit Support under Paragraph 3(a) or (ii) has Transferred Eligible Credit Support under Paragraph 3(a).

Local Business Day	A normal business day in the location required for the valuation of Transactions and collateral under the New York Law CSA and also a normal business day for the party receiving a Transfer of collateral.
Minimum Transfer Amount	The minimum amount that the Delivery Amount or Return Amount must reach prior to a party being obligated to return or deliver collateral.
Notification Time	The agreed deadline for making a collateral call in order to receive a Transfer by the deadline specified in the New York Law CSA.
Obligations	The present and future obligations of a party under the ISDA Master Agreement. Their scope may be expanded under Paragraph 13.
Other Eligible Support	This constitutes credit support that the parties may agree to such as letters of credit or surety bonds.
Other Posted Support	Other Eligible Support that is actually provided by the Pledgor to the Secured Party (i.e. the actual delivery of a letter of credit).
Pledgor	The party that receives a demand requiring it to post collateral or the party who currently has pledged collateral.

"Posted Collateral" means all Eligible Collateral, other property, Distributions, and all proceeds thereof that have been Transferred to or received by the Secured Party under this Annex and not Transferred to the Pledgor pursuant to Paragraph 3(b), 4(d)(ii) or 6(d)(i) or released by the Secured Party under Paragraph 8. Any Interest Amount or portion thereof not Transferred pursuant to Paragraph 6(d)(ii) will constitute Posted Collateral in the form of Cash.

"Posted Credit Support" means Posted Collateral and Other Posted Support.

"Recalculation Date" means the Valuation Date that gives rise to the dispute under Paragraph 5; *provided, however*, that if a subsequent Valuation Date occurs under Paragraph 3 prior to the resolution of the dispute, then the "Recalculation Date" means the most recent Valuation Date under Paragraph 3.

"Resolution Time" has the meaning specified in Paragraph 13.

"Return Amount" has the meaning specified in Paragraph 3(b).

"Secured Party" means either party, when that party (i) makes a demand for or is entitled to receive Eligible Credit Support under Paragraph 3(a) or (ii) holds or is deemed to hold Posted Credit Support.

"Specified Condition" means, with respect to a party, any event specified as such for that party in Paragraph 13.

"Substitute Credit Support" has the meaning specified in Paragraph 4(d)(i).

Posted Collateral	All collateral that has been pledged to, and is currently held by, the Secured Party.
Posted Credit Support	This includes Posted Collateral plus any Other Posted Support such as a letter of credit.
Recalculation Date	The Valuation Date that gave rise to the dispute.
Resolution Time	The deadline for resolving disputes i.e. one Local Business Day after the date on which the party receives a notice that it disputes.
Return Amount	See annotation under Paragraph 3.
Secured Party	The party making a demand to receive collateral or the party holding Posted Collateral.
Specified Condition	A Termination Event such as Illegality or Credit Event Upon Merger designated by the parties in Paragraph 13 as a Specified Condition.
Substitute Credit Support	Collateral transferred to the Secured Party in substitution for previously pledged collateral.

"Substitution Date" has the meaning specified in Paragraph 4(d)(ii).

"Threshold" means, with respect to a party, the amount specified as such for that party in Paragraph 13; if no amount is specified, zero.

"Transfer" means, with respect to any Eligible Credit Support, Posted Credit Support or Interest Amount, and in accordance with the instructions of the Secured Party, Pledgor or Custodian, as applicable:

(i) in the case of Cash, payment or delivery by wire transfer into one or more bank accounts specified by the recipient;

(ii) in the case of certificated securities that cannot be paid or delivered by book-entry, payment or delivery in appropriate physical form to the recipient or its account accompanied by any duly executed instruments of transfer, assignments in blank, transfer tax stamps and any other documents necessary to constitute a legally valid transfer to the recipient;

(iii) in the case of securities that can be paid or delivered by book-entry, the giving of written instructions to the relevant depository institution or other entity specified by the recipient, together with a written copy thereof to the recipient, sufficient if complied with to result in a legally effective transfer of the relevant interest to the recipient; and

(iv) in the case of Other Eligible Support or Other Posted Support, as specified in Paragraph 13.

"Valuation Agent" has the meaning specified in Paragraph 13.

"Valuation Date" means each date specified in or otherwise determined pursuant to Paragraph 13.

"Valuation Percentage" means, for any item of Eligible Collateral, the percentage specified in Paragraph 13.

Substitution Date	The date the Secured Party receives Substitute Credit Support.
Threshold	The unsecured risk exposure each party allows the other. Collateral may only be called or returned where the risk exposure exceeds the relevant party's Threshold and Minimum Transfer Amount.
Transfer	A Transfer occurs when collateral delivered to a Secured Party is deemed to be received by the Secured Party. For example, a Transfer of Cash occurs when the Cash is delivered to the Secured Party's bank account.
Valuation Agent	The Valuation Agent is the party calculating Exposure and the value of Posted Collateral. It is also the party that makes a request for collateral to be transferred.
Valuation Date	The Local Business Day upon which risk exposure calculations and collateral valuations are made (based upon those amounts as of the Valuation Time) to determine if a collateral delivery or return is needed.
Valuation Percentage	The remaining value of collateral expressed in percentage terms after the agreed haircut has been deducted.

"Valuation Time" has the meaning specified in Paragraph 13.

"Value" means for any Valuation Date or other date for which Value is calculated and subject to Paragraph 5 in the case of a dispute, with respect to:

(i) Eligible Collateral or Posted Collateral that is:

(A) Cash, the amount thereof; and

(B) a security, the bid price obtained by the Valuation Agent multiplied by the applicable Valuation Percentage, if any;

(ii) Posted Collateral that consists of items that are not specified as Eligible Collateral, zero; and

(iii) Other Eligible Support and Other Posted Support, as specified in Paragraph 13.

Valuation Time	The reference time at which calculations for collateral calls are made. They are often based on prices at the close of business on the Local Business Date before the Valuation Date.
Value	The agreed valuation bases for Cash and securities collateral in Paragraph 13(f).

Paragraph 13. Elections and Variables

This is the Elections and Variables paragraph where the parties provide information and make their elections, modifications and amendments to the standard form of the New York Law CSA. Paragraph 13 is the New York Law CSA equivalent of the ISDA Master Agreement Schedule.

For the purpose of illustrating market practice on various choices made in Paragraph 13, I have reviewed several dozen versions of Paragraph 13 to the New York Law CSA used by various dealers, sophisticated end users and hedge funds that I consider to be a reasonable cross-section of the documentation seen in the market.

Below is an example of Paragraph 13 that reflects market practice. In addition to annotating the provisions, this section also illustrates variations of them.

Many of the provisions set out in Chapter 5 with respect to Paragraph 11 of the English Law CSA may also be applicable to Paragraph 13 of the New York CSA. These provisions have not been repeated here. The author has flagged throughout the following discussion where the reader should also consult Paragraph 11 of the English Law CSA for other relevant provisions.

Paragraph 13. Elections and Variables

(a) ***Security Interest for "Obligations"***. The term ***"Obligations"*** as used in this Annex includes the following additional obligations:

With respect to Party A: ....

With respect to Party B: ....

(b) ***Credit Support Obligations.***

(i) ***Delivery Amount, Return Amount and Credit Support Amount.***

(A) ***"Delivery Amount"*** has the meaning specified in Paragraph 3(a), unless otherwise specified here: ....

(B) ***"Return Amount"*** has the meaning specified in Paragraph 3(b), unless otherwise specified here: ....

(C) ***"Credit Support Amount"*** has the meaning specified in Paragraph 3, unless otherwise specified here: ....

(ii) ***Eligible Collateral.*** The following items will qualify as ***"Eligible Collateral"*** for the party specified:

		Party A	Party B	Valuation Percentage
(A)	Cash	[ ]	[ ]	[ ]%
(B)	negotiable debt obligations issued by the U.S. Treasury Department having an original maturity at issuance of not more than one year ("Treasury Bills")	[ ]	[ ]	[ ]%
(C)	negotiable debt obligations issued by the U.S. Treasury Department having an original maturity at issuance of more than one year but not more than 10 years ("Treasury Notes")	[ ]	[ ]	[ ]%
(D)	negotiable debt obligations issued by the U.S. Treasury Department having an original maturity at issuance of more than 10 years ("Treasury Bonds")	[ ]	[ ]	[ ]%
(E)	other:	[ ]	[ ]	[ ]%

(iii) ***Other Eligible Support.*** The following items will qualify as ***"Other Eligible Support"*** for the party specified:

		Party A	Party B
(A)	....	[ ]	[ ]
(B)	....	[ ]	[ ]

(iv) ***Thresholds.***

(A) ***"Independent Amount"*** means with respect to Party A: $ ....
"Independent Amount" means with respect to Party B: $ ....

(B) ***"Threshold"*** means with respect to Party A: $ ....
"Threshold" means with respect to Party B: $ ....

(C) ***"Minimum Transfer Amount"*** means with respect to Party A: $ ....
"Minimum Transfer Amount" means with respect to Party B: $ ....

(D) **Rounding.** The Delivery Amount and the Return Amount will be rounded [down to the nearest integral multiple of $. . . ./up and down to the nearest integral multiple of $. . . ., respectively*].

(c) ***Valuation and Timing.***

(i) ***"Valuation Agent"*** means, for purposes of Paragraphs 3 and 5, the party making the demand under Paragraph 3, and, for purposes of Paragraph 6(d), the Secured Party receiving or deemed to receive the Distributions or the Interest Amount, as applicable, unless otherwise specified here: ....

(ii) ***"Valuation Date"*** means: ....

(iii) ***"Valuation Time"*** means:

[ ] the close of business in the city of the Valuation Agent on the Valuation Date or date of calculation, as applicable;

[ ] the close of business on the Local Business Day before the Valuation Date or date of calculation, as applicable;

provided that the calculations of Value and Exposure will be made as of approximately the same time on the same date.

(iv) ***"Notification Time"*** means 1:00 p.m., New York time, on a Local Business Day, unless otherwise specified here: ....

(d) ***Conditions Precedent and Secured Party's Rights and Remedies.*** The following Termination Event(s) will be a ***"Specified Condition"*** for the party specified (that party being the Affected Party if the Termination Event occurs with respect to that party):

	Party A	**Party B**
Illegality	[ ]	[ ]
Tax Event	[ ]	[ ]
Tax Event Upon Merger	[ ]	[ ]
Credit Event Upon Merger	[ ]	[ ]
Additional Termination Event(s):[1]		
....	[ ]	[ ]
....	[ ]	[ ]

* Delete as applicable.

[1] If the parties elect to designate an Additional Termination Event as a "Specified Condition", then they should only designate one or more Additional Termination Events that are designated as such in their Schedule.

(e) ***Substitution.***

(i) ***"Substitution Date"*** has the meaning specified in Paragraph 4(d)(ii), unless otherwise specified here: ....

(ii) ***Consent.*** If specified here as applicable, then the Pledgor must obtain the Secured Party's consent for any substitution pursuant to Paragraph 4(d): [applicable/inapplicable*][2]

(f) ***Dispute Resolution.***

(i) ***"Resolution Time"*** means 1:00 p.m., New York time, on the Local Business Day following the date on which the notice is given that gives rise to a dispute under Paragraph 5, unless otherwise specified here: ....

(ii) ***Value.*** For the purpose of Paragraphs 5(i)(C) and 5(ii), the Value of Posted Credit Support will be calculated as follows: ....

(iii) ***Alternative.*** The provisions of Paragraph 5 will apply, unless an alternative dispute resolution procedure is specified here: ....

(g) ***Holding and Using Posted Collateral.***

(i) ***Eligibility to Hold Posted Collateral; Custodians.*** Party A and its Custodian will be entitled to hold Posted Collateral pursuant to Paragraph 6(b); *provided* that the following conditions applicable to it are satisfied:

(1) Party A is not a Defaulting Party.

(2) Posted Collateral may be held only in the following jurisdictions: ....

(3) ....

Initially, the **Custodian** for Party A is ....

Party B and its Custodian will be entitled to hold Posted Collateral pursuant to Paragraph 6(b); *provided* that the following conditions applicable to it are satisfied:

(1) Party B is not a Defaulting Party.

(2) Posted Collateral may be held only in the following jurisdictions: ....

(3) ....

Initially, the **Custodian** for Party B is ....

(ii) ***Use of Posted Collateral.*** The provisions of Paragraph 6(c) will not apply to the [party/parties*] specified here:

[ ] Party A

[ ] Party B

and [that party/those parties*] will not be permitted to: ....

---

* Delete as applicable.

[2] Parties should consider selecting "applicable" where substitution without consent could give rise to a registration requirement to perfect properly the security interest in Posted Collateral (*e.g.*, where a party to the Annex is the New York branch of an English bank).

(h) ***Distributions and Interest Amount.***

(i) ***Interest Rate.*** The ***"Interest Rate"*** will be: ....

(ii) ***Transfer of Interest Amount.*** The Transfer of the Interest Amount will be made on the last Local Business Day of each calendar month and on any Local Business Day that Posted Collateral in the form of Cash is Transferred to the Pledgor pursuant to Paragraph 3 (b), unless otherwise specified here: ...

....

(iii) ***Alternative to Interest Amount.*** The provisions of Paragraph 6(d)(ii) will apply, unless otherwise specified here: ....

(i) ***Additional Representation(s).***

[Party A/Party B*] represents to the other party (which representation(s) will be deemed to be repeated as of each date on which it, as the Pledgor, Transfers Eligible Collateral) that:

(i) ....

(ii) ....

(j) ***Other Eligible Support and Other Posted Support.***

(i) ***"Value"*** with respect to Other Eligible Support and Other Posted Support means:..

(ii) ***"Transfer"*** with respect to Other Eligible Support and Other Posted Support means:..................................

(k) ***Demands and Notices.***

All demands, specifications and notices under this Annex will be made pursuant to the Notices Section of this Agreement, unless otherwise specified here:

Party A: ....

....

Party B: ....

....

(l) ***Addresses for Transfers.***

Party A: ....

....

Party B: ....

....

(m) ***Other Provisions.***

---

* Delete as applicable.

EXAMPLES OF PARAGRAPH 13 PROVISIONS

It is important to note that all calculations and amounts under the New York Law CSA are denominated in US dollars.

Obligations

(a) *Security Interest for "Obligations"*. The term "*Obligations*" as used in this Annex includes no additional obligations with respect to Party A and Party B.

Parties generally do not expand the definition of "Obligations." However, some dealers have begun to expand the definition to include other obligations of their counterparty that fall outside of the ISDA Master Agreement. Many dealers, for example, may also lend securities or enter into repurchase agreements with their counterparty. By expanding the definition of Obligations to include these other obligations, in the event that their counterparty defaults, collateral could be applied not only against the early termination amount payable by the counterparty under the ISDA Master Agreement but also against the other obligations of the counterparty to the dealer. The following is an example of this type of provision:

(a) *Security Interest for "Obligations*. The term "Obligations" as used in this Annex means, with respect to a party, all present and future obligations under this Agreement or any other contractual arrangement between the Pledgor and the Secured Party or the Pledgor and any Affiliate of the Secured Party.

Credit support obligations

(b) *Credit Support Obligations.*

(i) *Delivery Amount, Return Amount and Credit Support Amount.*

(A) "*Delivery Amount*" has the meaning specified in Paragraph 3(a).

Return Amount

(B) "*Return Amount*" has the meaning specified in Paragraph 3(b).

It is probably understood by the parties to the New York Law CSA that if the Credit Support Amount is zero, the Secured Party is obligated to return any Posted Collateral. Some Pledgors worry, however, that if the

Return Amount is less than the Pledgor's Minimum Transfer Amount, that a Secured Party will not be obligated to return the remaining Posted Collateral. The following provision expressly eliminates that concern:

(B) "*Return Amount*" has the meaning specified in Paragraph 3(b), except that such definition is hereby amended by adding in the fifth line thereof after the words "(rounded pursuant to paragraph 13)" the words "; *provided* that if the Credit Support Amount is zero the Secured Party will, upon the Pledgor's request, Transfer to the Pledgor all Posted Collateral".

Credit Support Amount

(C) "*Credit Support Amount*" has the meaning specified in Paragraph 3.

Similar to the changes suggested for the English Law CSA in Chapter 5 at pages 169–70, when dealing with hedge funds and other entities that are required to post Independent Amounts, the parties may want to amend the definition of Credit Support Amount and also add the "offset" provision in order to ensure that a Secured Party is always holding Posted Collateral equal to the Pledgor's Independent Amount regardless of its risk exposure on the Pledgor.

Eligible Collateral

(ii) *Eligible Collateral.* The following items will qualify as "*Eligible Collateral*" for the party specified, provided that the Secured Party shall be entitled at any time, and from time to time, not to accept as Eligible Collateral any of the following which constitute Ineligible Securities as defined below:

		Party A	Party B	Valuation percentage
(A)	*Cash*: US Dollars in depositary account form. {Note: a recent trend is that some dealers will only accept Cash as Posted Collateral}	YES	YES	100%

(B)	*Treasury Bills*: negotiable debt obligations issued by the US Treasury Department having a remaining maturity of not more than one year.	YES	YES	{99–98%}
(C)	*Treasury Notes*: negotiable debt obligations issued by the US Treasury Department having a remaining maturity of more than one year but not more than 10 years.	YES	YES	{98%–95%}
(D)	*Treasury Bonds*: negotiable debt obligations issued by the US Treasury Department having a remaining maturity of more than 10 years but not more than 30 years. {Note: for US Treasury securities, the above Valuation Percentages will fluctuate depending upon the institution.}	YES	YES	{94–90%}

The above definition for Eligible Collateral is very common for US counterparties. Although some counterparties look to the "original" versus "remaining" maturity for applying the Valuation Percentage, "remaining" maturity would appear to be more useful given that the remaining maturity is typically what will determine the volatility in the value of the US Treasury security.

(E)	*Agency Securities*: negotiable debt obligations of the Federal National Mortgage Association (FNMA), Federal Home Loan Mortgage Corporation (FHLMC), Federal Home Loan Banks (FHLB), Federal Farm Credit Banks (FFCB), Tennessee Valley Authority (TVA) having a remaining maturity of not more than 30 years. [Note: for US Agency debt securities, the above Valuation Percentages will fluctuate depending upon the institution. Some institutions may break down the maturities similar to what was done above for US Treasuries above.]	YES	YES	[97–92%]

Given their AAA ratings, these types of agency securities are still considered to be high quality collateral in spite of the crisis.

Parties often request that they can pledge additional types of collateral other than US Treasuries and cash. The most common of these have been debt securities of entities that are commonly referred to as "quasi-government" agencies or "government sponsored enterprises". The above provision lists the most common quasi-government agency securities that are requested for inclusion in the definition of Eligible Collateral. This list of possibilities, however, is often limited to the debt securities of the Federal National Mortgage Association and the Federal Home Loan Mortgage Corporation. These two agencies are most typically referred to as Fannie Mae and Freddie Mac, respectively.

Although the debt securities of quasi-government agencies do not have an express US government guarantee, quasi-government agencies are considered to be extremely creditworthy by the credit rating agencies and carry very high credit ratings. These agencies continue to have high credit ratings, primarily due to the US government's direct intervention through providing additional capital in the credit crunch. In agreeing to accept these securities, however, parties should be careful only to accept plain vanilla debt obligations and avoid debt securities that are principal or interest only, puttable or what are commonly referred to as "structured notes". The definition below of Ineligible Securities should cover any securities that would be inappropriate for a Secured Party to accept as collateral.

In addition to the debt obligations of quasi-government agency securities, US counterparties often request that mortgage-backed securities ("MBS") be added to the list of Eligible Collateral. Since the beginning of the financial crisis in 2007, however, many dealers now refuse to accept MBS. If they do agree to accept MBS, US counterparties will only agree to include as eligible collateral plain vanilla MBS certificates issued by FNMA, FHLMC and GNMA.

(F)	*FHLMC Certificates*. **Mortgage participation certificates issued by FHLMC evidencing undivided interests or participations in pools of first lien conventional or FHA/VA residential mortgages or deeds of trust, guaranteed by FHLMC, and having a remaining maturity of not more than 30 years.**	**YES**	**YES**	[94–92%]
(G)	*FNMA Certificates*. **Mortgage-backed pass-through certificates issued by FNMA evidencing undivided interests in pools of first lien mortgages or deeds of trust on residential properties, guaranteed by FNMA, and having a remaining maturity of not more than 30 years.**	**YES**	**YES**	[94–92%]

(H)	*GNMA Certificates*. Mortgage-backed pass-through certificates issued by private entities, evidencing undivided interests in pools of first lien mortgages or deeds of trust on single family residences, guaranteed by the Government National Mortgage Association (GNMA) with the full faith and credit of the United States, and having a remaining maturity of not more than 30 years.	YES	YES	[94–92%]

[Note: for US MBS securities, the above Valuation Percentages will fluctuate depending upon the institution.]

In addition, parties typically do not permit a party to pledge MBS collateral that constitutes an interest-only or principal only MBS, a real estate mortgage investment conduit or collateralised mortgage obligations. Structured notes and other similar securities are also usually not accepted. The following is an example of "ineligible securities" that a party would not be able to pledge:

> "*Ineligible Securities*" means any obligations, securities, certificates or instruments that (i) are denominated in a currency other than US Dollars, (ii) are issued other than in Federal Reserve book entry form, or (iii) constitute or include structured notes or other structured debt instruments, real estate mortgage investment conduits, collateralized mortgage obligations, guaranteed mortgage certificates, interest-only securities, principal-only securities or any securities representing interests in, or are composed in whole or in part of, residual or high risk mortgage derivatives or other derivatives.

A few parties use defined terms taken from the *ISDA Collateral Asset Definitions* developed originally in June 2003 (the definitions have not been updated since that time). The *Collateral Asset Definitions* are available on the ISDA website in the Bookstore section.

The definitions were drafted directly to reference statutory, regulatory and other primary sources of information that help identify the collateral in question. The idea is that, similar to what is done in Confirmations, the *Collateral Asset Definitions* would provide concise definitions that accurately describe the collateral in question. For example, rather than just referring to US Treasury Bills, Paragraph 13 would only list US-TBILL. Under the *Collateral Asset Definitions*, a US-TBILL is defined as the following:

Negotiable debt obligations issued pursuant to USC Title 31, Chapter 31, Section 3104 by the Department of the Treasury backed by the credit of the United States of America, having a maturity at issuance of no greater than 1 year.

Although this appears to be a potentially useful and efficient way to refer to Eligible Collateral, using the ISDA Collateral Asset Definitions has not become market standard.

Finally you occasionally see general wording for other "Other Eligible Support". It is highly unusual, however, that Other Eligible Support (such as a letter of credit or a surety bond) would ever actually be used.

Such other Eligible Credit Support as the parties may from time to time agree in writing as being acceptable.	**To be agreed by the parties on a case by case basis.**

In a bilateral New York Law CSA both boxes (for Party A and Party B) would be checked and the appropriate Valuation Percentage, determined by the credit function, entered alongside.

No haircut is normally applied to Cash and so its Valuation Percentage is usually 100%.

The Valuation Percentages for US Treasury securities and US Agency securities are the current market standards (June 2011).

The normal Valuation Percentages for guaranteed US agencies is generally between 90% and 95%. The normal Valuation Percentages for plain vanilla MBS collateral issued by FNMA, FHLMC and GNMA are also generally between 90% and 95%. It is important to remember that the haircut is applied against the fair market value of the Posted Collateral, which is generally already at a discount from the face amount of the Posted Collateral.

Sometimes at the end of the Eligible Credit Support table the following wording will be added:

Notwithstanding the foregoing, the Valuation Percentage with respect to all Eligible Credit Support shall be deemed to be 100% with respect to a Valuation Date which is an Early Termination Date designated or deemed to have occurred as a result of an Event of Default.

The purpose of this is to limit the recovery of a Non-defaulting Party to 100% of what he is owed and to value the collateral at its full market value. Haircuts are ignored in a termination situation. Variations of this wording may be found on pages 237–8.

Thresholds, Independent Amounts and Minimum Transfer Amounts

Independent amount

(A) "*Independent Amount*" means with respect to Party A:

....

"*Independent Amount*" means with respect to Party B:

....

As discussed earlier, less creditworthy parties are often required to post Independent Amounts before any trading takes place. In this case it is excluded from the Exposure calculations upon which any collateral call is based. Alternatively it can be a sum that is callable after trading has occurred and may affect either party, possibly as a result of a credit ratings downgrade. This type of Independent Amount will be included in the calculation of Exposure for collateral call purposes.

An Independent Amount may be a fixed monetary sum or a percentage of the notional amount of an individual Transaction or Transactions. This is usually graduated according to the maturity of the individual Transaction. Moreover, Independent Amounts are typically lower for Transactions involving fixed income derivatives than those for equity or credit derivatives.

The discussion and examples of Independent Amount found in Chapter 5 are equally relevant to negotiations involving the New York Law CSA (see pages 185–9).

Threshold

(B) "*Threshold*" means with respect to Party A: ....

"*Threshold*" means with respect to Party B: ....

The Threshold is the level of unsecured exposure each party is content to allow the other before any collateral is called. This unsecured exposure will be increased by any Minimum Transfer Amount applying to the parties.

Generally speaking Thresholds are recorded either as a monetary amount (or zero) or in the form of a credit ratings matrix. An example of the first is:

(B) "*Threshold*" means with respect to Party A: USD 10,000,000

"*Threshold*" means with respect to Party B: USD 5,000,000

An example of the second kind is:

(B) "*Threshold*" means the amounts determined on the basis of the lower ratings assigned by either Standard & Poor's Ratings Group ("S&P"), a division of McGraw-Hill Inc. or Moody's Investor Services, Inc. ("Moody's") to the long term, unsecured and unsubordinated

debt of Party B; provided that if (x) Party B has no such ratings or (y) an Event of Default has occurred and is continuing, the Threshold with respect to the relevant party shall be zero:

S&P Rating	Moody's Rating	Threshold (USD million)
AAA	Aaa	
AA+	Aa1	
AA	Aa2	
AA–	Aa3	
A+	A1	
A	A2	
A–	A3	
BBB+	Baa1	
BBB	Baa2	
BBB–	Baa3	
BB+	Ba1	
BB	Ba2	
BB– and below	Ba3 and below	

Again the credit function would supply the necessary figures. Many US dealers will require that the Threshold be zero below A– by S&P or below A3 by Moody's and almost all US dealers will require the Threshold to be zero below BBB– by S&P or below Baa3 by Moody's. Anything below BBB– by S&P or Baa3 by Moody's is generally not considered to be investment grade.

As shown in the example provision above, a common amendment is to include a zero Threshold if a party suffers an Event of Default or if a party is no longer rated by any credit rating agencies.

Although there are other credit rating agencies in the United States such as Duff & Phelps Credit Rating Agency, Fitch Ratings and A.M. Best, parties typically only reference S&P and Moody's. There may be situations, however, when a company may only be rated by one of the other credit rating agencies. A typical definition of a credit rating is as follows:

"*Rating*" means the rating issued by either Moody's Investor Services (Moody's) or Standard and Poor's Rating Group, a division of McGraw-Hill, Inc. (S&P) in respect of either party's long term, unsecured and unsubordinated debt securities.

From previous discussion (see page 193) you will recall that the CSA can be made unilateral by assigning a Threshold of Infinity to one of the parties.

Where the credit quality differential between the parties is broad, this can look quite stark:

(B) "*Threshold*" means with respect to Party A: Infinity

"*Threshold*" means with respect to Party B: Zero

You will also recall (see page 193) that a zero Threshold is not only used where a counterparty is considered to be a weak credit but also to maximise regulatory capital savings for a bank because collateral is callable all the sooner where there is a zero Threshold.

Typically, Thresholds appear to be larger in the United States than in Europe.

If a Threshold is not specified it is deemed to be zero.

Minimum Transfer Amount

(C) "*Minimum Transfer Amount*" means with respect to Party A: ....

"*Minimum Transfer Amount*" means with respect to Party B: ....

Minimum Transfer Amounts are designed to prevent costly transfers of low or "nuisance" amounts of collateral. Before a Delivery or Return Amount is required to be made under Paragraph 3, the amount must exceed the Minimum Transfer Amount.

Occasionally you see a Minimum Transfer Amount of zero which if combined with a zero Threshold means that you do not wish to take any unsecured risk on your counterparty.

Normally the Minimum Transfer Amount is expressed in a fixed monetary sum (e.g. US$250,000) or linked to a credit ratings matrix as in the following example:

(C) "*Minimum Transfer Amount*" means with respect to Party A and Party B, the amount determined on the basis of the lower of the Long Term Debt Ratings in the table set forth below; provided however that if (i) a party has no Long Term Debt Ratings or (ii) an Event of Default has occurred and is continuing with respect to such party, such party's Minimum Transfer Amount shall be zero.

S&P Rating	Moody's Rating	Minimum Transfer Amount
AAA to A–	Aaa to A3	US$
BBB+ to BB	Baa1 to Ba2	US$
BB– and below	Ba3 and below	US$

Minimum Transfer Amounts tend to be larger in the US than in Europe. Many dealers will permit relatively large Minimum Transfer Amounts for parties that are rated AA– by S&P or Aa3 or above by Moody's. These amounts can range from US$100,000 to several million dollars. Because the Minimum Transfer Amount has the indirect effect of extending additional unsecured credit to a Pledgor, the credit department will generally provide these numbers. Many US dealers will require that the Minimum Transfer Amount be zero below A– by S&P or A3 by Moody's and almost all US dealers will require the Minimum Transfer Amount to be zero below BBB– by S&P or Baa3 by Moody's.

As shown in the example above, a common amendment is to include a zero Minimum Transfer Amount if a party suffers an Event of Default. In addition, if a party is no longer rated by any credit rating agencies, the Minimum Transfer Amount will also go to zero.

The variations further discussed in Chapter 5 regarding Minimum Transfer Amounts are equally applicable to the New York Law CSA (see pages 195–7).

A completely different approach (although currently relatively uncommon) towards permitting an unsecured amount of credit involves setting the Threshold for both parties at zero and providing the unsecured amount as part of the Minimum Transfer Amount. Under this approach, a party is provided an unsecured amount of credit until the Minimum Transfer Amount is exceeded. At this point, the Pledgor is then required to secure the entire Credit Support Amount since the Threshold is zero. The amounts set out for the Minimum Transfer Amount provisions typically parallel the amounts set out for the Threshold provisions in more traditional provisions. The following is a typical provision:

> (C) "*Minimum Transfer Amount*" for purposes of computing a Delivery Amount pursuant to Paragraph 3(a), as of any date shall be as set forth in Schedule II hereto under the caption "Minimum Transfer Amount" and shall be, with respect to Party A, the amount set forth opposite the rating classification assigned to any long-term unsecured, unsubordinated debt securities of Party A, and, with respect to Party B, shall be the amount set forth opposite the rating classification assigned to any long-term unsecured unsubordinated debt securities of Party B by the Relevant Rating Agency. If at any time all outstanding long-term unsecured unsubordinated debt securities of Party A or Party B shall not be rated by either of the Relevant Rating Agencies, the Minimum Transfer Amount for such party shall be zero. In the event of a split rating classification by the Relevant Rating Agencies the Minimum Transfer Amount shall be the rating classification opposite the lower of the ratings in Schedule II hereto. "Relevant Rating Agency" for purposes hereof means Moody's Investors Service, Inc. ("Moody's") and Standard & Poor's Ratings Group, a division of McGraw Hill, Inc. ("S&P"). The Minimum Transfer Amount for purposes of computing a Return Amount pursuant to Paragraph 3(b) shall be US$500,000. If an Event of Default occurs and is continuing with respect to a party as Pledgor, its Minimum Transfer Amount shall be zero.

Schedule II in this provision would resemble the Threshold Schedule based on credit ratings that is shown above. One difficulty with this approach is that if the Minimum Transfer Amount is the same for both the Delivery Amount and the Return Amount; if the Minimum Transfer Amount is large, such as US$10,000,000, the Secured Party may end up being overcollateralised in the event that the Credit Support Amount were to decrease. This is because the Credit Support Amount would have to decrease by US$10,000,000 before the Secured Party was required to return Posted Collateral. In this example, the parties have resolved this concern by agreeing that the Minimum Transfer Amount for the purposes of a Return Amount is only US$500,000, a number which is probably much lower than the amounts found in Schedule II.

Because the Minimum Transfer Amount only establishes a floor for transfers it does not avoid transfers of uneven amounts of collateral. Applying a rounding convention overcomes this.

Rounding

> **(D) "*Rounding*". The Delivery Amount will be rounded up and the Return Amount will be rounded {down to the nearest integral multiple of ..../up and down to the nearest integral multiple of .... respectively}.**

One of the following options is usually selected:

- **round the Delivery and Return Amount down to the nearest integral multiple specified; or**
- **round the Delivery Amount up and the Return Amount down to the nearest integral multiple specified. (This is the more common choice.)**

If no rounding convention is specified, then the Delivery Amount and the Return Amount will not be rounded.

You would not normally specify that both Delivery and Return Amounts are to be rounded up as this could leave a Transferee undercollateralised after transferring a Return Amount.

A typical example of a rounding provision is:

> **(D) *Rounding*. The Delivery Amount and the Return Amount will be rounded up and down respectively to the nearest integral multiple of US$10,000.**

Although a rounding amount of US$10,000 is most common, rounding amounts of US$100,000 or even US$250,000 are seen in the market.

Valuation Agent

(c) *Valuation and Timing.*

(i) "*Valuation Agent*" means: for purposes of Paragraphs 3 and 5, the party making the demand under Paragraph 3; for purposes of paragraph 4(d)(ii), the Secured Party receiving the Substitute Credit Support; and, for purposes of Paragraph 6(d), the Secured Party receiving or deemed to receive the Distributions or the Interest Amount, as applicable;

The Valuation Agent calculates the Delivery Amount and the Return Amount and reports these calculations to the Pledgor and Secured Party so than they can fulfil their obligations under Paragraphs 3, 4, 5 and 6 of the New York Law CSA.

As described in the clause above, the party calling for the collateral (the Secured Party) under Paragraph 3(a) is the Valuation Agent. The Secured Party is also the Valuation Agent for transferring Distributions or Interest Amounts under Paragraph 6(d). The Pledgor would be the Valuation Agent if it were calling for a Return Amount under Paragraph 3(b). The standard wording is most commonly used.

In negotiations between US parties, it is relatively uncommon that a third party would ever be appointed as Valuation Agent. Although a less sophisticated end user would probably be more comfortable with a third party acting as Valuation Agent, dealers have been reluctant to permit such a provision probably due to the fees a Valuation Agent would charge and probable operational and back office headaches that would occur when involving a third party.

At times, one party will request that the other party act as the Valuation Agent for purposes of calculating Exposure and the Value of Posted Collateral. This situation would occur if one party did not have the ability or sophistication to make the necessary calculations itself. Many US dealers resist acting as Valuation Agent out of concern that they may be viewed as a fiduciary of the other party. They also are concerned about being liable for errors in making the required calculations. As a courtesy, a dealer will also often agree either formally or informally to provide the other party with the calculation of Exposure on a daily basis.

The variations further discussed in Chapter 5 regarding Valuation Agents are equally applicable to the New York Law CSA (see pages 201–3).

Valuation Date

(ii) "*Valuation Date*" means:..

This item must be completed as there is no ISDA fallback position here.

Valuation Date states the frequency at which Exposure is calculated and collateral is revalued under the ISDA Master Agreement and the New York Law CSA. On each Valuation Date the Valuation Agent must calculate the following and advise the other party/parties of:

- the Exposure,
- the Value of the Pledgor's Posted Collateral (if any),
- the Credit Support Amount,
- the Delivery Amount (if any); and
- the Return Amount (if any),

all as of the Valuation Time (see below).

A number of frequencies are, of course, possible (e.g. daily, weekly, monthly or on a particular day of each week or month).

The most common is:

(ii) "*Valuation Date*" means any Local Business Day.

This allows for daily exposure and collateral valuation. Most US dealers will calculate the Exposure and the Value of Posted Collateral each morning based on the close of business values on the previous day. Defining the Valuation Date to be any Local Business Day provides a dealer with the maximum amount of flexibility to call for a Delivery Amount.

The variations on the definition of Valuation Date set forth in Chapter 5 are equally applicable to the New York Law CSA (see pages 205–7).

As described in Chapter 5, some parties may also request that a particular day also be expressly designated as a Valuation Date. This is particularly important for parties that are not operationally set up to do the necessary calculations and valuations, and are dependent upon the other party to make certain calculations. These parties may need these calculations to close their books on a monthly basis, for example.

Valuation Time

(iii) "*Valuation Time*" means:

[ ] the close of business in the place of location of the Valuation Agent on the Valuation Date or date of calculation, as applicable;

[ ] the close of business on the Local Business Day immediately preceding the Valuation Date or date of calculation, as applicable;

provided that the calculations of Value and Exposure will, as far as practicable, be made as of approximately the same time on the same date.

The Valuation Time is the time at which the Valuation Agent calculates Exposure and the value of collateral held to determine if a Delivery Amount or Return Amount call is needed. The Valuation Agent will also factor in any Distributions or Interest Amounts due to the Transferor at the Valuation Time.

The parties have two main choices, viz:

- **as at the close of business on the Valuation Date or the date of calculation for Paragraph 6(d) payments to the Pledgor; or**
- **as at the close of business on the Local Business Day immediately before the Valuation Date or the date of calculation for Paragraph 6(d) payments to the Pledgor.**

They can, of course, choose another means for deciding the Valuation Time by amending this sub-paragraph.

Once they have made their choice, the New York Law CSA stipulates that the calculation of risk exposure and collateral values has to be made as of approximately at the same time on the selected date.

A Valuation Time as at the close of business on the Local Business Day immediately preceding the Valuation Date is the most common choice because collateral management units are then working from reports of exposure and collateral values at the close of that previous business day.

Notification Time

(iv) "*Notification Time*" means 1:00 p.m., New York time, on a Local Business Day, unless otherwise specified here:

..

This is the time by which, among other things, (1) the Valuation Agent must notify the parties of its calculations under Paragraph 4(b) on the Local Business Day following a Valuation Date and (2) a party must make a demand for a transfer of collateral so that the other party makes the appropriate transfer not later than the close of business on the next Local Business Day. If a demand for a transfer is made after the Notification Time then the transfer does not have to be made until the close of business on the second Local Business Day following the day on which the demand was made. Such transfers will be made if there is no dispute and no condition precedent being unfulfilled in Section 2(a)(iii) of the ISDA Master Agreement.

The Notification Time is specified to mean 1.00 p.m. New York time on the appropriate Local Business Day unless the parties agree otherwise. Sometimes parties arrange for the Notification Time for the Valuation Agent's Exposure calculations to be earlier than the Notification Time for collateral calls (at least where a third party acts as the Valuation Agent). In these circumstances, a party receiving notice of the Valuation Agent's calculations will be able to make a collateral call on the same day for a transfer to be made on the next Local Business Day.

Typically a Notification Time would not be later than 3.00 p.m. New York Time in order to give the parties sufficient time to meet their collateral transfer deadlines.

Many dealers and sophisticated parties prefer to amend the transfer provisions and require collateral to be transferred on the same Local Business Day. This minimises the time during which a Secured Party would be unsecured and would also speed up the return of collateral to a Pledgor. In these situations, the Notification Time would be much earlier in the day. Same day transfer of collateral also puts a burden on parties to make the demand for collateral earlier in the day. It also places stress on operations to make collateral transfers on the same day.

The following is language that would be used to require same day transfers of collateral

> **_Transfer Timing._ Paragraph 4(b) is amended by (A) deleting the word "next" in the third line thereof and replacing it with the word "same"; and (B) deleting the words "second Local Business Day hereafter" in the fifth line thereof and replacing them with the words "next Local Business Day".**

This next provision adjusts the time for transfers of collateral in order to deal with a party's operational needs:

> _Transfer Timing._ Subject to Paragraphs 4(a) and 5 and unless otherwise specified, (i) if a demand for Transfer of Eligible Credit Support or Posted Credit Support is made by the Notification Time, then the Transfer of Eligible Credit Support or Posted Credit Support will be completed prior to 6:00 p.m., New York time, on the Local Business Day following the Local Business Day on which the demand is made, (ii) if a demand for Transfer of Eligible Credit Support or Posted Credit Support is made by the Notification Time with respect to a foreign currency exchange Transaction, such Transfer shall be completed prior to 6:00 p.m., New York time, on the third (3rd) Local Business Day following the Local Business Day on which the demand is made and (iii) if a demand for Transfer of Eligible Credit Support or Posted Credit Support is made subsequent to the Notification Time, then the relevant Transfer will be made in accordance with the rules provided in the immediately preceding subparagraphs (i) and (ii), except that the demand will be treated as if made on the Local Business Day following the day the demand was actually made.

This provision makes timing adjustments with respect to the transfer of Distributions to the Pledgor:

(iii) *Certain Distributions Received.* If a Secured Party receives or is deemed to receive Distributions on a day that is not a Local Business Day, or after its close of business on a Local Business Day, it will Transfer the Distributions to the Pledgor on the following Local Business Day, subject to Paragraph 4(a), but only to the extent contemplated in Paragraph 6(d)(i) in connection with Distributions received or deemed received on a Local Business Day.

The following is an example of language requiring Posted Collateral in the form of Cash to be transferred on the same day:

(iv) *Notification Time*" means 9:00am New York time on the Valuation Date provided, however, that, notwithstanding Paragraph 3(a), (x) with regard to Transfers of Eligible Credit Support in the form of USD cash, if a request for delivery or return is made by the Notification Time, then the relevant Transfer shall be made not later than the close of business on the day on which such a request is received, or if such day is not a Local Business Day or if such request is made after the Notification Time, not later than the close of business on the next Local Business Day and (y) with regard to Transfers of other forms of Eligible Credit Support or posted credit support, the relevant Transfer shall be made in accordance with Paragraph 3(a).

Specified Conditions

(d) *Conditions Precedent and Secured Party's Rights and Remedies.* The following Termination Event(s) will be a "*Specified Condition*" for the party specified (that party being the Affected Party if the Termination Event occurs with respect to that party):

	Party A	Party B
Illegality	[X]	[X]
Tax Event	[ ]	[ ]
Tax Event Upon Merger	[ ]	[ ]
Credit Event Upon Merger	[X]	[X]
Additional Termination Event(s): . . .	[ ]	[ ]

By designating a Specified Condition, the parties agree that when it occurs:

- if the Affected Party (i.e. the condition has occurred to that party) is the Pledgor, the Secured Party's obligations to transfer collateral and interest payments to the Pledgor under Paragraphs 3, 4(d)(ii) and 6(d) are suspended;

- **if the Affected Party is the Secured Party, the Pledgor's obligation to transfer collateral under Paragraphs 3 and 5 is suspended;**
- **if the Affected Party is the Pledgor, the Secured Party may exercise its rights and remedies under Paragraph 8(a).**

The most common designated Specified Conditions are Illegality and Credit Event Upon Merger. Many parties are concerned about pledging collateral to a party that is affected by an Illegality through fears that the Pledgor may not be able to return the collateral pledged to it because of the Illegality.

Parties also do not want to pledge collateral to a party whose creditworthiness has become materially weaker due to a merger. They would be concerned that their counterparty might become insolvent because of the merger with the result that any pledged collateral might be trapped in an insolvency proceeding. Many parties also view the occurrence of a Credit Event Upon Merger as the fault of the Affected Party and think it should be treated in a similar way to an Event of Default for the purposes of the New York Law CSA.

Some dealers (a minority) are reluctant, however, to agree to the designation of Specified Conditions (other than Illegality). The dealer is concerned about a scenario where a Specified Condition has occurred with respect to it while it is also the Secured Party. If the dealer is exposed to the counterparty (i.e. the dealer is "in the money"), the dealer does not want the Pledgor's obligation to pledge collateral to be suspended because of the occurrence of the Specified Condition. The dealer is more concerned about the credit risk of its counterparty than the risk of having to pledge collateral to a counterparty that is subject to a Specified Condition.

If a dealer does agree to designate Illegality as a Specified Condition, one way to minimise the time during which it might be exposed is to limit the lengthy cure periods that apply to Illegality under the 1992 ISDA Master Agreement. The following is a provision that limits the lengthy cure periods with respect to an Illegality that is also a Specified Condition:

(d) *Conditions Precedent and Secured Party's Rights and Remedies.* The following Termination Event(s) will be a "*Specified Condition*" for the party specified (that party being the Affected Party if the Termination Event occurs with respect to that party):

	Party A	Party B
Illegality	YES	YES

provided that if the Affected Party would be entitled to receive Eligible Credit Support or Posted Credit Support but for that Specified Condition, then notwithstanding Sections 6(b)(ii) and (iii) of this Agreement, the Affected Party may designate an Early Termination Date in respect of all Affected Transactions pursuant to Section 6(b)(iv) as the result of any such Termination Event(s) regardless of whether the condition set forth in Section 6(b)(iv)(1) has been satisfied.

Substitution

(e) *Substitution.*

(i) "*Substitution Date*" has the meaning specified in Paragraph 4(d)(ii).

(ii) *Consent.* The Pledgor is not required to obtain the Secured Party's consent for any substitution.

The ability to substitute is an important right for Pledgors. Often a Pledgor requires the return of a particular security for business reasons that was previously pledged to the Secured Party. For example, the security may be collateral that the Pledgor had repledged to the Secured Party. The Pledgor may then need to return that same security to its original pledgor. Please see the discussion regarding rehypothecation in Chapter 3, page 66.

Many Secured Parties insist that they have the right to consent to a substitution. Even though the Secured Party will be receiving Substitute Credit Support, the substitution process is time consuming and uses up the limited back office resources of the Secured Party. By having the right to consent, a Secured Party hopes to limit the number of substitutions that it will be required to perform by the Pledgor. A possible compromise could be to require consent, but to provide that such consent shall be not unreasonably withheld:

(ii) *Consent.* The Pledgor is required to obtain the Secured Party's consent for any substitution pursuant to Paragraph 4(d), provided however, that such consent shall not be unreasonably withheld.

Resolution Time

(f) *Dispute Resolution.*

"*Resolution Time*" means 1:00 p.m., New York time, on the Local Business Day following the date on which the notice is given that gives rise to a dispute under Paragraph 5.

The Resolution Time is the deadline for the parties to resolve their dispute under Paragraph 5. If they fail the Valuation Agent makes certain recalculations under Paragraph 5(i).

The fallback dispute Resolution Time is 1:00 p.m. New York time on the Local Business Day after the date notice is given that gives rise to a dispute under Paragraph 5, although this wording is sometimes changed to "the date on which notice of dispute is given under Paragraph 5" to avoid confusion with the Valuation Agent's notice of Exposure or collateral valuation.

US counterparties are often asked by European counterparties to agree to an earlier Resolution time due to the time differences between New York and Europe.

Value

> (ii) *Value*. For the purpose of Paragraphs 5(i)(C) and 5(ii), the Value of Posted Credit Support other than Cash will be calculated based upon the mid-point between the bid and offered purchase rates or prices for that Posted Credit Support as reported on the Bloomberg electronic service as of the Resolution Time, or if unavailable, as quoted to the Valuation Agent as of the Resolution Time by a dealer in that Posted Credit Support of recognized standing selected in good faith by the Valuation Agent, which calculation shall include any unpaid interest on that Posted Credit Support.

Paragraph 5(ii) requires the parties to agree to a procedure to value Posted Collateral in the event that there is a dispute. Many US counterparties prefer to require the parties to look to published quotes such as Bloomberg, L.P., a Delaware limited partnership ("Bloomberg") for valuing Posted Collateral before going out to solicit quotes from dealers that trade in the disputed type of collateral.

Many parties, however, believe that if there were a dispute with respect to the Value of Posted Collateral, it is because the bid and offer prices are not available on Bloomberg or there is a disagreement over the quote that Bloomberg provides. In this case, the parties instead look directly to quotes:

> If the dispute relates to the Value of a security, the Valuation Agent will use the arithmetic mean of the bid prices for the security obtained by it from Reference Dealers selected by it as provided in the final sentence of Section 4.14 of the 2006 Definitions, subject to the Valuation Percentage indicated in Paragraph 13(b)(ii) of this Annex. For these purposes, "Reference Dealers" means three leading dealers in the principal market for the relevant kind of security; provided, that if three quotations are not available for a particular security, then the number of quotations obtained with respect to such security will be used. If no quotations are available for a particular security, then the Valuation Agent's original calculation of Value thereof will be used – subject to agreement by both parties – for that security, provided, that if the parties remain unable to agree on a particular calculation after five (5) Local Business Days for both parties after the party who is not the Valuation Agent has received notice that no quotations were available, another mutually acceptable Valuation Agent, which is a dealer in the relevant

market, will be appointed to determine such calculation (the "Mutually Acceptable Valuation Agent"). The determination by the Mutually Acceptable Valuation Agent, shall be binding on Party A and Party B. The fees and expenses of the Mutually Acceptable Valuation Agent shall be borne by the parties equally.

The discussion and example provisions of value found in Chapter 5 at pages 219–21 are also equally applicable to the New York Law CSA.

Alternative

(iii) *Alternative*. The provisions of Paragraph 5 will apply.

This provision enables the parties to adopt a different dispute resolution procedure to that contained in Paragraph 5. Normally parties adopt Paragraph 5. See Chapter 5 at pages 223–5 for a discussion of "Alternative" provisions.

Holding Posted Collateral

(g) *Holding and Using Posted Collateral.*

(i) *Eligibility to Hold Posted Collateral; Custodians.*

(A) Party A will be entitled to hold Posted Collateral itself or through a Custodian pursuant to Paragraph 6(b), *provided* that the following conditions applicable to it are satisfied:

(1) Party A is not a Defaulting Party.

(2) Posted Collateral may be held only in the following jurisdictions: New York.

(3) The party or entity holding the Posted Collateral maintains a Credit Rating of at least BBB+ from S&P and Baa1 from Moody's.

(4) The Custodian is a bank or trust company having total assets in excess of $10 billion.

(B) Party B will be entitled to hold Posted Collateral itself or through its Custodian pursuant to Paragraph 6(b), *provided* that the following conditions applicable to it are satisfied:

(1) Party B is not a Defaulting Party.

(2) Posted Collateral may be held only in the following jurisdictions: New York.

(3) The party or entity holding the Posted Collateral maintains a Credit Rating of at least BBB+ from S&P and Baa1 from Moody's.

(4) The Custodian is a bank or trust company having total assets in excess of $10 billion.

Parties frequently worry about the sophistication and credit quality of the Secured Party that is to hold the Posted Collateral. If the Secured Party itself is to hold the Posted Collateral, it is generally not permitted to be a Defaulting Party and often must have a high credit rating. Typically parties will request that a party or its Custodian have a credit rating of at least BBB+ from S&P and Baa1 from Moody's and hold either a certain amount of assets or have a certain net worth.

A Pledgor is concerned about pledging collateral to a party that is not creditworthy. This is because if the Secured Party were to become insolvent, it may be difficult for the Pledgor to obtain the return of the Posted Collateral. This is because the Pledgor would probably only be an unsecured creditor with respect to its contractual claim to the return of the collateral that it had pledged to the Secured Party.

As explained above in Paragraph 6(b), a custodian selected by the Secured Party is defined as an agent of the Secured Party and is not intended to have any fiduciary duties to the Pledgor. The parties would need to require that the Custodian enter into a custodial agreement with both the Pledgor and the Secured Party if the parties intend to create a fiduciary relationship among all three of them.

Paragraph 13(g)(i) also establishes where Posted Collateral can be held. As explained in Chapter 3 (see pages 67–8), as long as the Posted Collateral is held in the United States, the state laws governing the pledging and holding of collateral are consistent and uniform. However, many parties will still insist that Posted Collateral is held only in the State of New York. This is because parties are typically relying upon the ISDA collateral opinion given with respect to the State of New York or because they have only done due diligence with respect to the New York UCC.

Use of Posted Collateral

(ii) *Use of Posted Collateral.* The provisions of Paragraph 6(c) will apply to Party A and will apply to Party B.

Paragraph 6(c) provides that the parties agree to "rehypothecation" or use rights, unless otherwise specified in Paragraph 13. See Chapter 3 (page 66) for a discussion of the issues involving rehypothecation.

The following provisions provide additional protections for a Pledgor if it grants the Secured Party rehypothecation rights. The provision provides that a party must stop using the collateral if it no longer meets the eligibility requirements. A party may also want to consider a ratings trigger that would require the Secured Party to stop rehypothecating collateral in the event that its credit rating fell below a particular level.

(ii) *Use of Posted Collateral.* The provisions of Paragraph 6(c) will apply to both parties, and in addition to the other conditions set forth in Paragraph 6(c), the Secured Party's rights under Paragraph 6(c) are subject to the condition precedent that each of the conditions set forth in Paragraph 13(g)(i) is satisfied with respect to it.

If the parties do not want to permit rehypothecation, the following language could be used:

(ii) *Use of Posted Collateral.* The provisions of Paragraph 6(c)(i) will not apply.

Interest Amount

(h) *Distributions and Interest Amount.*

Interest Rate. The "*Interest Rate*" for any day will be the Federal Funds (Effective) rate published in N.Y. Federal Reserve Statistical Release H.15(519) for that day (or if that day is not a New York Business Day, then for the next preceding New York Business Day).

The Interest Rate is the interest which will be paid by the Secured Party on the Cash collateral received from the Pledgor plus or minus a spread. It will reflect the frequency of the Valuation Dates. This provision must be completed as there is no ISDA fallback.

The Interest Rate between US parties is typically based on the Federal Funds (Effective) rate. This represents the interest rate traditionally used when banks lend money to each other on the interbank market overnight. Because this represents the rate of return anticipated by most banks on their overnight cash balances, they are generally reluctant to agree to other interest rates such as LIBOR because of a fear that LIBOR will diverge from Federal Funds (Effective).

The Federal Funds (Effective) rate is published in numerous sources, including Reuters and Bloomberg.

Occasionally a dealer will request that the rate be Federal Funds (Effective) less a spread such as 25 basis points. A dealer may ask for this because of difficulties the derivatives desk in particular may have in earning Federal Funds (Effective). Often the derivatives desk will be charged a fee for having another part of the dealer invest the Cash collateral.

It is also possible for an Interest Rate to be negative (especially if a spread is deducted from the referenced interest rate at a time of historically low interest rates). To avoid any concerns of a negative interest rate, the following provision could be added:

> **If the Interest Rate for the relevant day is a negative number, such Interest Rate will be deemed to be zero.**

The calculation of the Interest Amount is based on "simple" as opposed to a "compounded" interest rate. The following provision provides for daily compounding if that is what the parties want:

> **For the purpose of computing the Interest Amount, the amount of interest computed for each day of the Interest Period shall be compounded daily.**

Some parties also request that the Secured Party deliver a notice to the Pledgor with respect to the amount of interest that will be paid:

> **Notice of Interest Amount. A notice of the Interest Amount due to the Pledgor (or a statement that no such interest is due) shall be delivered to the Pledgor from the Secured Party on the next to last Local Business Day of each calendar month that Posted Collateral in the form of Cash is being held by the Secured Party.**

A Pledgor that is a dealer, however, often will invoice the Secured Party for the amount of interest payable.

Transfer of Interest Amount

> **(ii) *Transfer of Interest Amount.* The Transfer of the Interest Amount will be made on the first Local Business Day of each calendar month and on any Local Business Day that Posted Collateral in the form of Cash is Transferred to the Pledgor pursuant to Paragraph 3(b).**

As long as the Secured Party does not become undersecured by transferring an Interest Amount, Paragraph 13(h)(ii) proposes that interest on cash collateral is transferred in arrears to the Secured Party on the first Local Business Day of each month and on any Local Business Day when a cash Return Amount is due to the Pledgor.

Whether this payment structure is acceptable will depend upon the parties' operational systems. Many parties prefer such interest transfers to take place on the second or third Local Business Day of the succeeding calendar month because they can spend the first or second Local Business Day of that month checking calculations and preparing the necessary electronic transfers.

The above language presupposes that that Interest Period is a calendar month. Some parties clarify that assumption by adding the following:

(iv) *Interest Period.* The definition of "Interest Period" in Paragraph 12 shall be deleted and replaced by the following:

" "*Interest Period*" means the period from (and including) the first Local Business Day of a calendar month to (and excluding) the first Local Business Day of the following calendar month."

Alternative to Interest Amount

(iii) *Alternative to Interest Amount.* The provisions of Paragraph 6(d)(ii) will apply.

Although the drafters of Paragraph 6(d)(ii) anticipated that parties may want to diverge from the standard provisions, it is rarely used.

Additional Representations

(i) *Additional Representation(s).* Not applicable.

Parties rarely add additional representations to the New York Law CSA.

Other Eligible Support

(j) *Other Eligible Support and Other Posted Support.* Not applicable.

This provision is also rarely used given that it is only applicable if the parties have agreed to include Other Posted Support. If Other Posted Support were pledged to the Secured Party, the parties may want to consider adding special provisions as to how to value or transfer that Other Posted Support.

Demands and Notices

(k) *Demands and Notices.* All demands, specifications and notices under this Annex will be made to a party as follows unless otherwise specified from time to time by that party for purposes of this Annex in a written notice given to the other party:

Party A: as set forth in the Notices section of the Agreement.

Party B: as set forth in the Notices section of the Agreement.

With large dealers, the collateral operation may be completely separate and administered apart from the derivatives desk or legal department. Accordingly, a party may want to designate additional addresses for notification if collateral is administered by another section of their operations.

Although uncommon, a party may also want to clarify how notices can be given with respect to the transfer of collateral in order to conform the document to that party's practices in transferring collateral:

> *Notices*. Notwithstanding Section 12 of the Agreement, any communication by a party ("X") to the other party ("Y") requesting the delivery or return of Eligible Credit Support or Posted Credit Support pursuant to Paragraph 3 of this Annex may be given orally (including telephonically to the telephone number of Y set forth in subparagraph (k) above, or any other telephone number Y may notify X of in writing) during normal business hours in the city in which Y is located on any Local Business Day to any officer, employee or agent of Y which identifies himself or herself as being permitted to receive oral communications on behalf of Y with respect to this Annex. Any such oral communication will be deemed received and effective when actually received by any such officer, employee or agent of Y. X shall deliver to Y, within one Local Business Day following receipt of an oral or written request by Y, a written confirmation of any such oral communication.

Addresses for Transfers

> (l) *Addresses for Transfers.*
>
> (i) For each Transfer hereunder to Party A, instructions will be provided by Party A for that specific Transfer.
>
> (ii) For each Transfer hereunder to Party B, instructions will be provided by Party B for that specific Transfer.

This must be completed if collateral transfers and interest payments and Distributions are to be correctly routed to the recipient. Sometimes these details are spelt out by currency for cash and securities. In large dealers, the collateral operation will have standard accounts for Cash and securities that will not change on a day to day basis. Often these transfer instructions will be added directly to Paragraph 13.

Other provisions

> (m) *Other provisions*

Paragraph 13(m) is similar to Part 5 of the ISDA Master Agreement Schedule – a place where other provisions may be inserted. There is no general market practice as to what should be added in Paragraph 13(m). There are, however, several general types of provisions that some parties will request to be added. Because these provisions are not always market standard, they often will be difficult and time consuming to negotiate.

In addition to the provisions listed below, please also carefully review the miscellaneous provisions of Paragraph 11(h) of the English Law CSA that are discussed in Chapter 5 at pages 235–48. Many of the provisions discussed there are equally applicable to the New York Law CSA.

Exposure

Some parties want to clarify the types of Transactions that will be included in the calculation of Exposure. The most common is to ensure that all Specified Transactions between the parties are included. This is important because some confirmations may not reference the ISDA Master Agreement. This addition would be unnecessary, however, if there is a Scope of Agreement provision in the Schedule that would include all Specified Transactions between the parties as being governed by the ISDA Master Agreement. An example of this is as follows:

> *Exposure*. All calculations of "Exposure" under this Annex shall *include* all Transactions, including all Specified Transactions that have been or will be entered into between the parties (whether or not evidenced by a Confirmation).

Some parties also are unable or unwilling to collateralise certain types of Transactions. The most common exclusion would be for Transactions such as spot FX Transactions that mature before a party has the ability to call or pledge collateral. Another situation involves Transactions that are difficult to value and thus are excluded in order to avoid disputes. An example from the past (which is no longer done as a practical matter), would be to exclude credit derivatives from the calculation.

The following are some common provision examples:

> *Exposure*. Without limiting the term "Obligations" as defined in this Annex, all calculations of "Exposure" under this Annex shall *exclude* the following:
>
> (A) {All Transactions (including Specified Transactions) that are bond options.}
>
> (B) {All Transactions (including Specified Transactions) that are FX Transactions maturing within ___ of their respective trade dates.}
>
> (C) {All Transactions (including Specified Transactions) that are either FX Transactions or Currency Option Transactions.}
>
> (D) ____.

OR

Exposure. The definition of "Exposure" in Paragraph 12 shall be amended by adding the following sentence at the end thereof: "For purpose of this definition, the term "Transaction" will only cover the following transactions: any rate swap transaction, basis-swap, forward rate transaction, bond option, interest rate option, cap transaction, floor transaction, collar transaction, cross-currency rate swap transaction (including any option with respect to any of these transactions), Equity Swap Transactions, Index Transactions, Share Transactions, Index Basket Transactions, Share Basket Transactions, Basket Option Transaction, and any Option Transaction (each as defined in the 2002 ISDA Equity Derivatives Definitions), any FX Transactions and Currency Options Transaction (each as defined in the 1998 FX and Currency Options Definitions)." For the avoidance of doubt the term "Transaction" will not cover foreign exchange spot dealings.

Cure Periods

Parties may want to reduce the amount of time permitted to transfer collateral or to cure defaults, especially given the reduction in cure period timescales in the 2002 ISDA Master Agreement.

The following provision reduces the cure period for failure to transfer collateral:

Grace Period. Clause (i) of Paragraph 7 is hereby amended by deleting the words "two Local Business Days" and substituting therefor "one Local Business Day".

OR

Events of Default. Paragraph 7 shall be amended so that the references in Paragraph 7(i), Paragraph 7(ii) and Paragraph 7(iii) to "two Local Business Days", "five Local Business Days", and "thirty days" respectively, shall instead be replaced by "one Local Business Day", "three Local Business Days" and "three Local Business Days" respectively.

OR

Events of Default. Paragraph 7(i) shall be amended and restated in its entirety as follows: "(i) that party fails (or fails to cause its Custodian) to make, when due any Transfer of Eligible Collateral, Posted Collateral or the Interest Amount as applicable, required to be made by it and that failure continues for one Local Business Day after notice of that failure is given to that party;".

Remedies

Parties often request provisions that clarify and amplify a party's remedies under the New York Law CSA.

> *Rights and Remedies under Paragraph 8(a).* The Secured Party will be entitled to exercise the rights and remedies provided for in Paragraph 8(a) if the Pledgor fails to pay when due any amount payable by it under Section 6 of this Agreement in connection with a Termination Event, even if the Pledgor is not the Affected Party.

AND

> *Set off.* For purposes of Paragraphs 2 and 8(a)(iii) of this Annex, the reference to any amount payable under Section 6 of this Agreement in the definition of "Set-off" in this Agreement shall be deemed a reference to any amount payable with respect to any Obligation, as described in Paragraph 8(a)(iii) of this Annex.

AND

> *Secured Party's Rights and Remedies.* (a) Supplementing the provisions of Paragraph 8(a), the Pledgor irrevocably appoints the Secured Party its attorney-in-fact, with full authority in its place and stead and in its name or otherwise, from time to time in the Secured Party's discretion, to take any action and to execute any instrument which the Secured Party may deem necessary or advisable to accomplish the purposes of this Annex, including without limitation:
>
> (i) to ask, demand, collect, sue for, recover, compromise, receive and give acquittance and receipts for moneys due and to become due under or in respect of any Posted Collateral and to perform all other acts as fully as though the Secured Party were the absolute owner of the Posted Collateral for all purposes,
>
> (ii) to receive, endorse, and collect any drafts or other instruments, documents and chattel paper, in connection with clause (i) above, and
>
> (iii) to file any claims or take any action or institute any proceedings which the Secured Party may deem necessary or desirable for the collection of any of the Posted Collateral or otherwise to enforce the rights of the Secured Party with respect to any Posted Collateral.
>
> (b) Further supplementing the provisions of Paragraph 8(a) and 13(a), the Secured Party may apply Eligible Credit Support or Posted Credit Support to pay any amounts due by Pledgor to Secured Party pursuant to this Agreement, including any Transaction, and any other amounts then due by Pledgor to Secured Party or its Affiliates under any other contractual arrangements between them.

Interest Amount and Taxes

Parties at times are concerned that the payment of the Interest Amount may trigger a Tax Event. Because the Interest Amount is typically insignificant in comparison with other payment obligations under the ISDA Master Agreement, the parties attempt to minimise any disruptions that such a Tax Event could cause on the parties:

> *Taxes in Connection with Interest Amounts*: Neither party will be entitled to designate an Early Termination Date on the ground of any Tax Event resulting from the party's obligation to pay additional amounts in respect of Indemnifiable Taxes imposed with respect to any Interest Amount it is required to Transfer under this Annex.

Dealings in relation to Posted Collateral

Secured Parties also often seek additional assurances with respect to the Posted Collateral that they have received from the Pledgor:

> *No further dealings by Pledgor.* So long as the Agreement is in effect, the Pledgor covenants that it:
>
> (i) will keep the Posted Collateral free from all security interests or other encumbrances created by the Pledgor, except the security interest created hereunder and any security interests or other encumbrances created by the Secured Party;
>
> (ii) will not sell, transfer, assign, deliver or otherwise dispose of, or grant any option with respect to any Posted Collateral or any interest therein, or create, incur or permit to exist any pledge, lien, mortgage, hypothecation, security interest, charge, option or any other encumbrance with respect to any Posted Collateral or any interest therein, without the prior written consent of the Secured Party.

Parties also attempt to further clarify the duty of care of a Secured Party:

> *Care of Posted Collateral.* Supplementing the provisions of Paragraph 6(a), the Secured Party shall also be deemed to have exercised reasonable care if it takes such action for that purpose as the Pledgor shall reasonably request in writing (but no omission to comply with any such request shall of itself be deemed a failure to exercise reasonable care).

OR

> *Duty of Secured Party to Preserve Collateral; Limit on Secured Party's Liability*: to the extent required by applicable law and subject to the remainder of this provision, the Secured Party will exercise reasonable care in the preservation of Posted Collateral held by it,

and the parties agree that the Secured Party will be deemed to have exercised reasonable care if it exercises at least the same degree of care it would exercise with respect to its own property. However, without limiting the generality of the final sentence of paragraph 6(a), each party, as Pledgor, acknowledges that it has the means to monitor all matters relating to all valuations, payments, defaults and rights without need to rely on the other party, in its capacity as Secured Party, and that, given the provisions of this Annex on substitution, responsibility for the preservation of the rights of the Pledgor with respect to all such matters is reasonably allocated hereby to the Pledgor. The Secured Party will not be liable for any losses or damages that the Pledgor may suffer as a result of any failure by the Secured Party to perform, or any delay by it in performing, any of its obligations under this Annex if the failure or delay results from circumstances beyond the reasonable control of the Secured Party or its Custodian, such as interruption or loss of computer or communication devices, labor disturbance, natural disaster or local or national emergency.

Amending and restating a Credit Support Annex

Parties may wish to completely amend and restate a Credit Support Annex during a later renegotiation of an ISDA Master Agreement. This is typically done by adding the following on the first page of Paragraph 13:

> This Credit Support Annex amends and restates the Credit Support Annex to the Schedule to the ISDA Master Agreement (Multicurrency-Cross Border) between Party A and Party B, dated as of XXX, as such may have been amended prior hereto.

Reconcilation of Posted Collateral

There may arise disputes between the parties with respect to the amounts of collateral held or other issues. The following provision is intended to allow these differences to be quickly resolved:

> Sharing of Information. The parties hereto agree that they shall, in the event of a margin call dispute and/or upon request of the other party, exchange (i) lists identifying all Transactions included in the calculation of Exposure hereunder and (ii) a statement of Posted Credit Support.

ISDA elections and fallbacks

At this point it might be useful to summarise the ISDA fallbacks for Paragraph 13 and the provisions which must be completed for the Annex to be operative (see Table 6.1).

Table 6.1

ISDA fallbacks

If no choice is made the following apply by default:	
Provision	**Fallback**
Specifying dispute resolution procedures in Paragraph 13	Paragraph 5 dispute resolution procedures apply
Consent for Substitution	No consent required
Eligibility to Hold Collateral	Secured Party cannot be a Defaulting Party
Independent Amount	Zero
Threshold	Zero
Minimum Transfer Amount	Zero
Notification Time	1.00 p.m. New York time
Notices	Pursuant to Notices Section of ISDA Master Agreement
Resolution Time	1.00 p.m. New York time
Rounding	No rounding
Specified Condition	No Specified Conditions apply
Substitution Date	Local Business Day following receipt of Substitute Credit Support
Transfer of Interest Amount	Last Local Business Day of a calendar month and any Local Business Day when a cash Return Amount is due to the Pledgor
Use or Rehypothecation of Posted Collateral	Use or rehypothecation permitted
Valuation Agent	The Secured Party for purposes of Paragraph 3(a) and the Pledgor for purposes of Paragraph 3(b)

The following are provisions that must be completed if there is no fallback:

- Addresses for Transfers
- Eligible Collateral
- Interest Rate
- Other Eligible Support
- Valuation Date

- Valuation Percentage
- Valuation Time
- Value.

COMPARISON OF THE NEW YORK LAW CSA WITH THE ENGLISH LAW CSA

The New York Law CSA and the English Law CSA are quite different conceptually as to how they secure and collateralise obligations under the ISDA Master Agreement. However, they share many common characteristics in their form, appearance and modus operandi.

Key similarities

There are several key similarities between the two documents. First, each document is an Annex to the ISDA Master Agreement Schedule and supplements, forms part of and is subject to the ISDA Master Agreement. Accordingly, they both conform much of their vocabulary and mechanics to the ISDA Master Agreement standard form and Schedule.

Second, the Transferee/Secured Party is free to use the collateral. For example, under the New York Law CSA, the Secured Party is often given use or rehypothecation rights. (See Chapter 3 at page 66 for a discussion of these rights.)

Because the Transferee under the English Law CSA is treated as the owner of the collateral, it is also free to deal with the collateral as it sees fit. Of course, both the Secured Party and the Transferee have a contractual obligation to return the collateral upon the counterparty making a Return Amount collateral call or satisfying all its obligations under the ISDA Master Agreement.

Third, neither Annex requires any registration formalities. For example, because Eligible Collateral under the New York Law CSA is typically cash and securities, the Secured Party is not even required to make a UCC filing in order to perfect its security interest in the collateral.

Fourth, both Annexes use the same vocabulary and similar provisions whenever possible. Negotiators, however, should be careful to appreciate subtle differences between provisions that might otherwise appear identical in order to avoid drafting errors.

Principal Differences

There are numerous important distinctions between the New York Law CSA and the English Law CSA that should be understood. Failure to appreciate these differences can result in drafting errors when a negotiator using one form of the Annex negotiates an ISDA Master Agreement using the other Annex.

(i) Unlike the New York Law CSA, the English Law CSA is not a Credit Support Document to the ISDA Master Agreement. It constitutes a Confirmation to the relevant Transaction under the ISDA Master Agreement. This distinction could affect how Events of Default and other provisions operate under either Annex. It is also important because any collateral held by the Transferee under the English Law CSA is treated as an Unpaid Amount upon the early termination of the Transactions under an ISDA Master Agreement.

(ii) In contrast to the New York Law CSA, the English Law CSA does not create a first priority security interest in and lien on the collateral transferred. The English Law CSA relies on transferring ownership and close-out netting for its effectiveness.

(iii) The English Law CSA is intended to cover cash collateral and securities denominated in various currencies while the New York Law CSA is intended to be used primarily with US Dollar cash and securities. This is why there are specific provisions to convert all values to a common Base Currency in the English Law CSA.

(iv) The English Law CSA contemplates taking securities located in various jurisdictions while the New York Law CSA is intended primarily to be used with US Treasury securities and quasi US government agency securities. Generally in the New York Law CSA, transfers must occur within one Local Business Day. This is done easily because these types of US securities are always held through book entry at a Federal Reserve Bank. In the English Law CSA transfers are required to occur as soon as practicable in accordance with custom in the relevant market. This is to allow, for example, for differences between settlement timing and practice in an international central securities depository like Euroclear as opposed to, say, a domestic settlement system for government bonds.

(v) The English Law CSA relies solely on close-out netting. Where a default occurs, collateral values are included within the close-out netting calculations under the ISDA Master Agreement as Unpaid Amounts. The Transferor therefore takes the credit risk on the Transferee since, in contrast to the New York Law CSA's security interest, the Transferee has no continuing proprietary interest in the collateral provided. It owns it.

(vi) In determining if a Delivery Amount or a Return Amount has arisen, the English Law CSA provides an adjustment to the value of the collateral already held by a Transferee on the Valuation Date that takes into account incomplete transfers at that time. The New York Law

CSA makes no such adjustment because settlement timescales are usually quicker in the US.

(vii) To illustrate this the English Law CSA requires the receipt of the demand and transfer to take place in accordance with the Settlement Day on which such demand is received while the New York Law CSA only requires such demand to be made and the transfer to take place on the next Local Business Day.

(viii) The New York Law CSA provides that the parties may agree that an event that constitutes a Specified Condition as a condition precedent with respect to the Pledgor's obligations. Under a Specified Condition the party affected by a stated Termination Event is not allowed to call for or substitute collateral nor receive dividends or interest on pledged collateral. The occurrence of a Specified Condition also permits a Secured Party to exercise its remedies under the New York Law CSA. The English Law CSA does not provide for a Specified Condition to be stated (but the English Law Deed Does).

(ix) The English Law CSA provides that if the Transferor wishes to transfer New Credit Support the Transferee's consent is required. The New York Law CSA provides that the Pledgor may substitute credit support upon notice to the Secured Party. Paragraph 13 may provide for the Secured Party's consent to the substitution but it is not an absolute requirement of the terms of the New York Law CSA.

(x) The English Law CSA requires that any Disputing Party must "reasonably" dispute the calculation of a Delivery or Return Amount or the value of a transfer. The New York Law CSA does not require this reasonableness standard. With respect to the transfer of the undisputed amount, the English Law CSA provides that the relevant transfer will be made not later than the close of business on the Settlement Day following the date the demand is received. The New York Law CSA, in contrast, provides for such transfer to take effect not later than the close of business on the Local Business Day following the call. This is because the New York Law CSA deals solely with US$ collateral and its transfer is more streamlined.

(xi) The title transfer approach of the English Law CSA allows the Transferee to use the collateral. In contrast, subject to the New York Law CSA's rehypothecation rights, the Secured Party is required to exercise reasonable care in its custody arrangements for the posted collateral. It can appoint a custodian. The Transferee under the English Law CSA cannot appoint a custodian as this would destroy close-out netting mutuality.

(xii) The English Law CSA requires the Transferee to transfer equivalent interest and dividend payments to the Transferor not later than the Settlement Day following each Distributions Date. Under the New York Law CSA the Secured Party must make such transfers on the Local Business Day following the one on which he received them.

(xiii) Close-out netting is the remedy for parties under the English Law CSA. A Secured Party under the New York Law CSA can look to rights under law as well as set off rights and the right to liquidate collateral through public or private sales. It can also buy it himself. In addition the Pledgor can exercise similar rights if the Secured Party defaults.

(xiv) The New York Law CSA obliges parties, if required under applicable law for particular collateral, to file or deliver any document or perform any act to enable a valid, enforceable security interest to be created. The Pledgor must also give notice and defend any action that involves collateral. The English Law CSA lacks these requirements.

(xv) In Paragraph 7(i) of the New York Law CSA there is a two Local Business Day grace period to remedy a failure to transfer collateral when due. There is no such grace period in the English Law CSA.

7

The ISDA English Law Credit Support Deed

The *ISDA Margin Survey 2009* (ISDA's last figures on this subject) estimated that the English Law Credit Support Deed was then used in only 0.5% of collateral arrangements although there is scope for this to increase if the market decides that Independent Amounts should be pledged and segregated in the keeping of a Secured Party or a Custodian (see pages 413–18 on that subject).

Given this minority usage and the space constraints in this book, it was considered appropriate to provide a summary treatment of the English Law Credit Support Deed rather than the type of extended expositions in Chapters 5 and 6 on the English Law CSA and New York Law CSA respectively. Nonetheless it is hoped that this chapter will still be useful.

PARAGRAPH BY PARAGRAPH SUMMARY OF THE ISDA ENGLISH LAW CREDIT SUPPORT DEED

The English Law Credit Support Deed (which we shall call the "Deed" from now on) was published by ISDA in autumn 1995.

It is a standalone document which relies for its effectiveness upon a security interest or pledge over the collateral received under it. It is also a Credit Support Document under the ISDA Master Agreement as its preamble states. This document is in the form of a Deed because under its Paragraph 8(b) if a power of attorney has to be executed it must, under English law, be executed pursuant to a deed. It also differs from the English Law CSA discussed in Chapter 5 that is treated as a Transaction as opposed to a Credit Support Document.

The Deed is a bilateral document in its standard form meaning that either party may pledge or receive collateral under it. Where it is desired that the Deed be one way, an amendment will need to be made in Paragraph 13 (see page 193 for how this is done with the English Law Credit Support Annex).

Let us now review the individual Paragraphs of the Deed.

Heading

Please note that the Deed should be dated with the date it is actually executed and not the same date as the ISDA Master Agreement (unless that Agreement is executed on the same day).

In contrast, the English law CSA is dated as of the same date as the ISDA Master Agreement itself which may have been executed some months or years before.

Paragraph 1. Interpretation

(a) Definitions and Inconsistency

Capitalised terms will have the same meanings in both the ISDA Master Agreement and the Deed. Where capitalised terms are not otherwise defined in the Deed or the Agreement they shall have the meanings given against them in Paragraph 12 of the Deed.

Where there is inconsistency, the Deed prevails over the Agreement and Paragraph 13 over the other provisions of the Deed.

The Deed covers payments of cash collateral and deliveries of securities and other assets.

(b) Secured Party and Chargor

The Deed is structured as a bilateral document. Therefore either party may act as Secured Party or Chargor at different times during the life of the Deed. In respect of Other Posted Support the Secured Party will be considered to hold it as beneficiary rather than chargee.

Paragraph 2. Security

(a) Covenant to Perform

Like any other English law security document, the Deed contains a covenant to perform the Obligations under the Agreement, the Deed or any other agreed relevant agreement referred to in Paragraph 13(b) of the Deed. This covenant is given by each party when acting as Chargor.

The purpose of this covenant is to provide a starting date for the limitation period for any payment demand under the Deed. A deed executed under seal extends the limitation period to 12 years from the normal 6 years for contractual debt claims under English law.

It is possible to use the Deed to secure obligations of a third party (e.g. one of the Chargor's Affiliates) by expanding the scope of the term "Obligations" in Paragraph 13(b). However, thought would need to be given as to whether the Chargor had received commercial consideration or benefit in these circumstances.

(b) Security

This is the charging clause. In order to secure performance of its Obligations, the Chargor charges by way of first fixed legal mortgage all Posted Collateral in the form of cash and securities.

The Chargor also assigns the Assigned Rights to the Secured Party under Paragraph 2(b)(iii). These are any rights (e.g. liens) that a securities clearance system or other third party may have over the Posted Collateral at any time.

As we saw in Chapter 3 the legal problems over the location of the collateral asset have been clarified through Article 8 of the Uniform Commercial Code in the USA, Article 9(2) of the European Union Settlement Finality Directive, the European Directive on Financial Collateral Arrangements and the Hague Convention on Indirectly Held Securities.

As drafted, Paragraph 2(b)(i) and (ii) deal respectively with non-cash Posted Collateral and Posted Collateral consisting of cash. This distinction was necessary at the time the Deed was drafted due to the 1986 *Re Charge Card Services Limited* case. This cast doubt on a chargor's ability to create a charge over cash in favour of a party holding that deposit. This was because the deposit represented a debt owed by the Secured Party to the Chargor and so it was "conceptually impossible" for the Secured Party to take a charge over a debt it owed. To avoid this problem cash collateral was often deposited with a third party bank and then assigned by way of security to the Secured Party – a circular route with the Secured Party ending up having a security interest in a debt owed by a third party rather than itself.

However, in 1997 in *Morris* v *Argrichemicals Ltd* the House of Lords overruled the *Charge Card* case. So now a cash depositor may charge its deposit to the deposit taker.

The granting of the charge is with full title guarantee. Up until July 1995 reference would have been made to the legal and beneficial owner granting the security interest.

However, there was a change in English statute law in 1994 in the Law of Property (Miscellaneous Provisions) Act 1994 to the effect that a legal and beneficial owner cannot give a full covenant for title to the property in question unless, from July 1995, the words "full title guarantee" are used instead of "legal and beneficial owner".

(c) Release of Security

When the Obligations are extinguished or reduced below the Threshold or the Minimum Transfer Amount (if the Threshold is zero), Paragraph 2(c) makes clear that the Secured Party must transfer back the Posted Collateral to the Chargor whereupon the security interest under the Deed is immediately released without further formality.

Paragraph 2(c) also makes clear that when securities are released, the Secured Party is obliged to return to the Chargor equivalent fungible securities (i.e. of the same type, class, issuer and issue) to the ones he received. The Secured Party does not have to return the identically numbered securities originally received as this would probably be impractical.

(d) Preservation of Security

This is the continuing security provision and is designed under English law to avoid the operation of the Rule in *Clayton's Case* (1816). That Rule provides that payments into a current account discharge debts in the account in the order in which they were incurred. Any fresh advances under the account would be unsecured.

In Paragraph 2(d) the security under the Deed is stated as unaffected by any intermediate payments in respect of the whole or part of the Obligations and shall continue to secure the outstanding Obligations. However, even if the security ceases to be a continuing security, the Secured Party can open a new account or continue an existing account with the Chargor who will remain responsible for its Obligations regardless of any debits or credits to the account.

It is also stressed that security under the Deed is additional to and unaffected by any other security held or to be held by the Secured Party in respect of the Obligations.

(e) Waiver of Defences

It is made clear that any acts or omissions which might in other circumstances give grounds to release the Chargor from its obligations under the Deed are waived and the Chargor will remain fully responsible under the Deed. These circumstances include:

- any time, indulgence or composition granted to the Chargor or a third party;
- any change in terms or inaction to perform or perfect any term of the ISDA Master Agreement or any security rights granted by the Chargor or a third party;
- any flaw in the regularity, validity or enforceability in the Chargor's obligations under the Agreement or any government action which results in this;
- any legal incapacity relating to the Chargor or any third party or any change to the terms of the Agreement or other document or security.

(f) Immediate Recourse

The Chargor waives any right it has which obliges the Secured Party to claim payment first from any third party or to call on any guarantee or enforce any other security before enforcing its rights under the Deed.

(g) Reinstatement

If it should happen that any discharge of security is made following a payment or is made in reliance on a payment or arrangement that is avoided or vitiated by insolvency or some other event and the payment made has to be returned, the security under the Deed and the Chargor's liability thereunder shall continue as if no such discharge had been made.

Paragraph 3. Credit Support Obligations

Basically this Paragraph concerns collateral calls and returns and how they are calculated. Choices need to be made in Paragraph 13 to make the mechanism fully effective.

In Paragraph 3(a) the collateral taker (the Secured Party) can call for collateral from the collateral giver (the Chargor) where his OTC derivatives risk exposure on the Chargor is greater that the Minimum Transfer Amount applicable to the Chargor.

The calculation of the Credit Support Amount will take into account:

- **the net mark-to-market valuation of all Transactions under the Agreements plus or minus;**
- **the net Independent Amounts between the parties and**
- **any Threshold applicable to the Chargor.**

When called upon and assuming there is no dispute, the Chargor will transfer the requested amount of collateral (the "Delivery Amount") to the Secured Party. Any transfers already in transit in respect of previous collateral calls are also taken into account in the calculation of the Delivery Amount.

Paragraph 3(b) covers the position where the Secured Party holds surplus collateral which it must return to the Chargor if it is above the Secured Party's Minimum Transfer Amount *and* the Chargor calls for the return of the collateral. Please note that if the Chargor fails to make a call, the Secured Party is not obliged to transfer the collateral or point this out to the Chargor. However, if a third party Valuation Agent is involved this, of course, will not arise if he is doing his job properly.

A Return Amount arises where the value of the collateral held by the Secured Party exceeds its risk exposure on the Chargor and is above the Secured Party's agreed Minimum Transfer Amount.

Again with a Return Amount any return collateral already in transit will be taken into account in the current Return Amount called.

Please note that collateral eligible for transfer is called Eligible Collateral or Other Eligible Support. When actually held by the Secured Party it is called Posted Collateral or Other Posted Support.

Paragraph 4. Conditions Precedent, Transfers, Calculations and Substitutions

A mixed bag of provisions appears in Paragraph 4.

(a) Conditions Precedent

Paragraph 4(a) is similar to the conditions precedent found in Section 2(a)(iii) of the ISDA Master Agreement in connection with payments or deliveries under it.

Each transfer obligation of the Chargor under Paragraph 3(a) (Delivery Amount) and 5 (in a dispute) or of the Secured Party under Paragraph 3(b) (Return Amounts), 4(d)(ii) (Substitutions), 5 (in a dispute) and 6(g) (payment of Interest Amounts or Distributions) is subject to the following pre-conditions:

- No potential or actual Event of Default or Specified Condition (see page 285 for an explanation of this term) has occurred or is continuing.
- No Early Termination Date due to unsatisfied payments has occurred or been designated following an Event of Default or Specified Condition impacting the other party.

(b) Transfers

Paragraph 4(b) describes how transfers are to be made for cash, certificated securities and book entry securities charged under the Deed.

(i) With cash this is by transfer to the recipient's nominated bank account(s).

(ii) With securities certificates this will involve physical delivery to the recipient or its account together with all necessary transfer documentation which will vest legal ownership with full title guarantee in the securities in the recipient.

(iii) With book entry or dematerialised securities this entails the transferring party giving written instructions in a choice of media to the recipient's central securities depository system (e.g. Euroclear or Clearstream) where he holds his account. A copy of such instructions (which must be sufficient to transfer legal ownership with full title guarantee in the securities) must be sent to the recipient.

(iv) With Other Eligible Support or Other Posted Support as required by Paragraph 13(j)(ii).

In the normal course of business (i.e. when there is no dispute) if a collateral call notice is received for a Delivery Amount or a Return Amount before the deadline (Notification Time) agreed in Paragraph 13(d)(iv) then with securities, the transfer must be made no later than the close of business on the first trade settlement day thereafter in the relevant market. If the deadline is missed, transfer will occur on the next following trade settlement day in that market. With cash the transfer must be made on the next Local Business Day if the call notice is received before the Notification Time and the following Local Business Day if not (see Paragraph 12 definition of Settlement Day).

(c) Calculations

Paragraph 4(c) provides for the calculation of risk exposure and the value of collateral held to be made by the relevant Valuation Agent stated in Paragraph 13 for the purposes of calculating Delivery Amounts and Return Amounts both in the normal course of business and in disputes. The Valuation Agent will notify its calculations to the other party (or to both parties if it is a third party) by the deadline (Notification Time) on the Local Business Day after it makes its calculations.

(d) Substitutions

Paragraph 4(d) is about substitutions of collateral.

(i) Unless stated otherwise in Paragraph 13(f), the Chargor may request by notice to the Secured Party a substitution of part or all of the collateral it has already transferred to the Secured Party in exchange for new collateral acceptable to the Secured Party.

(ii) If the Secured Party consents to this by written notice or orally to the Chargor, then the latter must transfer the substitute collateral to the Secured Party on the first trade settlement date thereafter. After it has received the new collateral, the Secured Party must return the original collateral which has been substituted no later than the trade settlement date after he has received the substitute collateral from the Chargor. This will usually be the following Local Business Day. In any case on the transfer date the collateral must be worth the same or the nearly the same and in no circumstances is he obliged to retransfer original collateral worth more than the new collateral. The consent point was important at least under English law because without it the Deed could have constituted a floating charge which would, in a liquidation, rank behind other fixed charges and behind certain preferential creditors such as liquidators (for their charges) and HM Revenue & Customs.

If the Deed were to be recharacterised as a floating charge it is likely to be void against a liquidator or other creditor of a Chargor because it failed to be registered at Companies House within 21 days of creation. Fines could also be levied for this.

This would also mean that the debt secured by the Deed would become immediately payable and could trigger close-out under the ISDA Master Agreement.

However, the Secured Party should have the right to consent or not for commercial reasons in case he has used the collateral to meet another counterparty's collateral call and it might be inconvenient for him to request a substitution.

Paragraph 5. Dispute Resolution

(a) If a party disputes the Valuation Agent's calculation of risk exposure or the value of collateral held, Paragraph 5 provides a framework for resolving the dispute if it cannot be settled informally.

Collateral disputes *always* relate to these two matters and the calculation of risk exposure is the more common kind of dispute.

Please note in Paragraph 5(a) the Disputing Party has to observe a standard of reasonableness in initiating a dispute with its counterparty.

The steps are outlined in Paragraph 5(a) (1)–(4) and involve:

1 A requirement for the Disputing Party to notify its counterparty or the third party Valuation Agent that it wishes to dispute the risk exposure calculation or collateral valuation not later than the close of business on the Local Business Day after either the date the collateral call notice is received or the date the collateral transfer has been made. The last point covers the situation where a party has agreed a collateral call; has made the transfer; and then realises that he has made a mistake.

2 In the case of disputes over exposure calculation for collateral calls, the Disputing Party agrees to transfer the undisputed amount to its counterparty not later than the close of business on the next trade settlement date following the date he receives the collateral call notice from its counterparty.

3 The parties will attempt to resolve the dispute by the deadline nominated in Paragraph 13(g)(i) – the Resolution Time.

4 If they fail then:

(i) (A) If the dispute involves the amount of collateral called for, the Valuation Agent will recalculate his figures for risk exposure and collateral value (including any haircut) by reusing any calculation of the undisputed part of the exposure.

(B) It will then approach four Reference Market-makers (i.e. leading dealers) for mid-market quotations (i.e. the average of the bid and offer prices of the Transactions concerned). Provided four quotations are received the arithmetic mean of these quotations is used. To this is added the risk exposure calculation which is undisputed. However, fewer than four quotations may be used in the recalculation of risk exposure, but if no quotations are available for a particular Transaction then the Valuation Agent's original calculation will be used for that Transaction because it is the only reasonable thing to do in the circumstances.

(C) The Valuation Agent will also follow the method specified in Paragraph 13(g) (ii) for calculating the value of collateral held. This method has to be stated in Paragraph 13 or the dispute resolution provisions will not work. There is no fallback.

(ii) The Valuation Agent will directly focus on Paragraph 13(g)(ii) where the dispute solely involves the value of collateral held.

When all the recalculations have been done, the Valuation Agent will notify each party (if it is a third party) and the other party (if it is not) of the revised figures not later than the deadline (Notification Time) on the Local Business Day after the Resolution Time (i.e. the dispute resolution deadline agreed in the Deed).

Once all is agreed a revised collateral call notice is sent and the necessary collateral transfer is made.

(b) Paragraph 5(b) clarifies that failure to transfer a disputed amount does not constitute an Event of Default while the above process is being carried out. However, when the process is ended and the transfer is still not made then Paragraph 7 of the Deed comes into play and a Relevant Event will have occurred which could lead to an Event of Default being declared and Paragraph 8 options being exercised.

Paragraph 6. Holding Posted Collateral

(a) Care of Posted Collateral

The Secured Party has a duty of care to keep Posted Collateral in safe custody but has no obligation to collect interest or dividends or preserve or enforce any rights the Posted Collateral might have.

(b) Eligibility to Hold Posted Collateral; Custodians

The Secured Party can itself hold Posted Collateral or appoint a Custodian, subject to Paragraph 13 conditions, to do so. The Chargor can discharge its collateral transfer obligations when it transfers collateral to the appointed Custodian. Transfer to another Custodian is necessary within five Local Business Days if the first Custodian fails to fulfil Paragraph 13 conditions and the Chargor demands this. The Secured Party is liable for the Custodian's acts or omissions as he would be for his own under the Deed.

It is important that the Custodian is notified of the Chargor's ownership interest in the Posted Collateral and, for the pledge to be perfected, the security interest is in favour of the Secured Party.

(c) Segregated Accounts

All non-cash Posted Collateral must be held in segregated accounts by the Secured Party or its Custodian. This protects the Secured Party because if the non-cash Posted Collateral was commingled the Chargor's ownership interest in the securities would be lost because the Secured Party relies upon the Chargor's equity of redemption for its own continuing security interest in the collateral.

Segregation was considered unnecessary for cash collateral because the charge is over the Secured Party's contractual obligation to repay the correct amount of cash and not over tangible cash itself. However, following the *Morris* v *Agrichemicals* case in 1997, the Secured Party could have a charge over cash collateral.

(d) No Use of Collateral

Paragraph 6(d) is a very strict prohibition on any sale, loan, repledging, assignment or other disposition by the Secured Party of the Posted Collateral it holds under the Deed. If it did any of these things it would wreck the security interest over the Posted Collateral.

This was the case before the European Directive on Financial Collateral Arrangements was implemented in England in December 2003. It does not apply now.

Nevertheless it is advisable for the parties to agree not to reuse collateral because the transfer of that collateral to a third party could cause the Chargor difficulties in reclaiming it if the Secured Party becomes insolvent.

(e) Rights Accompanying Posted Collateral

(i) Provided no Paragraph 7 Relevant Event or Specified Condition has occurred, the Chargor is entitled to all interest and dividend payments on Posted Collateral securities and to have the Secured Party follow its voting instructions where such rights attach to the Posted Collateral. However, it must indemnify the Secured Party for any expense arising in doing so.

(ii) However, after a Relevant Event or Specified Condition has happened, the Secured Party may exercise its rights, voting or otherwise, over the Posted Collateral without the Chargor's consent although he must notify the Chargor of such exercise.

(f) Calls and Other Obligations

(i) The Chargor is obliged to pay all calls in respect of the Posted Collateral securities and if it fails to do so must reimburse the Secured Party if it decides to pay the call on the Chargor's behalf. Before reimbursement such additional securities will form part of the Chargor's Obligations and will bear interest at the Default Rate from the date the Secured Party pays the call.

(ii) In addition, the Chargor is responsible for supplying the Secured Party with such information as it has in respect of a notice issued by a securities issuer under Section 793 of the Companies Act 2006. Such notices are normally issued by public companies wanting to find out the exact identity of holders of their shares. The sub-paragraph also extends to similar inquiries arising under Articles of Association or constituting documents. Where the Chargor fails to do this, the Secured Party may choose to volunteer such information as it has on the Chargor's behalf.

(iii) The Chargor has a continuing liability to perform and observe all the terms, conditions and obligations it has in relation to the collateral it has charged.

(iv) Paragraph 6(f)(iv) is a general disclaimer by the Secured Party. It is not liable to perform or fulfil any of the Chargor's obligations in relation to the collateral. It is not obliged to make any payment in connection with the collateral nor to file any claim or take any other action to collect or enforce any payment due to it under the Deed.

(g) Distributions and Interest Amount

(i) The Secured Party must transfer to the Chargor any distribution he receives from a securities issuer not later than the Settlement Day following its receipt provided that there are no collateral implications in doing so.

(b) Interest Amount is the interest payable by the Secured Party on cash deposits he holds as collateral from the Chargor. The frequency at which cash interest is paid over to the Chargor is stated in Paragraph 13(i)(ii). It is usually monthly. Again it will not be paid over if it creates or increases a collateral call and will continue to be held as part of the Chargor's collateral balance in those circumstances.

Indeed, if any distributions on securities or interest on cash collateral are not paid over to the Chargor by the Secured Party they will form part of the Posted Collateral balance or be set off in accordance with Paragraph 8(a)(ii) as described below.

Paragraph 7. Default

This Paragraph sets out the events which can trigger the Secured Party's enforcement rights under the Deed. These can arise if an Event of Default occurs or there is a failure to perform any obligation under the Deed. There is a grace period of two Local Business Days where the failure relates to collateral or interest/distribution transfers and 30 days in respect of any other obligation under the Deed. Both grace periods commence from the issue of a notice by the Non-defaulting Party to the Defaulting Party. These failures are individually called a "Relevant Event".

The term "Relevant Event" refers to both parties but in fact the Deed fails to state any consequences of a Relevant Event impacting a Secured Party. A Paragraph 13 amendment is sometimes made to address this.

Paragraph 8. Rights of Enforcement

(a) Secured Party's Rights

Paragraph 8 is the most important part of the Deed as it details the Secured Party's enforcement rights. These arise from a Relevant Event, Specified Condition (see page 285) or the designation of an Early Termination Date happening to the Chargor.

Paragraph 8(a)(i) deals with the Secured Party's enforcement rights with non-cash Posted Collateral.

If the Chargor fails to pay its Obligations in full when they are due, the Secured Party may immediately without notice exercise all its powers under the Deed, for example:

(A) to sell all or part of the Posted Collateral by any legal means and at its absolute discretion; and

(B) to receive payments or moneys due to the Chargor in respect of the Posted Collateral and to give a good discharge for them.

Sections 93 (partial redemption of charges) and 103 (regulation of the exercise of a power of sale) of the Law of Property Act 1925 are stated as not applying under the Deed. These exclusions commonly appear in other English law governed charge documentation.

Paragraph 8(a)(ii) gives the Secured Party the right to realise cash collateral by the following means:

(A) to discharge the Obligations due in any order it sees fit; or

(B) to offset the Chargor's payment of Obligations against any Return Amount owed by the Secured Party to the Chargor; or

(C) to debit any sole or joint accounts of the Chargor held at any of the Secured Party's offices with all or any part of amounts owing by the Chargor under its Obligations to the Secured Party; or

(D) to combine any such account referred to in (C) above with the account holding the Posted Collateral making any currency conversions, transfers or bookkeeping entries on the Chargor's account(s) as the Secured Party thinks are proper.

Finally the Secured Party may also exercise all applicable rights and remedies it has in respect of Other Posted Collateral stated in Paragraph 13(c)(iii).

(b) Power of Attorney

Paragraph 8(b) gives the Secured Party a power of attorney exclusively for the purpose of securing performance of the Obligations. As attorney, the Secured Party can act without limitation in its own name or in the name of the Chargor to:

(i) execute any transfer in relation to the Posted Collateral;

(ii) exercise all the Chargor's powers and rights in the same;

(iii) take various actions in relation to moneys due or arising out of the Posted Collateral and to give a good discharge for the same;

(iv) endorse cheques or similar instruments in relation to the Posted Collateral; and

(v) institute such proceedings, actions or claims as the Secured Party thinks necessary to protect or enforce the security interest under the Deed.

As mentioned before, the Secured Party can only execute a document as a deed under this power of attorney if the power of attorney is itself granted pursuant to a deed. This is why it is sensible to execute the Deed itself as a deed in its signing block on page 24.

(c) Protection of Purchaser

(i) Third parties purchasing collateral from an enforcing Secured Party are protected by this provision. Such a third party purchaser need not concern itself with:

- whether any of the Secured Party's powers has become exercisable;
- whether any Obligation is due;
- whether the Secured Party has acted properly or regularly; or
- how the Secured Party has dealt with any money paid to it.

(ii) Provided the third party purchaser has not acted in bad faith, it may assume that the Secured Party has dealt with the above matters in a valid manner under the Deed. If, however, the Chargor considers that the Secured Party has acted improperly, it may sue but, if successful, it may only claim damages and not receive back any collateral sold to the third party.

As well as protecting the third party collateral purchaser, this provision also indirectly shields the Secured Party from possible liabilities to the collateral purchaser which could otherwise arise.

(d) Deficiencies and Excess Proceeds

When all proceeds from collateral realisations have been received by the Secured Party, he must return any surplus to the Chargor (subject to any further set off or counterclaim rights the Secured Party may have). In any case where there is any shortfall in the amount raised by the collateral to cover the Obligations, the Chargor remains liable for that shortfall.

(e) Final Returns

When the Chargor owes nothing under any present or future Obligations (any liability to withholding tax under Section 2(d) of the ISDA Master Agreement is excluded from this) the Secured Party must return any collateral it is still holding to the Chargor.

Paragraph 9. Representations

In this Paragraph standard representations are made by each party when acting in the capacity of Chargor under the Deed in respect of the following matters:

- It has power to grant a security interest over the collateral and has taken all necessary authorising action.
- It has full legal title to the collateral charged under the Deed and such collateral is free from all encumbrances apart from securities liens in a clearing system.
- Following the Chargor's transfer of the collateral to the Secured Party, the Secured Party will have a valid security interest over the collateral.
- No third party security interests (except for securities' liens in a clearing system) will be created over the collateral following the performance of the Chargor's obligations under the Deed.

The New York CSA includes within its third representation a representation covering the perfection or priority of the security interest created under it. This is fine as far as New York law is concerned but is less practical with the Deed where the security interest could be taken over collateral in various countries and currencies and give rise to conflicts of laws issues.

Paragraph 10. Expenses

This is a simple but comprehensive expenses provision.

Each party will pay its own costs and expenses arising from performing its obligations under the Deed. However, the Chargor shall be liable for any taxes or charges imposed upon the collateral held by the Secured Party as soon as it becomes aware of them.

Following realisation or set off of collateral, the Defaulting Party will pay the liquidation costs unless there is no Defaulting Party in which case both parties will share them equally.

Paragraph 11. Other Provisions

This Paragraph brings together a number of "boilerplate" provisions that give additional protections to the parties.

(a) Default Interest

Where the Secured Party fails to transfer Posted Collateral or an Interest Amount promptly, it will be obliged to pay compensation to the Chargor at the Default Rate (1% over the Chargor's cost of funds). The default interest period includes the date on which such return or payment was due to but excluding the date on which it is actually made (in line with the normal practice in the OTC derivatives markets). In addition daily compounding of interest will also apply.

(b) Further Assurances

Promptly following a demand from the Secured Party, the Chargor will take any necessary action to ensure the security interest is validly created and perfected over the collateral. In addition, the Secured Party undertakes to arrange the release of the charge over any collateral to be returned or paid over to the Chargor under the Deed.

(c) Further Protection

The Chargor will promptly notify the Secured Party of any lawsuit or attachment relating to the collateral it has charged to the Secured Party and defend the same.

(d) Good Faith and Commercially Reasonable Manner

This describes the standard required of both parties for their performance under the Deed including any calculations or valuations they may make.

(e) Demands and Notices

Self-explanatory provision. All demands and notices under the Deed will be given in one of the traditional or electronic means stated in Section 12 of the Master Agreement unless provided otherwise under Paragraph 13.

(f) Specifications of Certain Matters

This provision states that any matter referred to in the Deed as being specified in Paragraph 13 could alternatively be referred to in a Confirmation or other document and, if so, the Deed will be interpreted accordingly. This use of a Confirmation could well cause monitoring problems for Risk or Operations Departments.

(g) Governing Law and Jurisdiction

The Deed is a standalone document and it is appropriate for it to have a separate governing law and jurisdiction clause.

Page 12 of *The User's Guide to the ISDA Credit Support Documents under English Law* points out that under English law there is no objection per se why the Deed cannot be used in conjunction with an ISDA Master Agreement subject to New York law. However, if this is done, greater expense and inconvenience could arise in litigation where two documents under different governing laws are involved.

Moreover, it would be inadvisable to make the Deed subject to New York law because:

- English and New York law have important differences over taking security interests; and
- the Deed was composed with English law principles in mind.

Paragraph 12. Definitions: Glossary of Terms

Assigned Rights	The Chargor's current and future rights to collateral transferred to or present in a securities clearance system or with a third party.
Base Currency	The currency into which risk exposure and collateral is converted to calculate if a collateral call needs to be made.
Base Currency Equivalent	If collateral is denominated in another currency, the amount in the Base Currency needed to buy the other currency at the spot rate of exchange so as to convert it into the Base Currency.
Chargor	The party pledging the collateral under the Deed.
Credit Support Amount	The net risk exposure the Secured Party has on the collateral giver and which needs to be collateralised.
Custodian	A third party who holds securities in a clearing system and administers them for the Secured Party.
Delivery Amount	The amount of collateral the Chargor needs to deliver if he agrees a collateral call from the Secured Party.
Disputing Party	A party who disputes the other party's calculation of Transaction values in determining risk exposure and/or the value of any collateral held or to be returned.
Distributions	Periodic payments of interest or dividends on bonds or shares by issuers of the same to their holders.
Distributions Date	The date upon which holders of bonds or shares are entitled to receive interest or dividends from their issuers.
Eligible Collateral	The collateral types and maturities agreed by the parties to be subject to the Deed

Eligible Credit Support	Eligible Collateral plus Other Eligible Support stated in Paragraph 13(c)(iii) of the Deed including proceeds from securities redeemed by their issuer.
Eligible Currency	The agreed currency or currencies for cash collateral transferred under the Deed.
Exposure	The estimated replacement value of all Transactions (using mid-market quotations from dealers) so as to calculate risk exposure. The calculation is made as if the Transactions were being closed out on the basis described in the definition.
Independent Amount	A confusing term meaning either initial margin taken at the start of a collateral relationship and not counted in risk exposure calculations or a sum taken later in the relationship and which is counted in the risk exposure calculations.
Interest Amount	The aggregate sum of interest due on cash collateral including its conversion into the Base Currency Equivalent where interest is due on cash collateral in various currencies.
Interest Period	The period from and including the date when interest was last paid on cash collateral to but excluding the date on which it is next due to be paid.
Interest Rate	The particular benchmark interest rate (e.g. Fed Funds) which the parties agree shall be paid on cash deposited as collateral. It may include a spread.
Local Business Day	A business day for commercial banks in the location required for the valuation of Transactions and non-securities collateral under the Deed. With securities transfers, a business day for securities clearance systems.
Minimum Transfer Amount	The agreed minimum level that the Credit Support Amount must reach before a party is obliged to deliver or return collateral.
Notification Time	The agreed deadline for making a collateral call.
Obligations	All obligations of either party under the ISDA Master Agreement and the Deed.
Other Eligible Support	Additional or alternative collateral stated in Paragraph 13(c)(iii) of the Deed.
Other Posted Support	Other Eligible Support when transferred and charged to the Secured Party.
Posted Collateral	All Eligible Collateral and Distributions transferred under the Deed to the Secured Party or received by it and under its control. Includes Distributions and Interest Amounts not yet paid over to the Chargor.
Posted Credit Support	The totality of collateral charged to and held by or on behalf of the Secured Party.
Recalculation Date	In a dispute the date or dates upon which recalculation of Transaction and collateral values are made.
Relevant Event	An Event of Default under the ISDA Master Agreement or a performance failure under the terms of the Deed.
Resolution Time	The agreed deadline for resolving disputes.

Return Amount	The collateral amount to be returned by the Secured Party to the Chargor if called by him because it is surplus to the Secured Party's risk exposure on the Chargor.
Secured Party	The party benefiting from the charging of the collateral under the Deed.
Settlement Day	For cash collateral transfers, the following Local Business Day. For securities collateral the next Local Business Day when transfer of such securities can be completed in the normal course of business in the market concerned.
Specified Condition	A pre-condition under which the party affected by a stated Termination Event cannot call for or substitute collateral nor receive dividends or interest on pledged collateral.
Substitute Credit Support	Where agreed by the Secured Party, collateral transferred by the Chargor in substitution for other collateral already held by the Secured Party.
Substitution Date	The deadline for the Secured Party to return designated previously delivered collateral to the Chargor following an agreed substitution.
Substitution Notice	The notice given by the Chargor to the Secured Party requesting the substitution of collateral previously charged with new collateral of equivalent value.
Threshold	The unsecured risk exposure each party allows the other. Collateral may only be called or returned where the risk exposure exceeds the relevant party's Threshold and Minimum Transfer Amount.
Valuation Agent	Either each party to the Deed performing their own valuations of Transactions and collateral and making collateral calls as appropriate or a third party doing this for them both.
Valuation Date	The Local Business Day upon which risk exposure calculations and collateral valuations are made to determine if a collateral call is needed.
Valuation Percentage	The remaining value of collateral expressed in percentage terms after the agreed haircut has been deducted.
Valuation Time	The reference time as at which calculations for collateral calls are made. They are often based on prices at the close of business on the Local Business Day before the Valuation Date.
Value	The agreed valuation bases in Paragraph 13(g)(ii) of the Deed for cash and securities collateral required to value collateral in a dispute.

Paragraph 13. Elections and Variables

In order to avoid repetition, I do not propose to go over the same ground covered in Chapter 5 relating to matters already covered in respect of Paragraph 11 of the English Law CSA. However, the following provisions are not found in that document:

(b) Security Interest for "Obligations"

Paragraph 13(b) allows the parties to expand the Paragraph 12 definition of Obligations (i.e. all obligations of either party under the ISDA Master Agreement and the Deed) to be covered by the security interest. This means that liabilities outside the ISDA Master Agreement and the Deed can be stated and brought within the ambit of the security interest under the Deed. This would, of course, require a legal analysis that such an arrangement would be enforceable under insolvency laws in the Chargor's jurisdiction of incorporation.

(c)(iii) Other Eligible Support

This allows the parties to state other acceptable collateral for a Chargor to supply, for example bank letters of credit, third party guarantees, investment grade corporate bonds or even gold. If Other Eligible Support applies then the parties must in Paragraph 13(j) describe how Value is to be calculated for these items. Any grace periods or Events of Default in the documentation for such assets/instruments should also be taken into account in the Deed provisions.

(e) Conditions Precedent and Secured Party's Rights and Remedies

Paragraph 4(a) sets out the pre-conditions for the parties' collateral call, substitution and distribution transfer rights under the Deed. If an Event of Default is called, an Early Termination Date designated or a Specified Condition occurs the normal run of things is interrupted.

Paragraph 13(e) enables the parties to choose one or more Termination Events as Specified Conditions. If these occur, then the Affected Party cannot call for or substitute collateral nor receive dividends or interest on pledged collateral until the position is cured. This is because a non-Affected Party would not wish, inter alia, to have to release collateral or distributions to an Affected Party in these circumstances. This is a useful protection for a Secured Party. This is an important concern because parties must designate an Additional Termination Event as a Specified Condition if they want this provision to apply. Many parties often erroneously think of an Additional Termination Event as an Event of Default and not realise that it must be specifically designated to enjoy the protections under this clause.

Amendments can be made to the Termination Events for this purpose, for example Credit Event Upon Merger impacts below a certain credit rating. Any Termination Event may be designated as a Specified Condition but Additional Termination Events should only be nominated as Specified Conditions if these mirror Additional Termination Events in the ISDA Master Agreement.

(h) Eligibility to hold Posted Collateral; Custodians

This provision usefully sets out conditions for the parties to hold collateral themselves and to use custodians. As for the parties themselves, they must not have defaulted. As for the Posted Collateral, it is likely to be held only in specified jurisdictions. The custodian is identified and often there is wording added stating minimum asset size or formal credit rating before the Custodian is eligible for appointment. The following is a full example of this:

> Party A and its Custodian will be entitled to hold Posted Collateral pursuant to Paragraph 6(b); provided that the following conditions applicable to it are satisfied:
>
> 1 Party A is not a Defaulting Party nor is subject to a Specified Condition which has occurred and is continuing.
>
> 2 Party A or its Custodian (as the case may be) has US$10 billion in assets
>
> 3 Party A or its Custodian (as the case may be) has a Rating of Baa1 or better from Moody's and BBB+ or better from S&P.
>
> 4 The Custodian is not an Affiliate of Party A.
>
> 5 Posted Collateral may only be held in the following jurisdictions: Germany, United Kingdom, The State of New York.
>
> Initially, the Custodian for Party A is {name of institution}.

The specifications for Party B's Custodian are usually the same.

(j)(i) Other Eligible Support and Other Posted Support

The definition of Value in Chapter 12 is inadequate to cover valuation of these items and so the necessary modus operandi needs to be specified here. Sometimes this might just be expressed as "as agreed between the parties from time to time".

Signing block

The footnotes on page 24 of the Deed give guidance on how it should be executed – under seal or under hand, as appropriate.

PRINCIPAL DIFFERENCES BETWEEN THE ISDA ENGLISH LAW CSA AND THE ISDA ENGLISH LAW CREDIT SUPPORT DEED

The English Law CSA (the "CSA") differs from the English Law Deed in the following main ways:

1 It is a title transfer agreement while the English Law Deed creates a security interest over the collateral.

2 It requires very few formalities for its perfection. It is probably best that the English Law Deed be registered at Companies House in the UK.

3 The English Law Deed is a standalone document (a Credit Support Document under the ISDA Master Agreement) while the CSA is characterised as a Transaction and forms part of the ISDA Master Agreement itself.

4 The CSA relies for its effectiveness on the close-out netting provisions of the ISDA Master Agreement. The English Law Deed relies upon the enforcement of a security interest.

5 The English Law Deed allows for a number of Termination Events to be added as Specified Conditions (i.e. extra events which can trigger the enforcement of a Secured Party's close-out rights). If a Specified Condition applies to a party he cannot call for collateral, substitute it or receive Distributions or interest on collateral posted by it while it lasts. The English Law CSA does not have Specified Conditions.

6 The English Law Deed imposes a duty of care on the Secured Party in holding collateral and allows him to use custodians. This is not permitted in the CSA as it would destroy the mutuality of the set off arrangements.

7 Under the English Law Deed the Chargor appoints the Secured Party as its power of attorney to complete any necessary documents in a close-out situation. There is no such arrangement in the CSA because it is not by nature a deed.

8 The English Law Deed contains a governing law clause (as it is a standalone document) while the CSA does not (as it is part of the ISDA Master Agreement).

9 The English Law Deed allows a separate category of collateral entitled Other Eligible Support to be specified in the Variables Paragraph. This could be a guarantee or letter of credit. The English Law CSA has no such provision.

10 Undoubtedly it would be costlier and more time consuming to enforce collateral under the English Law Deed than under the English Law CSA.

ISDA FALLBACKS FOR THE ENGLISH LAW CREDIT SUPPORT DEED

If no choice is made the following apply by default:

Provision	Fallback
Base Currency	US Dollars
Eligible Currency	Base Currency
Independent Amount	Zero
Threshold	Zero
Minimum Transfer Amount	Zero
Rounding	No rounding
Valuation Agent	The party making demand under Paragraph 3 and the Transferee for Paragraph 6 payments
Substitution Date	The Settlement Date following the Transferee's receipt of New Credit Support
Specified Condition	Does not apply if not specified
Alternative	Paragraph 5 dispute resolution procedures apply
Eligibility to Hold Posted Collateral: Custodians	Secured Party not a Defaulting Party
Transfer of Interest Amount	Last Local Business Day of a calendar month and any Local Business Day when a cash Return Amount is due to the Transferor
Alternative to Interest Amount	Paragraph 6(g)(ii) and Paragraph 12 definition of Interest Amount applies

The following are provisions that must be completed if there is no fallback:

- Eligible Collateral
- Other Eligible Support
- Valuation Date
- Valuation Time
- Notification Time
- Resolution Time
- Value
- Interest Rate
- Value and Transfer of Other Eligible Support and Other Posted Support
- Addresses for Transfers.

8

Developments since 2002

Results of ISDA collateral initiatives since 2001

ISDA Collateral Roadmaps 2010 and 2011 and their Constituents

Portfolio Reconciliation Plan

Collateralized Portfolio Reconciliation Operational Best Practices

Minimum Market Standards for Collateralized Portfolio Reconciliation

Standards for the Electronic Exchange of OTC Derivative Margin Calls

Market Review of OTC Derivative Bilateral Collateralization Practices

Best Practices for the OTC Derivatives Collateral Process

The Independent Amount White Paper

ISDA Dispute Resolution Procedure

Central clearing counterparties and collateralisation

The “Standardised CSA”

The future

RESULTS OF ISDA COLLATERAL INITIATIVES SINCE 2001

Before we look at the considerable activity in the past two years in the collateral space, it might be useful briefly to cover collateral initiatives that have taken place since the first edition of this book in 2002. The main ones are as follows:

The 2001 ISDA Margin Provisions

After two years of discussions the *2001 ISDA Margin Provisions* were published in May 2001. They take the form of a five-part definitional booklet structured as follows:

Part 1: Operational Provisions

This part contains the non-legal, operational provisions that are essentially common whether an outright title transfer or security interest approach to taking margin is adopted. These include transfer timing, dispute resolution and substitutions.

Part 2: Security Interest Approach (New York law)

Provisions necessary where the parties intend to create a security interest in margin under New York law.

Part 3: Title Transfer Approach (English law)

Provisions necessary where the parties intend to adopt a title transfer approach to taking margin under English law.

Part 4: Local Law Annex

Provisions added to address local legal requirements relevant to the chosen method of taking margin. Section 4.1 allows the parties to use the Provisions when using certain Japanese margin.

Part 5: Definitions

(51 of them.)

2001 ISDA Margin Supplement (Appendix A)

The core definitional booklet document is supplemented by a Margin Supplement that allows the parties to make various choices and amendments to the Provisions and in this way is similar to the Variables Paragraphs of the ISDA Credit Support Documents.

So the *2001 ISDA Margin Provisions* contain the governing text and the Supplement is exchanged between the parties. It becomes part of the ISDA

Master Agreement and incorporates the Provisions. It also states the elections and variables chosen from the Provisions.

The Provisions cannot be used with the English law Deed or the Japanese Credit Support Annex.

Because of their tight operational deadlines for collateral margin calls, transfers, substitutions and dispute resolutions, the Provisions have not caught on in the market and the *ISDA Market Survey 2009* reported that only 334 had been signed out of an estimated 150,100 global volume of collateral documents at the time. ISDA has published no updated figure since.

ISDA 2001 Credit Support Protocol

On 1 August 2001 ISDA published this Protocol which through the selection of 10 Annexes (5 each for the English Law Credit Support Annex and the New York Credit Support Annex) allowed parties to amend certain provisions in their CSAs on a multilateral basis to cater for the requirements of the *2001 ISDA Margin Provisions*.

The 10 Annexes were:

English Law CSA	New York Law CSA
Annex 1 Transfer Timing	Annex 1 Transfer Timing
Annex 2 Dispute Resolution	Annex 2 Dispute Resolution
Annex 3 Dispute Termination Event	Annex 3 Dispute Termination Event
Annex 4 Substitutions	Annex 4 Exchanges
Annex 5 Definitions	Annex 5 Definitions

The Protocol was open for adherence from 1 August 2001 until 28 February 2002. Only one party adhered to it and so it was not a success.

ISDA Collateral Asset Definitions

At its AGM in Berlin in April 2002, ISDA announced a new project to produce a definitions booklet for collateral assets that would complement the existing ISDA Credit Support Documents.

One of the problems that has arisen in the market was that even eligible collateral descriptions in CSAs could have unintended delivery consequences. The following example was quoted in the presentation. The CSA may state:

> **... negotiable debt obligations issued by the Government of the United States of America having a remaining maturity of more than one year but not more than 10 years.**

One imagines a delivery of US Treasury bills, notes or bonds depending upon tenor. However, a counterparty could deliver Treasury Inflation Protected Securities (TIPS) within this description. TIPS are issued by the US Treasury through auctions three times a year. Fixed interest is paid twice yearly upon the inflation adjusted principal of the bonds. The principal adjusted for inflation is paid out upon the maturity of these bonds after 10 years. With inflation adjustment to these securities every 6 months at coupon payment times, their valuation for haircutting purposes is a little more complex than usual.

The *Collateral Asset Definitions* deals with this by proposing a standard set of terms and definitions for collateral assets. The aim is to include eligible collateral lists in ISDA Credit Support Documents by making reference to the *Collateral Asset Definitions*. The *Collateral Asset Definitions* were published in June 2003 and there has been steady use of them in the market.

Form of Amendment to 1994 ISDA Credit Support Annex (Security Interest – New York Law) and the 1995 ISDA Credit Support Annex (Transfer – English Law)

These Amendments let parties with 1992 ISDA Master Agreements (which have been amended to include Close-out Amount) to amend their existing Credit Support Annex to take into account the addition of Close-out Amount and the deletion of Market Quotation and Loss where they appear in the Dispute Resolution and Default provisions and the definition of Exposure.

2005 ISDA Collateral Guidelines

The *2005 ISDA Collateral Guidelines* (the "2005 Guidelines") comprehensively updated the 1998 *Guidelines for Collateral Practitioners*.

The 2005 Guidelines did the following:

- documented the state of collateral management practice at the end of 2004;
- discussed the nature and mechanics of collateralisation;
- described the interaction of the collateral management unit with other areas in the firm;
- identified the benefits and risks of collateralisation;
- outlined then current trends and possible future developments in collateral management.

While perhaps a little dated now, the 2005 Guidelines contain much useful information and are very readable for an ISDA publication.

2008 ISDA Credit Support Annex (Loan/Japanese Pledge)

The latest Japanese Law CSA was published by ISDA on 21 October 2008. It is a stand-alone document (not an Annex to the Schedule).

The Annex reflects new netting, bankruptcy and securities clearing system legislation that were implemented in Japan after the 1995 ISDA Credit Support Annex (Security Interest – Japanese Law) was published. It is used in documenting bilateral security and other credit support arrangements between parties for transactions documented under an ISDA Master Agreement where the parties intend to use assets located in Japan as collateral. This Annex assumes that Japanese law will govern questions of perfection and priorities relating to posted collateral and is designed to cover collateral arrangements involving cash, deposit accounts, Japanese government bonds or other marketable securities located in Japan.

ISDA COLLATERAL ROADMAPS 2010 AND 2011 AND THEIR CONSTITUENTS

On 31 October and 31 December 2008, the management of the leading major derivative dealers wrote two letters to the Federal Reserve Bank of New York that set out a comprehensive set of commitments by major dealers to reform market practice in collateral management.

The main commitments were:

- promptly to put in place a Portfolio Reconciliation practice to detect major trade population and risk exposure differences that could lead to disputed collateral calls;
- to follow that up with a new industry-wide Dispute Resolution Procedure; and
- to set out a Roadmap for Collateral Management

The first Roadmap was published on 2 February 2009. It included specific implementation steps and deadlines for proposed actions many of which were completed in 2009 and early 2010, albeit after their deadlines in a few instances.

The Roadmap was reviewed, updated and published as the *2010 Roadmap for Collateral Management* on 15 April 2010. It was based on recommendations from three ISDA analytical documents, viz:

- *Market Review of Bilateral Collateralization Practices* (published on 1 March 2010);
- *Independent Amounts* White Paper (also published on 1 March 2010);
- *Portfolio Reconciliation Implementation Plan* (published on 15 April 2010).

On 1 March 2010 the series of Market Initiative commitments shown in Table 8.1 were made to global regulators in a letter:

Table 8.1

Target date	Item
15 April 2010	Update Roadmap and establish template for monthly report on disputed collateral and risk exposure amounts.
31 May 2010	(1) Start submitting such reports to supervisors. (2) Establish a working group to develop standard provisions on Independent Amount holding arrangements in Custodian and triparty collateral agent documentation for operational consistency when parties adopt these arrangements.
30 June 2010	Publish Best Practices for Collateral Management Process.
30 June 2010	Start monthly one-way portfolio reconciliation with OTC counterparties where 1000+ trades exist.
31 July 2010	Expand monthly regulatory portfolio reconciliation reports to show progress on this new commitment.
30 September 2010	Complete industry testing and refinement of the Dispute Resolution Procedure.
30 November 2010	ISDA to investigate if consent to substitution can be harmonised between the English Law and New York Law CSA possibly on a non-consensual basis.
31 December 2010	(1) Industry to develop a fully interoperable standardised electronic communication for margin calls. G14 to start to pilot this with their chosen vendors by 31 January 2010 if a commercially viable solution is available. (2) Complete detailed review of the Phase I of a two-phased Portfolio Reconciliation plan by 31 December 2010 to define targets for Phase II to be implemented in 2011.
31 January 2011	ISDA to develop a standard form of amendment agreement allowing parties to a New York Law CSA to deal with segregated Independent Amounts as a separate, protected pool of collateral including enforceability of netting and collateral provisions: avoidance of regulatory arbitrage; ensuring collateral held by a non-defaulting party is not subject to enforcement delays; and surplus collateral held by a defaulting party is returned promptly.
No deadline	A working group to be set up to address collateral requirements of central clearing counterparties (CCPs) and use of straight-through processing with them.
Ongoing	Liaison with regulators on matters and recommendations arising from ISDA collateral analytical documents.

On 30 June 2011 ISDA published its *2011 Roadmap for Collateral Management* and outlined the commitments for 2011 shown in Table 8.2.

Table 8.2

Target date	Item
31 March 2011	Amend the threshold of G14 dispute reporting from disputes over US$20 million and 15 days to disputes over US$15 million and 15 days, for reports starting in April 2011.
7 April 2011	Release a revised draft of the ISDA 2011 Convention on Portfolio Reconciliation and the Investigation of Disputed Margin Calls (the "Convention").
26 April 2011	Release a revised draft of the ISDA 2011 Formal Market Polling Procedure (the "MPP").
4 May 2011	Begin to trial the Convention and MPP for a three-month period ending 29 July 2011 between G14 members and other interested market participants on a bilateral basis.
31 May 2011	Enhance G14 reports to include disputes both where the reporting entity is calling for collateral and being disputed and where such a reporting entity is being called for collateral and is disputing. G14 members will report on the number of disputes that are undertaken through a polling process during the previous month.
30 June 2011	Investigate the feasibility of achieving a consolidated, no-name report of large disputes across industry participants.
30 June 2011	Reduce the threshold for routine portfolio reconciliation of collateralised portfolios from those exceeding 1,000 transactions to those exceeding 500 transactions and reconcile these portfolios at least monthly.
30 June 2011	Update the Collateral Roadmap.
15 July 2011	Complete analysis of whether treatment of consent to a substitution request can be standardised between the English Law and New York Law CSAs.
August 2011	Update ISDA Minimum Market Standards for Collateralized Portfolio Reconciliation. It is planned that these be adopted on a phased basis from December 2011 until 2013.
9 September 2011	Publish a revised draft of the ISDA Dispute Resolution Documents reflecting lessons learned in the trial period.
9 September 2011	Release a phased implementation plan for industry adoption of the revised Dispute Resolution Documents.
30 November 2011	Update the Best Practices for the OTC Derivatives Collateral Process document published in June 2010.
Ongoing	Continue developmental work with vendors and the industry to bring at least one commercially viable, robust and mature electronic messaging platform for collateral management to market.

Progress on matters during July–September 2011 has not been reported by ISDA at the time of writing (October 2011).

PORTFOLIO RECONCILIATION PLAN

Back in 2002 ISDA initiated an Electronic Data Interchange Project and formed a working group to design standard formats for portfolio information notices in Excel and XML to make reconciliations easier, both at the start of a collateralised relationship and in disputes. Some consideration was also given to proposing a standard format for margin call notices.

While progress was made on this, there was no industry-wide adoption of this work. Operational risk can arise if parties do not accurately record their OTC derivatives trade populations in their systems. Moreover regulators have introduced requirements to validate the accuracy of OTC derivatives portfolio populations.

In 2008 ISDA published a *Portfolio Reconciliation in Practice* paper followed by its *Best Practice Guidance for Collateralized Portfolio Reconciliation Between Derivatives Market Professionals.*

By mid-2009 the major derivative dealers (often referred to as the Fed 14 or the G14) had agreed to exchange daily collateralised portfolio reconciliation information where they had 500 trades or more with each other.

This was followed in December 2009 by the publication of a feasibility study entitled *Extending Collateralized Portfolio Reconciliations* which discussed the elements and infrastructure needed to increase portfolio reconciliation across the OTC derivatives market.

The Feasibility Study proposed to set common standards and adopt a consistent approach across the market to encourage wider use of portfolio reconciliation as a risk reduction tool. This aimed to reduce the then current lack of standardisation and the many different technological packages used in valuing transactions and concerns over security in data transmission.

The objective of collateralised portfolio reconciliation is to ensure that two organisations have one consistent record and approach in valuing positions by matching and comparing the portfolio deals through an agreed minimum set of information fields.

The main problems identified in the market were:

- multiple reconciliation solutions (i.e. vendor solutions and in house solutions yielding very different results due to different trade matching algorithms and data sets);
- different reconciliation models (i.e. bilateral sharing of reconciliation results or one party performing the function for both);
- competing break resolution deadline priorities;
- inconsistent expectations of the parties;
- lack of transparency;
- reconciliation frequency (i.e. major dealers daily but other market players weekly or ad hoc);

- **longer lead time for major players to implement IT solutions given high volume portfolios; and**
- **staff resourcing issues.**

Many of these issues would have been resolved bilaterally between parties. However, the two main problems were identified as Reconciliation Technology and Common Data Standards and Consistency.

Reconciliation Technology

The number of technology solutions used to perform reconciliations is a major problem to be addressed. At a high level, there are two basic options:

1 All participants use one technology solution. Or

2 All participants use different technology solutions but those solutions are inter-operable and perform on a consistent basis to provide consistent results.

Looking at current models, it is clear that there are applications (particularly in-house solutions) that were built for different and wider purposes beyond collateralised portfolio reconciliation. Such broader use would be a natural development of reconciliation activities in the future.

The immediate solution must be scaleable, i.e. able to deal efficiently with increasing volumes and will need to provide transparency over reconciliation results for both parties. Use of automated tools and secure transmission methods will need to support rollout in a high-volume environment. Many firms are using triResolve for portfolio reconciliation, margin calling and dispute resolution purposes.

Common data standards and consistency

The second fundamental issue is data standards, i.e. how trades are represented in the portfolio, the fields used to match trades accurately and field content and format. While different matching models can produce different results, unless trades can be presented in a standardised, consistent manner by all parties, portfolios cannot be reconciled accurately or in any automated fashion. Parties will be thrown back to manual investigation and exchange trade confirmations or other evidence in order to pair up trades. The delays caused by doing this are significant and the process eats up staff time.

ISDA published its *Minimum Market Standards for Collateralized Portfolio Reconciliation* ("MMS") on 20 January 2010. The market agreed minimum field requirements for collateralised OTC derivative reconciliations should be viewed as entry level criteria for wider market rollout.

The Feasibility Study made three recommendations, viz:

- OTC derivative markets players should adopt the *Collateralized Portfolio Reconciliation Best Operational Practices* (published on 20 January 2010).
- OTC derivatives players should adopt the *Minimum Market Standards for Collateralized Portfolio Reconciliation* (also published on 20 January 2010).
- ISDA should commission an Implementation Plan to develop a graduated approach to wider market adoption of portfolio reconciliation measures. This was published on 12 April 2010.

Let us look at each of these in turn.

COLLATERALIZED PORTFOLIO RECONCILIATION BEST OPERATIONAL PRACTICES

These Best Practices and the December 2009 Feasibility Study noted that portfolio reconciliation was done on a proactive basis to ensure portfolio valuations and populations remained in line to reduce disputes and on a reactive basis when a dispute arose. The standards set in these Best Practices are regarded as the minimum market entry level criteria for collateral portfolio reconciliations.

There are 25 Best Practices that are listed in Table 8.3.

Table 8.3

Best Practice No.	Description	Best Practice Main Comments
1	Parties to know size of teams for reconciliation purposes and exchange contact lists and advise escalation trigger points.	Both parties to work together co-operatively and make reconciliation a high priority.
2	Larger, active portfolios should be regularly reconciled	A proactive reconciliation strategy reduces both operational risk and the timescale during which portfolio discrepancies survive.
3	Portfolio reconciliation frequency should take account of portfolio size, activity and volatility and parties' creditworthiness.	Very active relationships should reconcile portfolios daily. Otherwise weekly, monthly or quarterly reconciliations might be appropriate. Where portfolios have little or no activity, an ad hoc annual reconciliation is proposed.

Best Practice No.	Description	Best Practice Main Comments
4	Both parties should use reconciliation technology (in-house or vendor provided) that involves them in reconciling portfolios, gives transparency and reduces staff time.	Automated processes such as market vendor services are recommended for large, active portfolios. In-house solutions are more appropriate for low-volume, low-activity portfolios.
5	Parties to agree portfolio tolerances for mark-to-market booking differences.	This reduces the potential for disputes.
6	OTC derivatives industry to adopt Minimum Market Standards for data presentation in collateral portfolio reconciliation.	Consistent format and agreed standards for this are vital for successful reconciliation.
7	One confirmation = one trade resulting in one line of data in a reconciliation file.	Work needed to reduce booking of complex trades as there are multiple transaction legs.
8	Portfolios should be populated and valued as at the close of business on the previous business day.	It has to be a business day for both parties.
9	Reconcilable portfolio trade populations should be as contemplated by the governing Master Agreement documentation.	A trade would normally be described as a "Transaction" in an ISDA style Confirmation.
10	Individual trades should at least have a product classification when being reconciled.	Trades should as a minimum be described as a generic product class. This applies to structured trades too.
11	Counterparty trade IDs and any common market product IDs should be stated in the reconciliation file.	Trade IDs should apply for the life of the trade and not be reused for later trades. A structured trade should have an additional common ID applying to all its legs.
12	Reconciliation files should be transmitted securely.	Use of automated and vendor services appropriate for large-volume portfolios. With small portfolios exchange of information by email normal but these files should be password protected and read receipt enabled.
13	Reconciliation files to be sent in an industry standard format agreed between the parties.	Nothing significant added.

Best Practice No.	Description	Best Practice Main Comments
14	Portfolios should be available for reconciliation on any mutual business day upon either party's request.	It must be a mutual business day for both parties where their collateral relationship is managed or where reconciliation takes place.
15	Parties agree the time for files to be exchanged or uploaded.	With daily or frequent reconciliations, the deadline should be 12 noon in the place where their collateral relationship is managed or where reconciliation takes place.
16	Full results of all breaks arising from a reconciliation should be made available to a requesting counterparty.	Where firms use an internal automated portfolio reconciliation solution it should connect to a single technology source to view results.
17	Parties should agree mutual priorities for break resolution and their focus for addressing main break categories.	Breaks tend to concern mark-to-market differences, misbooking and unmatched trades.
18	Priority and staff resourcing should be provided by firms to ensure prompt investigation of breaks when requested.	Parties can agree deadlines and actions to resolve breaks. The industry expects reconciliation results on the same day as the reconciliation itself. Parties should raise queries by the next business day and the whole process should be completed within five business days after the reconciliation.
19	Break resolution progress to be tracked and who is responsible for making each move. Requested information should be provided within one business day of a party's request.	Parties are mutually responsible for break management.
20	Where a break involves other functional areas in a firm, there must be a process for co-operation to take place.	Communication lines and procedures need to be established firm-wide to resolve breaks and capture root causes that may create future breaks.
21	Escalation procedures should be established by firms.	A cross-departmental escalation procedure should be in place to address unreasonable delays in the break resolution process. Counterparty to be advised of contact points for escalation.

Best Practice No.	Description	Best Practice Main Comments
22	Where an internal system or process causes a trade break, the firm concerned is expected to act in good faith to resolve the data issue concerned promptly.	System issues cause many breaks (e.g. one-off feed or recurring feed issues and slow inputting and removal of trades).
23	For break resolution purposes, firms need to understand their whole trade booking and recording process in order to filter out break causes.	Unmatched trades are a major cause of breaks but many systems filter them out after five days. However, earlier identification is better.
24	Firms should agree minimum standards and methods for reporting breaks to support transparency of reconciliation results.	Parties should exchange results no later than the business day following the reconciliation taking place. Breaks should be aged by both parties from the date first discovered.
25	Firms should measure their compliance against these Best Practices and identify shortcomings.	Nothing significant added.

While these Best Practices recognise that parties should be free to decide between themselves which parameters for portfolio reconciliation best suit them mutually, the new ISDA Dispute Resolution Procedures, if triggered by either party, may supersede Best Practice terms in certain areas.

MINIMUM MARKET STANDARDS FOR COLLATERALIZED PORTFOLIO RECONCILIATION

These Minimum Market Standards were also published on 20 January 2010 in the form of a table or matrix.

They have the following fields:

- Asset Class (e.g. Interest Rate Derivatives)
- Product Sub-Group (e.g. Interest Rate Swap (Vanilla))
- Your Trade ID
- Counterparty Trade ID
- 1st Notional (i.e. Notional Amount)
- 1st Currency
- 2nd Notional
- 2nd Currency

- Price (i.e. Fixed Rate)
- Reference Entity/Underlying (i.e. Floating Rate source, e.g. LIBOR)
- Trade Date
- Start Date (i.e. Effective Date)
- End Date (i.e. Maturity Date)
- MTM (i.e. mark-to-market value as per CSA Base Currency)
- Group ID (only applies to multiple transaction legs, e.g. with a structured deal)
- Pay/Rec or Buy Sell (i.e. Pay/Rec on Fixed Leg)
- Independent Amount Required (if yes it must be stated in the CSA Base Currency)
- External Match ID (include if confirmed electronically and it is available)
- Confirmation status
- Upfront fees (include if applicable)
- Fee Settlement Date (include if applicable)
- Final Settlement Date (include if applicable).

The Feasibility Study recommended that OTC derivative market players should adopt these Minimum Market Standards, and the Fed 14 have.

Feasibility Study Implementation Plan: Extending Collateralized Portfolio Reconciliation

This Implementation Plan was published on 12 April 2010 and is a short seven-page document. Its objective is "to recommend a phased approach to extending the discipline of portfolio reconciliation as best practice throughout the OTC derivative market, giving consideration to any infrastructure and standardisation of practices which may be needed to support this". The Fed 14 already reconcile portfolios with each other every business day.

Following the Feasibility study there was a clear view among firms already reconciling regularly that their existing technology choices should be respected because they had developed internal workflows and processes to support high-volume trading. It would be most efficient for both parties to perform reconciliations if required. Greater standardisation of data was also useful in this context.

However, questions about the interoperability of in-house technology and vendor platform solutions for file exchange and reconciliation purposes to reach a shared bilateral review of results are hard to resolve and dialogue is continuing in the market on this issue.

The Implementation Plan also comments on secure transmission of data and the means for doing this, adding that market vendors could consider designing secure connections for parties reconciling their portfolios infrequently.

The Implementation Plan proposed a two-phase market roll out for portfolio reconciliation in the broader market (i.e. beyond the Fed 14). The following minimum commitments were proposed by 30 June 2010:

- Collateralised portfolios with any OTC counterparty comprising more than 1,000 trades should be reconciled at least monthly by 30 June 2010.
- Both parties should provide a portfolio data file to a pre-agreed schedule without further request and should be able to provide a file of sufficient data (inclusive of net present values by trade) to a quality standard that allows the file to be readily reconciled.
- Each party should be able to reconcile on a platform or technology of their choice (vendor managed or in-house infrastructure).
- Each party is to provide results on request in a mutually agreed form.
- To maintain efficiency, scalability and security of the process, counterparties will need mutually to agree a method of secure data delivery that should be to the destination of each party's choice.
- The Fed 14 dealers will expand current monthly Portfolio Reconciliation reports submitted to their regulators to reflect the above commitment by 31 July 2010.

The Phase I results were to be reviewed until 31 December 2010 before Phase II started. This was to gauge the level of market support and readiness, and the scope of further market infrastructure and standardisation needed.

In April 2010 the following Phase II targets were envisaged:

- a decision to increase the frequency of reconciling individual collateralised portfolios of over 1,000 trades from a minimum of monthly to weekly;
- a decision around expanding commitments to reconcile any collateralised portfolio comprising more than 500 trades at least monthly;
- a decision around expanding commitments to reconcile collateralised portfolios comprising more than 1,000 trades across multiple funds at the Credit Support Annex (CSA) level with buy-side firms (e.g. hedge funds) at least monthly;
- an assessment of requirements to allow introduction of periodic reconciliation of portfolios with less than 500 trades following the Phase II implementation.

ISDA's Collateral Steering Committee and Infrastructure Working Group also considered the following points for implementation in or after Phase II:

- The market should consider if it can move towards a bilateral view of reconciliation results at some future stage. This could include working with vendors to obtain a satisfactory degree of interoperability.
- Files for reconciliation should comply with the Minimum Market Standards ("MMS") for Collateralized Portfolio Reconciliation and the market should adopt the Collateralized Portfolio Reconciliation Best Practices.
- If sufficient demand develops, vendor services could be encouraged to support normalising of data to MMS standards.
- Potential development of secure data transfer options should be encouraged with vendors to mitigate breaches of security for client data and eliminate the practice of email exchange for reconciliation files.

STANDARDS FOR THE ELECTRONIC EXCHANGE OF OTC DERIVATIVE MARGIN CALLS

This 46-page document was published by ISDA on 12 November 2009. It noted that margin call notices, interest settlement confirmations and requests for collateral substitutions were often sent by email "without the use of any centrally-defined standard message format" and "with precious little security in data transmission".

The document proposes that collateral messages be exchanged in an open standard format electronically which permits interoperability between existing platforms so that a party can use its chosen vendor and exchange messages with another market player even if they use a different vendor platform. The document advocates the use of Financial products Markup Language ("FpML") which is supported by ISDA and is established as an open standard of electronic data principally relating to trade capture and confirmations for OTC derivatives.

The document sets out the data requirements for key collateral processes to facilitate interoperability between market players and vendors. It includes:

- a proposal defining the sequence of messages to be exchanged electronically between parties for the following: Margin Call, Interest Payment and Collateral Substitution; and

- **For each message exchange in relation to these processes, a definition of the standard attributes of each message, including a proposal for the optimal timing and frequency of each message.**

The second paragraph is optional between parties. They are meant to be technical definitions to facilitate standardised electronic messaging between parties. It is expected that these definitions will be translated into FpML messages to support them but they are not intended to amend or limit the rights of any party under its CSA or other collateral agreement.

It is anticipated that in due course these standards will be extended for the instruction of settlement of collateral movements and interest payments. In addition they may be used in exchanging electronic messages with central clearing counterparties once their requirements are finalised.

ISDA encourages the use of these standardised messages, but recognises the technical hurdles to implementation that firms and vendors will encounter and that it may take some time for them to be used widely in the market. However, the intention is for the collateral management industry to work with vendors in applying the use of FpML messages based on the standards defined within this document.

The main body of the document describes the step-by-step process of a margin call, interest payment message and substitution request, and the sequence and format of messages to be used. It excludes instructions for collateral settlement which, of course, will vary in each case.

MARKET REVIEW OF OTC DERIVATIVE BILATERAL COLLATERALIZATION PRACTICES

This important wide-ranging document was published on 1 March 2010 and reviewed the use of collateral in the OTC derivative market and the likelihood of systemic risks, and if any reforms to collateral practices were needed.

Much of the generic content of the paper's market review appears in the previous chapters of this book, but the Review made the 12 recommendations shown in Table 8.4.

Table 8.4

Recommendation No.	Recommendation	Current status
1	Subject to relevant capital standards and supervisory oversight (where applicable) parties active in the bilateral OTC derivative markets should have the responsibility and the authority to decide regarding the credit risk they assume, including the potential use of credit risk mitigation measures such as collateralisation, insurance or other credit enhancement techniques.	It was decided that this was a matter for firms themselves to decide.
2	National, Regional, and State legislative bodies should review applicable laws within their jurisdiction and take steps to ensure that netting and collateral provisions (including those relating to security interests), typically used in the bilateral OTC derivative market are promptly enforceable in the event of insolvency, bankruptcy, administration, conservatorship and other similar proceedings affecting all market participants.	Roadmap commitment to work with legislators and regulators.
3	Consideration should be given to ensure there is harmonisation of policy and regulation to avoid regulatory and legislative arbitrage across jurisdiction and entity types.	Roadmap commitment to work with legislators and regulators.
4	ISDA, SIFMA, MFA and market participants should work together to develop standard provisions that may be incorporated into documents for Third Party Custodian and Tri-Party Collateral Agent Independent Amount holding arrangements.	Roadmap commitment to work with legislators and regulators.
5	ISDA should continue the drive towards standardisation of format and electronic communication of margin calls in the market, coordinating across market participant firms and vendors who should create fully interoperable solutions that improve market efficiency and reduce systemic risk.	Ongoing.

Recommendation No.	Recommendation	Current status
6	The requirement to receive consent ahead of agreeing to a substitution differs depending upon the choice of ISDA Credit Support Document and the terms of that particular document. ISDA should investigate whether the treatment of consent can be standardised between the English CSA and the New York CSA and determine whether a template English CSA or New York CSA can be developed that treats substitution requests as non-consensual (for new collateral agreements or existing agreements that are subject to renegotiation).	Ongoing. See Standardised CSA section towards the end of this chapter.
7	A party receiving a reasonable request from their counterparty to provide their view of portfolio content and valuation in order to facilitate a portfolio reconciliation for the purpose of the collateralisation process or resolution of a margin dispute should provide the requested data on a timely basis, according to the relevant documentation and consistent with the ISDA Portfolio Reconciliation Best Practices and Minimum Market Standards papers.	Ongoing.
8	A party in receipt of portfolio content and valuation details from its counterparty to facilitate the collateralisation process or resolution of a margin dispute should take commercially reasonable measures so that its sales and trading personnel do not have access in the ordinary course of business to trade details or valuations, except for the purpose of margin dispute resolution, investigation of portfolio differences and similar issue-driven situations, and then only to the limited extent necessary in the circumstances.	Added to *Best Practices for the OTC Derivatives Collateral Process*.
9	In order to promote market efficiency and to reduce systemic risk through standardisation, ISDA should nominate a Working Group to develop, in partnership with clearing house operators, a set of guiding principles and practical recommendations for common Straight Through Processing to be adopted by all entities that interact with the bilateral collateralisation process (including central clearing houses).	Ongoing.

Recommendation No.	Recommendation	Current status
10	The use of credit-based Thresholds that reduce as credit ratings decline or credit spreads widen should be carefully considered. Parties that elect to use these elements in collateral arrangements should recognise that they may have a ratcheting effect that reduces credit risk to one party while simultaneously increasing liquidity demands on the other party if the latter suffers credit deterioration. Accordingly, both parties should ensure that they have in place appropriate monitoring to (a) detect and respond to credit deterioration in their counterparty and (b) forecast and manage the liquidity impact of their own credit deterioration. Alternatively, the use of fixed thresholds and/or frequent margin calls should also be considered, and all collateral structures should be considered in the context of guarantees and other credit risk mitigants that may be available.	It was decided that this was a matter for firms themselves to decide.
11	Firms should consider the quality and liquidity of collateral when including assets in the eligible collateral schedule for each credit support arrangement. In particular, in the case of new collateral agreements and as existing agreements are subject to substantial re-negotiation, for non-cash collateral firms should perform analysis and apply appropriate haircuts and concentration limits such that post-liquidation proceeds of collateral will probably be sufficient to cover expected credit exposure and can be realised in a reasonable period even in distressed market conditions.	Ongoing.
12	All parties should, subject to local law requirements, continue to be able to hold collateral to cover Variation Margin free of any segregation requirement, restriction on rehypothecation or other limitation.	Ongoing.

BEST PRACTICES FOR THE OTC DERIVATIVES COLLATERAL PROCESS

In June 2009 ISDA members decided to re-examine the collateral management function based on the events of the 2008 financial crisis and published their Best Practices document on 30 June 2010.

The document covers bilateral OTC derivatives trades collateralised under a New York Law CSA, English Law CSA and English Law Credit Support Deed. It does *not* cover OTC derivatives given up by clearing members on behalf of their clients to CCPs.

There are a total of 73 recommendations in these Best Practices. They are numbered and described in Table 8.5. Comments in the third column are paraphrased in most cases from the Best Practices document but also at times include my own comments.

Table 8.5

Best Practice No.	Best Practice	Comment
1.1	Newly signed CSA terms to be promptly input on to internal systems.	Client boarding on to internal systems should be done promptly and accurately ideally within 2–3 days. Once done, there should be a procedure in place that lets the collateral management unit access all executed agreements and verify that operational terms have been captured correctly within the collateral management system. The CSA terms that have been entered in the legal documentation system should automatically feed into the collateral calculation system. Where no system interface exists between the legal documentation and collateral systems, the collateral team must have access to copies of executed documents.
1.2	General contact information for collateral operations should be included in the CSA.	Each party should provide a group email address, phone number and initial operations contact and maintain a current list of daily contacts.

Best Practice No.	Best Practice	Comment
1.3	Standard settlement instructions (SSIs) should be exchanged before the first collateral delivery.	Institutions should, as a minimum, call back someone other than the individual who originally supplied the SSIs. The call-back process also applies to amended SSIs.
1.4	Any CSA or Long Form Confirmation with non-standard terms should be reviewed by collateral operations before execution.	This is in case extended manual support is needed. Such terms are likely to be reviewed by a Legal Department too.
1.5	ISDA/CSA should be used for collateral terms. Otherwise they should be stated in a Long Form Confirmation if a credit officer agrees to trades beforehand.	Collateral terms in a Long Form Confirmation should be reviewed by Legal, Credit and Collateral Management before signing to ensure that they can each support them.
1.6	Long Form Confirmations should at least contain the standard CSA definitions.	The collateral terms included in the Long Form Confirmation should be captured in the collateral management system to facilitate an automated collateral call process.
2.1	For new trades, initial and variation margin should be included in collateral calculations on a T+1 basis.	Nothing added.
2.2	Variation Margin and Initial Margin on Terminated or Matured Trades.	Nothing stated in Best Practice. To be added in future.
2.3	All OTC derivative product types to be included in the collateral call process.	Parties can exclude certain product types by mutual agreement. Spot FX is normally excluded.
2.4	Collateral should be revalued daily beginning on the Valuation Date with haircuts applied in line with the CSA. Collateral should be clearly defined in the CSA. Securities collateral should be valued including accrued interest while cash collateral values should generally exclude accrued interest. Reporting should be available to enable regular reconciliation of collateral amounts between the parties to assist with dispute resolution.	Securities collateral should be maintained at the ISIN/CUSIP level with market recognised pricing feeds to enable daily recalculation of collateral values at each day's closing values.

Best Practice No.	Best Practice	Comment
3.1	Vital that data used in collateral calculation be received in the collateral management system in a timely manner so that collateral calls can be made as soon as possible.	It is critical to establish firm cut off times for delivery and receipt of trade level details into collateral management systems. All business areas should be made aware of timeframes for the delivery of data and that trades booked after the cut off time will not feed into systems and will not be included in the collateral call. Calls must be issued by the Notification Time in the CSA. However, it is better for a call to be issued as soon as operationally possible.
3.2	Collateral practitioners must ensure that robust data integrity controls and processes are in place so that completely accurate data is transmitted in a collateral call and disputes are avoided.	Collateral call calculations rely on several data sources: trade and exposure data, collateral positions, agreement terms, market data, and instrument data. Firms should have in place controls to measure the accuracy of such data.
3.3	For the issuance of non-electronic exchanged collateral calls, the following minimum standard data fields should be included: 1. Principal Counterparty Reference – Reference of the client issuing the collateral call 2. Counterparty Reference – Reference of the client receiving the collateral call 3. Valuation Date – The close of business date for which the principal counterparty is issuing the collateral call 4. MTA – Minimum amount to pay/ receive as specified in the CSA in the Base Currency. 5. Threshold – Amount of exposure a counterparty will accept before issuing a collateral call in the Base Currency 6. Independent Amount – Required Credit Support, in addition to the Variation Margin, included in the MTM in the Base Currency 7. Total MTM – Net market value of the portfolio in the Base Currency 8. Margin Requirement – Value of the requested collateral transfer in the Base Currency.	Nothing added in Best Practice.

Best Practice No.	Best Practice	Comment
3.4	Counterparty collateral calls should be checked when received.	Nothing significant added in Best Practice.
3.5	Generally speaking, counterparties should provide a response at latest by close of business on the day a call is received, provided settlement is call date +1. Where call issuance and settlement of collateral is same day, wherever possible, responses should be received no later than one hour before the closing of the securities market and two hours prior to cash deadlines.	Parties should have the systems' capability and procedures in place for delivery of collateral within the timeframes agreed in the CSA. If a party has agreed a delivery and is aware that it will be late in being made, every effort should be made to notify the receiving party to avoid unnecessary loss due to positioning of funds.
3.6	If a party is responding to a collateral call in a non-electronically exchanged message then parties should include, as a minimum, the fields below in their collateral call response: 1. Counterparty Reference – Reference of the client responding to the collateral call 2. Indication of agreement or a full or partial dispute 3. Collateral Amount – Amount of collateral agreed to and being sent 4. Collateral Type – e.g. EUR/USD cash or security ID and par value 5. Settlement Date – The business date for which the counterparty is delivering the agreed collateral 6. Total MTM – Net market value of the portfolio in the Base Currency if anything other than agreed in full.	Nothing added in Best Practice.
3.7	Revised collateral calls, when required, should be issued as early as possible during the day. The receiving party should try to review and respond to the revised collateral call in a timely manner to meet delivery timings in the CSA on a reasonable efforts basis.	It may be that the parties will agree a different Notification Time than the one in the CSA to achieve this.

Best Practice No.	Best Practice	Comment
3.8	From time to time counterparties may experience technical difficulties preventing them from answering collateral calls within the agreed deadlines. Wherever possible, parties should try to communicate the existence of technical difficulties impeding call response as soon as possible.	This will avoid the other party calling an Event of Default unnecessarily.
4.1	Once the collateral type to be delivered has been agreed by both parties settlement instructions for collateral movements should be effected including both deliveries and receipts of collateral, cash and securities.	This may involve the release of instructions from collateral systems linked directly to payment systems or providing settlement instructions to an independent settlement function for execution. Instructions should be input to the appropriate settlement systems for both the receipt and the delivery of securities to facilitate matching between both parties to the transfer. This principle equally applies to the movement of cash collateral but matching is not required.
4.2	Where payments are effected in a settlements/payment system which is not embedded within the collateral management system, a reconciliation of collateral balances should be performed between the systems on a daily basis.	Nothing significant added in Best Practice.
5.1	Firms should be able easily to access a trade file from their collateral management system to facilitate a portfolio reconciliation in a collateral dispute, or otherwise. Where possible, trade portfolios should be reconciled proactively on a regular basis.	Nothing significant added in Best Practice.
5.2	Firms should ensure there is an internal investigation process in place to identify valuation and/or operational trade breaks causing a collateral dispute.	Escalation should be made if necessary.
5.3	Firms should establish internal processes for the investigation and resolution of trade breaks causing collateral disputes across all relevant areas.	Interdepartmental responsibilities and co-operation to be established.

Best Practice No.	Best Practice	Comment
5.4	Firms should establish internal guidelines and policies to ensure that trading desk access to counterparty portfolio content and valuation details takes place only on a valid need to know basis.	Nothing significant added in Best Practice. Chinese wall recommendation.
5.5	Collateral disputes should be monitored, tracked and reported from both a party and counterparty perspective.	Collateral dispute ageing should be available on a calendar day basis.
5.6	Proper governance and/or escalation procedures should be in place to ensure proper senior management insight into collateral disputes and associated resolution activities.	Nothing significant added in Best Practice.
6.1	Systems and procedures should be in place to actively monitor settlement status of all forms of collateral transfers.	This is to reduce settlement failures. SWIFT or other electronic communication methods can be utilised automatically to update settlement status on collateral transfers. Fail reports generated by these systems should be actively reviewed by a firm's settlements team. Otherwise manual procedures should be established to check on settlement failures. Custodians should be required to provide information for failed transactions on a settlement date +1 basis.
6.2	Once a failed collateral delivery has been identified, the party that has identified it should promptly notify its counterparty to allow ample time to resolve the issue.	Both parties should be aware of a failed transaction if the proper identification steps are in place. However, the party that has failed to receive collateral should advise the party that has failed to deliver it to ensure that appropriate steps to resolve the fail have been initiated and should supply, at a minimum, the following information: Account Name, Security ID (or cash), and Quantity. Also, once identified, pending settlements should be noted on outgoing collateral calls.

Best Practice No.	Best Practice	Comment
6.3	Failed collateral transactions should be resolved on the day they are identified or the next available settlement date determined by market settlement cycles (ex Japanese Government Bond or Euroclear transfers).	The cause of any recurring settlement issue (incorrect SSI, problems with custodians, etc.) should be investigated and steps should be taken to eliminate these issues going forward.
6.4	Failed collateral settlements should be recorded on an end of day fails report which should be distributed to operations managers and credit officers with escalation procedures in place to address aged fail items.	Nothing significant added in Best Practice.
7.1	The Transferor in exiting the trade no longer has any collateralised exposure to the Remaining Party as of the Novation Effective Date. All collateralised exposure related to the trade in question should be removed from the portfolio of the Transferor as of the Novation Effective Date +1.	As Best Practice, the settlement/fee related to an assignment should be collateralised between the Transferor and the Transferee. If the Transferor removes its position from the portfolio of the Remaining Party on the Novation Effective Date +1, the exposure related to the settlement/fee should remain collateralised with the Transferee until the applicable settlement date.
7.2	The Transferee entering the trade will collateralise the full exposure of the swap with the Remaining Party on trade date +1 of the assignment subject to its CSA with the Remaining Party.	The settlement/fee related to the assignment is collateralised between the Transferee and the Transferor until the applicable settlement date. The Transferee will continue to collateralise its new position *vis à vis* the Remaining Party following current market standards.
7.3	The Remaining Party simply moves the exposure from the Transferor to the Transferee. Its exposure on the transaction does not change in an assignment.	The consistent collateralisation of the settlement/fee between the Transferor and Transferee will result in more accurate calls between the parties. The Transferor would no longer hesitate to remove its trades as its settlement risk would be fully collateralised *vis à vis* the Transferee.

Best Practice No.	Best Practice	Comment
8.1	All new trades are to be included in the collateral calculation on trade date +1. All upfront fees on new trades should be included in the calculation until settlement date.	All new trades and upfront fees should be included in the relevant collateralised portfolios on Trade Date +1 regardless of the Effective Date. Parties should not be able to claim that deals are not included in the collateralised deal population on T+1 because their Effective Date is T+2.
8.2	Exposure related to trades that are unwound should stay in the portfolio through the settlement date.	One reason for collateral call differences is due to one party dropping unwound trades from its collateral calculation on the unwind date while the other party drops the same trade on the settlement date. Exposure related to the unwound trades should remain in the collateralised portfolio through the settlement date.
8.3	Exposure related to trades that are subject to a Credit Event should remain in the collateralised portfolio through the settlement date.	This mainly relates to credit default swaps. Credit Events can cause collateral call differences by one party dropping the impacted trades from the collateral calculation on the auction date while the other collateralises them through the settlement date. In addition, if a trade is live at the time of an applicable Credit Event and then subsequently matures before the Auction Date, it should remain in the portfolio until the settlement date as the Credit Event occurred before the Maturity Date.
8.4	Trades that are subject to industry-wide compression should be removed from the portfolio on the day the compression occurs. This should be in line with governing documentation for the applicable compression process.	Again this mainly relates to credit default swaps. All replacement trades should be booked according to the relevant compression guidelines and subsequent exposure for replacement trades should be included in collateralised exposure on the date following execution.

Best Practice No.	Best Practice	Comment
9.1	It is the obligation of the Secured Party to ensure that all assets, whether eligible for rehypothecation or not, are tracked in line with the agreed terms of the CSA. Where appropriate this obligation can be assigned to an agent but responsibility in a bilateral CSA remains with the Secured Party. The correct reuse rights of secured assets should be checked regularly.	A critical element of the collateral process, especially involving securities pledged, is the ability to differentiate between those that are delivered by a Pledgor that has granted reuse rights and those that have been delivered without them. If this differentiation is not in place, the risk is that ineligible assets may be inadvertently reused inappropriately.
9.2	Where rehypothecation rights are granted, to avoid settlement fails, it is advisable to ensure that the settlement convention of the market where the assets are being reused is aligned with the settlement convention of the CSA.	Reuse of securities collateral opens up the possibility of taking those securities from one set of settlement rules, very specific to the OTC derivatives market, into shorter or longer settlement and recall environments thereby increasing the chance of a settlement fail.
9.3	Parties should try to make substitution requests as soon as possible but no later than 5 p.m. in the time zone in which the Secured Party is located. Wherever possible, the Secured Party should try to return items of posted collateral on the same day on which the Secured Party receives the substitute collateral but no later than the next local business day.	Same day return is appropriate if the substitute securities use the same settlement convention in the same country.
9.4	Where the Secured Party cannot source and return the pledged asset, unless otherwise agreed by the parties it must provide an exact ISIN/CUSIP not later than one local business day after the substitute collateral is received.	If the Pledgor requests that specific securities be returned for substitution, the Secured Party is obliged to deliver collateral with that specific ISIN/CUSIP no later than the next local business day after which the substitute collateral is received.
10.1	Both parties should understand the size and structure of their respective teams and agree which resources will be allocated to working on reconciliations. Exchanging organisation charts and contact lists and discussing trigger points for escalation is also advised.	No commentary added in Best Practice.

Best Practice No.	Best Practice	Comment
10.2	A proactive and regular reconciliation strategy rather than a reactive (dispute or Credit Event driven) reconciliation strategy should be pursued for larger actively traded portfolios.	No commentary added in Best Practice.
10.3	The frequency of reconciling portfolios should depend on the size, volatility and trading activity in them as well as the type and credit standing of the parties involved.	No commentary added in Best Practice.
10.4	Whether an in-house or outsourced solution or both, counterparties should make use of reconciliation technology for reconciling their portfolios to facilitate bilateral involvement and transparency over results. Automated solutions reduce significantly the level of resources needed to reconcile portfolios and result in a more efficient, timely and controlled process.	No commentary added in Best Practice.
10.5	Parties should discuss and agree tolerances between themselves in order to determine what they judge to be significant mark-to-market differences as well as material trade booking discrepancies and any other differences that may arise.	No commentary added in Best Practice.
10.6	The OTC derivatives industry should move to adopt Market Minimum Standards for data presentation in collateralised portfolio reconciliation.	No commentary added in Best Practice.
10.7	Parties should be able to represent any type of trade as a single line of data in their reconciliation files. This follows the principle of "one confirmation = one trade".	Nothing significant added in Best Practice.
10.8	Portfolios should be valued and populated as of close of business on the previous business day.	No commentary added in Best Practice.
10.9	The trade population of portfolios to be reconciled should be consistent with the trade population under the governing ISDA Master Agreement or other collateralised OTC agreement.	No commentary added in Best Practice.

Best Practice No.	Best Practice	Comment
10.10	Individual trades within the portfolio should be identified using a product classification at the point of reconciliation.	No commentary added in Best Practice.
10.11	Each trade in the portfolio should contain that counterparty's unique trade ID (as referenced, if applicable, in the Confirmation) together with any common market IDs that may have been assigned by an electronic confirmation platform. Where available, unique counterparty IDs should be submitted as part of the reconciliation file. It is best practice that these should be captured as part of the confirmation/affirmation process. Structured trades recorded using multiple legs with multiple IDs should have an additional common ID assigned to all legs to facilitate the matching process.	No commentary added in Best Practice.
10.12	Files for reconciliation should be transmitted by secure means recognising that flexibility may be required and even desirable in certain situations.	No commentary added in Best Practice.
10.13	Files for reconciliation should be sent in a commonly available standard industry format and agreed between the parties at the start of their reconciliation activities.	No commentary added in Best Practice.
10.14	To facilitate timely dispute resolution and to encourage the development of a proactive reconciliation strategy across the market, portfolios should be available for reconciliation on any mutual business day by request of either counterparty.	No commentary added in Best Practice.

Best Practice No.	Best Practice	Comment
10.15	Parties should agree the time by which files are to be exchanged or uploaded, which should be as soon as possible following the portfolio Valuation Date and not later than noon in the location of the collateral call or the location where the reconciliation is undertaken, if different.	Breaks may occur simply due to timing differences in allocating a trade to a portfolio or taking it out of the portfolio. In that event, only one party will show the trade at the time of the reconciliation. Also parties may see mismatches in trade populations due to system constraints although the trade is actually recognised by both parties. Alternatively the reconciliation process may uncover genuine breaks between the parties such as parameter differences, i.e. differences in trade booking or valuation differences where parties may be adopting different valuation models. Break resolutions should be done as a high priority.
10.16	To assist break resolution, full results of all breaks arising from any reconciliation should be available if requested by the counterparty. This includes trades with field differences, MTM differences and unmatched trades. This principle applies irrespective of the technology used to perform the reconciliation, whether performed in-house or through a vendor-serviced external platform.	No commentary added in Best Practice.
10.17	Parties should agree mutual priorities for break resolution and their focus for addressing the main categories of breaks.	No commentary added in Best Practice.
10.18	Firms should give priority to and be adequately resourced to provide a timely response to a request for investigation of breaks.	No commentary added in Best Practice.

Best Practice No.	Best Practice	Comment
10.19	Parties should clearly identify which of them is assigned to action a particular break and they should track the progress of resolving agreed breaks. Documentation, confirmations or information requested by the firm investigating the break should be provided in a timely manner and no later than one business day following a request from them.	No commentary added in Best Practice.
10.20	Firms should have a process in place which reaches across relevant functional areas in order to resolve issues or root causes uncovered in the reconciliation process.	No commentary added in Best Practice.
10.21	Firms should have formal escalation procedures in place for addressing and actioning breaks in the portfolio promptly. Escalation procedures should focus on timeframes and the process for communicating with affected departments, for example Operations, Middle Office, Credit, product controllers and Front Office.	No commentary added in Best Practice.
10.22	When the reconciliation process establishes that the cause of the trade break is an internal system or process at one of the counterparties, it is expected that such counterparty will work in good faith to resolve the underlying data issue in a timely fashion.	Trades requiring investigation which are not true breaks (e.g. late bookings, novations, tear-ups, settlements) create what is called "noise" in the portfolio. This noise is worst in the 1–2 day period but can last up to 5 days or more. With actively traded portfolios it is important to know the source of recurring issues and to understand the nature of the problems involved. The ultimate goal is to reduce the time spent in managing regular reconciliations and to focus on resolving any real breaks between the parties.

Best Practice No.	Best Practice	Comment
10.23	Flawed data and process standards contribute a lot of noise to the reconciliation process with new or maturing trades and system issues underlying many of the breaks between the parties. It is therefore important that parties understand their internal front-to-back process and data and pricing sources in order successfully to filter out these issues from the population of breaks to be addressed.	No commentary added in Best Practice.
10.24	Firms should agree minimum standards and methods for reporting breaks in order to support transparency of results following portfolio reconciliation.	No commentary added in Best Practice.
10.25	Firms should measure their compliance against these Best Practices and identify gaps to be addressed.	In the Best Practices, ISDA says: "While these Best Practices are not intended to be obligatory, they seek to harmonise the current range of bespoke procedures and individual priorities and create consistency and efficiency in the market. Generally, the OTC derivatives industry should move towards adopting these guidelines which utilize proactive collateralized portfolio reconciliation as a tool to reduce operational risk and counterparty exposure."
11.1	Interest on the collateral balance is accrued on a daily basis using the CSA agreed interest rate and spread. All interest accrued will be paid monthly to the party pledging collateral or as mutually agreed between the parties. The party receiving interest is obliged to raise any dispute on the amount received within 30 days of receipt.	Advice of the amount to be paid will be sent on the first business day of the month if operationally feasible with actual delivery occurring as mutually agreed between the parties. Delivery of the interest amount will be made to the relevant party's original settlement instructions. The following month's starting balance, interest rate and account spread should all be reconfirmed. Interest should not be rolled into the principal balance unless specifically agreed by both parties.

Best Practice No.	Best Practice	Comment
11.2	At no point should the interest accrual (rate minus spread) drop into a negative figure. If this occurs the rate should be floored at zero.	Many CSA agreements were written and agreed when it was not anticipated that interest rates would reach extremely low levels. However, market conditions have occurred where the interest accrual formula could result in a negative number with a collateral provider obliged to pay interest to a collateral holder. At no point should the interest accrual (rate minus spread) drop into a negative figure. If it does then the best practice is to floor the interest rate at zero.
11.3	When closing a client relationship and returning collateral, the full amount of collateral should be returned including any accrued interest.	To avoid having any future payable amount at the end of a client relationship, when returning any collateral balance in full all interest should be included at the same time.
11.4	Absent specific wording to the contrary in the CSA, interest should be calculated using a standard formula. The formula should be (Principal Balance * (Interest Rate/100))/(360 or 365) * number of days relevant to the currency of collateral held.	Market practice is that interest should be calculated using actual days. All decimals should be rounded to 2 places to avoid rounding issues.

Best Practice No.	Best Practice	Comment
11.5	All requests for interest should include the information necessary for a client to be able to evaluate and agree any interest amount.	Request for interest delivery should be standardised around a single electronic message format. A list of fields to include in the interest message are included in the *Standards for the Electronic Exchange of OTC Derivative Margin Calls*. If the interest statement is sent via email, the body of the email should include the interest period, legal entity, amount of interest (payable or receivable), contact name/phone/email address and wire instructions. The interest statements should include: rate, daily principal amount, date, accrued interest amount and daily interest amount. The interest statement should be included in the communication as an attachment.
11.6	Interest should be calculated on a full month basis only unless otherwise agreed between the parties.	ISDA members consider as a best practice that interest calculations should be from the first day of the month to the last day of the month with interest accrued to the last day of the month. However, other periods have and can be agreed.
12.1	Where collateral movements are effected in a Third Party or Tri-Party system a reconciliation of collateral balances should be performed between the parties on a daily basis.	Nothing significant added in Best Practice.

THE INDEPENDENT AMOUNT WHITE PAPER

Independent Amounts overcollateralise OTC derivatives risk exposure. They provide a cushion of additional collateral to protect against certain risks including a decline in a counterparty's creditworthiness below an agreed rating or because a particular transaction may be more than normally risky or volatile in nature and a credit officer wants more collateral to cover that risk.

The parties may agree any sum for an Independent Amount ("IA") which can be a fixed money sum, a percentage of the notional principal amount of a portfolio or a single Transaction, or even a Value at Risk calculation. They can also agree not to have any IAs at all.

The amount of an IA can be stated in the CSA itself or in a Confirmation. They will normally only apply to one party because if they are equal and apply to both they will cancel each other out when the Credit Support Amount is calculated.

Exposure and IAs are two of several terms netted together in the calculation of Credit Support Amount. Some market players might think of them as two pools of collateral – one covering the Exposure and the other the IA. In fact, under the CSA there is just one pool of collateral and its constituent elements are generally not held separately.

ISDA's Independent Amount Working Group was formed in early 2009 to address concerns that arose in the Lehman Brothers' insolvency and that highlighted new risks. ISDA published a White Paper on the subject on 22 October 2009 and followed it up with a final paper on 1 March 2010. They both looked at the question of whether IAs should be maintained separately so that they would be better protected from loss by a party entitled to them arising from its counterparty's default or insolvency.

For example, while a Dealer receiving an IA will benefit from the additional collateral cushion, the End User may incur added risk of loss if that Dealer goes bankrupt. In a Dealer insolvency if the End User delivered collateral directly to him and such an IA was rehypothecated or commingled with that Dealer's assets and it is overcollateralised by that IA, then the End User will only be a general unsecured creditor and may recover less than 100% of what they are owed.

This was illustrated in the Lehman Brothers' insolvency where IAs posted to Lehman and reused by them proved not to be recoverable by Pledgors in many cases. This was because the Pledgor's legal title to the IA was essentially neutralised when it was reused by Lehman and they became general unsecured creditors. Secondly, receivers of this IA from Lehman could offset it against their own risk exposure on Lehman and so the original Pledgor could not claim it back as legal owner.

ISDA's final Independent Amount paper proposed four ways in which risk could be reduced, viz:

1 Segregated Direct Dealer Holding of Independent Amount
2 Segregated Dealer Affiliate Holding of Independent Amount
3 Third Party Custodian Holding of Independent Amount
4 Tri-Party Collateral Agent Holding of Independent Amount.

In all four options we are talking about a security interest or pledge approach.

Segregated Direct Dealer Holding of Independent Amount

Where an IA is delivered directly from an End User to a Dealer with rehypothecation rights and no formal arrangements for its segregation, it is impossible to distinguish between the IA and the Dealer's other assets. In the Dealer's insolvency the IA is unlikely to have any special protection and the End User will be treated as a general unsecured creditor.

With this first option:

- the IA is delivered directly by the End User to the Dealer;
- the dealer must segregate the IA from its own assets and those it holds for third parties;
- the dealer cannot reuse the IA himself but the End User can agree that cash can be reinvested in investment vehicles (e.g. money market funds) but returns are likely to be low; securities can be repoed out or loaned.

Features of this arrangement are:

- no third party is involved;
- the IA is traceable because of segregation;
- this is evidenced by account numbers and periodic bank statements;
- the dealer has full possession and control of the IA and can seize and liquidate it if the End User defaults.

Segregated Dealer Affiliate Holding of Independent Amount

Here:

- the IA is delivered by the End User to an Affiliate of the Dealer;
- it is held pursuant to a contract between the Dealer and its Affiliate;
- both the Dealer and the Affiliate must segregate the IA from their own assets and those they hold for third parties;
- neither the Dealer nor the Affiliate can reuse the IA;
- reinvestment of the IA is agreed for the End User's benefit.

Features of this arrangement are:

- a third party is involved – the Affiliate of the Dealer;
- ideally it should be at arm's length from the Dealer and separately regulated;
- the insolvency of the Affiliate should not inevitably lead to the insolvency of the Dealer or vice versa: this should give the End User a measure of comfort and protection;
- segregation makes the IA traceable in the books of the Affiliate backed up by account numbers and statements;
- however, the Dealer probably has contractual and practical control over the Affiliate and can get the IA back on request and then liquidate it.

Third Party Custodian Holding of Independent Amount

In this case:

- the IA is delivered to a Third Party Custodian;
- there is a contract between the Dealer and the Third Party Custodian;
- the End User's ownership of the IA is established by the IA being held in an account with the Third Party Custodian;
- the Dealer has a security interest over the IA in that account;
- the Third Party Custodian must segregate the IA from its own assets;
- the Third Party Custodian cannot reuse the IA;
- however, reinvestment of the IA is agreed for the End User's benefit.

Features of this arrangement are:

- a third party is involved;
- however, the contract is with the Dealer not the End User;
- segregation makes the IA traceable in the Third Party Custodian's books: account numbers and statements would be provided;
- the Third Party Custodian only has limited rights against the IA (e.g. a lien for non-payment of its fees);
- the contract the Dealer has with the Third Party Custodian means he can request the return of the IA and liquidate it.

Alternatively an End User could appoint a Third Party Custodian under a bilateral contract and notify the Third Party Custodian of the Dealer's interest in the IA in the account. This is only likely to be done rarely.

Tri-Party Collateral Agent Holding of Independent Amount

Here:

- the IA is delivered to a Tri-Party Collateral Agent;
- the contract is between the Tri-Party Collateral Agent, the Dealer and the End User;
- the Tri-Party Collateral Agent holds the IA in an account in the End User's name;
- the Dealer has a security interest over the IA in the account;
- the Tri-Party Collateral Agent must segregate the IA from its own assets;
- no reuse of the IA is allowed;
- however, reinvestment of the IA is agreed for the End User's benefit.

Features of this arrangement are:

- once again a third party is involved;
- however, this time the contract is trilateral between the Tri-Party Collateral Agent, the Dealer and the End User;
- the IA is segregated in the books of the Tri-Party Collateral Agent and the Dealer and evidenced by identifying account numbers and statements;
- the Tri-Party Collateral Agent has limited rights against the IA (e.g. a lien for non-payment of its fees);
- where the End User or the Dealer defaults, the Non-defaulting Party must issue a notice of exclusive control to the Tri-Party Collateral Agent who must then return the IA to the Non-defaulting Party who can liquidate it. In practice, an End User may find this more difficult to achieve than a Dealer and may have to go through the Dealer's insolvency procedure first which may, in turn, classify the End User as a general unsecured creditor who may be unable to recover all his IA.

Only with this final option – Tri-Party Collateral Agent Holding of Independent Amount – does the End User have any control over the IA.

ISDA has essentially left firms to decide which, if any, of these choices they will adopt if they want their IA to be segregated and not reused. Segregation of the IA may well be safer but it will also be more expensive. Nevertheless it is important to note that an IA is required in the minority of cases in the market.

However, there is an issue with cash IAs whichever route is chosen. Cash is, by its nature, fungible, i.e. one euro is worth the same as another euro.

IA cash will be difficult to segregate on the balance sheet of the party receiving it. Of course, it is possible to overcome this where cash is held in a segregated account by a third party custodian and not reinvested or reused in any way. However, the Pledgor would probably not earn any interest on the cash and even if the third party custodian offers investment of IA cash, investment returns are likely to be low.

To circumvent this return issue, sometimes IA cash is delivered with instructions only to invest that cash in a defined range of investments with reasonable returns. This might include mutual funds or short-term commercial paper with minimum credit ratings. When this is done it is not always clear over which asset the Secured Party has an interest. For example, if the End User delivered the IA cash to the Dealer who instructed his custodian to invest the cash in money market funds, does the Dealer have a security interest over the cash or the money market fund units? – an interesting question.

Segregation and title transfer arrangements like the English Law CSA

Independent Amounts feature under both the New York Law CSA and the English Law CSA.

The English Law CSA is a title transfer document under which legal ownership and use of the collateral passes from the collateral giver (the Transferor) to the collateral taker (the Transferee). The collateral belongs to the Transferee at the point of delivery.

In contrast, under the New York Law CSA when the Pledgor delivers collateral it retains legal title in that collateral which may be effectively extinguished when/if the collateral is commingled or rehypothecated.

Because of the title transfer nature of the English Law CSA, if one was to segregate IA or indeed any collateral under it, it would theoretically create recharacterisation risk which would, in adhering countries like England, be neutralised by the European Directive on Financial Collateral Arrangements that outlaws recharacterisation. However, outside the EU if title transfer collateral assets were segregated it would invite recharacterisation of the CSA as a pledge or security interest that had not been perfected.

The market has explored possible ways of overcoming this problem, viz:

- take collateral for Exposure as normal under an English Law CSA; and
- take IA and segregate and prohibit its reuse under an English Law Credit Support Deed.

OR

- Make use of the *2001 ISDA Margin Provisions* that include both title transfer and security interest options for taking collateral, although the security interest option is under the New York Law CSA and not the English Law Credit Support Deed.

Given the low take up of the *2001 ISDA Margin Provision*, we know of nobody who has taken the latter course.

As regards the first option, some market players have followed it after taking legal advice. They have used an English Law CSA modified to define Exposure to be just the variation margin element of the total collateral required plus a parallel English Law Credit Support Deed modified to define Exposure as just the IA element of the total collateral requirement.

IA collateral would be fully segregated and not reusable and possibly covered by investor protection rules such as the UK Financial Services Authority's Client Asset Rules.

In other countries statutory changes to existing close-out netting and collateral holding laws may be necessary to achieve this result.

Conclusion

There are operational challenges with all four of the proposed solutions with segregating IA where pledges or security interests are involved. The features of each are compared in Table C-1 on page 22 of ISDA's *Independent Amounts* Paper of 1 March 2010 that has not been reproduced here owing to space constraints.

Direct Dealer Holding without any restrictions (such as a segregation requirement or a limitation on reuse) is the most common current market practice in the USA and Asia. By contrast title transfer collateral is the most common current market practice in Europe. It is estimated that more than 90% of all current security-interest-based OTC derivative collateral agreements are based on non-segregation and the reuse of collateral.

Segregation of IA could leave an end user facing higher transaction costs and custody fees through forbidding a dealer reusing IA. Moreover, with greater volume of documentation this may increase both negotiation time and the potential for gaps and mistakes in legal agreements.

It should be borne in mind that nothing stops parties from negotiating different IA holding structures to the ones mentioned above or indeed just carrying on as the market did before the Lehman Brothers' insolvency.

However, section 724(c) of the Dodd-Frank Act states that, with respect to uncleared swaps, dealers are required, upon a counterparty's request, to segregate IA collateral with an independent third party custodian or under a tri-party arrangement. Please note that the Dodd-Frank segregation requirement only applies to IA and not top-up margin.

ISDA DISPUTE RESOLUTION PROCEDURE

Although most disputes are settled informally, it was found during the financial crisis in Autumn 2008 that Dispute Resolution terms in CSAs were not being applied by collateral managers at a time when disputes were becoming more frequent.

This was because:

- **there was no requirement for parties to exchange portfolio information;**
- **the nature of "consultation" to resolve the dispute was neither formalised nor clear;**
- **there was a lack of participation by dealers in providing market quotations;**
- **there was no shelf life for the results of a dispute – a counter dispute could start on the following day resulting in another dispute process.**

ISDA set up a Dispute Resolution Procedures Working Group in late 2008 to develop a new structured framework for dispute resolution in the OTC derivative market.

On 30 September 2009 a draft procedure was published by ISDA outlining best practice terms (the *ISDA 2009 Collateral Dispute Resolution Procedure*) and this led to more active interaction with regulators. This Procedure aimed to:

- **make the exchange of portfolio information mandatory early on in the dispute resolution process;**
- **promote transparency in resolving disputes;**
- **involve market players in committing to provide firm, two-way executable quotations or indicative prices in resolving disputes.**

There was an initial three-month pilot period between some dealers to test the best practice procedures. The results of this pilot showed that most disputes were reconciliation issues.

The Procedure has now been split into three, viz:

1 ***The ISDA 2011 Convention on Portfolio Reconciliation and the Investigation of Disputed Margin Calls* (the "Convention");**
2 ***The ISDA 2011 Formal Market Polling Procedure* (the "MPP"); and**
3 ***The ISDA 2011 Portfolio Reconciliation and Dispute Resolution Protocol* (the "2011 Protocol").**

ISDA had initially made a commitment to regulators to publish these documents by 30 September 2010. However, this commitment was not met, mainly due to MPP issues regarding what was classified as an "executable quote". The regulators understood and accepted that this commitment was not met because of these issues and were quite comfortable with the deadline being missed because advanced drafts of the first two documents existed.

So far it has taken more than two years to agree the procedures and a lot of work has been done by the ISDA committees involved.

During a second pilot period in August and September 2010 there were very few disputes. Some dealers even put fake disputes through their systems to try and test the procedures. However, many agreed that the MPP process needs to be trialled properly before it could be implemented.

In April 2011 draft Convention and MPP documents were published by ISDA for review with no specific deadline. ISDA called these two documents collectively the *ISDA Collateral Dispute Resolution Documents* and they will replace the *2009 ISDA Collateral Dispute Resolution Procedure*, when finalised.

The Convention and the MPP are complex documents and being drafts are subject to further amendment by the ISDA Working Group. Therefore, the following summary should be regarded as ISDA's interim proposals on these documents.

Convention

The draft Convention is in three parts covering:

- Portfolio Reconciliation of Transactions under the relevant ISDA Master Agreement;
- disputed Margin Calls under a CSA;
- general provisions covering both of these.

It is envisaged that by adhering to the forthcoming 2011 Protocol parties will be bound by the terms of the Convention.

Where there is a dispute there will be a 20 calendar day Administrative Review to resolve the dispute and this has the following steps:

- each party promptly to exchange Portfolio Data and Margin Data and perform a Portfolio Reconciliation; and
- investigate the following:
  - that each Disputed Transaction is in the Exposure calculation and its value;
  - that each Disputed Transaction is referred to relevant personnel so as to resolve the dispute;
  - that each Disputed Transaction is checked for incorrect matching;
  - that all unmatched Disputed Transactions are identified; and
  - that the next steps are agreed for resolving the dispute.

During this period or 20 calendar days after the Administrative Review has started either party may request an escalation to Senior Consultation.

It is expected that the relevant departments will be actively involved in resolving disputes during the Administrative Review period. For example, if there is a valuation issue then the relevant trader will be involved.

The Senior Consultation period lasts for 10 calendar days and is where senior management get involved in the process. It is important to note that during the Senior Consultation period the Administrative Review can continue in order to resolve the issue. This is a "building blocks" model so additional levels are added when needed, i.e. Senior Consultation added to Administrative Review.

If the dispute is still not resolved after this 10 calendar day period then the Secondary Resolution Start Date commences.

It is important to note that the process can be accelerated if one party is in "distress" or perceived to be and the other party wants to speed up the process. They can move quickly from Administrative Review to the Senior Consultation period or even straight to Secondary Resolution.

Secondary Resolution essentially means finding some other way to resolve the dispute. At this stage a Tolerance Level for the Disputed Amount appears on the scene which for an English Law CSA is the Base Currency Equivalent of US$20 million. However, the only significance of this is who can issue the Secondary Resolution Selection Notice, although in fact both parties can if they wish. If they cannot agree on a Secondary Resolution Method within four hours of the notice becoming effective it will be the Market Polling Procedure.

Market Polling Procedure ("MPP")

A draft of the MPP was circulated by ISDA on 27 April 2011. It is even more complex than the Convention.

First of all it states that if there is any clash in the terms of the documents, the MPP will prevail over the Convention and the Protocol but all three of them will prevail over the Master Agreement with the Convention having priority over the Protocol. The MPP comes into play if the dispute is not primarily resolved under the Convention.

The MPP starts when one party gives a notice to the other which will cover all Disputed Transactions. It is a three-stage process covering:

1 Polling Process Consultation;

2 Quote Gathering;

3 Quote Evaluation.

The Polling Process Consultation involves the following:

- The notifying party telephones the other party's senior personnel after the notice is delivered.
- The Polling Process Consultation ends two Local Business Hours after it starts unless the parties agree to extend it.
- The parties consult on who is to provide Quotes. These providers are called Reference Independent Price Sources ("RIPS").

- Either or both parties can obtain Quotes from RIPS. If they both do, both Quotes will be used in the MPP process.
- Parties agree a deadline (the "Announcement Time") when Quote Gathering will cease. If they fail to agree, the fallback is six Local Business Hours after the Quote Gathering Period starts.
- Only RIPS can provide Executable Quotes.
- Only Third Party RIPS can provide Indicative Quotes.

The Quote Gathering period starts when the Polling Process Consultation finishes. It is possible to extend Quote Gathering for one Local Business Day beyond the Announcement Time.

Each party can solicit as many Quotes as it wishes as long as this is done in good faith and a commercially reasonable manner. All Quotes must conform to standards set out in the MPP document. No RIPS may be remunerated for their efforts.

Quote Evaluation

All Quotes obtained by each party must be disclosed. They cannot just pick the best ones. Conforming Quotes will be classified as Executable Quotes, Indicative Quotes or Mid-Market Values at the Quote Evaluation stage. If a Quote does not fit these categories it is discarded.

There are very detailed provisions on how each of these will be evaluated depending upon the number of Quotes. There is a basic six Local Business Hour deadline for Quote Evaluation.

The basic choices are:

- If there are two or more Executable Quotes, these are compared to the Mid-Market Values. The highest Bid and lowest Offer are taken from the Executable Quotes and averaged to calculate the Implied Mid which is compared with the Mid-Market Values. If the Implied Mid lies between them, then it is the result. If it is higher than the higher Mid-Market Value, the latter is used and if it is lower than the lower Mid-Market Value, then again the latter is used.
- If there is one Executable Quote its Bid and Offer are averaged to produce an Executable Mid. Then it, the Indicative Average and the Mid-Market Values are averaged to calculate the Blended Average. This is then compared to the Bid and Offer of the Executable Quote to calculate the Interim Result. If the Blended Average lies between the Bid and Offer, it is the Interim Result. If it is higher than the Offer then the Offer is the Interim Result. If it is lower than the Bid, then the Bid is the Interim Result. The Interim Result is then compared to the Mid-Market Values. If it lies between them, the Interim

Result is the result. If it is higher than the higher Mid-Market Value, the latter is used and if it is lower than the lower Mid-Market Value, then again the latter is used.

- **[If there are no Executable Quotes, Indicative Quotes and Mid-Market Values are retained. The Indicative Quotes and the Mid-Market Values are then averaged to become the Non-Executable Average and this is then compared with the Mid-Market Values. If the Non-Executable Average lies between the Mid-Market Values, it is used. If it is higher than the higher Mid-Market Value, the latter is used and if it is lower than the lower Mid-Market Value, then again the latter is used.]**

This last provision is square bracketed because it is open for further discussion.

Failure to comply with the Convention or the MPP will not result in an Event of Default under the ISDA Master Agreement but parties will have to disclose disputes to regulators. The current proposal for reporting to regulators is to report all disputes greater than US$15 million or its equivalent (the Convention's Tolerance Level) and which have been outstanding for 15 or more calendar days.

According to the ISDA *2011 Roadmap for Collateral Management* published on 30 June 2011 the Convention and MPP are to be trialled for a period of three months until 29 July 2011 and on 9 September 2011 revised drafts of the ISDA Dispute Resolution Documents and a phased implementation plan for them will be published. At the time of writing (October 2011) this has not happened.

CENTRAL CLEARING COUNTERPARTIES AND COLLATERALISATION

This is a big subject but initially there is not a lot I can say concretely until the Dodd-Frank Act implementers in the USA decide how they wish to deal with this subject. It is possible that ESMA may adopt a similar or a different approach in Europe.

What is clear is that central clearing counterparties ("CCPs") will increase trade transparency: they will require high-quality collateral and this could well lead to higher costs for OTC derivatives firms.

Clearing members need to post two types of collateral to CCPs – initial margin and variation margin. They have their own proprietary trading accounts under which they will be required to post collateral and also their client accounts.

For their part, clearing members want more collateral from clients so as to reduce their CCP default fund charges. Clients want the opposite as only the clearing member makes CCP default fund contributions.

If a clearing member defaults then the CCP will use the margin posted by the clearing member first and then use the default fund to which all clearing members must contribute. However, in theory, if the CCP has done its calculations correctly then only the margin posted by the clearing member will be needed to cover defaults.

Clearing members may also be required to transform collateral posted to them from the client into collateral which is eligible for the CCPs. If this is the case then the clearing member will be left holding (CCP) ineligible collateral and this would mean the client would incur higher costs.

Clearing houses will only accept cash collateral as variation margin.

Central clearing will see members of the buyside community post variation margin to their clearing brokers on a daily basis. This would require many clearing members to transform, for instance, corporate bond collateral into cash collateral to meet these obligations where the clearing house demands this.

LCH.Clearnet takes this a step further, requiring that the cash collateral matches the currency of the underlying swap, adding another layer of operational complexity. However, some buyside firms (e.g. pension funds and mutual funds) may not have surplus cash to post as collateral. They are often asset rich but cash poor. With CCPs unlikely to move away from cash for variation margin, clients will either have to convert assets into cash through repoing the bonds out on a short-term basis for cash or pay for help. Whoever does the repo takes on market risk during its life.

Transforming bond collateral into cash collateral will be a new service banks could offer their clients but they may not be the cheapest source for doing so as collateral transformation has capital implications for banks providing this service because it uses up the balance sheet and banks are conscious of the growing capital constraints under Basel III and will need to price in their balance sheet usage for this purpose appropriately.

Regulators require CCPs to take high quality collateral to protect themselves from systemic risk. Prime brokers, custodians and clearing members planning to provide collateral transformation services will include stress testing in their models, which may also quietly factor in a higher cost for the client.

These clients will need to work out what is best for them to do in each individual case.

In Europe the Principal Model for clearing is mainly used. There is mandatory netting. Following an insolvency, set-off is applied.

There is a bilateral contractual relationship between the clearing member and the CCP and between the clearing member and the client. The clearing member has a principal-to-principal relationship with the CCP.

The Agency Model for clearing is used more in the US. The client (in theory) has a direct contractual relationship with the CCP. However, in practice the clearing member manages the process on behalf of the client. Therefore the two models look similar in practice with the clearing member standing in the middle.

Under the Principal Model the client has no direct recourse to the CCP; they would in theory under the Agency Model.

In the Principal Model the collateral is posted directly to the CCP (i.e. the client through to the clearing member then through to the CCP). In the Agency Model the collateral is segregated and held with a third party custodian. It is not held at the clearing house.

In the event of a default of a clearing member the client may port (transfer) the trades to another clearing member. This was the case with Lehmans. This works for the trades but there are implications for the collateral. The client needs to make a claim against the defaulting clearing member to receive their collateral back. They will also be required to post collateral to the new clearing member at the same time.

The legislation being drafted should allow both the positions and collateral to be moved. Under the Principal Model (e.g. SwapClear Model) the clearing member owns the collateral in the eyes of the CCP even though it is segregated. A Security Deed needs to be signed by the client in order to make porting/close-out work and to make a claim to the CCP.

Each CCP will have its own regulation and jurisdiction issues and a lot of work is being done to iron these issues out.

When parties clear trades they require an ISDA Master Agreement (or a deemed ISDA). This cleared ISDA needs to be in line with the CCP's rules and have provisions that state what will happen if the CCP defaults. Certain terms in the CSA also need to be amended to match the CCP's clearing/collateral requirements.

At the moment, CCP documents are not hardcoded and in some cases certain provisions can be amended. However this is likely to change when the market standard documentation is finalised after legislation is finalised.

There are therefore impacts on collateral when it comes to central clearing. When trades are executed bilaterally under a CSA, risk exposure and collateral are netted across asset classes. By separating trades out into cleared and non-cleared trades and then further splitting them into different asset classes (and therefore different CCPs) there is a high margin impact.

Often when exotic trades are entered into there are standardised trades (e.g. plain vanilla IRS) used to hedge certain elements of the bespoke trades. The trades can then be netted and less collateral is required. With cleared and non-cleared trades separated this netting relief is removed.

For example, a medium- or long-term structured transaction is likely to be collateralised and hedged by one or a series of interest rate swaps, all of which are captured by an ISDA Master Agreement and a CSA. Collateralisation of all these Transactions (i.e. the structured one and the hedging one(s)) will be collateralised under the same CSA.

However, if the plain vanilla interest rate swaps are cleared and collateralised through a CCP it is possible that the CCP will impose higher haircuts (lower Valuation Percentages) and require a narrower range of Eligible Credit Support, both of which could increase trading costs and lower profitability.

Apparently LCH Clearnet performed a test to see what impact there would be on collateral requirements if they segregated (pure vanilla) US$ trades from other currencies for one dealer. The impact on margin was 2.5 times more than the original margin requirement.

One interesting thing is that despite the recent US government ratings downgrade by Standard & Poor's, US CCPs have said that they see no need to change their haircut levels or policies for accepting US Treasuries as collateral.

The extra-territorial reach of the Dodd-Frank Act proposals are also currently a problem. Extra-territoriality means applying national rules of one country (here the US) to other national markets and firms in the global OTC derivatives markets. The concern here is that the Dodd-Frank Act in its current form does not just cover US banks operating in the US market but also foreign subsidiaries of US banks operating globally and US subsidiaries of foreign banks doing business in the US.

These rules cover trading and collateralisation and, if not revised, may mean that US markets could be at a serious competitive disadvantage as foreign market players may decide to avoid doing business with swap dealers affiliated to US banks and companies if this means higher capital costs.

The EMIR and Dodd-Frank collateral requirements are not yet finalised but when they are regulators are currently proposing that the market will have 60 days to implement them, which may also cause problems.

So there is much to exercise the minds of collateral managers in this brave new world of regulation. We shall see what happens.

THE "STANDARDISED CSA"

On 17 June 2011 the *International Financing Review* carried an article that ISDA was at an advanced stage of establishing a market standard Credit Support Annex for use between dealers and hoped to publish it by the end of 2011.

The standardised CSA has been composed to overcome certain cash collateral valuation difficulties identified by major dealers.

Where a counterparty had the option under a CSA to post cash collateral in any of the G3 currencies (i.e. US$, Euro and Sterling) this caused valuation headaches for dealers. Many disputes arose over trade valuation where the currency of the collateral posted was different to that of the underlying swap leading to both traders valuing the swap differently.

Moving to a standardised CSA will remove this issue for banks because they will be posting collateral in the currency of the underlying trade.

The standardised CSA will have five currency buckets, viz:

1 **US$**
2 **Euro**
3 **Sterling**

4 Swiss Franc

5 Japanese Yen.

Collateral, as mentioned above, will be posted in the currency of the underlying swap. Any multicurrency deals and all other collateral currencies will fall into the US$ bucket.

The standardised CSA will have the following standard terms:

- no Independent Amounts;
- zero Thresholds;
- US$10,000 Minimum Transfer Amount.

Currency settlement risk is the main difficulty in finalising the standardised CSA. Euro payments are normally settled in the morning European time and US$ in the morning US time.

The ISDA Working Group on this project continues to work on this issue.

THE FUTURE

In the previous edition of this book we referred to a likely trend of concentration and centralisation of collateral activities within firms and a break up of separate product fiefdoms that have developed over the years but which essentially do the same thing vis-à-vis collateralisation. If implemented successfully, this should optimise the use of collateral and lead to improvements in operational efficiencies and, of course, staff allocation. Doubtless, it will need a high IT content to develop the necessary systems. It would, of course, end the so-called silo approach to taking collateral among various separate functions in firms that led to problems in the 2008 financial crisis.

Since 2002 this trend has been called enterprise-wide collateralisation and it has recently come to the fore again in the context of collateralisation with CCPs.

For several years some banks have been offering Collateral Management services to customers but clearly there is scope to expand this to a management service across various OTC derivatives and securities products. Such a service would provide customers with a single contact point for common reporting and position management for many different products. The service would, of course, need secure electronic information delivery systems. It would also offer enhanced payment netting opportunities across products. Prime brokerage is offering many aspects of this service. The Market Review estimated that 20% of the market used third party Valuation Agents and this may grow if smaller counterparties increase in number due to the regulatory push for OTC derivatives transactions to be cleared and collateralised via CCPs.

The roles of collateral management staff will become more complex, at least in the short term, as they battle with all these factors. They will need greater product knowledge and state of the art risk management systems to monitor and control the various inherent risks, both old and new.

The drivers of this are, therefore, better use of collateral resources within firms and even greater focus on costs and compliance with regulators' rules and expectations.

It is a time of opportunity for those who want to embrace it and an exciting time to be a collateral manager!

ANNEXES

ISDA Credit Support Annex subject to English Law

ISDA Credit Support Annex subject to New York Law

List of countries where ISDA has obtained collateral legal opinions

Relevant extracts from the New York Uniform Commercial Code

ANNEXES

We have provided these four Annexes in the hope that they might provide useful reference material in one place.

Annex 1

A facsimile of the ISDA Credit Support Annex (Bilateral Form – Transfer. Subject to English Law) (reproduced with the permission of the International Swaps and Derivatives Association, Inc.).*

Annex 2

A facsimile of the ISDA Credit Support Annex (Bilateral Form. Subject to New York Law) (reproduced with the permission of the International Swaps and Derivatives Association, Inc.).

Annex 3

List of countries where ISDA has obtained collateral legal opinions.

Annex 4

Relevant extracts from the New York Uniform Commercial Code.

* ISDA® is the registered trademark of the International Swaps and Derivatives Association, Inc.

ANNEX 1 ISDA CREDIT SUPPORT ANNEX SUBJECT TO ENGLISH LAW

(Bilateral Form - Transfer)[1] **(ISDA Agreements Subject to English Law)**[2]

ISDA®

International Swaps and Derivatives Association, Inc.

CREDIT SUPPORT ANNEX

to the Schedule to the

ISDA Master Agreement

dated as of ……………………………………

between

…………………………………… and ……………………………………
("Party A") **("Party B")**

This Annex supplements, forms part of, and is subject to, the ISDA Master Agreement referred to above and is part of its Schedule. For the purposes of this Agreement, including, without limitation, Sections 1(c), 2(a), 5 and 6, the credit support arrangements set out in this Annex constitute a Transaction (for which this Annex constitutes the Confirmation).

Paragraph 1. Interpretation

Capitalised terms not otherwise defined in this Annex or elsewhere in this Agreement have the meanings specified pursuant to Paragraph 10, and all references in this Annex to Paragraphs are to Paragraphs of this Annex. In the event of any inconsistency between this Annex and the other provisions of this Schedule, this Annex will prevail, and in the event of any inconsistency between Paragraph 11 and the other

1 This document is not intended to create a charge or other security interest over the assets transferred under its terms. Persons intending to establish a collateral arrangement based on the creation of a charge or other security interest should consider using the ISDA Credit Support Deed (English law) or the ISDA Credit Support Annex (New York law), as appropriate.

2 This Credit Support Annex has been prepared for use with ISDA Master Agreements subject to English law. Users should consult their legal advisers as to the proper use and effect of this form and the arrangements it contemplates. In particular, users should consult their legal advisers if they wish to have the Credit Support Annex made subject to a governing law other than English law or to have the Credit Support Annex subject to a different governing law than that governing the rest of the ISDA Master Agreement (e.g., English law for the Credit Support Annex and New York law for the rest of the ISDA Master Agreement).

provisions of this Annex, Paragraph 11 will prevail. For the avoidance of doubt, references to "transfer" in this Annex mean, in relation to cash, payment and, in relation to other assets, delivery.

Paragraph 2. Credit Support Obligations

(a) ***Delivery Amount.*** Subject to Paragraphs 3 and 4, upon a demand made by the Transferee on or promptly following a Valuation Date, if the Delivery Amount for that Valuation Date equals or exceeds the Transferor's Minimum Transfer Amount, then the Transferor will transfer to the Transferee Eligible Credit Support having a Value as of the date of transfer at least equal to the applicable Delivery Amount (rounded pursuant to Paragraph 11(b)(iii)(D)). Unless otherwise specified in Paragraph 11(b), the "Delivery Amount" applicable to the Transferor for any Valuation Date will equal the amount by which:

(i) the Credit Support Amount

exceeds

(ii) the Value as of that Valuation Date of the Transferor's Credit Support Balance (adjusted to include any prior Delivery Amount and to exclude any prior Return Amount, the transfer of which, in either case, has not yet been completed and for which the relevant Settlement Day falls on or after such Valuation Date).

(b) ***Return Amount.*** Subject to Paragraphs 3 and 4, upon a demand made by the Transferor on or promptly following a Valuation Date, if the Return Amount for that Valuation Date equals or exceeds the Transferee's Minimum Transfer Amount, then the Transferee will transfer to the Transferor Equivalent Credit Support specified by the Transferor in that demand having a Value as of the date of transfer as close as practicable to the applicable Return Amount (rounded pursuant to Paragraph 11(b)(iii)(D)) and the Credit Support Balance will, upon such transfer, be reduced accordingly. Unless otherwise specified in Paragraph 11(b), the "Return Amount" applicable to the Transferee for any Valuation Date will equal the amount by which:

(i) the Value as of that Valuation Date of the Transferor's Credit Support Balance (adjusted to include any prior Delivery Amount and to exclude any prior Return Amount, the transfer of which, in either case, has not yet been completed and for which the relevant Settlement Day falls on or after such Valuation Date)

exceeds

(ii) the Credit Support Amount.

Paragraph 3. Transfers, Calculations and Exchanges

(a) ***Transfers.*** All transfers under this Annex of any Eligible Credit Support, Equivalent Credit Support, Interest Amount or Equivalent Distributions shall be made in accordance with the instructions of the Transferee or Transferor, as applicable, and shall be made:

(i) in the case of cash, by transfer into one or more bank accounts specified by the recipient;

(ii) in the case of certificated securities which cannot or which the parties have agreed will not be delivered by book-entry, by delivery in appropriate physical form to the recipient or its account accompanied by any duly executed instruments of transfer, transfer tax stamps and any other documents necessary to constitute a legally valid transfer of the transferring party's legal and beneficial title to the recipient; and

(iii) in the case of securities which the parties have agreed will be delivered by book-entry, by the giving of written instructions (including, for the avoidance of doubt, instructions given by telex, facsimile transmission or electronic messaging system) to the relevant depository institution or other entity specified by the recipient, together with a written copy of the instructions to the recipient, sufficient, if complied with, to result in a legally effective transfer of the transferring party's legal and beneficial title to the recipient.

Subject to Paragraph 4 and unless otherwise specified, if a demand for the transfer of Eligible Credit Support or Equivalent Credit Support is received by the Notification Time, then the relevant transfer will be made not later than the close of business on the Settlement Day relating to the date such demand is received; if a demand is received after the Notification Time, then the relevant transfer will be made not later than the close of business on the Settlement Day relating to the day after the date such demand is received.

(b) ***Calculations.*** All calculations of Value and Exposure for purposes of Paragraphs 2 and 4(a) will be made by the relevant Valuation Agent as of the relevant Valuation Time. The Valuation Agent will notify each party (or the other party, if the Valuation Agent is a party) of its calculations not later than the Notification Time on the Local Business Day following the applicable Valuation Date (or, in the case of Paragraph 4(a), following the date of calculation).

(c) ***Exchanges.***

(i) Unless otherwise specified in Paragraph 11, the Transferor may on any Local Business Day by notice inform the Transferee that it wishes to transfer to the Transferee Eligible Credit Support specified in that notice (the "New Credit Support") in exchange for certain Eligible Credit Support (the "Original Credit Support") specified in that notice comprised in the Transferor's Credit Support Balance.

(ii) If the Transferee notifies the Transferor that it has consented to the proposed exchange, (A) the Transferor will be obliged to transfer the New Credit Support to the Transferee on the first Settlement Day following the date on which it receives notice (which may be oral telephonic notice) from the Transferee of its consent and (B) the Transferee will be obliged to transfer to the Transferor Equivalent Credit Support in respect of the Original Credit Support not later than the Settlement Day following the date on which the Transferee receives the New Credit Support, unless otherwise specified in Paragraph 11(d) (the "Exchange Date"); *provided* that the Transferee will only be obliged to transfer Equivalent Credit Support with a Value as of the date of transfer as close as practicable to, but in any event not more than, the Value of the New Credit Support as of that date.

Paragraph 4. Dispute Resolution

(a) ***Disputed Calculations or Valuations*** . If a party (a "Disputing Party") reasonably disputes (I) the Valuation Agent's calculation of a Delivery Amount or a Return Amount or (II) the Value of any transfer of Eligible Credit Support or Equivalent Credit Support, then:

(1) the Disputing Party will notify the other party and the Valuation Agent (if the Valuation Agent is not the other party) not later than the close of business on the Local Business Day following, in the case of (I) above, the date that the demand is received under Paragraph 2 or, in the case of (II) above, the date of transfer;

(2) in the case of (I) above, the appropriate party will transfer the undisputed amount to the other party not later than the close of business on the Settlement Day following the date that the demand is received under Paragraph 2;

(3) the parties will consult with each other in an attempt to resolve the dispute; and

(4) if they fail to resolve the dispute by the Resolution Time, then:

(i) in the case of a dispute involving a Delivery Amount or Return Amount, unless otherwise specified in Paragraph 11(e), the Valuation Agent will recalculate the Exposure and the Value as of the Recalculation Date by:

(A) utilising any calculations of that part of the Exposure attributable to the Transactions that the parties have agreed are not in dispute;

(B) calculating that part of the Exposure attributable to the Transactions in dispute by seeking four actual quotations at mid-market from Reference Market-makers for purposes of calculating Market Quotation, and taking the arithmetic average of those obtained; *provided* that if four quotations are not available for a particular Transaction, then fewer than four quotations may be used for that Transaction, and if no quotations are available for a particular Transaction, then the Valuation Agent's original calculations will be used for the Transaction; and

(C) utilising the procedures specified in Paragraph 11(e)(ii) for calculating the Value, if disputed, of the outstanding Credit Support Balance;

(ii) in the case of a dispute involving the Value of any transfer of Eligible Credit Support or Equivalent Credit Support, the Valuation Agent will recalculate the Value as of the date of transfer pursuant to Paragraph 11(e)(ii).

Following a recalculation pursuant to this Paragraph, the Valuation Agent will notify each party (or the other party, if the Valuation Agent is a party) as soon as possible but in any event not later than the Notification Time on the Local Business Day following the Resolution Time. The appropriate party will, upon demand following such notice given by the Valuation Agent or a resolution pursuant to (3) above and subject to Paragraph 3(a), make the appropriate transfer.

(b) ***No Event of Default.*** The failure by a party to make a transfer of any amount which is the subject of a dispute to which Paragraph 4(a) applies will not constitute an Event of Default for as long as the procedures set out in this Paragraph 4 are being carried out. For the avoidance of doubt, upon completion of those procedures, Section 5(a)(i) of this Agreement will apply to any failure by a party to make a transfer required under the final sentence of Paragraph 4(a) on the relevant due date.

Paragraph 5. Transfer of Title, No Security Interest, Distributions and Interest Amount

(a) ***Transfer of Title.*** Each party agrees that all right, title and interest in and to any Eligible Credit Support, Equivalent Credit Support, Equivalent Distributions or Interest Amount which it transfers to the other party under the terms of this Annex shall vest in the recipient free and clear of any liens, claims, charges or encumbrances or any other interest of the transferring party or of any third person (other than a lien routinely imposed on all securities in a relevant clearance system).

(b) ***No Security Interest.*** Nothing in this Annex is intended to create or does create in favour of either party any mortgage, charge, lien, pledge, encumbrance or other security interest in any cash or other property transferred by one party to the other party under the terms of this Annex.

(c) ***Distributions and Interest Amount.***

(i) ***Distributions.*** The Transferee will transfer to the Transferor not later than the Settlement Day following each Distributions Date cash, securities or other property of the same type, nominal value, description and amount as the relevant Distributions ("Equivalent Distributions") to the extent that a Delivery Amount would not be created or increased by the transfer, as calculated by the Valuation Agent (and the date of calculation will be deemed a Valuation Date for this purpose).

(ii) ***Interest Amount.*** Unless otherwise specified in Paragraph 11(f)(iii), the Transferee will transfer to the Transferor at the times specified in Paragraph 11(f)(ii) the relevant Interest Amount to the extent that a Delivery Amount would not be created or increased by the transfer, as calculated by the Valuation Agent (and the date of calculation will be deemed a Valuation Date for this purpose).

Paragraph 6. Default

If an Early Termination Date is designated or deemed to occur as a result of an Event of Default in relation to a party, an amount equal to the Value of the Credit Support Balance, determined as though the Early Termination Date were a Valuation Date, will be deemed to be an Unpaid Amount due to the Transferor (which may or may not be the Defaulting Party) for purposes of Section 6(e). For the avoidance of doubt, if Market Quotation is the applicable payment measure for purposes of Section 6(e), then the Market Quotation determined under Section 6(e) in relation to the Transaction constituted by this Annex will be deemed to be zero, and, if Loss is the applicable payment measure for purposes of Section 6(e), then the Loss determined under Section 6(e) in relation to the Transaction will be limited to the Unpaid Amount representing the Value of the Credit Support Balance.

Paragraph 7. Representation

Each party represents to the other party (which representation will be deemed to be repeated as of each date on which it transfers Eligible Credit Support, Equivalent Credit Support or Equivalent Distributions) that it is the sole owner of or otherwise has the right to transfer all Eligible Credit Support, Equivalent Credit Support or Equivalent Distributions it transfers to the other party under this Annex, free and clear of any security interest, lien, encumbrance or other restriction (other than a lien routinely imposed on all securities in a relevant clearance system).

Paragraph 8. Expenses

Each party will pay its own costs and expenses (including any stamp, transfer or similar transaction tax or duty payable on any transfer it is required to make under this Annex) in connection with performing its obligations under this Annex, and neither party will be liable for any such costs and expenses incurred by the other party.

Paragraph 9. Miscellaneous

(a) ***Default Interest.*** Other than in the case of an amount which is the subject of a dispute under Paragraph 4(a), if a Transferee fails to make, when due, any transfer of Equivalent Credit Support, Equivalent Distributions or the Interest Amount, it will be obliged to pay the Transferor (to the extent permitted under applicable law) an amount equal to interest at the Default Rate multiplied by the Value on the relevant Valuation Date of the items of property that were required to be transferred, from (and including) the date that the Equivalent Credit Support, Equivalent Distributions or Interest Amount were required to be transferred to (but excluding) the date of transfer of the Equivalent Credit Support, Equivalent Distributions or Interest Amount. This interest will be calculated on the basis of daily compounding and the actual number of days elapsed.

(b) ***Good Faith and Commercially Reasonable Manner.*** Performance of all obligations under this Annex, including, but not limited to, all calculations, valuations and determinations made by either party, will be made in good faith and in a commercially reasonable manner.

(c) ***Demands and Notices.*** All demands and notices given by a party under this Annex will be given as specified in Section 12 of this Agreement.

(d) ***Specifications of Certain Matters.*** Anything referred to in this Annex as being specified in Paragraph 11 also may be specified in one or more Confirmations or other documents and this Annex will be construed accordingly.

Paragraph 10. Definitions

As used in this Annex:

"Base Currency" means the currency specified as such in Paragraph 11(a)(i).

"Base Currency Equivalent" means, with respect to an amount on a Valuation Date, in the case of an amount denominated in the Base Currency, such Base Currency amount and, in the case of an amount denominated in a currency other than the Base Currency (the "Other Currency"), the amount of Base Currency required to purchase such amount of the Other Currency at the spot exchange rate determined by the Valuation Agent for value on such Valuation Date.

"Credit Support Amount" means, with respect to a Transferor on a Valuation Date, (i) the Transferee's Exposure plus (ii) all Independent Amounts applicable to the Transferor, if any, minus (iii) all Independent Amounts applicable to the Transferee, if any, minus (iv) the Transferor's Threshold; *provided, however,* that the Credit Support Amount will be deemed to be zero whenever the calculation of Credit Support Amount yields a number less than zero.

"Credit Support Balance" means, with respect to a Transferor on a Valuation Date, the aggregate of all Eligible Credit Support that has been transferred to or received by the Transferee under this Annex, together with any Distributions and all proceeds of any such Eligible Credit Support or Distributions, as reduced pursuant to Paragraph 2(b), 3(c)(ii) or 6. Any Equivalent Distributions or Interest Amount (or portion of either) not transferred pursuant to Paragraph 5(c)(i) or (ii) will form part of the Credit Support Balance.

"Delivery Amount" has the meaning specified in Paragraph 2(a).

"Disputing Party" has the meaning specified in Paragraph 4.

"Distributions" means, with respect to any Eligible Credit Support comprised in the Credit Support Balance consisting of securities, all principal, interest and other payments and distributions of cash or other property to which a holder of securities of the same type, nominal value, description and amount as such Eligible Credit Support would be entitled from time to time.

"Distributions Date" means, with respect to any Eligible Credit Support comprised in the Credit Support Balance other than cash, each date on which a holder of such Eligible Credit Support is entitled to receive Distributions or, if that date is not a Local Business Day, the next following Local Business Day.

"Eligible Credit Support" means, with respect to a party, the items, if any, specified as such for that party in Paragraph 11(b)(ii) including, in relation to any securities, if applicable, the proceeds of any redemption in whole or in part of such securities by the relevant issuer.

"Eligible Currency" means each currency specified as such in Paragraph 11(a)(ii), if such currency is freely available.

"Equivalent Credit Support" means, in relation to any Eligible Credit Support comprised in the Credit Support Balance, Eligible Credit Support of the same type, nominal value, description and amount as that Eligible Credit Support.

"Equivalent Distributions" has the meaning specified in Paragraph 5(c)(i).

"Exchange Date" has the meaning specified in Paragraph 11(d).

"Exposure" means, with respect to a party on a Valuation Date and subject to Paragraph 4 in the case of a dispute, the amount, if any, that would be payable to that party by the other party (expressed as a positive number) or by that party to the other party (expressed as a negative number) pursuant to Section 6(e)(ii)(1) of this Agreement if all Transactions (other than the Transaction constituted by this Annex) were being terminated as of the relevant Valuation Time, on the basis that (i) that party is not the Affected Party and (ii) the Base Currency is the Termination Currency; *provided* that Market Quotations will be determined by the Valuation Agent on behalf of that party using its estimates at mid-market of the amounts that would be paid for Replacement Transactions (as that term is defined in the definition of "Market Quotation").

"Independent Amount" means, with respect to a party, the Base Currency Equivalent of the amount specified as such for that party in Paragraph 11 (b)(iii)(A); if no amount is specified, zero.

"Interest Amount" means, with respect to an Interest Period, the aggregate sum of the Base Currency Equivalents of the amounts of interest determined for each relevant currency and calculated for each day in that Interest Period on the principal amount of the portion of the Credit Support Balance comprised of cash in such currency, determined by the Valuation Agent for each such day as follows:

(x) the amount of cash in such currency on that day; multiplied by

(y) the relevant Interest Rate in effect for that day; divided by

(z) 360 (or, in the case of pounds sterling, 365).

"Interest Period" means the period from (and including) the last Local Business Day on which an Interest Amount was transferred (or, if no Interest Amount has yet been transferred, the Local Business Day on which Eligible Credit Support or Equivalent Credit Support in the form of cash was transferred to or received by the Transferee) to (but excluding) the Local Business Day on which the current Interest Amount is transferred.

"Interest Rate" means, with respect to an Eligible Currency, the rate specified in Paragraph 11(f)(i) for that currency.

"Local Business Day", unless otherwise specified in Paragraph 11(h), means:

(i) in relation to a transfer of cash or other property (other than securities) under this Annex, a day on which commercial banks are open for business (including dealings in foreign exchange and foreign currency deposits) in the place where the relevant account is located and, if different, in the principal financial centre, if any, of the currency of such payment;

(ii) in relation to a transfer of securities under this Annex, a day on which the clearance system agreed between the parties for delivery of the securities is open for the acceptance and execution of settlement instructions or, if delivery of the securities is contemplated by other means, a day on which commercial banks are open for business (including dealings in foreign exchange and foreign currency deposits) in the place(s) agreed between the parties for this purpose;

(iii) in relation to a valuation under this Annex, a day on which commercial banks are open for business (including dealings in foreign exchange and foreign currency deposits) in the place of location of the Valuation Agent and in the place(s) agreed between the parties for this purpose; and

(iv) in relation to any notice or other communication under this Annex, a day on which commercial banks are open for business (including dealings in foreign exchange and foreign currency deposits) in the place specified in the address for notice most recently provided by the recipient.

"Minimum Transfer Amount" means, with respect to a party, the amount specified as such for that party in Paragraph 11(b)(iii)(C); if no amount is specified, zero.

"New Credit Support" has the meaning specified in Paragraph 3(c)(i).

"Notification Time" has the meaning specified in Paragraph 11(c)(iv).

"Recalculation Date" means the Valuation Date that gives rise to the dispute under Paragraph 4; *provided, however,* that if a subsequent Valuation Date occurs under Paragraph 2 prior to the resolution of the dispute, then the ***"Recalculation Date"*** means the most recent Valuation Date under Paragraph 2.

"Resolution Time" has the meaning specified in Paragraph 11(e)(i).

"Return Amount" has the meaning specified in Paragraph 2(b).

"Settlement Day" means, in relation to a date, (i) with respect to a transfer of cash or other property (other than securities), the next Local Business Day and (ii) with respect to a transfer of securities, the first Local Business Day after such date on which settlement of a trade in the relevant securities, if effected on such date, would have been settled in accordance with customary practice when settling through the clearance system agreed between the parties for delivery of such securities or, otherwise, on the market in which such securities are principally traded (or, in either case, if there is no such customary practice, on the first Local Business Day after such date on which it is reasonably practicable to deliver such securities).

"Threshold" means, with respect to a party, the Base Currency Equivalent of the amount specified as such for that party in Paragraph 11(b)(iii)(B); if no amount is specified, zero.

"Transferee" means, in relation to each Valuation Date, the party in respect of which Exposure is a positive number and, in relation to a Credit Support Balance, the party which, subject to this Annex, owes such Credit Support Balance or, as the case may be, the Value of such Credit Support Balance to the other party.

"Transferor" means, in relation to a Transferee, the other party.

"Valuation Agent" has the meaning specified in Paragraph 11(c)(i).

"Valuation Date" means each date specified in or otherwise determined pursuant to Paragraph 11(c)(ii).

"Valuation Percentage" means, for any item of Eligible Credit Support, the percentage specified in Paragraph 11(b)(ii).

"Valuation Time" has the meaning specified in Paragraph 11(c)(iii).

"Value" means, for any Valuation Date or other date for which Value is calculated, and subject to Paragraph 4 in the case of a dispute, with respect to:

(i) Eligible Credit Support comprised in a Credit Support Balance that is:

(A) an amount of cash, the Base Currency Equivalent of such amount multiplied by the applicable Valuation Percentage, if any; and

(B) a security, the Base Currency Equivalent of the bid price obtained by the Valuation Agent multiplied by the applicable Valuation Percentage, if any; and

(ii) items that are comprised in a Credit Support Balance and are not Eligible Credit Support, zero.

Paragraph 11. Elections and Variables

(a) ***Base Currency and Eligible Currency.***

(i) "Base Currency" means United States Dollars unless otherwise specified here:

…………………………………………………….

(ii) "Eligible Currency" means the Base Currency and each other currency specified here:

…………………………………………………….

…………………………………………………….

(b) ***Credit Support Obligations.***

(i) ***Delivery Amount, Return Amount and Credit Support Amount.***

(A) ***"Delivery Amount"*** has the meaning specified in Paragraph 2(a), unless otherwise specified here: ……………………………………………………

(B) ***"Return Amount"*** has the meaning specified in Paragraph 2(b), unless otherwise specified here: ………………………………………………..

(C) ***"Credit Support Amount"*** has the meaning specified in Paragraph 10, unless otherwise specified here: ……………………………………………………

(ii) ***Eligible Credit Support***. The following items will qualify as ***"Eligible Credit Support"*** for the party specified:

		Party A	**Party B**	**Valuation Percentage**
(A)	cash in an Eligible Currency	[ ]	[ ]	[ ]%
(B)	negotiable debt obligations issued by the Government of [ ] having an original maturity at issuance of not more than one year	[ ]	[ ]	[ ]%
(C)	negotiable debt obligations issue by the Government of [ ] having an original maturity at issuance of more than one year but not more than 10 years	[ ]	[ ]	[ ]%

(D)	negotiable debt obligation issued by the Government of [ ] having an original maturity at issuance of more than 10 years	[ ]	[ ]	[ ]%
(E)	other:	[ ]	[ ]	[ ]%

(iii) ***Thresholds.***

(A) ***"Independent Amount"*** means with respect to Party A: ....
"Independent Amount" means with respect to Party B: ....

(B) ***"Threshold"*** means with respect to Party A: ....
"Threshold" means with respect to Party B: ....

(C) ***"Minimum Transfer Amount"*** means with respect to Party A: ....
"Minimum Transfer Amount" means with respect to Party B: ....

(D) ***Rounding.*** The Delivery Amount and the Return Amount will be rounded [down to the nearest integral multiple of ..../up and down to the nearest integral multiple of ...., respectively[3]].

(c) ***Valuation and Timing.***

(i) ***"Valuation Agent"*** means, for purposes of Paragraphs 2 and 4, the party making the demand under Paragraph 2, and, for purposes of Paragraph 5(c), the Transferee, as applicable, unless otherwise specified here: ....

(ii) ***"Valuation Date"*** means: ....

(iii) ***"Valuation Time"*** means:

[ ] the close of business in the place of location of the Valuation Agent on the Valuation Date or date of calculation, as applicable;

[ ] the close of business on the Local Business Day immediately preceding the Valuation Date or date of calculation, as applicable;

provided that the calculations of Value and Exposure will, as far as practicable, be made as of approximately the same time on the same date.

(iv) ***"Notification Time"*** means 1:00 p.m., London time, on a Local Business Day, unless otherwise specified here: ....

[3] Delete as applicable.

(d) ***Exchange Date. "Exchange Date"*** has the meaning specified in Paragraph 3(c)(ii), unless otherwise specified here: ……………………………………………………………………….

(e) ***Dispute Resolution.***

(i) ***"Resolution Time"*** means 1:00 p.m., London time, on the Local Business Day following the date on which the notice is given that gives rise to a dispute under Paragraph 4, unless otherwise specified here: ……………………………………………

(ii) ***Value.*** For the purpose of Paragraphs 4(a)(4)(i)(C) and 4(a)(4)(ii), the Value of the outstanding Credit Support Balance or of any transfer of Eligible Credit Support or Equivalent Credit Support, as the case may be, will be calculated as follows: ………………………………..

(iii) ***Alternative.*** The provisions of Paragraph 4 will apply, unless an alternative dispute resolution procedure is specified here: ………………………………………………………………………

(f) ***Distributions and Interest Amount.***

(i) ***Interest Rate.*** The "Interest Rate" in relation to each Eligible Currency specified below will be:

Eligible Currency	***Interest Rate***
……………………………………..	…………………………………….
……………………………………..	…………………………………….
……………………………………..	…………………………………….

(ii) ***Transfer of Interest Amount.*** The transfer of the Interest Amount will be made on the last Local Business Day of each calendar month and on any Local Business Day that a Return Amount consisting wholly or partly of cash is transferred to the Transferor pursuant to Paragraph 2(b), unless otherwise specified here: ……………………………………….

(iii) ***Alternative to Interest Amount.*** The provisions of Paragraph 5(c)(ii) will apply, unless otherwise specified here: …………………………………………………………

(g) ***Addresses for Transfers.***

Party A: ....
....

Party B: ....
....

(h) ***Other Provisions.***

ANNEX 2 ISDA CREDIT SUPPORT ANNEX SUBJECT TO NEW YORK LAW

(Bilateral Form) **(ISDA Agreements Subject to New York Law Only)**

ISDA®

International Swaps and Derivatives Association, Inc.

CREDIT SUPPORT ANNEX

to the Schedule to the

....

dated as of ....

between

.... and ....

("Party A") ("Party B")

This Annex supplements, forms part of, and is subject to, the above-referenced Agreement, is part of its Schedule and is a Credit Support Document under this Agreement with respect to each party.

Accordingly, the parties agree as follows:—

Paragraph 1. Interpretation

(a) ***Definitions and Inconsistency.*** Capitalized terms not otherwise defined herein or elsewhere in this Agreement have the meanings specified pursuant to Paragraph 12, and all references in this Annex to Paragraphs are to Paragraphs of this Annex. In the event of any inconsistency between this Annex and the other provisions of this Schedule, this Annex will prevail, and in the event of any inconsistency between Paragraph 13 and the other provisions of this Annex, Paragraph 13 will prevail.

(b) ***Secured Party and Pledgor.*** All references in this Annex to the "Secured Party" will be to either party when acting in that capacity and all corresponding references to the "Pledgor" will be to the other party when acting in that capacity; *provided, however*, that if Other Posted Support is held by a party to this Annex, all references herein to that party as the Secured Party with respect to that Other Posted Support will be to that party as the beneficiary thereof and will not subject that support or that party as the beneficiary thereof to provisions of law generally relating to security interests and secured parties.

Paragraph 2. Security Interest

Each party, as the Pledgor, hereby pledges to the other party, as the Secured Party, as security for its Obligations, and grants to the Secured Party a first priority continuing security interest in, lien on and right of Set-off against all Posted Collateral Transferred to or received by the Secured Party hereunder. Upon the Transfer by the Secured Party to the Pledgor of Posted Collateral, the security interest and lien granted hereunder on that Posted Collateral will be released immediately and, to the extent possible, without any further action by either party.

Paragraph 3. Credit Support Obligations

(a) ***Delivery Amount.*** Subject to Paragraphs 4 and 5, upon a demand made by the Secured Party on or promptly following a Valuation Date, if the Delivery Amount for that Valuation Date equals or exceeds the Pledgor's Minimum Transfer Amount, then the Pledgor will Transfer to the Secured Party Eligible Credit Support having a Value as of the date of Transfer at least equal to the applicable Delivery Amount (rounded pursuant to Paragraph 13). Unless otherwise specified in Paragraph 13, the ***"Delivery Amount"*** applicable to the Pledgor for any Valuation Date will equal the amount by which:

(i) the Credit Support Amount

exceeds

(ii) the Value as of that Valuation Date of all Posted Credit Support held by the Secured Party.

(b) ***Return Amount.*** Subject to Paragraphs 4 and 5, upon a demand made by the Pledgor on or promptly following a Valuation Date, if the Return Amount for that Valuation Date equals or exceeds the Secured Party's Minimum Transfer Amount, then the Secured Party will Transfer to the Pledgor Posted Credit Support specified by the Pledgor in that demand having a Value as of the date of Transfer as close as practicable to the applicable Return Amount (rounded pursuant to Paragraph 13). Unless otherwise specified in Paragraph 13, the ***"Return Amount"*** applicable to the Secured Party for any Valuation Date will equal the amount by which:

(i) the Value as of that Valuation Date of all Posted Credit Support held by the Secured Party

exceeds

(ii) the Credit Support Amount.

"Credit Support Amount" means, unless otherwise specified in Paragraph 13, for any Valuation Date (i) the Secured Party's Exposure for that Valuation Date plus (ii) the aggregate of all Independent Amounts applicable to the Pledgor, if any, minus (iii) all Independent Amounts applicable to the Secured Party, if any, minus (iv) the Pledgor's Threshold; *provided, however*, that the Credit Support Amount will be deemed to be zero whenever the calculation of Credit Support Amount yields a number less than zero.

Paragraph 4. Conditions Precedent, Transfer Timing, Calculations and Substitutions

(a) ***Conditions Precedent.*** Each Transfer obligation of the Pledgor under Paragraphs 3 and 5 and of the Secured Party under Paragraphs 3, 4(d)(ii), 5 and 6(d) is subject to the conditions precedent that:

(i) no Event of Default, Potential Event of Default or Specified Condition has occurred and is continuing with respect to the other party; and

(ii) no Early Termination Date for which any unsatisfied payment obligations exist has occurred or been designated as the result of an Event of Default or Specified Condition with respect to the other party.

(b) ***Transfer Timing.*** Subject to Paragraphs 4(a) and 5 and unless otherwise specified, if a demand for the Transfer of Eligible Credit Support or Posted Credit Support is made by the Notification Time, then the relevant Transfer will be made not later than the close of business on the next Local Business Day; if a demand is made after the Notification Time, then the relevant Transfer will be made not later than the close of business on the second Local Business Day thereafter.

(c) ***Calculations.*** All calculations of Value and Exposure for purposes of Paragraphs 3 and 6(d) will be made by the Valuation Agent as of the Valuation Time. The Valuation Agent will notify each party (or the other party, if the Valuation Agent is a party) of its calculations not later than the Notification Time on the Local Business Day following the applicable Valuation Date (or in the case of Paragraph 6(d), following the date of calculation).

(d) *Substitutions.*

(i) Unless otherwise specified in Paragraph 13, upon notice to the Secured Party specifying the items of Posted Credit Support to be exchanged, the Pledgor may, on any Local Business Day, Transfer to the Secured Party substitute Eligible Credit Support (the "Substitute Credit Support"); and

(ii) subject to Paragraph 4(a), the Secured Party will Transfer to the Pledgor the items of Posted Credit Support specified by the Pledgor in its notice not later than the Local Business Day following the date on which the Secured Party receives the Substitute Credit Support, unless otherwise specified in Paragraph 13 (the "Substitution Date"); *provided* that the Secured Party will only be obligated to Transfer Posted Credit Support with a Value as of the date of Transfer of that Posted Credit Support equal to the Value as of that date of the Substitute Credit Support.

Paragraph 5. Dispute Resolution

If a party (a "Disputing Party") disputes (I) the Valuation Agent's calculation of a Delivery Amount or a Return Amount or (II) the Value of any Transfer of Eligible Credit Support or Posted Credit Support, then (1) the Disputing Party will notify the other party and the Valuation Agent (if the Valuation Agent is not the other party) not later than the close of business on the Local Business Day following (X) the date that the demand is made under Paragraph 3 in the case of (I) above or (Y) the date of Transfer in the case of (II) above, (2) subject to Paragraph 4(a), the appropriate party will Transfer the undisputed amount to the other party not later than the close of business on the Local Business Day following (X) the date that the demand is made under Paragraph 3 in the case of (I) above or (Y) the date of Transfer in the case of (II) above, (3) the parties will consult with each other in an attempt to resolve the dispute and (4) if they fail to resolve the dispute by the Resolution Time, then:

(i) In the case of a dispute involving a Delivery Amount or Return Amount, unless otherwise specified in Paragraph 13, the Valuation Agent will recalculate the Exposure and the Value as of the Recalculation Date by:

(A) utilizing any calculations of Exposure for the Transactions (or Swap Transactions) that the parties have agreed are not in dispute;

(B) calculating the Exposure for the Transactions (or Swap Transactions) in dispute by seeking four actual quotations at mid-market from Reference Market-makers for purposes of calculating Market Quotation, and taking the arithmetic average of those obtained; *provided* that if four quotations are not available for a particular Transaction (or Swap Transaction), then fewer than four quotations may be used for that Transaction (or Swap Transaction); and if no quotations are available for a particular Transaction (or Swap Transaction), then the Valuation Agent's original calculations will be used for that Transaction (or Swap Transaction); and

(C) utilizing the procedures specified in Paragraph 13 for calculating the Value, if disputed, of Posted Credit Support.

(ii) In the case of a dispute involving the Value of any Transfer of Eligible Credit Support or Posted Credit Support, the Valuation Agent will recalculate the Value as of the date of Transfer pursuant to Paragraph 13.

Following a recalculation pursuant to this Paragraph, the Valuation Agent will notify each party (or the other party, if the Valuation Agent is a party) not later than the Notification Time on the Local Business Day following the Resolution Time. The appropriate party will, upon demand following that notice by the Valuation Agent or a resolution pursuant to (3) above and subject to Paragraphs 4(a) and 4(b), make the appropriate Transfer.

Paragraph 6. Holding and Using Posted Collateral

(a) ***Care of Posted Collateral.*** Without limiting the Secured Party's rights under Paragraph 6(c), the Secured Party will exercise reasonable care to assure the safe custody of all Posted Collateral to the extent required by applicable law, and in any event the Secured Party will be deemed to have exercised reasonable care if it exercises at least the same degree of care as it would exercise with respect to its own property. Except as specified in the preceding sentence, the Secured Party will have no duty with respect to Posted Collateral, including, without limitation, any duty to collect any Distributions, or enforce or preserve any rights pertaining thereto.

(b) ***Eligibility to Hold Posted Collateral; Custodians.***

(i) ***General.*** Subject to the satisfaction of any conditions specified in Paragraph 13 for holding Posted Collateral, the Secured Party will be entitled to hold Posted Collateral or to appoint an agent (a "Custodian") to hold Posted Collateral for the Secured Party. Upon notice by the Secured Party to the Pledgor of the appointment of a Custodian, the Pledgor's obligations to make any Transfer will be discharged by making the Transfer to that Custodian. The holding of Posted Collateral by a Custodian will be deemed to be the holding of that Posted Collateral by the Secured Party for which the Custodian is acting.

(ii) ***Failure to Satisfy Conditions.*** If the Secured Party or its Custodian fails to satisfy any conditions for holding Posted Collateral, then upon a demand made by the Pledgor, the Secured Party will, not later than five Local Business Days after the demand, Transfer or cause its Custodian to Transfer all Posted Collateral held by it to a Custodian that satisfies those conditions or to the Secured Party if it satisfies those conditions.

(iii) ***Liability.*** The Secured Party will be liable for the acts or omissions of its Custodian to the same extent that the Secured Party would be liable hereunder for its own acts or omissions.

(c) ***Use of Posted Collateral.*** Unless otherwise specified in Paragraph 13 and without limiting the rights and obligations of the parties under Paragraphs 3, 4(d)(ii), 5, 6(d) and 8, if the Secured Party is not a Defaulting Party or an Affected Party with respect to a Specified Condition and no Early Termination Date has occurred or been designated as the result of an Event of Default or Specified Condition with respect to the Secured Party, then the Secured Party will, notwithstanding Section 9-207 of the New York Uniform Commercial Code, have the right to:

(i) sell, pledge, rehypothecate, assign, invest, use, commingle or otherwise dispose of, or otherwise use in its business any Posted Collateral it holds, free from any claim or right of any nature whatsoever of the Pledgor, including any equity or right of redemption by the Pledgor; and

(ii) register any Posted Collateral in the name of the Secured Party, its Custodian or a nominee for either.

For purposes of the obligation to Transfer Eligible Credit Support or Posted Credit Support pursuant to Paragraphs 3 and 5 and any rights or remedies authorized under this Agreement, the Secured Party will be deemed to continue to hold all Posted Collateral and to receive Distributions made thereon, regardless of whether the Secured Party has exercised any rights with respect to any Posted Collateral pursuant to (i) or (ii) above.

(d) ***Distributions and Interest Amount.***

(i) ***Distributions.*** Subject to Paragraph 4(a), if the Secured Party receives or is deemed to receive Distributions on a Local Business Day, it will Transfer to the Pledgor not later than the following Local Business Day any Distributions it receives or is deemed to receive to the extent that a Delivery Amount would not be created or increased by that Transfer, as calculated by the Valuation Agent (and the date of calculation will be deemed to be a Valuation Date for this purpose).

(ii) ***Interest Amount.*** Unless otherwise specified in Paragraph 13 and subject to Paragraph 4(a), in lieu of any interest, dividends or other amounts paid or deemed to have been paid with respect to Posted Collateral in the form of Cash (all of which may be retained by the Secured Party), the Secured Party will Transfer to the Pledgor at the times specified in Paragraph 13 the Interest Amount to the extent that a Delivery Amount would not be created or increased by that Transfer, as calculated by the Valuation Agent (and the date of calculation will be deemed to be a Valuation Date for this purpose). The Interest Amount or portion thereof not Transferred pursuant to this Paragraph will constitute Posted Collateral in the form of Cash and will be subject to the security interest granted under Paragraph 2.

Paragraph 7. Events of Default

For purposes of Section 5(a)(iii)(1) of this Agreement, an Event of Default will exist with respect to a party if:

(i) that party fails (or fails to cause its Custodian) to make, when due, any Transfer of Eligible Collateral, Posted Collateral or the Interest Amount, as applicable, required to be made by it and that failure continues for two Local Business Days after notice of that failure is given to that party;

(ii) that party fails to comply with any restriction or prohibition specified in this Annex with respect to any of the rights specified in Paragraph 6(c) and that failure continues for five Local Business Days after notice of that failure is given to that party; or

(iii) that party fails to comply with or perform any agreement or obligation other than those specified in Paragraphs 7(i) and 7(ii) and that failure continues for 30 days after notice of that failure is given to that party.

Paragraph 8. Certain Rights and Remedies

(a) ***Secured Party's Rights and Remedies.*** If at any time (1) an Event of Default or Specified Condition with respect to the Pledgor has occurred and is continuing or (2) an Early Termination Date has occurred or been designated as the result of an Event of Default or Specified Condition with respect to the Pledgor, then, unless the Pledgor has paid in full all of its Obligations that are then due, the Secured Party may exercise one or more of the following rights and remedies:

(i) all rights and remedies available to a secured party under applicable law with respect to Posted Collateral held by the Secured Party;

(ii) any other rights and remedies available to the Secured Party under the terms of Other Posted Support, if any;

(iii) the right to Set-off any amounts payable by the Pledgor with respect to any Obligations against any Posted Collateral or the Cash equivalent of any Posted Collateral held by the Secured Party (or any obligation of the Secured Party to Transfer that Posted Collateral); and

(iv) the right to liquidate any Posted Collateral held by the Secured Party through one or more public or private sales or other dispositions with such notice, if any, as may be required under applicable law, free from any claim or right of any nature whatsoever of the Pledgor, including any equity or right of redemption by the Pledgor (with the Secured Party having the right to purchase any or all of the Posted Collateral to be sold) and to apply the proceeds (or the Cash equivalent thereof) from the liquidation of the Posted Collateral to any amounts payable by the Pledgor with respect to any Obligations in that order as the Secured Party may elect.

Each party acknowledges and agrees that Posted Collateral in the form of securities may decline speedily in value and is of a type customarily sold on a recognized market, and, accordingly, the Pledgor is not entitled to prior notice of any sale of that Posted Collateral by the Secured Party, except any notice that is required under applicable law and cannot be waived.

(b) ***Pledgor's Rights and Remedies.*** If at any time an Early Termination Date has occurred or been designated as the result of an Event of Default or Specified Condition with respect to the Secured Party, then (except in the case of an Early Termination Date relating to less than all Transactions (or Swap Transactions) where the Secured Party has paid in full all of its obligations that are then due under Section 6(e) of this Agreement):

(i) the Pledgor may exercise all rights and remedies available to a pledgor under applicable law with respect to Posted Collateral held by the Secured Party;

(ii) the Pledgor may exercise any other rights and remedies available to the Pledgor under the terms of Other Posted Support, if any;

(iii) the Secured Party will be obligated immediately to Transfer all Posted Collateral and the Interest Amount to the Pledgor; and

(iv) to the extent that Posted Collateral or the Interest Amount is not so Transferred pursuant to (iii) above, the Pledgor may:

(A) Set-off any amounts payable by the Pledgor with respect to any Obligations against any Posted Collateral or the Cash equivalent of any Posted Collateral held by the Secured Party (or any obligation of the Secured Party to Transfer that Posted Collateral); and

(B) to the extent that the Pledgor does not Set-off under (iv)(A) above, withhold payment of any remaining amounts payable by the Pledgor with respect to any Obligations, up to the Value of any remaining Posted Collateral held by the Secured Party, until that Posted Collateral is Transferred to the Pledgor.

(c) ***Deficiencies and Excess Proceeds.*** The Secured Party will Transfer to the Pledgor any proceeds and Posted Credit Support remaining after liquidation, Set-off and/or application under Paragraphs 8(a) and 8(b) after satisfaction in full of all amounts payable by the Pledgor with respect to any Obligations; the Pledgor in all events will remain liable for any amounts remaining unpaid after any liquidation, Set-off and/or application under Paragraphs 8(a) and 8(b).

(d) ***Final Returns.*** When no amounts are or thereafter may become payable by the Pledgor with respect to any Obligations (except for any potential liability under Section 2(d) of this Agreement), the Secured Party will Transfer to the Pledgor all Posted Credit Support and the Interest Amount, if any.

Paragraph 9. Representations

Each party represents to the other party (which representations will be deemed to be repeated as of each date on which it, as the Pledgor, Transfers Eligible Collateral) that:

(i) it has the power to grant a security interest in and lien on any Eligible Collateral it Transfers as the Pledgor and has taken all necessary actions to authorize the granting of that security interest and lien;

(ii) it is the sole owner of or otherwise has the right to Transfer all Eligible Collateral it Transfers to the Secured Party hereunder, free and clear of any security interest, lien, encumbrance or other restrictions other than the security interest and lien granted under Paragraph 2;

(iii) upon the Transfer of any Eligible Collateral to the Secured Party under the terms of this Annex, the Secured Party will have a valid and perfected first priority security interest therein (assuming that any central clearing corporation or any third-party financial intermediary or other entity not within the control of the Pledgor involved in the Transfer of that Eligible Collateral gives the notices and takes the action required of it under applicable law for perfection of that interest); and

(iv) the performance by it of its obligations under this Annex will not result in the creation of any security interest, lien or other encumbrance on any Posted Collateral other than the security interest and lien granted under Paragraph 2.

Paragraph 10. Expenses

(a) ***General.*** Except as otherwise provided in Paragraphs 10(b) and 10(c), each party will pay its own costs and expenses in connection with performing its obligations under this Annex and neither party will be liable for any costs and expenses incurred by the other party in connection herewith.

(b) ***Posted Credit Support.*** The Pledgor will promptly pay when due all taxes, assessments or charges of any nature that are imposed with respect to Posted Credit Support held by the Secured Party upon becoming aware of the same, regardless of whether any portion of that Posted Credit Support is subsequently disposed of under Paragraph 6(c), except for those taxes, assessments and charges that result from the exercise of the Secured Party's rights under Paragraph 6(c).

(c) ***Liquidation/Application of Posted Credit Support.*** All reasonable costs and expenses incurred by or on behalf of the Secured Party or the Pledgor in connection with the liquidation and/or application of any Posted Credit Support under Paragraph 8 will be payable, on demand and pursuant to the Expenses Section of this Agreement, by the Defaulting Party or, if there is no Defaulting Party, equally by the parties.

Paragraph 11. Miscellaneous

(a) ***Default Interest.*** A Secured Party that fails to make, when due, any Transfer of Posted Collateral or the Interest Amount will be obligated to pay the Pledgor (to the extent permitted under applicable law) an amount equal to interest at the Default Rate multiplied by the Value of the items of property that were required to be Transferred, from (and including) the date that Posted Collateral or Interest Amount was required to be Transferred to (but excluding) the date of Transfer of that Posted Collateral or Interest Amount. This interest will be calculated on the basis of daily compounding and the actual number of days elapsed.

(b) ***Further Assurances.*** Promptly following a demand made by a party, the other party will execute, deliver, file and record any financing statement, specific assignment or other document and take any other action that may be necessary or desirable and reasonably requested by that party to create, preserve, perfect or validate any security interest or lien granted under Paragraph 2, to enable that party to exercise or enforce its rights under this Annex with respect to Posted Credit Support or an Interest Amount or to effect or document a release of a security interest on Posted Collateral or an Interest Amount.

(c) ***Further Protection.*** The Pledgor will promptly give notice to the Secured Party of, and defend against, any suit, action, proceeding or lien that involves Posted Credit Support Transferred by the Pledgor or that could adversely affect the security interest and lien granted by it under Paragraph 2, unless that suit, action, proceeding or lien results from the exercise of the Secured Party's rights under Paragraph 6(c).

(d) ***Good Faith and Commercially Reasonable Manner.*** Performance of all obligations under this Annex, including, but not limited to, all calculations, valuations and determinations made by either party, will be made in good faith and in a commercially reasonable manner.

(e) ***Demands and Notices.*** All demands and notices made by a party under this Annex will be made as specified in the Notices Section of this Agreement, except as otherwise provided in Paragraph 13.

(f) ***Specifications of Certain Matters.*** Anything referred to in this Annex as being specified in Paragraph 13 also may be specified in one or more Confirmations or other documents and this Annex will be construed accordingly.

Paragraph 12. Definitions
As used in this Annex:—

"Cash" means the lawful currency of the United States of America.

"Credit Support Amount" has the meaning specified in Paragraph 3.

"Custodian" has the meaning specified in Paragraphs 6(b)(i) and 13.

"Delivery Amount" has the meaning specified in Paragraph 3(a).

"Disputing Party" has the meaning specified in Paragraph 5.

"Distributions" means with respect to Posted Collateral other than Cash, all principal, interest and other payments and distributions of cash or other property with respect thereto, regardless of whether the Secured Party has disposed of that Posted Collateral under Paragraph 6(c). Distributions will not include any item of property acquired by the Secured Party upon any disposition or liquidation of Posted Collateral or, with respect to any Posted Collateral in the form of Cash, any distributions on that collateral, unless otherwise specified herein.

"Eligible Collateral" means, with respect to a party, the items, if any, specified as such for that party in Paragraph 13.

"Eligible Credit Support" means Eligible Collateral and Other Eligible Support.

"Exposure" means for any Valuation Date or other date for which Exposure is calculated and subject to Paragraph 5 in the case of a dispute, the amount, if any, that would be payable to a party that is the Secured Party by the other party (expressed as a positive number) or by a party that is the Secured Party to the other party (expressed as a negative number) pursuant to Section 6(e)(ii)(2)(A) of this Agreement as if all Transactions (or Swap Transactions) were being terminated as of the relevant Valuation Time; *provided* that Market Quotation will be determined by the Valuation Agent using its estimates at mid-market of the amounts that would be paid for Replacement Transactions (as that term is defined in the definition of "Market Quotation").

"Independent Amount" means, with respect to a party, the amount specified as such for that party in Paragraph 13; if no amount is specified, zero.

"Interest Amount" means, with respect to an Interest Period, the aggregate sum of the amounts of interest calculated for each day in that Interest Period on the principal amount of Posted Collateral in the form of Cash held by the Secured Party on that day, determined by the Secured Party for each such day as follows:

(x) the amount of that Cash on that day; multiplied by

(y) the Interest Rate in effect for that day; divided by

(z) 360.

"Interest Period" means the period from (and including) the last Local Business Day on which an Interest Amount was Transferred (or, if no Interest Amount has yet been Transferred, the Local Business Day on which Posted Collateral in the form of Cash was Transferred to or received by the Secured Party) to (but excluding) the Local Business Day on which the current Interest Amount is to be Transferred.

"Interest Rate" means the rate specified in Paragraph 13.

"Local Business Day", unless otherwise specified in Paragraph 13, has the meaning specified in the Definitions Section of this Agreement, except that references to a payment in clause (b) thereof will be deemed to include a Transfer under this Annex.

"Minimum Transfer Amount" means, with respect to a party, the amount specified as such for that party in Paragraph 13; if no amount is specified, zero.

"Notification Time" has the meaning specified in Paragraph 13.

"Obligations" means, with respect to a party, all present and future obligations of that party under this Agreement and any additional obligations specified for that party in Paragraph 13.

"Other Eligible Support" means, with respect to a party, the items, if any, specified as such for that party in Paragraph 13.

"Other Posted Support" means all Other Eligible Support Transferred to the Secured Party that remains in effect for the benefit of that Secured Party.

"Pledgor" means either party, when that party (i) receives a demand for or is required to Transfer Eligible Credit Support under Paragraph 3(a) or (ii) has Transferred Eligible Credit Support under Paragraph 3(a).

"Posted Collateral" means all Eligible Collateral, other property, Distributions, and all proceeds thereof that have been Transferred to or received by the Secured Party under this Annex and not Transferred to the Pledgor pursuant to Paragraph 3(b), 4(d)(ii) or 6(d)(i) or released by the Secured Party under Paragraph 8. Any Interest Amount or portion thereof not Transferred pursuant to Paragraph 6(d)(ii) will constitute Posted Collateral in the form of Cash.

"Posted Credit Support" means Posted Collateral and Other Posted Support.

"Recalculation Date" means the Valuation Date that gives rise to the dispute under Paragraph 5; *provided, however*, that if a subsequent Valuation Date occurs under Paragraph 3 prior to the resolution of the dispute, then the "Recalculation Date" means the most recent Valuation Date under Paragraph 3.

"Resolution Time" has the meaning specified in Paragraph 13.

"Return Amount" has the meaning specified in Paragraph 3(b).

"Secured Party" means either party, when that party (i) makes a demand for or is entitled to receive Eligible Credit Support under Paragraph 3(a) or (ii) holds or is deemed to hold Posted Credit Support.

"Specified Condition" means, with respect to a party, any event specified as such for that party in Paragraph 13.

"Substitute Credit Support" has the meaning specified in Paragraph 4(d)(i).

"Substitution Date" has the meaning specified in Paragraph 4(d)(ii).

"Threshold" means, with respect to a party, the amount specified as such for that party in Paragraph 13; if no amount is specified, zero.

"Transfer" means, with respect to any Eligible Credit Support, Posted Credit Support or Interest Amount, and in accordance with the instructions of the Secured Party, Pledgor or Custodian, as applicable:

(i) in the case of Cash, payment or delivery by wire transfer into one or more bank accounts specified by the recipient;

(ii) in the case of certificated securities that cannot be paid or delivered by book-entry, payment or delivery in appropriate physical form to the recipient or its account accompanied by any duly executed instruments of transfer, assignments in blank, transfer tax stamps and any other documents necessary to constitute a legally valid transfer to the recipient;

(iii) in the case of securities that can be paid or delivered by book-entry, the giving of written instructions to the relevant depository institution or other entity specified by the recipient, together with a written copy thereof to the recipient, sufficient if complied with to result in a legally effective transfer of the relevant interest to the recipient; and

(iv) in the case of Other Eligible Support or Other Posted Support, as specified in Paragraph 13.

"Valuation Agent" has the meaning specified in Paragraph 13.

"Valuation Date" means each date specified in or otherwise determined pursuant to Paragraph 13.

"Valuation Percentage" means, for any item of Eligible Collateral, the percentage specified in Paragraph 13.

"Valuation Time" has the meaning specified in Paragraph 13.

"Value" means for any Valuation Date or other date for which Value is calculated and subject to Paragraph 5 in the case of a dispute, with respect to:

(i) Eligible Collateral or Posted Collateral that is:

(A) Cash, the amount thereof; and

(B) a security, the bid price obtained by the Valuation Agent multiplied by the applicable Valuation Percentage, if any;

(ii) Posted Collateral that consists of items that are not specified as Eligible Collateral, zero; and

(iii) Other Eligible Support and Other Posted Support, as specified in Paragraph 13.

Paragraph 13. Elections and Variables

(a) ***Security Interest for "Obligations"***. The term ***"Obligations"*** as used in this Annex includes the following additional obligations:

With respect to Party A: ....

With respect to Party B: ....

(b) ***Credit Support Obligations.***

(i) ***Delivery Amount, Return Amount and Credit Support Amount.***

(A) ***"Delivery Amount"*** has the meaning specified in Paragraph 3(a), unless otherwise specified here: ....

(B) ***"Return Amount"*** has the meaning specified in Paragraph 3(b), unless otherwise specified here: ....

(C) ***"Credit Support Amount"*** has the meaning specified in Paragraph 3, unless otherwise specified here: ....

(ii) ***Eligible Collateral.*** The following items will qualify as ***"Eligible Collateral"*** for the party specified:

		Party A	**Party B**	**Valuation Percentage**
(A)	Cash	[ ]	[ ]	[ ]%
(B)	negotiable debt obligations issued by the U.S. Treasury Department having an original maturity at issuance of not more than one year ("Treasury Bills")	[ ]	[ ]	[ ]%
(C)	negotiable debt obligations issued by the U.S. Treasury Department having an original maturity at issuance of more than one year but not more than 10 years ("Treasury Notes")	[ ]	[ ]	[ ]%
(D)	negotiable debt obligations issued by the U.S. Treasury Department having an original maturity at issuance of more than 10 years ("Treasury Bonds")	[ ]	[ ]	[ ]%
(E)	other:	[ ]	[ ]	[ ]%

(iii) ***Other Eligible Support.*** The following items will qualify as ***"Other Eligible Support"*** for the party specified:

		Party A	**Party B**
(A)	....	[ ]	[ ]
(B)	....	[ ]	[ ]

(iv) ***Thresholds.***

(A) ***"Independent Amount"*** means with respect to Party A: $ ....
"Independent Amount" means with respect to Party B: $ ....

(B) ***"Threshold"*** means with respect to Party A: $ ....
"Threshold" means with respect to Party B: $ ....

(C) ***"Minimum Transfer Amount"*** means with respect to Party A: $ ....
"Minimum Transfer Amount" means with respect to Party B: $ ....

(D) **Rounding.** The Delivery Amount and the Return Amount will be rounded [down to the nearest integral multiple of $. . . ./up and down to the nearest integral multiple of $. . . ., respectively*].

(c) ***Valuation and Timing.***

(i) ***"Valuation Agent"*** means, for purposes of Paragraphs 3 and 5, the party making the demand under Paragraph 3, and, for purposes of Paragraph 6(d), the Secured Party receiving or deemed to receive the Distributions or the Interest Amount, as applicable, unless otherwise specified here: ....

(ii) ***"Valuation Date"*** means: ....

(iii) ***"Valuation Time"*** means:

[ ] the close of business in the city of the Valuation Agent on the Valuation Date or date of calculation, as applicable;

[ ] the close of business on the Local Business Day before the Valuation Date or date of calculation, as applicable;

provided that the calculations of Value and Exposure will be made as of approximately the same time on the same date.

(iv) ***"Notification Time"*** means 1:00 p.m., New York time, on a Local Business Day, unless otherwise specified here: ....

(d) ***Conditions Precedent and Secured Party's Rights and Remedies.*** The following Termination Event(s) will be a ***"Specified Condition"*** for the party specified (that party being the Affected Party if the Termination Event occurs with respect to that party):

	Party A	**Party B**
Illegality	[ ]	[ ]
Tax Event	[ ]	[ ]
Tax Event Upon Merger	[ ]	[ ]
Credit Event Upon Merger	[ ]	[ ]
Additional Termination Event(s):[1]		
....	[ ]	[ ]
....	[ ]	[ ]

* Delete as applicable.

[1] If the parties elect to designate an Additional Termination Event as a "Specified Condition", then they should only designate one or more Additional Termination Events that are designated as such in their Schedule.

(e) ***Substitution.***

(i) ***"Substitution Date"*** has the meaning specified in Paragraph 4(d)(ii), unless otherwise specified here: ....

(ii) ***Consent.*** If specified here as applicable, then the Pledgor must obtain the Secured Party's consent for any substitution pursuant to Paragraph 4(d): [applicable/inapplicable*][2]

(f) ***Dispute Resolution.***

(i) ***"Resolution Time"*** means 1:00 p.m., New York time, on the Local Business Day following the date on which the notice is given that gives rise to a dispute under Paragraph 5, unless otherwise specified here: ....

(ii) ***Value.*** For the purpose of Paragraphs 5(i)(C) and 5(ii), the Value of Posted Credit Support will be calculated as follows: ....

(iii) ***Alternative.*** The provisions of Paragraph 5 will apply, unless an alternative dispute resolution procedure is specified here: ....

(g) ***Holding and Using Posted Collateral.***

(i) ***Eligibility to Hold Posted Collateral; Custodians.*** Party A and its Custodian will be entitled to hold Posted Collateral pursuant to Paragraph 6(b); *provided* that the following conditions applicable to it are satisfied:

(1) Party A is not a Defaulting Party.

(2) Posted Collateral may be held only in the following jurisdictions: ....

(3) ....

Initially, the **Custodian** for Party A is ....

Party B and its Custodian will be entitled to hold Posted Collateral pursuant to Paragraph 6(b); *provided* that the following conditions applicable to it are satisfied:

(1) Party B is not a Defaulting Party.

(2) Posted Collateral may be held only in the following jurisdictions: ....

(3) ....

Initially, the **Custodian** for Party B is ....

(ii) ***Use of Posted Collateral.*** The provisions of Paragraph 6(c) will not apply to the [party/parties*] specified here:

[ ] Party A

[ ] Party B

and [that party/those parties*] will not be permitted to: ....

* Delete as applicable.

[2] Parties should consider selecting "applicable" where substitution without consent could give rise to a registration requirement to perfect properly the security interest in Posted Collateral (*e.g.*, where a party to the Annex is the New York branch of an English bank).

(h) ***Distributions and Interest Amount.***

(i) ***Interest Rate.*** The ***"Interest Rate"*** will be: ....

(ii) ***Transfer of Interest Amount.*** The Transfer of the Interest Amount will be made on the last Local Business Day of each calendar month and on any Local Business Day that Posted Collateral in the form of Cash is Transferred to the Pledgor pursuant to Paragraph 3 (b), unless otherwise specified here: ...

....

(iii) ***Alternative to Interest Amount.*** The provisions of Paragraph 6(d)(ii) will apply, unless otherwise specified here: ....

(i) ***Additional Representation(s).***

[Party A/Party B*] represents to the other party (which representation(s) will be deemed to be repeated as of each date on which it, as the Pledgor, Transfers Eligible Collateral) that:

(i) ....

(ii) ....

(j) ***Other Eligible Support and Other Posted Support.***

(i) ***"Value"*** with respect to Other Eligible Support and Other Posted Support means:.......................................

(ii) ***"Transfer"*** with respect to Other Eligible Support and Other Posted Support means:................................

(k) ***Demands and Notices.***

All demands, specifications and notices under this Annex will be made pursuant to the Notices Section of this Agreement, unless otherwise specified here:

Party A: ....

....

Party B: ....

....

(l) ***Addresses for Transfers.***

Party A: ....

....

Party B: ....

....

(m) ***Other Provisions.***

---

* Delete as applicable.

ANNEX 3 LIST OF COUNTRIES WHERE ISDA HAS OBTAINED COLLATERAL LEGAL OPINIONS

The following is a list of jurisdictions where ISDA has obtained completed collateral legal opinions on the English Law CSA and the New York Law CSA (as at October 2011).

Australia	Mallesons Stephens Jaques
Austria	Weiss-Tessbach
Bahamas	Higgs & Johnson
Belgium	Loyens
Bermuda	Conyers, Dill & Pearman
Canada	Stikeman, Elliott
Cayman Islands	Maples & Calder
Channel Islands (Guernsey)	Ogier
Channel Islands (Jersey)	Ogier
Czech Republic	Allen & Overy
Denmark	Gorrissen Federspiel Kierkegaard
England	Allen & Overy
Finland	Peltonen, Ruokonen & Itainen
France	Gide Loyrette Nouel
Germany	Hengeler Mueller Weitzel Wirtz
Greece	Karatzas & Partners
Hong Kong	Allen & Overy
Hungary	Allen & Overy
India	Juris Corp.
Indonesia	Ali Budjiardo, Nugroho, Reksodiputro
Ireland	McCann Fitzgerald
Israel	Yigal Arnon & Co
Italy	Allen & Overy
Japan	Linklaters
Luxembourg	Linklaters Loesch
Malaysia	Shearn Delamore & Co
Mexico	Ritch Heather y Mueller
Netherlands	Nauta Dutilh
New Zealand	Bell Gully
Norway	Wiersholm, Mellbye & Bech
Philippines	SyCip Salazar Hernandes & amp; Gatmaitan
Portugal	Cardigos e Associados
Quebec	Stikeman, Elliott

Scotland	Dundas & Wilson
Singapore	Allen & Gledhill
South Africa	Deneys Reitz
South Korea	Kim & Chang
Sweden	Mannheimer Swartling Advokatbyra AB
Switzerland	Lenz & Staehelin
Taiwan	Russin & Vecchi
Thailand	Baker & McKenzie
Turkey	Pekin & Pekin
United States of America	Mayer Brown

45 completed opinions; 4 others commissioned from lawyers in Brazil, Cyprus, Iceland and Poland.

ANNEX 4 RELEVANT EXTRACTS FROM THE NEW YORK UNIFORM COMMERCIAL CODE

Section 8–102. Definitions.

(a) In this Article:

(1) "Adverse claim" means a claim that a claimant has a property interest in a financial asset and that it is a violation of the rights of the claimant for another person to hold, transfer, or deal with the financial asset.

(2) "Bearer form", as applied to a certificated security, means a form in which the security is payable to the bearer of the security certificate according to its terms but not by reason of an indorsement.

(3) "Broker" means a person defined as a broker or dealer under the federal securities laws, but without excluding a bank acting in that capacity.

(4) "Certificated security" means a security that is represented by a certificate.

(5) "Clearing corporation" means:

(i) a person that is registered as a "clearing agency" pursuant to 15 United States Code S 78-c(a)(23), as from time to time amended;

(ii) a federal reserve bank; or

(iii) any other person that provides clearance or settlement services with respect to financial assets that would require it to register as a clearing agency under the federal securities laws but for an exclusion or exemption from the registration requirement, if its activities as a clearing corporation, including promulgation of rules, are subject to regulation by a federal or state governmental authority.

(6) "Communicate" means to:

(i) send a signed writing; or

(ii) transmit information by any mechanism agreed upon by the persons transmitting and receiving the information.

(7) "Entitlement holder" means a person identified in the records of a securities intermediary as the person having a security entitlement against the securities intermediary. If a person acquires a security entitlement by virtue of Section 8–501(b) (2) or (3), that person is the entitlement holder.

(8) "Entitlement order" means a notification communicated to a securities intermediary directing transfer or redemption of a financial asset to which the entitlement holder has a security entitlement.

(9) "Financial asset", except as otherwise provided in Section 8–103, means:
  (i) a security;
  (ii) an obligation of a person or a share, participation, or other interest in a person or in property or an enterprise of a person, which is, or is of a type, dealt in or traded on financial markets, or which is recognized in any area in which it is issued or dealt in as a medium for investment; or
  (iii) any property that is held by a securities intermediary for another person in a securities account if the securities intermediary has expressly agreed with the other person that the property is to be treated as a financial asset under this Article. As context requires, the term means either the interest itself or the means by which a person's claim to it is evidenced, including a certificated or uncertificated security, a security certificate, or a security entitlement.

(10) "Good faith", for purposes of the obligation of good faith in the performance or enforcement of contracts or duties within this Article, means honesty in fact and the observance of reasonable commercial standards of fair dealing.

(11) "Indorsement" means a signature that alone or accompanied by other words is made on a security certificate in registered form or on a separate document for the purpose of assigning, transferring, or redeeming the security or granting a power to assign, transfer, or redeem it.

(12) "Instruction" means a notification communicated to the issuer of an uncertificated security which directs that the transfer of the security be registered or that the security be redeemed.

(13) "Registered form", as applied to a certificated security, means a form in which:
  (i) the security certificate specifies a person entitled to the security; and
  (ii) a transfer of the security may be registered upon books maintained for that purpose by or on behalf of the issuer, or the security certificate so states.

(14) "Securities intermediary" means:
  (i) a clearing corporation; or
  (ii) a person, including a bank or broker, that in the ordinary course of its business maintains securities accounts for others and is acting in that capacity.

(15) "Security", except as otherwise provided in Section 8–103, means an obligation of an issuer or a share, participation, or other interest in an issuer or in property or an enterprise of an issuer:

(i) which is represented by a security certificate in bearer or registered form, or the transfer of which may be registered upon books maintained for that purpose by or on behalf of the issuer;
(ii) which is one of a class or series or by its terms is divisible into a class or series of shares, participations, interests, or obligations; and
(iii) which:
(A) is, or is of a type, dealt in or traded on securities exchanges or securities markets; or
(B) is a medium for investment and by its terms expressly provides that it is a security governed by this Article.

(16) "Security certificate" means a certificate representing a security.
(17) "Security entitlement" means the rights and property interest of an entitlement holder with respect to a financial asset specified in Part 5.
(18) "Uncertificated security" means a security that is not represented by a certificate.

(b) Other definitions applying to this Article and the sections in which they appear are:

"Appropriate person".	Section 8–107.
"Control".	Section 8–106.
"Delivery".	Section 8–301.
"Investment company security".	Section 8–103.
"Issuer".	Section 8–201.
"Overissue".	Section 8–210.
"Protected purchaser".	Section 8–303.
"Securities account".	Section 8–501.

(c) In addition, Article 1 contains general definitions and principles of construction and interpretation applicable throughout this Article.
(d) The characterization of a person, business, or transaction for purposes of this Article does not determine the characterization of the person, business, or transaction for purposes of any other law, regulation, or rule.
(e) The following definitions in Article 9 apply to this article:

Cooperative interest	Section 9–102(a)(27–b)
Cooperative organization	Section 9–102(a)(27–c)
Cooperative record	Section 9–102(a)(27–e)

Section 8–104. Acquisition of Security or Financial Asset or Interest Therein.

(a) A person acquires a security or an interest therein, under this Article, if:
  (1) the person is a purchaser to whom a security is delivered pursuant to Section 8–301; or
  (2) the person acquires a security entitlement to the security pursuant to Section 8–501.

(b) A person acquires a financial asset, other than a security, or an interest therein, under this Article, if the person acquires a security entitlement to the financial asset.

(c) A person who acquires a security entitlement to a security or other financial asset has the rights specified in Part 5, but is a purchaser of any security, security entitlement, or other financial asset held by the securities intermediary only to the extent provided in Section 8–503.

(d) Unless the context shows that a different meaning is intended, a person who is required by other law, regulation, rule, or agreement to transfer, deliver, present, surrender, exchange, or otherwise put in the possession of another person a security or financial asset satisfies that requirement by causing the other person to acquire an interest in the security or financial asset pursuant to subsection (a) or (b).

Section 8–106. Control.

(a) A purchaser has "control" of a certificated security in bearer form if the certificated security is delivered to the purchaser.

(b) A purchaser has "control" of a certificated security in registered form if the certificated security is delivered to the purchaser, and:
  (1) the certificate is indorsed to the purchaser or in blank by an effective indorsement; or
  (2) the certificate is registered in the name of the purchaser, upon original issue or registration of transfer by the issuer.

(c) A purchaser has "control" of an uncertificated security if:
  (1) the uncertificated security is delivered to the purchaser; or
  (2) the issuer has agreed that it will comply with instructions originated by the purchaser without further consent by the registered owner.

(d) A purchaser has "control" of a security entitlement if:
  (1) the purchaser becomes the entitlement holder;
  (2) the securities intermediary has agreed that it will comply with entitlement orders originated by the purchaser without further consent by the entitlement holder; or

(3) another person has control of the security entitlement on behalf of the purchaser or, having previously acquired control of the security entitlement, acknowledges that it has control on behalf of the purchaser.

(e) If an interest in a security entitlement is granted by the entitlement holder to the entitlement holder's own securities intermediary, the securities intermediary has control.

(f) A purchaser who has satisfied the requirements of subsection (c) or (d) has control even if the registered owner in the case of subsection (c) or the entitlement holder in the case of subsection (d) retains the right to make substitutions for the uncertificated security or security entitlement, to originate instructions or entitlement orders to the issuer or securities intermediary, or otherwise to deal with the uncertificated security or security entitlement.

(g) An issuer or a securities intermediary may not enter into an agreement of the kind described in subsection (c)(2) or (d)(2) without the consent of the registered owner or entitlement holder, but an issuer or a securities intermediary is not required to enter into such an agreement even though the registered owner or entitlement holder so directs. An issuer or securities intermediary that has entered into such an agreement is not required to confirm the existence of the agreement to another party unless requested to do so by the registered owner or entitlement holder.

Section 8–110. Applicability; Choice of Law.

(a) The local law of the issuer's jurisdiction, as specified in subsection (d), governs:
  (1) the validity of a security;
  (2) the rights and duties of the issuer with respect to registration of transfer;
  (3) the effectiveness of registration of transfer by the issuer;
  (4) whether the issuer owes any duties to an adverse claimant to a security; and
  (5) whether an adverse claim can be asserted against a person to whom transfer of a certificated or uncertificated security is registered or a person who obtains control of an uncertificated security.

(b) The local law of the securities intermediary's jurisdiction, as specified in subsection (e), governs:
  (1) acquisition of a security entitlement from the securities intermediary;
  (2) the rights and duties of the securities intermediary and entitlement holder arising out of a security entitlement;

(3) whether the securities intermediary owes any duties to an adverse claimant to a security entitlement; and
(4) whether an adverse claim can be asserted against a person who acquires a security entitlement from the securities intermediary or a person who purchases a security entitlement or interest therein from an entitlement holder.

(c) Except with respect to cooperative interests, the local law of the jurisdiction in which a security certificate is located at the time of delivery governs whether an adverse claim can be asserted against a person to whom the security certificate is delivered.

(d) "Issuer's jurisdiction" means the jurisdiction under which the issuer of the security is organized or, if permitted by the law of that jurisdiction, the law of another jurisdiction specified by the issuer. An issuer organized under the law of this State may specify the law of another jurisdiction as the law governing the matters specified in subsection (a)(2) through (5).

(e) The following rules determine a "securities intermediary's jurisdiction" for purposes of this section:
(1) If an agreement between the securities intermediary and its entitlement holder governing the securities account expressly provides that a particular jurisdiction is the securities intermediary's jurisdiction for purposes of this part, this article, or this act, that jurisdiction is the securities intermediary's jurisdiction.
(2) If paragraph (1) does not apply and an agreement between the securities intermediary and its entitlement holder governing the securities account expressly provides that the agreement is governed by the law of a particular jurisdiction, that jurisdiction is the securities intermediary's jurisdiction.
(3) If neither paragraph (1) nor paragraph (2) apply and an agreement between the securities intermediary and its entitlement holder governing the securities account expressly provides that the securities account is maintained at an office in a particular jurisdiction, that jurisdiction is the securities intermediary's jurisdiction.
(4) If none of the preceding paragraphs apply, the securities intermediary's jurisdiction is the jurisdiction in which the office identified in an account statement as the office serving the entitlement holder's account is located.
(5) If none of the preceding paragraphs apply, the securities intermediary's jurisdiction is the jurisdiction in which the chief executive office of the securities intermediary is located.

(f) A securities intermediary's jurisdiction is not determined by the physical location of certificates representing financial assets, or by the jurisdiction in which is organized the issuer of the financial asset with respect to which an entitlement holder has a security entitlement, or by the location of facilities for data processing or other record keeping concerning the account.

Section 8–301. Delivery.

(a) Delivery of a certificated security to a purchaser occurs when:
  (1) the purchaser acquires possession of the security certificate;
  (2) another person, other than a securities intermediary, either acquires possession of the security certificate on behalf of the purchaser or, having previously acquired possession of the certificate, acknowledges that it holds for the purchaser; or
  (3) a securities intermediary acting on behalf of the purchaser acquires possession of the security certificate, only if the certificate is in registered form and is (i) registered in the name of the purchaser, (ii) payable to the order of the purchaser, or (iii) specially indorsed to the purchaser by an effective indorsement and has not been indorsed to the securities intermediary or in blank.

(b) Delivery of an uncertificated security to a purchaser occurs when:
  (1) the issuer registers the purchaser as the registered owner, upon original issue or registration of transfer; or
  (2) another person, other than a securities intermediary, either becomes the registered owner of the uncertificated security on behalf of the purchaser or, having previously become the registered owner, acknowledges that it holds for the purchaser.

Section 8–501. Securities Account; Acquisition of Security Entitlement from Securities Intermediary.

(a) "Securities account" means an account to which a financial asset is or may be credited in accordance with an agreement under which the person maintaining the account undertakes to treat the person for whom the account is maintained as entitled to exercise the rights that comprise the financial asset.

(b) Except as otherwise provided in subsections (d) and (e), a person acquires a security entitlement if a securities intermediary:
  (1) indicates by book entry that a financial asset has been credited to the person's securities account;
  (2) receives a financial asset from the person or acquires a financial asset for the person and, in either case, accepts it for credit to the person's securities account; or
  (3) becomes obligated under other law, regulation, or rule to credit a financial asset to the person's securities account.

(c) If a condition of subsection (b) has been met, a person has a security entitlement even though the securities intermediary does not itself hold the financial asset.

(d) If a securities intermediary holds a financial asset for another person, and the financial asset is registered in the name of, payable to the order of, or specially indorsed to the other person, and has not been indorsed to the securities intermediary or in blank, the other person is treated as holding the financial asset directly rather than as having a security entitlement with respect to the financial asset.

(e) Issuance of a security is not establishment of a security entitlement.

Section 8–503. Property Interest of Entitlement Holder in Financial Asset held by Securities Intermediary.

(a) To the extent necessary for a securities intermediary to satisfy all security entitlements with respect to a particular financial asset, all interests in that financial asset held by the securities intermediary are held by the securities intermediary for the entitlement holders, are not property of the securities intermediary, and are not subject to claims of creditors of the securities intermediary, except as otherwise provided in Section 8–511.

(b) An entitlement holder's property interest with respect to a particular financial asset under subsection (a) is a pro rata property interest in all interests in that financial asset held by the securities intermediary, without regard to the time the entitlement holder acquired the security entitlement or the time the securities intermediary acquired the interest in that financial asset.

(c) An entitlement holder's property interest with respect to a particular financial asset under subsection (a) may be enforced against the securities intermediary only by exercise of the entitlement holder's rights under Sections 8–505 through 8–508.

(d) An entitlement holder's property interest with respect to a particular financial asset under subsection (a) may be enforced against a purchaser of the financial asset or interest therein only if:
   (1) insolvency proceedings have been initiated by or against the securities intermediary;
   (2) the securities intermediary does not have sufficient interests in the financial asset to satisfy the security entitlements of all of its entitlement holders to that financial asset;
   (3) the securities intermediary violated its obligations under Section 8–504 by transferring the financial asset or interest therein to the purchaser; and

(4) the purchaser is not protected under subsection (e). The trustee or other liquidator, acting on behalf of all entitlement holders having security entitlements with respect to a particular financial asset, may recover the financial asset, or interest therein, from the purchaser. If the trustee or other liquidator elects not to pursue that right, an entitlement holder whose security entitlement remains unsatisfied has the right to recover its interest in the financial asset from the purchaser.

(e) An action based on the entitlement holder's property interest with respect to a particular financial asset under subsection (a), whether framed in conversion, replevin, constructive trust, equitable lien, or other theory, may not be asserted against any purchaser of a financial asset or interest therein who gives value, obtains control, and does not act in collusion with the securities intermediary in violating the securities intermediary's obligations under Section 8–504.

Section 8–504. Duty of Securities Intermediary to Maintain Financial Asset.

(a) A securities intermediary shall promptly obtain and thereafter maintain a financial asset in a quantity corresponding to the aggregate of all security entitlements it has established in favor of its entitlement holders with respect to that financial asset. The securities intermediary may maintain those financial assets directly or through one or more other securities intermediaries.

(b) Except to the extent otherwise agreed by its entitlement holder, a securities intermediary may not grant any security interests in a financial asset it is obligated to maintain pursuant to subsection (a).

(c) A securities intermediary satisfies the duty in subsection (a) if:

(1) the securities intermediary acts with respect to the duty as agreed upon by the entitlement holder and the securities intermediary; or

(2) in the absence of agreement, the securities intermediary exercises due care in accordance with reasonable commercial standards to obtain and maintain the financial asset.

(d) This section does not apply to a clearing corporation that is itself the obligor of an option or similar obligation to which its entitlement holders have security entitlements.

Section 8–505. Duty of Securities Intermediary with Respect to Payments and Distributions.

(a) A securities intermediary shall take action to obtain a payment or distribution made by the issuer of a financial asset. A securities intermediary satisfies the duty if:

(1) the securities intermediary acts with respect to the duty as agreed upon by the entitlement holder and the securities intermediary; or
(2) in the absence of agreement, the securities intermediary exercises due care in accordance with reasonable commercial standards to attempt to obtain the payment or distribution.

(b) A securities intermediary is obligated to its entitlement holder for a payment or distribution made by the issuer of a financial asset if the payment or distribution is received by the securities intermediary.

Section 8–506. Duty of Securities Intermediary to Exercise Rights as Directed by Entitlement Holder.

A securities intermediary shall exercise rights with respect to a financial asset if directed to do so by an entitlement holder. A securities intermediary satisfies the duty if:

(1) the securities intermediary acts with respect to the duty as agreed upon by the entitlement holder and the securities intermediary; or
(2) in the absence of agreement, the securities intermediary either places the entitlement holder in a position to exercise the rights directly or exercises due care in accordance with reasonable commercial standards to follow the direction of the entitlement holder.

Section 8–507. Duty of Securities Intermediary to Comply with Entitlement Order.

(a) A securities intermediary shall comply with an entitlement order if the entitlement order is originated by the appropriate person, the securities intermediary has had reasonable opportunity to assure itself that the entitlement order is genuine and authorized, and the securities intermediary has had reasonable opportunity to comply with the entitlement order. A securities intermediary satisfies the duty if:
(1) the securities intermediary acts with respect to the duty as agreed upon by the entitlement holder and the securities intermediary; or
(2) in the absence of agreement, the securities intermediary exercises due care in accordance with reasonable commercial standards to comply with the entitlement order.

(b) If a securities intermediary transfers a financial asset pursuant to an ineffective entitlement order, the securities intermediary shall reestablish a security entitlement in favor of the person entitled to it, and pay or credit any payments or distributions that the person did not receive as a result of the wrongful transfer. If the securities intermediary does not reestablish a security entitlement, the securities intermediary is liable to the entitlement holder for damages.

Section 8–508. Duty of Securities Intermediary to Change Entitlement Holder's Position to Other Form of Security Holding.

A securities intermediary shall act at the direction of an entitlement holder to change a security entitlement into another available form of holding for which the entitlement holder is eligible, or to cause the financial asset to be transferred to a securities account of the entitlement holder with another securities intermediary. A securities intermediary satisfies the duty if:

(1) the securities intermediary acts as agreed upon by the entitlement holder and the securities intermediary; or
(2) in the absence of agreement, the securities intermediary exercises due care in accordance with reasonable commercial standards to follow the direction of the entitlement holder.

Section 8–511. Priority Among Security Interests and Entitlement Holders.

(a) Except as otherwise provided in subsections (b) and (c), if a securities intermediary does not have sufficient interests in a particular financial asset to satisfy both its obligations to entitlement holders who have security entitlements to that financial asset and its obligation to a creditor of the securities intermediary who has a security interest in that financial asset, the claims of entitlement holders, other than the creditor, have priority over the claim of the creditor.
(b) A claim of a creditor of a securities intermediary who has a security interest in a financial asset held by a securities intermediary has priority over claims of the securities intermediary's entitlement holders who have security entitlements with respect to that financial asset if the creditor has control over the financial asset.
(c) If a clearing corporation does not have sufficient financial assets to satisfy both its obligations to entitlement holders who have security entitlements with respect to a financial asset and its obligation to a creditor of the clearing corporation who has a security interest in that financial asset, the claim of the creditor has priority over the claims of entitlement holders.

Section 9–103. Purchase-money Security Interest; Application of Payments; Burden of Establishing.

(a) Definitions. In this section:
    (1) "purchase-money collateral" means goods or software that secures a purchase-money obligation incurred with respect to that collateral; and
    (2) "purchase-money obligation" means an obligation of an obligor incurred as all or part of the price of the collateral or

for value given to enable the debtor to acquire rights in or the use of the collateral if the value is in fact so used.

(b) Purchase-money security interest in goods. A security interest in goods is a purchase-money security interest:

(1) to the extent that the goods are purchase-money collateral with respect to that security interest;

(2) if the security interest is in inventory that is or was purchase-money collateral, also to the extent that the security interest secures a purchase-money obligation incurred with respect to other inventory in which the secured party holds or held a purchase-money security interest; and

(3) also to the extent that the security interest secures a purchase-money obligation incurred with respect to software in which the secured party holds or held a purchase-money security interest.

(c) Purchase-money security interest in software. A security interest in software is a purchase-money security interest to the extent that the security interest also secures a purchase-money obligation incurred with respect to goods in which the secured party holds or held a purchase-money security interest if:

(1) the debtor acquired its interest in the software in an integrated transaction in which it acquired an interest in the goods; and

(2) the debtor acquired its interest in the software for the principal purpose of using the software in the goods.

(d) Consignor's inventory purchase-money security interest. The security interest of a consignor in goods that are the subject of a consignment is a purchase-money security interest in inventory.

(e) Application of payment in non-consumer-goods transaction. In a transaction other than a consumer-goods transaction, if the extent to which a security interest is a purchase-money security interest depends on the application of a payment to a particular obligation, the payment must be applied:

(1) in accordance with any reasonable method of application to which the parties agree;

(2) in the absence of the parties' agreement to a reasonable method, in accordance with any intention of the obligor manifested at or before the time of payment; or

(3) in the absence of an agreement to a reasonable method and timely manifestation of the obligor's intention, in the following order:

(A) to obligations that are not secured; and
(B) if more than one obligation is secured, to obligations secured by purchase-money security interests in the order in which those obligations were incurred.

(f) No loss of status of purchase-money security interest in non-consumer-goods transaction. In a transaction other than a consumer-goods transaction, a purchase-money security interest does not lose its status as such, even if:
(1) the purchase-money collateral also secures an obligation that is not a purchase-money obligation;
(2) collateral that is not purchase-money collateral also secures the purchase-money obligation; or
(3) the purchase-money obligation has been renewed, refinanced, consolidated, or restructured.

(g) Burden of proof in non-consumer-goods transaction. In a transaction other than a consumer-goods transaction, a secured party claiming a purchase-money security interest has the burden of establishing the extent to which the security interest is a purchase-money security interest.

(h) Non-consumer-goods transactions; no inference. The limitation of the rules in subsections (e), (f), and (g) to transactions other than consumer-goods transactions is intended to leave to the court the determination of the proper rules in consumer-goods transactions. The court may not infer from that limitation the nature of the proper rule in consumer-goods transactions and may continue to apply established approaches.

Section 9–104. Control of Deposit Account.

(a) Requirements for control. A secured party has control of a deposit account if:
(1) the secured party is the bank with which the deposit account is maintained;
(2) the debtor, secured party, and bank have agreed in an authenticated record that the bank will comply with instructions originated by the secured party directing disposition of the funds in the deposit account without further consent by the debtor; or
(3) the secured party becomes the bank's customer with respect to the deposit account.

(b) Debtor's right to direct disposition. A secured party that has satisfied subsection (a) has control, even if the debtor retains the right to direct the disposition of funds from the deposit account.

Section 9–105. Control of Electronic Chattel Paper.

A secured party has control of electronic chattel paper if the record or records comprising the chattel paper are created, stored, and assigned in such a manner that:

(1) a single authoritative copy of the record or records exists which is unique, identifiable and, except as otherwise provided in paragraphs (4), (5), and (6), unalterable;
(2) the authoritative copy identifies the secured party as the assignee of the record or records;
(3) the authoritative copy is communicated to and maintained by the secured party or its designated custodian;
(4) copies or revisions that add or change an identified assignee of the authoritative copy can be made only with the participation of the secured party;
(5) each copy of the authoritative copy and any copy of a copy is readily identifiable as a copy that is not the authoritative copy; and
(6) any revision of the authoritative copy is readily identifiable as an authorized or unauthorized revision.

Section 9–203. Attachment and Enforceability of Security Interest; Proceeds; Supporting Obligations; Formal Requisites.

(a) Attachment. A security interest attaches to collateral when it becomes enforceable against the debtor with respect to the collateral, unless an agreement expressly postpones the time of attachment.
(b) Enforceability. Except as otherwise provided in subsections (c) through (i), a security interest is enforceable against the debtor and third parties with respect to the collateral only if:
    (1) value has been given;
    (2) the debtor has rights in the collateral or the power to transfer rights in the collateral to a secured party; and
    (3) one of the following conditions is met:
        (A) the debtor has authenticated a security agreement that provides a description of the collateral and, if the security interest covers timber to be cut, a description of the land concerned;
        (B) the collateral is not a certificated security and is in the possession of the secured party under Section 9–313 pursuant to the debtor's security agreement;
        (C) the collateral is a certificated security in registered form and the security certificate has been delivered to

the secured party under Section 8–301 pursuant to the debtor's security agreement; or

(D) the collateral is deposit accounts, electronic chattel paper, investment property, or letter-of-credit rights, and the secured party has control under Section 9–104, 9–105, 9–106, or 9–107 pursuant to the debtor's security agreement.

(c) Other UCC provisions. Subsection (b) is subject to Section 4–210 on the security interest of a collecting bank, Section 5–118 on the security interest of a letter-of-credit issuer or nominated person, Section 9–110 on a security interest arising under Article 2 or 2-A, and Section 9–206 on security interests in investment property.

(d) When a person becomes bound by another person's security agreement. A person becomes bound as debtor by a security agreement entered into by another person if, by operation of law other than this article or by contract:

(1) the security agreement becomes effective to create a security interest in the person's property; or

(2) the person becomes generally obligated for the obligations of the other person, including the obligation secured under the security agreement, and acquires or succeeds to all or substantially all of the assets of the other person.

(e) Effect of new debtor becoming bound. If a new debtor becomes bound as debtor by a security agreement entered into by another person:

(1) the agreement satisfies subsection (b)(3) with respect to existing or after-acquired property of the new debtor to the extent the property is described in the agreement; and

(2) another agreement is not necessary to make a security interest in the property enforceable.

(f) Proceeds and supporting obligations. The attachment of a security interest in collateral gives the secured party the rights to proceeds provided by Section 9–315 and is also attachment of a security interest in a supporting obligation for the collateral.

(g) Lien securing right to payment. The attachment of a security interest in a right to payment or performance secured by a security interest or other lien on personal or real property is also attachment of a security interest in the security interest, mortgage, or other lien.

(h) Security entitlement carried in securities account. The attachment of a security interest in a securities account is also attachment of a security interest in the security entitlements carried in the securities account.

(i) Commodity contracts carried in commodity account. The attachment of a security interest in a commodity account is also attachment of a security interest in the commodity contracts carried in the commodity account.

Section 9–204. After-acquired Property; Future Advances.

(a) After-acquired collateral. Except as otherwise provided in subsection (b), a security agreement may create or provide for a security interest in after-acquired collateral.
(b) When after-acquired property clause not effective. A security interest does not attach under a term constituting an after-acquired property clause to:
    (1) consumer goods, other than an accession when given as additional security, unless the debtor acquires rights in them within 10 days after the secured party gives value; or
    (2) a commercial tort claim.
(c) Future advances and other value. A security agreement may provide that collateral secures, or that accounts, chattel paper, payment intangibles, or promissory notes are sold in connection with, future advances or other value, whether or not the advances or value are given pursuant to commitment.

Section 9–207. Rights and Duties of Secured Party Having Possession or Control of Collateral.

(a) Duty of care when secured party in possession. Except as otherwise provided in subsection (d), a secured party shall use reasonable care in the custody and preservation of collateral in the secured party's possession. In the case of chattel paper or an instrument, reasonable care includes taking necessary steps to preserve rights against prior parties unless otherwise agreed.
(b) Expenses, risks, duties, and rights when secured party in possession. Except as otherwise provided in subsection (d), if a secured party has possession of collateral:
    (1) reasonable expenses, including the cost of insurance and payment of taxes or other charges, incurred in the custody, preservation, use, or operation of the collateral are chargeable to the debtor and are secured by the collateral;
    (2) the risk of accidental loss or damage is on the debtor to the extent of a deficiency in any effective insurance coverage;
    (3) the secured party shall keep the collateral identifiable, but fungible collateral may be commingled; and

(4) the secured party may use or operate the collateral:
    (A) for the purpose of preserving the collateral or its value;
    (B) as permitted by an order of a court having competent jurisdiction; or
    (C) except in the case of consumer goods, in the manner and to the extent agreed by the debtor.

(c) Duties and rights when secured party in possession or control.

Except as otherwise provided in subsection (d), a secured party having possession of collateral or control of collateral under Section 9–104, 9–105, 9–106, or 9–107:

(1) may hold as additional security any proceeds, except money or funds, received from the collateral;
(2) shall apply money or funds received from the collateral to reduce the secured obligation, unless remitted to the debtor; and
(3) may create a security interest in the collateral.

(d) Buyer of certain rights to payment. If the secured party is a buyer of accounts, chattel paper, payment intangibles, or promissory notes or a consignor:
(1) subsection (a) does not apply unless the secured party is entitled under an agreement:
    (A) to charge back uncollected collateral; or
    (B) otherwise to full or limited recourse against the debtor or a secondary obligor based on the nonpayment or other default of an account debtor or other obligor on the collateral; and
(2) subsections (b) and (c) do not apply.

Section 9–304. Law Governing Perfection and Priority of Security Interests in Deposit Accounts

(a) Law of bank's jurisdiction governs. The local law of a bank's jurisdiction governs perfection, the effect of perfection or nonperfection, and the priority of a security interest in a deposit account maintained with that bank.
(b) Bank's jurisdiction. The following rules determine a bank's jurisdiction for purposes of this part:
(1) If an agreement between the bank and the debtor governing the deposit account expressly provides that a particular jurisdiction is the bank's jurisdiction for purposes of this part, this article, or this chapter, that jurisdiction is the bank's jurisdiction.

(2) If paragraph (1) does not apply and an agreeemnt between the bank and its customer governing the deposit account expressly provides that the agreement is governed by the law of a particular jurisdiction, that jurisdiction is the bank's jurisdiction.
(3) If neither paragraph (1) nor paragraph (2) applies and an agreement betwen the bank and its customer governing the deposit account expressly provides that the deposit account is maintained at an office in a particular jurisdiction, that jurisdiction is the bank's jurisdiction.
(4) If none of the preceding paragraphs apply, the bank's jurisdiction is the jurisdiction in which the office identified in an account statement as the office serving the customer's account is located.
(5) If none of the preceding paragraphs apply, the bank's jurisdiction is the jurisdiction in which the chief executive office of the bank is located.

Section 9–305. Law Governing Perfection and Priority of Security Interests in Investment Property.

(a) Governing law: general rules. Except as otherwise provided in subsections (c) and (d), the following rules apply:
   (1) While a security certificate is located in a jurisdiction, the local law of that jurisdiction governs perfection, the effect of perfection or nonperfection, and the priority of a security interest in the certificated security represented thereby.
   (2) The local law of the issuer's jurisdiction as specified in Section 8–110(d) governs perfection, the effect of perfection or nonperfection, and the priority of a security interest in an uncertificated security.
   (3) The local law of the securities intermediary's jurisdiction as specified in Section 8–110(e) governs perfection, the effect of perfection or nonperfection, and the priority of a security interest in a security entitlement or securities account.
   (4) The local law of the commodity intermediary's jurisdiction governs perfection, the effect of perfection or nonperfection, and the priority of a security interest in a commodity contract or commodity account.
(b) Commodity intermediary's jurisdiction. The following rules determine a commodity intermediary's jurisdiction for purposes of this part:
   (1) If an agreement between the commodity intermediary and commodity customer governing the commodity account expressly provides that a particular jurisdiction is the

commodity intermediary's jurisdiction for purposes of this part, this article, or this chapter, that jurisdiction is the commodity intermediary's jurisdiction.

(2) If paragraph (1) does not apply and an agreement between the commodity intermediary and commodity customer governing the commodity account expressly provides that the agreement is governed by the law of a particular jurisdiction, that jurisdiction is the commodity intermediary's jurisdiction.

(3) If neither paragraph (1) nor paragraph (2) applies and an agreement between the commodity intermediary and commodity customer governing the commodity account expressly provides that the commodity account is maintained at an office in a particular jurisdiction, that jurisdiction is the commodity intermediary's jurisdiction.

(4) If none of the preceding paragraphs apply, the commodity intermediary's jurisdiction is the jurisdiction in which the office identified in an account statement as the office serving the commodity customer's account is located.

(5) If none of the preceding paragraphs apply, the commodity intermediary's jurisdiction is the jurisdiction in which the chief executive office of the commodity intermediary is located.

(c) When perfection governed by law of jurisdiction where debtor located. The local law of the jurisdiction in which the debtor is located governs:

(1) perfection of a security interest in investment property by filing;

(2) automatic perfection of a security interest in investment property created by a broker or securities intermediary; and

(3) automatic perfection of a security interest in a commodity contract or commodity account created by a commodity intermediary.

(d) Cooperative interests. Subsections (a) through (c) do not apply to cooperative interests.

Section 9–504. Indication of Collateral.

A financing statement sufficiently indicates the collateral that it covers if the financing statement provides:

(1) a description of the collateral pursuant to Section 9–108; or

(2) an indication that the financing statement covers all assets or all personal property.

Section 9–505. Filing and Compliance with Other Statutes and Treaties for Consignments, Leases, Other Bailments, and Other Transactions.

(a) Use of terms other than "debtor" and "secured party". A consignor, lessor, or other bailor of goods, a licensor, or a buyer of a payment intangible or promissory note may file a financing statement, or may comply with a statute or treaty described in Section 9–311(a), using the terms "consignor", "consignee", "lessor", "lessee", "bailor","bailee", "licensor", "licensee", "owner", "registered owner", "buyer", "seller", or words of similar import, instead of the terms "secured party" and "debtor".

(b) Effect of financing statement under subsection (a). This part applies to the filing of a financing statement under subsection (a) and, as appropriate, to compliance that is equivalent to filing a financing statement under Section 9–311(b), but the filing or compliance is not of itself a factor in determining whether the collateral secures an obligation. If it is determined for another reason that the collateral secures an obligation, a security interest held by the consignor, lessor, bailor, licensor, owner, or buyer which attaches to the collateral is perfected by the filing or compliance.

Section 9–506. Effect of Errors or Omissions.

(a) Minor errors and omissions. A financing statement substantially satisfying the requirements of this part is effective, even if it has minor errors or omissions, unless the errors or omissions make the financing statement seriously misleading.

(b) Financing statement seriously misleading. Except as otherwise provided in subsection (c), a financing statement that fails sufficiently to provide the name of the debtor in accordance with Section 9–503(a) is seriously misleading.

(c) Financing statement not seriously misleading. If a search of the records of the filing office under the debtor's correct name, using the filing office's standard search logic, if any, would disclose a financing statement that fails sufficiently to provide the name of the debtor in accordance with Section 9–503(a), the name provided does not make the financing statement seriously misleading.

(d) "Debtor's correct name". For purposes of Section 9–508(b), the "debtor's correct name" in subsection (c) means the correct name of the new debtor.

Bibliography

Allen & Overy, *New Law on Financial Collateral* (January 2004).

Ashurst, *Changes to the UK financial collateral regime* (January 2011).

Basel Committee on Banking Supervision, *Basel III: A global regulatory framework for more resilient banks and banking systems* (December 2010).

Dr. Joanna Benjamin, 'Recharacterisation Risk and Conflict of Laws', *Journal of International Banking & Financial Law*, Special Supplement (September 1998).

Warren N. Davis, *Issues Frequently Negotiated by End-Users in Connection with ISDA Master Agreements and the Credit Support Annex*, 1769 PLI/Corp 115 (19 October 2009).

Anthony C. Gooch and Linda B. Klein, *Documentation for Derivatives: Credit Support Supplement,* Euromoney Books (1994).

Lauren Teigland-Hunt, *ISDA's Credit Support Annex Overview*, 1769 PLI/Corp 137 (19 October 2009).

International Financing Review, *ISDA edges closer to standardized CSA* (17 June 2011).

International Swaps & Derivatives Association Inc., *User's Guide to the 1994 ISDA Credit Support Annex* (1994).

International Swaps & Derivatives Association Inc., *User's Guide to the ISDA Credit Support Documents under English Law* (1999).

International Swaps & Derivatives Association Inc., *Collateral Asset Definitions* (June 2003).

International Swaps & Derivatives Association Inc. (2005), *2005 ISDA Collateral Guidelines.*

International Swaps & Derivatives Association Inc. (2009), *Guidelines for Implementation of the ISDA 2009 Collateral Dispute Resolution Procedure* (30 September 2009).

International Swaps & Derivatives Association Inc. (2009), *Standards for the Electronic Exchange of OTC Derivative Margin Calls* (12 November 2009).

International Swaps & Derivatives Association Inc. (2010), *Collateralized Portfolio Reconciliation Best Operational Practices* (20 January 2010).

International Swaps & Derivatives Association Inc. (2010), *Market Review of OTC Derivative Bilateral Collateralization Practices* (1 March 2010).

International Swaps & Derivatives Association Inc. (2010), *Independent Amounts* (1 March 2010).

International Swaps & Derivatives Association Inc. (2010), *Feasibility Study Implementation Plan: Extending Collateralized Portfolio Reconciliations* (12 April 2010).

International Swaps & Derivatives Association Inc. (2010) *2010 Roadmap for Collateral Management* (15 April 2010).

International Swaps & Derivatives Association Inc. (2010), *Best Practices for the OTC Derivatives Collateral Process* (30 June 2010).

International Swaps & Derivatives Association Inc. (2011) *ISDA Margin Survey 2011.*

International Swaps & Derivatives Association Inc. (2011), *2011 Roadmap for Collateral Management* (30 June 2010).

Christian Johnson, 'Derivatives and Rehypothecation Failure – It's 3:00pm, Do You Know Where Your Collateral Is?', *Arizona Law Review* 39 (949) (1997), available at http://ssrn.com/abstract=584102.

Christian Johnson, *A Guide to Using and Negotiating OTC Derivatives Documentation*, Chapter 5, Euromoney Books (2005).

Christian Johnson, 'Collateralizing Over-The-Counter Derivative Obligations' in *Secured Finance Transactions*, edited by Paul Ali (2007).

Christian Johnson, 'The Enigma of Clearing Buy Side OTC Derivatives', *Futures & Derivatives Law Report* (December 2009), available at: http://ssrn.com/abstract=1544017.

Robin Powers, 'Exploring Title VII of the Dodd-Frank Act & the Impact on Margin Posted by End Users' (2011), www.derivsource.com/node/7690.

Secretariat of the Basel Committee on Banking Supervision, *The New Basel Capital Accord: an explanatory note* (January 2001).

Dermot Turing, *Risk Management Handbook*, Butterworths (2000).

Unidroit, *Background to the UNIDROIT Convention on Substantive Rules for Intermediated Securities* (2009).

White & Case, *Basel III rules published* (January 2011).

Scott Willoughby, *The ISDA New York Law Credit Support Annex*, 1631 PLI 153 (15 October, 2007).

Index